Plehve

V. K. Plehve

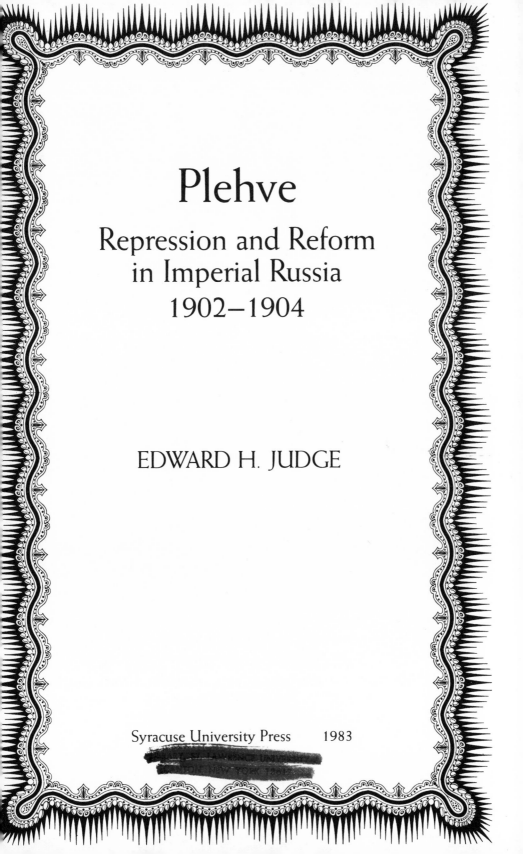

Plehve

Repression and Reform
in Imperial Russia
1902–1904

EDWARD H. JUDGE

Syracuse University Press   1983

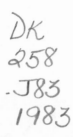

DK
258
.J83
1983

This manuscript was recommended for publication by the American Historical Association's Committee on the First Books Program, a joint project with the Association of American University Presses, to encourage publication of first works by younger historians.

SOURCES FOR PHOTOGRAPHS

Frontispiece:
Russia. Gosudarstvennaia kantseliariia. *Gosudarstvennaia kantseliariia, 1810–1910*, Saint Petersburg: Gosudarstvennaia tipografiia, 1910.

All Other Photos:
Obninskii, Viktor Petrovich. *Posliednii samoderzhets; ocherki zhizni i tsarstvovanie imperatora Rossii Nikolaia II-go*. Berlin: Eberhard Frowein, [1912].

Library of Congress Cataloging in Publication Data

Judge, Edward H.
Plehve : repression and reform in imperial Russia,
1902–1904.

Bibliography: p.
Includes index.
1. Soviet Union—Politics and government—1894–1917.
2. Plehve, Viacheslav Konstantinovich, 1846–1904.
I. Title.
DK258.J83   1983   947.08'3   83-670
ISBN 0-8156-2295-3

Manufactured in the United States of America

To John, Stephen, Matthew, and Christopher

Edward H. Judge is Associate Professor of History, LeMoyne College.

Contents

Preface   ix

1   The Minister of Interior   1

2   Viacheslav Konstantinovich Plehve   12

3   The Peasant Question and the Zemstvos   38

4   Plehve, Witte, and Society   62

5   The Jewish, Finnish, and Armenian Questions   93

6   The Worker Question and the Police   122

7   The Fall of Witte and the Far Eastern Question   150

8   The Plehve System   175

9   Repression Versus Reform   199

10   The Minister and the Terrorists   218

11   The Legacy of Plehve   238

Notes   247

Bibliographical Note   271

Bibliography   275

Index   287

Preface

A critical test of any political system is its ability to respond to the challenge of social and economic change. In the twentieth century, this challenge has been particularly acute for regimes which govern traditional societies that are undergoing modernization. Such regimes are often faced with an awkward situation. On one hand, modernization is desirable and necessary if they are to overcome backwardness, poverty, and impotence—indeed, if they are to survive. On the other hand, it is fraught with danger: the forces of modernization, if unchecked, can undermine traditional values, bring widespread suffering and dislocation, and provoke social and political unrest. The challenge for these regimes, then, is not so much to prevent change, but to manage it, direct it, and bring it under control.

At the beginning of the twentieth century, the Russian Empire was in transition. The preceding half century had witnessed the abolition of serfdom; major reforms in the judiciary, the military, and local self-government; an influx of Western liberal and socialist ideals; an intensification of nationalism among Russians and non-Russians; a rapid increase in population; and the beginnings of an industrial revolution. The tsarist regime was confronted with a profound social and economic transformation, some of which it had itself initiated. In seeking to guide the empire through this difficult transition, tsarist officials urgently strove to create new institutions, systems, and relationships that would make possible economic and social modernization without violent political upheaval.

One such official was Viacheslav Konstantinovich Plehve. An intelligent bureaucrat with broad legal, police, and administrative ex-

ix

perience, Plehve was appointed in 1902 to the empire's most influential administrative post. This was a critical juncture: the processes of modernization, industrialization, and social transformation had created severe problems for the imperial regime. The government was confronted simultaneously with diplomatic defeat, peasant disorders, labor unrest, discontent among subject nationalities, oppositional activity within educated society, growing revolutionary organizations, and outbursts of political terrorism. Plehve's mandate was to impose order, resolve the pressing problems, and assert state control.

Employing a mixture of repression and reform, Plehve strove to divide the opposition, co-opt the leaders of society, and gain full command over the ship of state. His efforts to revise peasant and factory legislation, to reform local administration, to regulate peasant resettlement, and to sponsor worker organizations were accompanied by stern and brutal repression of dissident workers, peasants, opposition leaders, Jews, and national minorities. His efforts to expand the power of the state bureaucracy were accompanied by an ongoing struggle to expand his own power within that bureaucracy. His methods of operation left him with an unsavory reputation which, although not entirely unwarranted, has tended to overshadow his accomplishments and to obscure his policies and programs.

The present work, then, is an account of the efforts of an intelligent and responsible official to come to grips with a host of bewildering problems, and to bring under control the forces of change that threatened to engulf the imperial order. It is neither a full study of the imperial bureaucracy nor a full biography of Plehve—though it contains elements of both. It seeks not so much to rehabilitate his reputation as to provide some understanding of the problems he faced, some explanation of his attempts to solve them, and some insight into why he failed.

In the interest of readability, I have adopted several conventions, a few of which may cause difficulties for purists. I have chosen to use English translations wherever possible, even in cases such as "county" (*uezd*) and "township" (*volost'*) where they are a bit imprecise. I have shortened the titles of several major ministries, from Internal Affairs to Interior, from Public Education to Education, and from Agriculture and State Domains to Agriculture. I have used the common, westernized spelling of Plehve, rather than the direct transliteration (Pleve) or the original germanic (von Plehwe). Dates throughout are given in the Old Style (Julian Calendar), except in a few citations referring to Western periodicals.

I am deeply indebted to a number of persons whose support and assistance made this work possible. Professors Arthur Mendel, William Rosenberg, Horace Dewey, William Zimmerman, George Yaney, Boris Anan'ich, John Langdon, and Joseph Curran all read this work at various stages of its development and offered valuable advice and encouragement. The archivists and librarians at the Hoover Library, the University of Michigan Libraries, the Columbia University Archives, the Saltykov-Shchedrin State Public Library, the Central State Historical Archive, the State Lenin Library, and the Central State Archive of the October Revolution provided courteous cooperation and assistance. The American Council of Learned Societies, through the International Research and Exchanges Board, made possible my studies in the Soviet archives. The LeMoyne College Faculty Research Committee provided some financial support. The American Historical Association, through its First Books Program, provided critical review and helpful recommendations. Joyce Bell and Susan Judge assisted greatly in preparing the manuscript. To these, and to all the colleagues and friends who contributed encouragement and advice, I am sincerely grateful.

I owe my family the greatest debt of all. The years in which this book was in preparation brought continual travel and dislocation, moderate financial hardship, some awkward living accommodations, and various other stresses and strains. Through their tolerance, patience, good humor, and common sense, my parents, wife, and children made far more important contributions than they will ever realize.

Syracuse, New York   EHJ
Fall 1982

Plehve

1

The Minister of Interior

THE IMPERIAL BUREAUCRACY

At one o'clock in the afternoon on Tuesday, April 2, 1902, the leading officials of the Imperial Russian Government gathered at the Mariinskii Palace in Saint Petersburg for a meeting of the Committee of Ministers. As the ministers congregated in the entrance hall, a young man in uniform approached the Minister of Interior, D. S. Sipiagin, with a package. Sipiagin held out his hand to accept it, but the uniformed youth suddenly produced a gun and fired several shots from point-blank range. The minister slumped to the floor. After several moments of confusion, the youth was forcibly detained, and the wounded minister was placed in a carriage and taken to a nearby hospital. A short time later, word came back that he had died.[1]

The news of Sipiagin's murder spread rapidly. At Tsarskoe Selo, a saddened and beleaguered emperor was informed of this latest tragedy by close advisors. Bad news was nothing new: the reign of Nicholas II had been beset with difficulties from its very beginning. Lately, however, the problems and disappointments seemed to be multiplying. On the international scene, only a week earlier, pressure from various powers had forced the Russians to back down in the Far East, and to agree to evacuate their troops from Manchuria. In the Russian countryside, a growing crisis in peasant agriculture had been intensified by the previous year's crop failure, and at that very moment officials in the Ukraine were having difficulty quelling a large-scale peasant revolt. In Finland, dissatisfaction with the Russian nationality policy was surfacing in street riots, which were beginning to erupt in several of the

1

major cities. In manufacturing areas, hard-pressed industrial workers were starting to organize themselves: a recent mass demonstration in Moscow, though peaceful and legal, had illustrated the growing potential of the worker movement. Even the upper circles of Russian society were rebelling: at present, one group was laying the groundwork for a national "zemstvo congress" while another was preparing to publish, abroad, the first edition of an oppositional newspaper. Most ominous, perhaps, the dormant revolutionary movement had revived, and revolutionary parties were already organizing, consolidating, and publishing. With this had come a rebirth of terrorism, witnessed in 1901 by the murder of the Minister of Education and now, in April 1902, by the assassination of the Minister of Interior. Sipiagin's successor, whoever he might be, would not be faced with an easy task.

In the capital, expressions of shock and outrage soon gave way to lively speculation as to the identity of the successor.[2] The importance of this appointment was readily apparent: the Minister of Interior was, at least potentially, the single most powerful official in the imperial government. An intelligent and capable new minister might be able to make full use of the powers of this office, powers which had languished under the weak stewardship of Sipiagin and his immediate predecessors. An astute and clever politician might be able to challenge the recent dominance of government affairs by the Minister of Finance. Above all, a strong and resolute appointee might be able to unify and coordinate the workings of the Russian state, and bring under control the forces of change that threatened the imperial order.

The official powers of the Minister of Interior were formidable indeed.[3] Under his jurisdiction were departments responsible for peasant economy and rural life, mails and telegraphs, medicine and statistics, non-Orthodox religions, the prison system, and censorship of the press. The provincial governors, in theory direct representatives of the tsar, in practice functioned largely as subordinates of this minister. The zemstvos and town councils, elected institutions designed to deal with certain local needs, were subject in many ways to his supervisory authority. Even the peasant masses, far removed from the bureaucratic world of Saint Petersburg, were under the general control of a network of "land captains," appointed and assigned by the Minister of Interior.

The minister's police powers were perhaps even more impressive. The Department of Police of the Ministry of Interior had jurisdiction over rural district police, city governors and city police, the departments of security, search, and inquest, the detective sections, the river police, the factory police, and even the fire brigades. It also employed a number of foreign agents, operating in the major European cities. Its most notorious branches, however, were the "security sections" or "Okhranas" which used spies and *provocateurs* to combat oppositional movements in the major cities. Another police agency, the separate Corps of Gendarmes, conducted formal investigations of political crimes. Organizationally it was part of the army, but it took its marching orders from the Minister of Interior.

Since the Minister of Interior had all this authority, it might have seemed that full control of the Russian government was within his grasp. This, however, had not been the case: numerous factors also tended to limit his power. These included the complexity and disunity of imperial government, the residual autonomy of the "estate" and "self-governing" institutions, and the power and personality of the emperor himself.

The imperial government in 1902 consisted of a wide array of departments, committees, councils, and chanceries, many acting more or less independently of the others. Established in various reigns to respond to diverse needs and philosophies, they formed no truly unified or coherent structure. The State Council, a body of seasoned officials appointed by the emperor, was a kind of advisory legislature: it discussed new proposals submitted by the ministers before they went to the tsar. The Ruling Senate, a larger group of imperial appointees, was responsible for the promulgation of laws, and acted as a court of appeals. The Committee of Ministers, made up of the various department heads, was designed to coordinate government activities. Despite the superficial similarity, however, it was in no sense a cabinet: there was no collective responsibility or united policy, and its chairman—far from being a Prime Minister—was little more than a figurehead. Added to these were agencies such as the Holy Synod, His Majesty's Personal Chancery, the Siberian Railway Committee, and various temporary conferences and commissions, each enjoying a fair amount of authority within its own realm. Finally, on the local level, there existed a complex system of quasi-official hierarchies, loyalties, and traditions, which had grown up over the centuries, and which militated against any far-reaching change.

The most important centers of bureaucratic power were the individual ministries. Each was an entity unto itself, although their assigned spheres often overlapped. The larger ministries, like Interior, Finance, Justice, War, and Agriculture, each had their own councils, chanceries, and local organs. At the head of each was a minister who possessed extensive powers: he could hire and fire subordinates at will, he could issue "clarifying" decrees which had the full force of law, and he could act in emergencies without awaiting imperial approval. Above all, each minister had the privilege of making regular, private reports to the tsar, who was the final authority for all state policy.

The very power and independence of the individual ministers, however, served as a check on the accumulation of too much power by any single one. Even the Minister of Interior needed the support and cooperation of the others to make his policies effective. If enough of them disagreed with his programs, or merely wished to limit his power, his projects might be in trouble. It was not unusual for several ministers to form an alliance in order to further their own ambitions and thwart those of others. They might combine to block a certain minister's proposals in the State Council or Committee of Ministers; they might use their regular imperial audiences to turn the emperor against the particular minister; or they might simply instruct their local agents to work at cross-purposes with this minister's goals. They might influence the emperor to form new conferences, committees, or departments through which they could pursue their own ends and frustrate those of their opponent. Since each minister reported independently, little could be done to prevent this; an ambitious minister's only recourse was to resort to similar tactics. For this reason, the higher bureaucracy sometimes functioned as much by means of intrigues and alliances as by regular administrative procedure.

The lower bureaucracy, too, presented problems for the minister. Although the government claimed extensive powers, it did not employ nearly enough officials on the provincial and local level to exercise these powers effectively. Despite its growing size, the Russian state bureaucracy still employed fewer than half as many officials *per capita* as the corresponding organizations in France or Germany. The large, diverse, multi-national and multi-lingual population, the vast size of the empire, and the lack of a fully-developed communications system made central state control more a matter of theory than practice. Governors, police officials, land captains, and other agents, burdened with the administration of large areas and multifarious functions, could scarcely exercise the sort of control needed for coordinated state policy or systematic reform. As a result, the government had little choice but to rely on the assistance of the traditional estate institutions and the more recently established "organs of local self-government."

The estate institutions represented, in some respects, a different concept of governance than the bureaucratic model. In theory, at least, the tsar related to his people, not as individuals, but as members of corporate social classes or "estates." The nobles and peasants, for instance, each had their own elected assemblies: the county and province assemblies of the nobility, and the peasant village and township assemblies. The peasant assemblies, led by elected "elders" and "foremen," had practical jurisdiction over village and township affairs, since the government largely depended on them to enforce its laws and perform its police and administrative functions. The nobility assemblies, through their elected marshals, also had administrative responsibilities, and the county and provincial marshalls of the nobility either chaired or served on all the main governmental councils and boards. Whatever their obligations to the state, however, the assemblies and their leaders often felt a greater allegiance to the persons who elected them than to distant ministers and officials. Furthermore, the nobility assemblies formally enjoyed the right to petition the tsar directly, and the nobles—especially those from long-established and prestigious families—tended to chafe at any suggestion that they were mere subordinates to Saint Petersburg bureaucrats.

Alongside the estate institutions there had existed since the 1860s another form of elected governing body: the county and provincial *zemstvo* assemblies and (since 1870) the town councils. These "self-governing" organizations were elected from, and had jurisdiction over, all estates—although in practice they were dominated by the nobility. They were responsible, in general, for matters pertaining to the health, education, and welfare of their county or province: roads, sanitation, schools, medicine, fire protection, food storage, surveying, and the like. Although technically subordinate to the central government, they operated with some autonomy in purely local affairs and, like the estate institutions, they were frequently concerned more with the needs of their constituents than with policies emanating from the capital. They were under the supervision of the Minister of Interior, but not necessarily under his control.

The legal source of a minister's power was, of course, the emperor himself. The monarch, after all, was the one person who did have the authority to coordinate government policy, if he were so inclined. The tsar was theoretically all-powerful; a minister who enjoyed his full support could use it to eliminate opponents or overcome opposition, to bypass or expedite the legislative process, or to assume jurisdiction over the affairs of other departments. Indeed, the most effective ministers often were those who managed to curry favor with the emperor, and then use his good will and authority to eliminate "red-tape" and ram their programs through.

Unfortunately, this need to retain imperial support could also add a large element of uncertainty to ministerial affairs. As strong as a minister might be, he served only at the pleasure of his monarch. He could be dismissed at any time, for any reason—or for no particular reason at all. He might find his most prized programs cancelled, and his best advice ignored. He might even find that the emperor initiated policies affecting his area of jurisdiction without consulting him. Furthermore, his own success might prove his undoing: not only his colleagues, but even the monarch himself, tended to resent any official who accumulated too much power. A minister could achieve great prominence by winning the sovereign's favor, but his position was built on the sand of the emperor's changing moods and fancies.

This problem was particularly acute for the ministers who served the vacillating young man who occupied the throne in 1902. By all accounts, Emperor Nicholas II was a man of moderate intelligence and great personal charm, but he had no taste for politics and little understanding of state affairs. As a consequence, he lacked the firmness of purpose necessary to give his government unity and direction. His extreme sensitivity made it difficult for him to criticize or even disagree with a minister to his face; this led him to approve projects which contradicted each other, or to frustrate his ministers by going back on his word and rejecting policies he had previously approved. His mystical religious inclinations brought an added touch of unpredictability to imperial affairs. He was impressed by strong personalities and relied heavily on ministerial favorites, yet at the same time he tended to play his ministers against each other, and to undermine even the policies of those he favored the most.[4]

The new Minister of Interior, then, would have to be a man of enormous strength and talent to bring any sense of unity to the Russian government. For one thing, he would require the ability and finesse to win and keep the confidence of the irresolute young emperor. For another thing, he would have to assert his control over the other ministers, either by force of his leadership or by bureaucratic intrigue —or by both. At the same time, he must confront a whole host of bewildering problems with intelligent and effective programs, and he must somehow compel the slow-moving bureaucracy to implement his policies. Even then, his success or failure might depend on factors beyond his control, such as the willingness of the various estate and self-governing institutions to cooperate with his programs. It might also depend, for that matter, on his relations with the person who had

provided what measure of direction there was in Nicholas's early reign:
Sergei Iul'evich Witte.

INTERIOR VERSUS FINANCE

Surprisingly enough, the man who had dominated affairs in the decade
before 1902 was not the Minister of Interior. After a remarkable career
as a railroad administrator, Sergei Witte had come to Saint Petersburg
in 1889 to manage the railways of the entire empire. He had achieved
such notable success that in 1892 Emperor Alexander III had appointed
him first Minister of Communications, and then Minister of Finance.
By dint of his enormous energy and ability he had soon established his
ascendancy over the other ministers; and by the time of Nicholas II's
accession in 1894, Witte had become one of the most powerful forces
in the capital. Although somewhat taken aback by the minister's un-
polished manner, the inexperienced young monarch had at first relied
heavily on Witte's advice, and had fully supported his programs.

It was Witte's conviction that Russia must industrialize in order
to survive in competition with the technically advanced Western nations. He had therefore bent every effort to transform the backward,
agrarian Russian Empire into a modern industrial power. He had encouraged and assisted the nascent Russian industries by forming councils to discuss their problems, founding industrial banks to grant them
credit, and lowering internal customs while retaining a high foreign
tariff. To provide transport and unlock Russia's resources, he had built
railroads at a feverish pace—his most grandiose project being the
5,400 mile Trans-Siberian line. He had stabilized the currency by
restricting imports, building up the gold supply, and placing Russia on
the gold standard. He had attacked the empire's fiscal problems by
sharply increasing indirect taxes on consumer items such as matches,
sugar, tobacco, and tea; and he had established a state liquor monop-
oly. At the same time, he had engaged in heavy domestic and foreign
borrowing to finance his costly projects.[5]

In many ways the "Witte system" had been a remarkable success.
During Witte's ten-year administration, government revenues had
more than doubled, and the length of the Russian railway system had
increased by fifty percent. Foreign capital had flowed into Russia.
Hundreds of new corporations and companies had been organized and

put into operation. The Russian currency was stable, and Russian credit was high. Coal production had doubled during Witte's tenure, and output of pig-iron had more than tripled. Russia had risen to fifth place among the world's steel producers. By 1902, the Russian Empire was taking its place as one of the industrial powers.[6]

Yet the reaction to these achievements had not been entirely favorable. The Minister of Finance had made many enemies. His rude and impatient manner had infuriated many of his colleagues, not to mention the emperor himself. In expanding the power and influence of the Ministry of Finance, he had incurred the jealousy of the other ministers. In putting government to work for industry, he had antagonized the powerful agrarian interests: many blamed Witte's combination of high consumer taxes and low grain prices for the apparent crisis in agriculture. In striving for rapid economic change, he had aroused the hostility of the traditionalists, who felt he was destroying the fabric of Russian society. This perception was shared by those concerned with social control: Witte's policies, whatever their merits, were causing severe economic dislocation, and paving the way for political and social unrest.[7]

In recent years, a series of external events had served to underscore the vulnerability of Witte's system. For a time all had gone fairly well, but in 1897, 1898, and again in 1901 the Russian crops had failed. The poor harvests were scarcely Witte's fault, but the resulting misery did lend credence to claims that Witte's policies were harming agriculture and increasing rural poverty. More importantly, the poor harvests had combined with an international monetary scarcity to produce a severe economic depression. The crop failures had depressed the domestic market for industrial goods, while the tightness of money had made large foreign loans unavailable and forced the government to curtail its spending. Industries which produced consumer goods and those which relied on government contracts had both suffered; many newer industries had failed to survive.

The deepening depression had been accompanied by a rise of popular discontent and a return of revolutionary activity. Student demonstrations, worker strikes, zemstvo agitation, peasant uprisings, and revolutionary terrorism all had added to the growing sense of crisis. Although Witte was not entirely responsible, as the major architect of government policy he was saddled with much of the blame.[8]

Within the government, opposition to Witte centered in the Ministry of Interior. This ministry was charged with social control, and thus deeply resented the disruption caused by Witte's economic policies. This ministry portrayed itself as a defender of agrarian interests, while the Ministry of Finance was championing the industrialist cause. And this ministry stood in danger of being surpassed by Finance as the most influential department of state. It is little wonder that the Witte years had witnessed a prolonged and intensive rivalry between the two ministries.[9]

Fortunately for Witte, none of his first three colleagues at Interior had been particularly capable or vigorous. I. N. Durnovo, the Minister of Interior when Witte took over at Finance, was a man of limited ability. His ministry (1889–95) had been concerned primarily with bringing to fruition certain "counter-reforms" proposed by his predecessor: it was under Durnovo that measures had been enacted placing the zemstvos and town councils more directly under state control. An avowed supporter of the landowning nobility, Durnovo had opposed Witte's attempts to colonize Siberia, fearing that this might harm the landlords by depleting the supply of cheap peasant labor. He had also criticized the practice of borrowing large sums abroad. Although he had differed from the Minister of Finance on these and other issues, Durnovo had managed to do little to obstruct Witte's programs.[10]

Durnovo's successor, I. L. Goremykin, had proved to be more of a threat. Concerned with the rising level of worker agitation, Goremykin had proposed government action to better the lot of the industrial workers, combined with closer police supervision of their activities. He had also revived an old demand that the Department of Factory Inspection, often "misused" by Witte to further interests of factory owners, be transferred from Finance to Interior. Witte, of course, had opposed any interference in his domain. He had continued to side with the manufacturers, arguing that the benefits of industrial growth far outweighed the temporary problems of worker unrest. He had managed to block the transfer of the inspectorate, and to tone down pro-worker legislation, but he had been unable to prevent the establishment of a special factory police force in Goremykin's ministry.[11]

On another major issue, however, Witte had emerged victorious. Goremykin had seen great value in the zemstvos, and had tried to maintain good relations with them: he had even permitted a national conference of zemstvo chairmen in 1896. Witte, on the other hand, disliked and distrusted the zemstvos, which had often criticized his policies, and which impressed him as little more than an inefficient duplication of government services. When, in 1898, Goremykin had proposed the extension of the zemstvo system into the western provinces, Witte had countered with a long memorandum to the tsar, arguing that zemstvos were incompatible with autocracy. Persuaded by this argument, Nicholas had rejected Goremykin's proposal, and had gone on to dismiss him from his post in October of 1899. [12]

Goremykin had been replaced by D. S. Sipiagin, a nobleman, former governor, and a personal friend of Witte's. This appointment, which marked a high point of Witte's influence, had ushered in a brief era of relative goodwill between the two ministries. Although the two men did not always agree, the brilliant Finance Minister had often been able to mold the opinions of his duller colleague, and to gain his cooperation on important matters. They had worked together, for instance, to limit the powers of the zemstvos, taking away zemstvo control of emergency food provisions and restricting zemstvo taxation rights. Even on the labor issue, although Sipiagin had shared his predecessor's views, he and Witte had managed to agree on a proposal concerning worker representation. The internal situation, however, had continued to deteriorate, as economic depression joined with rising discontent to intensify the atmosphere of crisis. [13]

Now, in April 1902, Sipiagin was gone, and his responsibilities were soon to be placed on someone else's shoulders. Witte, and all of Saint Petersburg, anxiously awaited the tsar's selection. If the emperor appointed a friend of Witte's, like Sipiagin, this would be seen as a reaffirmation of the Finance Minister's influence, and government policy would proceed in the same general direction. If the new minister, even though hostile, was a man of modest ability, Witte would probably still be able to dominate affairs as he had in the Durnovo and Goremykin years. But if the appointee turned out to be someone who was both hostile and capable, Witte was in for trouble. Such an appointment would be a clear signal from Nicholas II that he wished to abandon his reliance on the Minister of Finance, and to alter the course of government policy. In the latter case, unless Witte himself were simultaneously dismissed, a classic power struggle was bound to ensue.

The answer to these riddles was not long in coming. On the evening of April 4, only two days after Sipiagin's death, the identity of the new appointee was announced. The emperor's choice, as it turned out, confirmed Witte's worst fears. For the new man was not only an opponent of the Finance Minister, he was a bitter enemy. Unlike his predecessors, the new minister possessed the intelligence, vigor, and determination to take on a foe like Witte. Furthermore, he knew how to hold his own in the world of bureaucratic intrigue: if anything he was more unscrupulous and more ruthless than Witte himself. To make matters worse, the new man had the ear of the emperor, and he was not above using his position of favor to discredit the Minister of Finance. For the first time since his arrival in Saint Petersburg, Witte was confronted with an opponent whose powers and abilities rivalled his own. This opponent was the new Minister of Interior, Viacheslav Konstantinovich Plehve.

2

Viacheslav Konstantinovich Plehve

THE YOUNG PROCURATOR

Viacheslav Plehve was a few days short of his fifty-sixth birthday when he took over the Ministry of Interior. He was a big, impressive-looking man, broad-shouldered and stout; a man of powerful build and stately bearing. His complexion was sallow and pale; his thinning hair was silver-grey. His mouth was nearly covered by a thick, greyish-white mustache. His facial appearance was dominated by his eyebrows, which characteristically knit while he was in thought, and by his "remarkably youthful, energetic brown eyes." He reminded one visitor "not so much of an authoritative minister as of a stately country gentleman of the good old days."[1]

Despite his appearance and his high office, V. K. Plehve was of relatively modest origins.[2] His grandfather, a scion of the German family *von Plehwe*, apparently had moved to Russia in the 1820s from the Poznan region of Prussian Poland. His father, the immigrant's oldest son, was raised in Russia, educated at the University of Moscow, and employed by the government as a schoolteacher. His mother, Elizaveta, was the daughter of a minor Russian landowner named Shamaev. Not far from the Shamaev estate, about 130 miles southwest of Moscow, was the town of Meshchovsk, where Konstantin Plehve taught history and geography in the local school. It was here, on April 8, 1846, that the future minister was born, the only son of Konstantin Grigor'evich and Elizaveta Mikhailovna Plehve.

Plehve was destined to spend only five years in Meshchovsk: in 1851 his father accepted a job as a teacher in the Warsaw gymnasium,

12

and the small family moved to the Polish capital. In Warsaw young Viacheslav spent his formative years, from the age of five to the age of sixteen. As he later reminisced, he grew up among Jews. "I lived in a big house with my parents, who were in very modest circumstances. We had a small apartment, and we children had to play in the big courtyard. There I played with Jewish children exclusively."[3] In 1862, with Poland on the verge of rebellion, his parents sent him back to Russia to finish his education. Young Plehve was a brilliant student; in 1863 he graduated first in his class from the Kaluga provincial gymnasium. The same year he entered Moscow University.[4]

V. K. Plehve was only seventeen years of age when he entered the juridical department of Moscow University, and barely twenty-one when he was awarded the Candidate of Laws degree four years later. Apparently these were happy years for the future minister; he always took a great deal of pride in his association with the famous institution. In later years he regularly attended the annual dinners in Petersburg for Moscow University graduates, and in 1894 he chose to have a scholarship for study there established in his name.[5]

In August of 1867, shortly after his graduation, the young lawyer entered state service. These were exciting times for the legal profession: the implementation of the Judicial Reform of 1864 was providing a wealth of opportunities for talented and ambitious jurists.[6] Plehve, who had more than his share of talent and ambition, made rapid progress.

The judicial statutes of 1864 had set up two court systems: the Justices of the Peace, who were to deal with minor offenses, and the regular courts for more serious matters. The regular court system consisted of criminal and civil "Circuit Courts" in each province, and higher courts of appeal known as "Chambers of Justice," each of which covered several provinces. The reforming statutes also called for the introduction of public trials, judicial tenure, trial by jury in criminal cases, and separation of the judiciary from the administrative authority.

The new system was not entirely free of administrative control. Attached to each of the regular courts was an official of the Ministry of Justice known as the procurator, or public prosecutor. The procurator's primary function was to maintain the strict legality of court proceedings and, subsequently, of all administrative activity. The procurator's office was also responsible for the public prosecution of criminal cases, as well as the supervision of preliminary investigations and the preparation of bills of indictment. The procurators were part of a special central administration headed by the Minister of Justice, who was considered the Procurator-General. It was in this area, the procuracy, that young Plehve made his career.

The fact that Plehve became a procurator rather than a trial lawyer or a judge had great significance for his future career. As a procurator he was an employee of the state and was compelled to defend the interests of the state; as a procurator he would be involved in the investigation and prosecution of political crimes. Also significant was the fact that his career in the procuracy largely coincided with Count K. I. Pahlen's tenure as Minister of Justice (1867–78). Pahlen, who had replaced the reformer D. N. Zamiatnin, was opposed in principle to many aspects of the new system, particularly judicial independence. Pahlen had the reputation of appointing and promoting only men who were willing to follow orders from above and to cooperate with the local administrative authorities.[7] Plehve, apparently, possessed these credentials.

The first fourteen years of Plehve's career were spent in the Ministry of Justice. He began with a minor post in the investigating department under the Moscow Circuit Court Procurator. In this post he quickly distinguished himself, and within a year he was transferred to a similar position in Vladimir. Plehve's three years in the Vladimir post were highlighted by an important personal event: on April 27, 1869, he married the former Zinaida Nikolaevna Uzhumetskoi-Gritsevich. "Zina" was the daughter of an imperial officer of moderate rank and wealth, a fact which no doubt appealed to her status-conscious husband. Within a year, she presented him with a daughter, Elizaveta; a son, Nikolai, was born two years later.[8]

In 1870, shortly after the birth of his daughter, the young attorney received his first major promotion: he became the Assistant Procurator of the Tula circuit court, and was awarded a higher rank. Three years later came another promotion and another move, this time to Vologda province, where Plehve became the provincial procurator. In Vologda, he was called upon to investigate the province's outdated court system and, subsequently, to supervise the transition from the old system to the new. His skill in handling this assignment brought him to the attention of the Minister of Justice, who in 1876 appointed him Assistant Procurator of the Warsaw Chamber of Justice.[9] Plehve's Polish background was no doubt instrumental in this choice.

In the higher court, Plehve demonstrated the same energy and ability he had in the circuit courts. More importantly, his activities in Warsaw brought him into the investigation of political crimes—the area where he would make his reputation. He earned particular distinction with his handling of the case of the "proletarians," a group of revolutionary students with Marxist ideals. His interrogation of the youths was especially skillful: picturing himself as a convinced constitutionalist, he persuaded the prisoners that radical activity itself was the biggest obstacle to meaningful reform. When Plehve's superior was called to Saint Petersburg to receive an award for this case, he respectfully declined: his ambitious assistant, he admitted, had done all the work. As a result of his accomplishments in Warsaw, Plehve received several promotions and honors, and was entrusted with the inspection of the Kiev provincial procuracy. Finally, in 1879, he was again promoted, this time to Saint Petersburg, where he became Procurator of the Chamber of Justice. [10]

The transfer to Saint Petersburg brought the young procurator at last to the center of power, influence, and intrigue. It gave him, for the first time, a chance to make an impression on those who mattered the most: the tsar and his closest advisors. Plehve was not one to let an opportunity like this pass him by: the remainder of his career, in fact, would be spent in the Russian capital. In Petersburg Plehve would flourish; in Petersburg he would reach the heights of power; in Petersburg, eventually, he would die.

During Plehve's short tenure (1879–81) as Procurator of the Saint Petersburg Chamber of Justice, there occurred a series of attempts on the life of Emperor Alexander II. The most audacious of these took place on February 5, 1880, when an enormous explosion destroyed several rooms in the emperor's Winter Palace. The attempt was a failure: although a number of workers and soldiers were killed, the Emperor himself escaped unharmed. But the explosion did give an indirect boost to the career of Viacheslav Plehve.

As procurator, Plehve was called upon to supervise the investigation of the bombing and report on its results to the emperor. This was an important break for the young official: it gave him an opportunity to demonstrate his talents to the tsar himself. Apparently he made a very favorable impression. According to one report he presented the intricate details of the case from memory, without relying on a single note or document. Alexander II was impressed enough to mention the procurator's abilities to others, including M. T. Loris-Melikov, the "dictator" of Russia and soon-to-be Minister of Interior. [11]

In the wake of the Winter Palace blast Loris-Melikov, a former war hero and governor-general, had been given extraordinary powers in an effort to restore public order. He had not been faced with an easy task. The excitement generated by the reforms of the 1860s had given way to general disillusionment: as the government appeared to draw back from further reform, and as the general welfare failed to improve, several opposition groups had begun to emerge. Some were merely seeking an enhanced role for educated society; others called for the end of autocracy. One group of frustrated young radicals had turned to terror and—as the recent bombing made all too evident— were determined to murder the tsar. Meanwhile the state bureaucracy, after the early flush of reform activity, was finding it difficult to re- spond effectively to the challenge.

Determined to restore state control, Loris set out to crush the revolutionary movement, streamline the imperial bureaucracy, and win the support of educated society. His chosen vehicle was the Ministry of Interior, the one department with potential power to dominate affairs. By August of 1880 all the various police agencies had been consolidated under its control, and Loris himself had secured the post of minister. Armed with the tsar's support, he then undertook to con- centrate in the ministry sufficient power to unify and direct the gov- ernment, and to carry out reforms. Meanwhile, anxious both to accommodate and to better exploit the institutions of self-government, in January of 1881 he put forth a scheme which would have given them a voice in the law-making process. Zemstvos and town councils, he proposed, should elect representatives to a special commission formed to examine legislation before it went to the State Council. This modest "constitution" was approved in essence by the tsar, but it was fated never to go into effect. [12]

On March 1, 1881, the terrorists made another attempt on the life of the emperor. This time they did not fail. In the frantic days that followed the assassination, Procurator Plehve once again came to the fore, distinguishing himself by his level-headedness and energetic ac- tivity. Acting as a special prosecutor, on the orders of the Minister of Justice, he calmly took charge of the investigation. Under his direction arrests were made, apartments were searched, evidence was gathered, and suspects were questioned. Plehve himself took part in these inter- rogations, sometimes in the early hours of the morning, and quickly pieced together the details of the crime. [13] Within little more than a month, the leaders of the conspiracy were arrested, tried, convicted, and hanged.

Even before the assassination, Loris-Melikov had reorganized the police for an all-out attack on the forces of sedition and revolution. To lead this attack, the minister now called upon Plehve, whose con-

cise and pointed reports on the assassination had attracted the attention of the new tsar. Plehve at first hesitated, but finally agreed to
accept the offer and abandon his juridical career. [14] So it was that on
April 15, 1881—twelve days after the execution of the regicides—the
new tsar, Alexander III, made his first important change in personnel:
V. K. Plehve was appointed Director of the Department of State
Police of the Ministry of Interior. [15]

THE DIRECTOR OF POLICE

The appointment as police director marked an important turning point
for Plehve. As a procurator, his performance had been brilliant, and
his rise had been swift. "As a result of his extraordinary talent, his basic
juridical knowledge, and his detailed acquaintance with the handling
of state crimes," Loris-Melikov had written, "Plehve enjoys an outstanding reputation in the justice department." Now he was forsaking
all this and launching upon a new career in a new ministry, assuming
very difficult responsibilities at a very difficult time. The challenge was
great, but so was the potential for influence and impact on policy and
events. The Minister of Interior, for one, was confident that he would
succeed: "His administrative and moral qualifications serve as a guarantee that he will bring to his new sphere of activity the same energy
and reasonable approach to affairs which constantly characterized his
service in the judicial department." [16]

Loris could scarcely have chosen a better man for the job. When
Plehve assumed his leadership of the department, he was faced with
one overriding task: to destroy the revolutionary movement. This task
called for perseverance, dedication, and ruthlessness. Plehve devoted
himself wholeheartedly to his job: he worked incessantly—often day
and night—to smash the terrorist "People's Will" organization and
restore the prestige of the Russian police. His work was crowned with
success: by the time he left the Department of Police in 1884 the
terrorists were utterly crushed, calm had been restored to the empire,
and Plehve's reputation as a brilliant administrator-policeman was
firmly established. [17]

Loris-Melikov, however, was destined to derive no benefit from
his protégé's success. Two weeks after Plehve's appointment, the new
tsar issued a manifesto sternly reaffirming autocratic absolutism, and
implicitly denouncing Loris' "constitutional" proposals. Plehve, in

fact, drew the unpleasant task of transmitting this news to the minister, who immediately resigned.[18] Like Loris, Alexander III was anxious to enhance the real power of the state, but he was unwilling to countenance any plan calling for elected representation, no matter how restricted.

Loris' successor, the "Slavophile" Count N. P. Ignat'ev, also saw the need to involve enlightened local persons in the workings of the state. Unlike Loris, however, he preferred the traditional estate system to the newer, all-class zemstvos. Turning to Russia's past, he called for convocation of a *zemskii sobor*, a large, consultative "assembly of the land" representing each of the several estates. Although this proposal was inherently conservative, it too raised the spectre of representation, public criticism, and limits on autocratic power. It too was rejected by the tsar, who in 1882 replaced Ignat'ev with Count Dmitri Tolstoi. Tolstoi, a champion of unrestricted bureaucratic absolutism, soon put to rest all talk of representation and consultation.

Not all of the work of Loris-Melikov, however, was undone. The reorganized police, and the concentration of police and administrative power in the Ministry of Interior, remained key features of the bureaucratic system. At the helm of the police, despite the changing political winds, the versatile Plehve remained in his post, seeking further to consolidate the mechanisms of control. While continuing his hunt for revolutionaries, he energetically began to push such policies as expanded police authority, stricter control of universities, and a crackdown on the press.

One of Plehve's first major accomplishments was to secure additional powers for his police. He was convinced that only the strictest measures could stem the revolutionary tide, and that martial-law type provisions were needed, especially in the capital. Appointed in May 1881, to a special commission on public security, he played a leading role in drafting a measure to broaden the scope of police activity. In July, after the legislative draft had been completed, he pushed for its speedy implementation. "In my opinion," he wrote, "certain features of the new statute should be put into effect by September 1, consequently there exists an urgent need to hasten its confirmation."[19] The measure was confirmed into law on August 14, 1881.

The new law was known as the "Statute Concerning Measures for the Preservation of State Security and Public Order" or, more commonly, the "Law on Exceptional Measures." It provided that certain areas of the empire, where there existed the danger of revolutionary activity, could be placed under emergency rule. There were to be two degrees of emergency rule: "strengthened security," in which the police and local officials were given the right to arrest "suspicious persons," prohibit meetings, and conduct searches and seizures at will; and "extraordinary security," which was tantamount to martial law. Despite the fact that the law was passed as a temporary measure, it remained in force until the end of the empire.[20]

Several weeks after the law was confirmed, a state of "strengthened security" was declared in ten provinces, including Moscow and Saint Petersburg. This was a slight disappointment for Plehve, who had wished to see the capital placed under "extraordinary protection"; nevertheless it marked a significant increase in the powers of the police to deal with "sedition." Before long, to assist local enforcement, special "security sections," or "Okhranas" were established in Moscow, Saint Petersburg, and Warsaw.[21]

As Director of Police, Plehve also took a lively interest in the affairs of higher education. This is not really surprising: "almost all the regicides, and a very large number of those involved in political crimes," according to his information, were students. Much of the responsibility, therefore, must lie with the universities. In the words of a May 1881 memo, found among Plehve's papers, all police surveillance would be fruitless as long as the ranks of the revolutionaries were "constantly replenished by new recruits, unknown to the police, prepared at treasury expense by the institutes of higher education." Furthermore, as Plehve later pointed out, the practice of expelling and exiling students only made matters worse: part-time student rebels, deprived of their careers and embittered against society, became full-time political revolutionaries.[22]

The student problem, therefore, was of paramount concern to the police. As a member of the 1881 Delianov commission on supervision of students, Plehve helped work out a program intended to restrict the number of students to those who were politically reliable and independently wealthy. The commission also proposed measures to bring the universities themselves more directly under state control. Plehve himself felt the measures were so indispensable that he sought, unsuccessfully, to have the opening of schools in 1881 postponed until they could be implemented.[23] In 1882, the director of police took part in another commission, this one under Prince M. S. Volkonskii, which recommended that expelled student rebels be inducted into the army.[24] The work of these commissions, although not immediately effective, did pave the way for the University Statute of 1884 and later restrictive measures.

Plehve's search for the roots of the revolutionary movement, however, focused not so much on the university students as on the periodic press. The young rebels, in his view, were only "cannon fodder" in the war against the government.[25] The real cause of sedition, he wrote in an 1882 memo to Count Tolstoi, was "that peculiar world of ideas and notions which envelops that part of Russian educated society that has access to the theorists of extreme materialism and socialist utopias." These ideas, he added, finding widespread support in "literary circles," were then communicated to students by the liberal press. "A whole decade of . . . Russian youth, reading the newspapers and journals which espouse these views, is nourished on the fruits of immature political thought, made out to be the last word in Western culture." Unless such influences were destroyed, concluded Plehve, government efforts to root out sedition would "only disturb the external form" of the "hostile force."[26]

Plehve's memo, later forwarded by the minister to Tsar Alexander III, appears to have had the desired effect. In the years that followed, the Ministry of Interior's Main Office on Affairs of the Press, assisted at times by the Department of Police, led a vigorous attack on the liberal-radical press. Early in 1883, N. K. Mikhailovsky, one of the foremost oppositional writers, was exiled from Saint Petersburg. Later that year, a number of liberal journals were closed down, and several writers were arrested. In 1884 the journal *Notes of the Fatherland* was banned by the government, largely at Plehve's initiative. The police director was also instrumental in forcing the journal *The Cause (Delo)* out of existence several months later.[27]

As important as all these activities might be, Plehve's most immediate concern as Police Director was the struggle against the revolutionaries themselves. Here he scored his most visible triumph. Actually, thanks to the revelations of several political-prisoners-turned-informer, the police had been able to arrest most of the leaders of the "People's Will" before Plehve even took office. Unaware of the extreme weakness of their adversary, Plehve and gendarme Lieutenant Colonel G. D. Sudeikin, head of the Saint Petersburg Okhrana, determined to find out all they could about the revolutionary group. Fortified by the Law on Exceptional Measures, the police continued to make arrests and question suspects, hoping to find new informers. Plehve and Sudeikin themselves interrogated prisoners, asking them to indicate what reforms were necessary to end the terror, and insisting that many of these reforms would be effected as soon as the terror ceased.[28]

Their work eventually paid off. In December of 1882 Sudeikin succeeded in winning the confidence of a newly arrested prisoner named Sergei Degaev, who occupied a high position in the "People's Will." He convinced Degaev that the best way to achieve a liberal regime in Russia was for the "People's Will" to ally with the secret police in an elaborate scheme to raise Sudeikin to supreme power. The first part of the plan called for Degaev to further Sudeikin's ambitions by helping the latter achieve the destruction of the terrorist organization. A fake escape was arranged, and for a while Degaev cooperated by successfully playing the dual role of revolutionary and police informer. His information enabled the police to round up numerous members of the terrorist group, including the indomitable Vera Figner, its heart and soul. Although the "People's Will" continued to have a shadowy existence for several more years, it never recovered from this blow. [29]

The technique of using a double agent had succeeded in breaking up the "People's Will"; it would later be used extensively under Plehve to combat other revolutionary groups. But if the *Degaevshchina* had demonstrated to Plehve the usefulness of this technique, it should also have alerted him to its dangers. For in December of 1883 the guilt-ridden Sergei Degaev, in an effort to atone for the betrayal of his comrades, accomplished the murder of Sudeikin himself. The complex intrigue had cost Plehve his most valuable assistant. [30] By this time, however, the damage had been done to the revolutionary group, and the young Police Director was about to move on to better things. In July of 1884, Plehve became a senator—a high honor for a man still in his thirties. Six months later he was appointed Assistant Minister of Interior under Count Dmitri Tolstoi. [31]

THE ASSISTANT MINISTER OF INTERIOR

For nine years, Plehve would remain in this office. By all accounts his role in the ministry was a major one, despite his relative youth. This was due partly to his own outstanding ability, and partly to the character of his colleagues. Minister Tolstoi was in his sixties and in poor health; as time went on he relied increasingly on his assistants. Assistant Minister I. N. Durnovo—who would become minister after Tolstoi's death in 1889—was a sincere man, but very limited in ability and education. Gendarme Commander Orzhevskii was intelligent enough, but hampered by his own rancor and bitterness. Prince K. D. Gagarin, another assistant, was "distinguished neither by talent nor intelligence." Of the men at the head of the ministry, Plehve was doubtless the most intelligent, and certainly the most energetic.[32]

Furthermore, he enjoyed the special esteem and trust of Count Tolstoi. As early as 1882, Plehve had been instrumental in persuading the new minister not to give up control of the police, despite Tolstoi's fears of assassination. By 1884, thanks largely to the success of these police, the police director had won the minister's profound appreciation. As assistant minister, Plehve went on to become Tolstoi's most valuable aide—the man he could turn to to get things done. Plehve was called upon to advise the minister on important issues, to supervise the preparation of legislation, and to chair the most important committees. Beginning in 1886, when a prolonged illness limited Tolstoi's activity, an increasing share of the minister's duties fell on Plehve's shoulders. He made reports to the tsar, handled both routine and urgent affairs, and kept the absent minister abreast of current developments. He often became the ministry's spokesman in the State Council, since his lawyer's argumentative skills far excelled those of his colleagues.[33] "He was an absolute Godsend to Count Tolstoi," wrote one observer. "Especially when illness befell the count, I have no idea how business could have gone on had not Plehve rescued him at every step."[34]

After Tolstoi's death in 1889 the tsar, having been advised against appointing the "enchanting but frightfully clever" Plehve, made I. N. Durnovo Minister of Interior. This, however, only increased Plehve's influence. Durnovo was dedicated to completing Tolstoi's work, but the job of minister was beyond his abilities. Plehve was kept on as assistant because, in the words of the empress, "the good Durnovo needs help."[35] Recognizing his own shortcomings, the new minister relied heavily on Plehve's advice and assistance. He entrusted his assistant with the most important work, as had Tolstoi before him, and he consulted Plehve on decisions ranging from the most momentous to the most trivial. So extensive was Plehve's role that several observers contended it was he, and not Durnovo, who was the real minister. "For all intents and purposes," according to Sergei Witte, "he ran the entire ministry."[36]

There can be little doubt as to the importance of Plehve's role during this period. True, he did not occupy a position of great formal authority, nor did he enjoy the confidence of Alexander III.[37] But, through Tolstoi and Durnovo, and especially through his chairmanship of important commissions, he did have substantial input into the decision-making process. In fact, Plehve was involved, in one way or another, with almost every major piece of legislation enacted during these years. The commissions he chaired dealt with such issues as the treatment of factory workers, foreign ownership of Russian lands, falling grain prices, peasant resettlement, administration of the Steppes and Baltic Regions, emergency food provisioning, and protection of peasant allotment lands. He also played a leading role in producing the major "counterreforms" of Alexander III's reign: the land captain law of 1889 and the revised zemstvo and town council statutes of 1890 and 1892. In addition to all this he was, for a time, chairman of a High Commission on regulations pertaining to Jews, and business manager of the Special Committee on Famine Relief. [38]

In general, although Plehve's commission work covered a broad range of diverse subjects, it all sought, in some way, to strengthen government control. The laws drafted by his factory commission, although "progressive" in the sense that they guaranteed workers' rights, expanded the government's factory inspection and made strikers liable to police arrest. The commission on the rights of foreigners led to increased restrictions on the acquisition of Russian property or citizenship. The commission on falling grain prices called for wholesale government involvement, and led to the formation of a Ministry of Agriculture. The resettlement commission strove, above all, to control and limit peasant migration. The commission on food provisions, critical of zemstvo failures to meet public need, sought to bring this function more directly under state control. The commissions on the Steppes and Baltic Provinces, in seeking to restrict local autonomy, "followed the principle of Russian State predominance with steadfast consistency." And the new law on peasant allotments, drafted by a commission which Plehve chaired, prohibited peasants from selling their lands without permission from the authorities. [39]

Administrative control was also the primary concern of the major "counterreforms." Although these measures have often been portrayed as reactionary class legislation designed to insure nobility domination, their main thrust was actually to increase the power of the state bureaucracy. Despite his stated sympathies and his own aristocratic background, Count Tolstoi was not really willing to allow the nobility much independence or influence. The land captain law, for instance, created a new local office, to be staffed by local noblemen, that would control and supervise all peasant affairs. The nobles would play a key role, to be sure, but less as representatives of their estate than as subordinates of the imperial bureaucracy. They were to be appointed by the Minister of Interior, who could also discipline or dismiss them, and supervised jointly by his ministry, the governors, and the marshalls of the nobility.[40]

The zemstvo reform of 1890, and the town council reform of 1892, both reveal a similar pattern. These institutions would continue to exist, but they would be deprived of their autonomy and brought directly under administrative control. Electoral laws were revised to insure nobility domination, primarily in hopes of excluding "unreliables." Even then, however, these bodies were not to be trusted: the Minister of Interior and governors were given broad powers to interfere in their activity, reverse their decisions, and dismiss their officials. Although zemstvo and council members were still to be elected, the law made clear they were in no sense representatives: they were merely a different variety of civil servant owing their allegiance, like all other bureaucrats, directly to the central government. As if to emphasize this, the law set forth that their elected officials must also be confirmed by the imperial administration.[41]

The enactment of all these measures was due, in large part, to the work of V. K. Plehve. The concepts, it is true, were not his; indeed, he had at first been critical of the land captain project. But when the time came for the proposals to be debated in commission and conferences, much of the burden fell upon his shoulders. Although originally considered ignorant of peasant affairs, he tackled the problems with characteristic energy and, within a short time, he thoroughly mastered the issues. As a frequent stand-in for the dying Tolstoi, he helped explain and defend the land captain law, and make it more palatable to those who had reservations. He also took the lead in revising the peasant court system to accommodate the land captains, who received judicial as well as administrative powers. His role in pushing through the later reforms on the zemstvos, town councils, and peasant land allotments was even more substantial. As chairman of the commissions which drafted these laws, and as their most effective advocate in the State Council, he bore a major share of the responsibility for the shaping, substance, and survival of these reforms.[42]

The activities of the Plehve Commission on the Jewish question were of a slightly different character. This commission had originally been constituted under K. I. Pahlen to draw up new laws concerning the Jews. Instead, it had recommended the repeal of existing restrictions, as obstructive to the cause of Jewish assimilation. This apparently displeased the anti-Semitic tsar: in any event the proposals were rejected, Pahlen stepped down and, in 1890, Plehve was appointed chairman in his stead. Within a short time the Commission evidently produced some very different proposals. According to several sources, Plehve worked out a plan calling for the gradual expulsion of all Jews from the larger cities, and the strengthening of earlier repressive laws. At any rate, consideration of these "new restrictive measures against the Jews" was soon blocked by the Minister of Finance, who feared they would jeopardize Russia's chances of securing foreign loans.[43]

Plehve's work also had its more positive side. In 1891, Russia was hit by severe drought and crop failure, and this was followed by widespread hunger. When he finally realized the scope of the tragedy, the tsar responded by naming his son, the future Nicholas II, to head a Special Committee on Famine Relief. The competent and versatile Plehve was chosen as business manager. As such, he was not only responsible for the committee's clerical work and agendas, he also oversaw the enormous task of coordinating all the various public and private relief efforts in Russia. Although the committee's efforts were too modest to prevent extensive suffering, they did help to facilitate and expedite the delivery of food and supplies to the affected regions. Needless to say, they also sought to establish government control over these operations.[44]

These committee assignments and legislative activities were by no means Plehve's only accomplishments as Assistant Minister. He was, of course, involved in many lesser projects and debates, within the ministry and without. He also received several awards and decorations for his various activities, and he managed to improve his social status. In 1891, based on the service achievements of his father, Plehve was formally registered as belonging to the hereditary nobility. The same year, as an imperial official, a landowner, and a nobleman, Plehve took part in a Special Commission for the Support of Noble Landownership, which proposed several measures to check the decline of noble landholdings in Russia. Plehve's stress, as usual, was on the political benefits this class provided to the Russian State.[45]

All in all, Plehve's years in the Ministry of Interior were good years for him, full of accomplishment and success. By 1893 he had proven himself a reliable, trustworthy, and energetic servant of four different ministers. Under Durnovo, especially, he had shown himself quite capable of running the ministry when the minister was gone; some would say he ran it even when Durnovo was there. It certainly seemed reasonable to expect that, sooner or later, Durnovo would step aside and Plehve himself would become minister, assuming the position he had been grooming for. But the tsar, apparently, had other ideas: Plehve's day had not yet arrived.

THE IMPERIAL SECRETARY AND MINISTER FOR FINLAND

On January 1, 1894, after nearly thirteen years in the Ministry of Interior, Viacheslav Plehve was appointed to the post of Imperial Secretary.[46] This appointment was theoretically a promotion: as head of the Imperial Chancery, a special secretarial body attached to the State Council, the Imperial Secretary was a very important official. Through his hands passed almost all of the imperial legislation, along with the appointments and salaries of State Council appointees. He even enjoyed "ministerial" status, and sat on the Committee of Ministers.

The Imperial Chancery had a major role in the legislative process. It sorted incoming proposals and sent them to the proper department. It edited and reworded proposals once they had been approved —an important function, considering the fact that the Council often approved laws in principle without dictating their exact wording. It compiled the minutes of department meetings, and it maintained the Council's archives. It was also responsible for the codification of laws. This latter duty, acquired shortly before Plehve's arrival, doubled the size of the Chancery and added greatly to its significance. It likewise increased the influence of the Imperial Secretary, leading to fears in some quarters that this office was becoming much too powerful.[47]

In spite of all this, Plehve does not seem to have been particularly pleased with his new position. For one thing, considering the influence he had accumulated as Assistant Minister, the new post was more of a transfer than a promotion—he still would not be making regular direct reports to the tsar. For another thing, the Imperial Chancery was held in rather low esteem by many, and Plehve may have shared this perception. Perhaps he was disturbed that he was stepping into the shoes of a former protégé, N. V. Murav'ev, who now moved on to a major ministerial post. No doubt he was concerned, now that "the last clever man" had left the Ministry of Interior, that the way was open for the ascendancy of Witte's Ministry of Finance. Most likely, it appears, Plehve was simply disappointed: he had set his sights on becoming the empire's chief administrator, not merely its chief secretary.[48]

As a result, there was a rather obvious contrast between his farewell address to the Ministry of Interior and his introduction to the

Imperial Chancery. In the former, he spoke warmly of his years at the ministry, and graciously accepted his colleagues' offer to fund a scholarship in his name. In the latter, by comparison, he came across as "sullen and unsociable," limiting himself to a rather perfunctory shaking of hands.[49]

Be that as it may, Plehve did manage to acquire a great deal of influence in his new post. This was due not so much to his direction of the ordinary business of the Chancery, in which he involved himself very little, but to the role he played in appointing new Council members. Appointments were made by the emperor on the recommendation of the Chairman of the State Council, who at that time was Grand Duke Mikhail Nikolaevich. By working through the Grand Duke, Plehve managed to obtain considerable voice in the selection of Council members. He was also able to influence the composition of the special commissions set up by the Council, and was himself a member of several of the most important commissions.[50]

Plehve's years at the Imperial Chancery were relatively quiet, but they were by no means uneventful. Under his direction, work proceeded on such projects as the third edition of the *Complete Collection of Laws*, a State Council reorganization plan, and a centennial history of the State Council. In 1894 he took part in a special commission for the revision of the judicial statutes which, had its recommendations been adopted, would have done away with judicial independence and severely restricted the use of the jury. Several years later he participated in a special conference chaired by E. V. Frish concerned with the promulgation of a new civil law code. He was also a member of the Special Conference on the Needs of the Nobility, which was established under I. N. Durnovo in 1897, and which met until 1901. In 1899, moreover, Plehve attained the rank of Right Privy Counsellor, the second-highest rank in the Russian Civil Service.[51]

Meanwhile, important changes were taking place in Russia's political and social climate. With the ascendancy of Witte, government emphasis was shifting from administrative counter-reform to economic progress, from agriculture to industry, and from nobility to bourgeoisie. Social tensions and revolutionary violence—almost dormant since Plehve's days at the Police Department—were beginning to re-emerge. At the head of the state, Alexander III's premature death in October of 1894 brought a young and inexperienced new monarch to the throne.

One of Nicholas II's first major decisions involved the career of Plehve. Early in 1895, a few months after his father's death, Nicholas

dismissed I. N. Durnovo from his post as Minister of Interior, subsequently appointing him Chairman of the Committee of Ministers.
However, he did not immediately name a successor.

The most obvious candidate for the post, and the one recommended by the outgoing minister, was the Imperial Secretary.[52]
Plehve's competence and intelligence were recognized by all, as was
his enormous energy. His experience was unmatched by any of his
rivals: during his three years as Police Director and nine as Assistant
Minister he had become thoroughly familiar with the operation of the
ministry. At 49 he was no longer too young to be considered for a
ministerial post. Under Tolstoi and Durnovo he had been groomed
for the top job, and now that it was vacant he seemed the logical
choice. His major rival, Dmitrii Sipiagin, was seven years younger
than he, and possessed neither his knowledge nor his ability. Furthermore, although Sipiagin did have some experience as a governor, he
had been Assistant Minister of Interior for only a year.

Before making his decision, Nicholas discussed the appointment
with two of his closest advisors. One of these was Witte, the other
Pobedonostsev, the Procurator of the Holy Synod. Neither was an
admirer of Plehve. Witte told the tsar that Plehve had great intelligence and was a good lawyer, but that he was an unprincipled career-
maker: "I do not think that anyone knows what Plehve's real opinions
and convictions are, and I suppose even Plehve himself does not know.
He will hold those opinions which he considers to be to his personal
advantage at a given moment, or which will be advantageous when he
is in a position of authority." Pobedonostsev, according to Witte, was
much more succinct. "Sipiagin is a fool," he told the emperor, "and
Plehve is a scoundrel."[53]

After several months of hesitation the young emperor finally decided to choose neither, and instead gave the post to acting Minister
I. L. Goremykin on a permanent basis. Like Sipiagin, Goremykin had
been an assistant minister for only a year. According to Witte, this
appointment won for the Finance Minister the undying enmity of
Plehve, who was convinced that Witte had turned the sovereign
against him.[54] In view of the conversation related above, it would seem
that Plehve's grudge was not entirely without foundation.

Frustrated in his hopes to become Minister of Interior, V. K.
Plehve began to search for other ways to increase his influence. One
of these was commission work, in which he had excelled as Assistant
Minister. Even here, however, he ran into the opposition of Witte.
The Special Conference on the Needs of the Nobility, begun in 1897,

for a time disintegrated into a series of intense, often bitter debates between Plehve and Witte. The Minister of Finance, by this time, had become the leading advocate of industrial capitalism in Russia. Plehve, one of the few officials who could hold their own in debate against Witte, assumed the role of spokesman for the opposition. The conference itself accomplished little, but it did reveal an interesting anomaly: Witte, the nobles' "enemy," was willing to give them broader scope in the creation of new noblemen than Plehve, their supposed "friend." The latter, fearing that "alien" elements (such as industrialists and merchants) might penetrate the nobility, favored strict qualifications to insure the moral and political reliability of members of the first estate.[55]

In fall of 1899 the Ministry of Interior again changed hands. Once more Plehve was passed up, this time in favor of Sipiagin. Although Witte insisted he had done nothing to influence this selection, his antipathy toward Plehve and preference for Sipiagin were well-known.[56] The Imperial Secretary, meanwhile, had found another way to increase his influence, securing a position which provided him with regular access to the emperor.

Plehve's opportunity came as a result of the government's decision to strengthen its control over Finland. The Finns, who had been under Russian rule since 1808, were accustomed to considering themselves as an autonomous entity whose ruling Grand Duke happened also to be the Emperor of Russia. They had their own language, their own laws, their own religion, their own army—they even had their own legislative body, or Diet. For nearly a century Russian emperors had honored a promise not to tamper with their "fundamental laws," and the Finns, in return, had been loyal subjects. But this quasi-constitutional set up, and the growing Finnish sense of national identity, ran counter to the Russian notion of centralized autocratic power. In 1898, after several years of study, the Ministry of War proposed to abolish the Finnish army and draft Finns into the Russian military. Tsar Nicholas II was readily supportive. In July, he summoned a special session of the Finnish Diet to consider this plan, and the following month he appointed an ardent Russian nationalist named N. I. Bobrikov to be Governor-General of Finland.[57]

At this juncture, V. K. Plehve began to get involved in Finnish affairs. The emperor, aware that the Diet was unlikely to approve his project, called into existence a special commission to revise the system of Finnish legislation. A prominent role in this commission was played by the Imperial Secretary. Sensing the tsar's desire to deal harshly with the Finns, and seizing upon this as a vehicle for his own ambitions, Plehve took the lead in composing a new legal order for Finland. The result was an Imperial Manifesto, written by Plehve, which was issued, along with certain "Fundamental Statutes," on February 3, 1899. Together these documents declared that all legislation which touched on "the common interests of the Empire"—even if it was to be applied only in Finland—must henceforth be examined by the Russian State Council. The Diet was reduced to a purely advisory function.[58]

The publication of these acts resulted in general turmoil in Finland, where the Diet had just begun consideration of the military bill. Numerous public and private protests were made, but to no avail: Nicholas remained adamant.

Meanwhile, on April 6, 1899, Plehve received permission from the tsar to form, under the auspices of the Imperial Chancery, a commission for the codification of Finnish laws. If the State Council was now going to legislate for Finland, he reasoned, it must have access to previous Finnish legislation. "Such a commission," he added, "would no doubt contribute to the calm and gradual clarification of those misunderstandings which obscure the whole question of the Fundamental Laws of Finland."[59] Although the commission, in fact, neither calmed nor clarified the situation, it did provide Plehve with frequent access to the emperor. Then, with the support of Governor-general Bobrikov, he pressed his candidacy for the Office of Minister-State Secretary for the Grand Duchy of Finland. On August 17, 1899, Nicholas finally appointed him to this post, while instructing him to stay on as Imperial Secretary.[60] At long last, V. K. Plehve was in a position to make regular reports to the tsar.

Plehve's new position was a difficult one. The Minister-State Secretary was Finland's representative in Saint Petersburg; as such, he had traditionally been a Finn. The Finns were not disposed to look kindly on a Russian bureaucrat sitting in this position, especially one who had been responsible for the Manifesto of February 3, 1899. Their irritation was compounded by the provocative activities of Governor-General Bobrikov, who seemed determined to force the Finns into either full submission or full rebellion.[61]

In the beginning, at least, Plehve proceeded rather cautiously, apparently hoping to avoid complete alienation of the Finns. "We do not propose to abolish either their legislative or administrative autonomy," he wrote to a colleague in September 1899. "We only desire that this autonomy does not exclude our own state laws, according to which Finland is a division of the state ruled by the autocratic authority. . . ." He tried to establish good relations with certain Finnish statesmen of the "Compliant" party—those who were willing to meet the Russians half-way. He even advised Bobrikov to use a bit more tact. "I am in favor of strict measures, taken from time to time," he wrote the governor-general, "but I am opposed to partial vivisection. . . . It seems to me that the former is a sobering scare, while the latter is a gradual irritation, only adding to distrust of the authorities."[62] Nevertheless, Plehve's attempts to calm the situation and win Finnish confidence came to naught.

Perhaps the main reason for the failure of his efforts was that the actions of his government belied his moderate words. Although he was at times critical of Bobrikov's haste and harshness, Plehve collaborated closely with the governor-general, and their policies earned the full support of Emperor Nicholas II. With Plehve's acquiescence—indeed, with his active support—the Russians took steps designed to bring the Finns directly under the control of the imperial government. Wholesale changes were made in the personnel of the Finnish administration. The Finnish Senate was directed to keep all its records in Russian. Measures were taken to increase the study of the Russian language in Finnish schools. In August 1900 a commission on the internal administration of Finland was set up under Plehve's chairmanship; it eventually produced legislation which opened up the Finnish civil service to Russian applicants and increased the powers of the governor-general.[63]

Other aspects of Plehve's activity could scarcely have mollified the Finns. In December of 1899 he secured an additional appointment as Chancellor of Helsingfors University, and quickly pressed the school's officials to prevent political action by the students. The following spring, on a visit to the university, he upbraided a professor for having the audacity to evaluate the work of Catherine the Great. Meanwhile, in Saint Petersburg, he warned visiting Finnish dignitaries that anti-Russian protests could lead to the closing of the Finnish Diet.[64]

Finally, in 1901, the military issue that had begun the whole affair was tackled by the Russian government. Although the idea of incorporating the Finns into the Russian army had originated with War Minister A. N. Kuropatkin, Plehve supported it as if it were his own. Once again, he found himself in conflict with Witte, who put forth his own, "more moderate" version. In the debates that followed, in a special committee and in the State Council, Plehve was very cautious and discreet. Witte, in fact, was able to win much support for his "compromise" plan, and his proposal carried the day by a wide margin. Unfortunately for Witte, his victory proved hollow: Plehve, Bobrikov, and Kuropatkin had lined up the one vote that really counted. On June 29, 1901, Nicholas II formally sanctioned the opinion of the minority, confirming Kuropatkin's project into law. At the same time he ordered the dissolution of the separate Finnish army.[65]

The passage of the military incorporation law, coming on top of the "reforms" of Plehve and Bobrikov, called forth a storm of protest in Finland. A campaign of mass petitions and passive resistance was waged against the Russians. The first Russian attempt at conscription of Finns, on April 2, 1902, met with almost total non-compliance. Street riots followed in various Finnish cities.[66] Plehve's hopes of a calm transition had failed to materialize. By this time, however, the Minister-State Secretary had other things on his mind.

On April 2, 1902, along with the Finnish conscription, came the murder of Sipiagin. Once more, the tsar would have to choose a Minister of Interior. But who would get the call this time? Witte's name was mentioned, as were those of Bobrikov and several others. But the name "on everybody's lips" was that of the Imperial Secretary: Plehve's hour had finally arrived. Not long after the assassination, he was summoned to the emperor's residence and offered the most influential office in the Russian Empire.[67] His acceptance was a foregone conclusion.

CHARACTER, ABILITY, AND OUTLOOK

Such was the background of the new Minister of the Interior. He had vast experience in several areas of government. His thirty-five years in state service included legislative, judicial, and administrative work. This experience would help him, now that he had reached the top, but there were other considerations of equal significance to his contemporaries. What sort of a man was he? What were his views, and what were his goals? In what direction was he likely to lead Russia?

Foremost among Plehve's attributes was his intelligence. Friend and foe alike paid tribute to his mental ability. "Plehve was unquestionably an intelligent and talented man . . ." admitted his arch-rival Witte. Others saw him as "adroit, crafty, and intelligent"; "intelligent and efficient"; a man of "extraordinary intellect." "He possessed many qualities," wrote one colleague, "a remarkable mind, a vast memory, the ability to work without rest. There was no matter which was so difficult that he could not master it in a short time."[68]

This "ability to work without rest" was his other outstanding quality. Throughout his career, he had impressed observers with his enormous energy and vigor. "Plehve's outstanding capacity for work was universally recognized," wrote a labor expert commissioned by him. "My memo-reports were sometimes very thick. . . . I could not help but be amazed at his interest . . . and his astonishing patience. . . ." According to Plehve's eulogist: "Those closest to him in government work could not but attest to his exceptional energy [and] his inexhaustible capacity for work."[69]

Other qualities possessed by the new minister included a large share of administrative talent, a calm and unexcitable nature, a frank and businesslike disposition, and even a certain degree of charm. Long years in various bureaucratic positions had made him, in the words of a close associate, a "superlative clerk." He was a capable organizer, a demanding boss, and a good judge of men.[70] His ability to keep his head in a crisis, evident at the time of Alexander II's assassination, was but one manifestation of the cautious imperturbability he brought to all his posts. "Neither one-sided passion nor hasty decisions and measures are in the character of the new Minister of Interior," wrote the influential *New Times* on the occasion of his appointment.[71]

Although he could be cruel to his subordinates, he respected those who stood their ground before him. He placed great value on forthrightness and candor, and he "was able to listen to the truth when it was told him to his face." He was "extraordinarily plain-spoken in conversation," and he disliked "ingratiating flattery." Furthermore, he was able to combine this plain-spokenness and lack of airs with friendliness and sincerity when the occasion demanded. He possessed good manners and a great deal of polish—traits which distinguished him sharply from his less accomplished colleague at the Ministry of Finance. He was well-read and sophisticated—and he was always well-informed. Above all, he "had the talent of tacitly suggesting that a great deal of genuine, enlightened statesmanship lay hidden under the smooth surface of his cautious reserve."[72]

On the negative side of the ledger, despite his intelligence and experience, Plehve was a man of narrow scope and limited vision. His entire career had been spent in the imperial bureaucracy, and he suffered from bureaucratic myopia. His solutions to problems tended to be bureaucratic solutions; he "apparently thought that the most efficient way to insure the future peaceful and systematic development of

Russia would be to perfect the state machinery." He did not have many contacts outside the government, in business or intellectual circles, or even among the nobility. As a consequence, there was no group among the population whom he could readily count on for support.[73]

Plehve evidently had few close friends; his personal life seems to have been overshadowed by his political career. Although he had lived in Saint Petersburg for 23 years, he apparently participated little in the social life of the capital. He owned a modest country estate, and was formally a member of the nobility, but he had never participated actively in the affairs of that class. He was, in fact, one of a growing number of high officials who did not have extensive landholdings. His own family was small: a wife, a son, and a daughter. His son, Nikolai, was involved in government, ultimately becoming Assistant Minister of Interior a decade after his father's death. His daughter, Elizaveta, was married to N. I. Vuich, who later became business manager of the Committee of Ministers and eventually a senator.[74]

Among his colleagues, although he was widely respected, Plehve was neither well-liked nor well-trusted. Despite the fact that he could be charming and courteous with visitors, he was often sarcastic and cruel towards his own subordinates. Conscious of his own ability, he held many of his colleagues in rather low esteem and, unless he needed their support for some reason or other, made little attempt to hide it. On one hand he cultivated the favor of highly-placed persons; on the other he "kept his subordinates in constant awe of him" and at times "gave vent to a caustic humor at their expense." These traits, combined with his driving ambition, had made him many enemies, even among those who shared his political views. "From my first meeting with Plehve I felt distrust toward him," wrote Prince V. P. Meshcherskii, ". . . he is an unreliable and even dangerous man, clever and resourceful like Beelzebub."[75]

Some in fact, would have said that Plehve had no political views. Sergei Witte, for one, cited his early career as evidence of this:

> When Plehve was Procurator of the Chamber of Justice his ideals were liberal enough, and as a result of this Count Loris-Melikov . . . made him Director of the Police Department. . . . Then Loris-Melikov was replaced by Count Ignat'ev. Plehve became Ignat'ev's right-hand man, and kow-towed to Count Ignat'ev, even though . . . Ignat'ev's opinions were completely at odds with those of Loris-Melikov. . . . Later Count Ignat'ev was replaced by Minister of Interior Tolstoi. Tolstoi . . . was a representative of autocratic bureau-

cracy in the fullest sense of the word, and Plehve became the greatest admirer and supporter of his system.

Alexander III himself had shared Witte's appraisal of Plehve. "Of course he has excellent convictions when you are around," he once told Count Tolstoi, "but when you are gone his convictions are different." Many felt Plehve would hold any view which happened to be in vogue. "It takes courage to go against the current," went the popular assessment of him, "but even a dead fish can swim with the stream."[76] Even those who were more kindly disposed toward Plehve recognized him as a man "determined to elevate himself at any cost." He was ambitious, opportunistic, and career-minded, and he was aware that he must please the right people in order to get ahead. "[H]e knew perfectly well that it was impossible to accomplish anything unless one was willing to humor influential persons by granting some of their demands." Therefore, according to one associate, "he strove to be on the same good terms with one and all, so as not to close off any of the various paths for his career."[77]

This desire to please led him to be extremely cautious about expressing his own opinions or committing himself to any definite stand. He tended to speak in the "polished phrases characteristic of a lawyer bureaucrat," and with "the evasiveness distinguishing anyone who has pretensions of an official career in Petersburg." As one observer noted in 1894: "His opinion is very difficult to find out, since he does not express it. He knows how to avoid a direct reply, and does this so skillfully that the listener is not offended by his cautiousness."[78] This did not always work to Plehve's advantage—colleagues often perceived this cautiousness as a sign of lack of principle. "This man, with his excellent manners and imperturbable calm, was not apt to let drop one superfluous word in a conversation. He never raised the intonation of his voice, which was like a cold wind. Everyone instinctively recognized that it was very dangerous to trust him."[79]

On the whole, it is true, Plehve preferred to think of himself as a man of action rather than a man of dreams, as a practical worker rather than as a theoretician, and as a problem solver rather than as an ideologue. He saw "abstract ideas" and "immature political thought" as diseases affecting Russian life, and he had little use for any approach that was not "forged by practical experience." In making his career, and in shaping state policy, he was more likely to be persuaded by the effectiveness of an action than by its conformity with a set of preconceived principles.[80]

This does not mean, of course, that he lacked political convictions. In his attitude toward governance he was a product of the Ministry of Interior, in which he had served so well, and he considered himself a "pupil" of Ministers Tolstoi and Durnovo.[81] He surpassed even his mentors, however, in his cleverness, energy, and opportunism, in his recognition of the need for change, and in his determination to concentrate power in the hands of the imperial bureaucracy.

Plehve was, above all, a supporter of autocratic absolutism and paternalistic bureaucratic control. Compared to Tolstoi and Durnovo, he had few close connections with the landed gentry, and less real empathy with the needs and views of that estate. He possessed, moreover, a passion for unity, harmony, and order, which he saw as both the source of Russia's strength and the key to her future survival. He disliked the pluralism, competition, and individualism of the West, and he hoped that Russia could somehow avoid "the oppression of capital, bourgeoisie, and class struggle." This could be done, he was convinced, if only all the emperor's subjects could be compelled to work together for the common goals of Russian power, prosperity, and stability.[82]

In spite of all this, he was not necessarily an opponent of modernization and reform. Plehve was well aware of the fact that Russia was undergoing profound economic and social changes which could neither be ignored nor prevented. He did feel, though, that they must be controlled. The very circumstance of these changes made firm state direction even more necessary, since only strict autocratic discipline could prevent the sort of fragmentation and disunity he feared would destroy the Russian state. As he would later contend, all of the progressive and modernizing reforms of the past century had been carried out by the autocratic government, often in the face of opposition from the educated classes. In his view, "neither the Russian people in general nor the educated circles in particular were sufficiently well-trained to be allowed to govern their country." Only a well-organized and powerful government could be expected to provide unity, direction, and purpose to Russian life. If the government had so far failed to solve Russia's problems, it was because it did not yet have the necessary public support and sufficient political control.[83]

Political control, of course, was Plehve's forte. He was known as an advocate of "decisive measures": severe, repressive actions taken all at once, as opposed to hesitation and piecemeal retreat. He had made his reputation as a policeman, and as an advocate of "strict social discipline in all areas of the people's lives which are accessible to control by the government."[84] He had once helped restore order and reassert control at a time of internal crisis. Now, with a similar crisis threatening Russia, he had again been called to the fore.

In truth, then, Plehve was something more than just a self-seeking opportunist. He was a careerist, admittedly, but he worked as hard or harder than anyone in Saint Petersburg. He sought power, to be sure, but he was also willing to sacrifice: he had few friends, little time for relaxation, and no social life to speak of. He was, apparently, a man of financial integrity: at least he did not use his high office as a means of amassing wealth. Nor does he seem to have been a seeker of fame or recognition: he made little effort to improve, or even protect, his public image.[85] Besides, the post of Minister of Interior was neither a pleasant nor a popular one, and it involved no small amount of danger to its occupant's own life. To pursue and accept such a position required not just ambition and opportunism; it also took dedication and courage. "Everything was present," observed one contemporary, "intelligence, character, honor, efficiency, experience."[86]

3

The Peasant Question and
the Zemstvos

THE KHAR'KOV AND POLTAVA RIOTS

Imperial Secretary Plehve was at work in his office at the Mariinskii Palace when the news came that the Minister of Interior had been shot. He rushed through the palace corridors to the Committee of Ministers hall, where the incident had occurred. He was one of the first to arrive. After issuing instructions to have the wounded Sipiagin taken to the hospital, he remained at the palace, discussing the event with the ministers and other dignitaries on hand. [1]

Later that afternoon, according to one account, Plehve was summoned to the imperial palace. Angered by the act of terrorism, Nicholas II was anxious to choose a new minister. "You have long been a candidate for the post of Minister of Interior," the tsar reportedly declared. "Now I know you better and I have decided to appoint you." [2] Although the announcement was not made for several days, observers were struck by Plehve's confident bearing at Sipiagin's funeral. Finally, on the evening of April 4, 1902, came the formal announcement: it was "benevolently ordained" that "State Secretary, Imperial Secretary, Minister State-Secretary for the Grand Duchy of Finland, Senator, and Right Privy Counsellor von Plehve" was to be the new Minister of Interior. [3]

As might have been expected, Plehve proceeded rather cautiously in his first few days in office. On Saturday, April 6, he met briefly with the key officials of the ministry and made a short, noncommittal speech. He eulogized his late predecessor and, in a rather somber note, declared that the "historical significance" of contemporary events was such that "actions, not words" were required. "I invite you to judicious, well-intentioned, and harmonious work," he told his new subordinates, "and I demand honest and skillful cooperation."[4]

Although the use of the word "demand" raised a few eyebrows, the public reaction to the speech—and to the appointment itself—was not unfavorable. The publisher of the *Citizen* applauded Plehve's "brief but forceful remarks" and noted that "everyone seems satisfied with this appointment." The publisher of the *New Times* remarked to an associate that he admired the new minister's "honesty" in admitting the current difficulties. The Minister of War, in a congratulatory message, expressed a similar sentiment. "I am happy for the Tsar, and for Russia, but not for you," he wrote. "Your new activity will bring many difficulties and concerns."[5]

Indeed it would. The murder of Sipiagin, the riots in Finland, the peasant revolts in the Ukraine—these were only the most recent and most visible manifestations of widespread unrest in the Russian Empire. University students, factory workers, national minorities, and educated society in general all were dissatisfied, all demanded change. Plehve's mandate seemed clear enough. He must restore order, reassert government authority, bring the situation back under control. And he must take steps to end the discontent, and to satisfy the real needs and legitimate demands of the populace.[6] But therein lay the rub. If he used authoritative, repressive measures to quell dissent and assert control, might this not serve only to increase discontent, and heighten resentment and hostility?

Authoritative, repressive measures, however, were Plehve's stock in trade, and few doubted that his appointment signalled a new, "get-tough" policy. On April 10, as if to underscore this impression, the tsar dismissed Minister of Education P. S. Vannovsky for reasons of "health." Vannovsky, who had aroused the emperor's ire by proposing a rather liberal reform of the secondary schools, was replaced by a hard-line traditionalist named G. E. Zenger. That same day it was announced that Sipiagin's murderer, at Plehve's behest, would be turned over to the military for trial. As a minor, the assassin would not have faced the death penalty in a civil court. And this, according to Plehve, was not a time for leniency. "I was brought to the ministry as a strongman," he confided to the French ambassador. "If I manifest the slightest hesitation in repression, I shall lose my *raison d'être.*"[7]

A third development of April 10, 1902, dealt with an even more serious concern: the peasant riots in the Ukraine. In recent years, unrest had surfaced among workers, students, intellectuals, and Finns, but the vast multitudes of "dark" peasants had remained relatively silent. Now, suddenly, the spectre of massive peasant revolt seemed very real. Plehve's response was characteristic: moving quickly, he decided to go to the troubled areas himself and determine the nature and scope of the problem. That evening, only six days into his tenure, he left Saint Petersburg for a visit to the riot-torn provinces of Khar'kov and Poltava. "Now there is a minister," remarked one admiring observer. "Not many would have done that!"[8]

The first stop on Plehve's itinerary, however, was Moscow. There he paid a visit to the governor-general, and he discussed the worker situation with local officials. He then travelled to the nearby Holy Trinity Monastery, where he spent the next three days—Good Friday, Holy Saturday, and Easter Sunday. He fasted, confessed his sins, and received the sacrament. He was presented with an icon by archimandrite Nikon, who described Plehve's appointment as "a new holy penance imposed on you by our devout sovereign."[9]

This "pilgrimage" to the ancient monastery caused considerable comment. The former Imperial Secretary had not been known for his piety, and the trip was seen by some as a blatant attempt to curry favor with the religiously-inclined emperor. It certainly could do him no harm in this regard. But, as with so many of Plehve's actions, his cynical opportunism was almost certainly mixed with an element of sincerity. After all, his predecessor had been brutally murdered the week before, and he himself was aware that his appointment made him a primary target of the revolutionary terrorists. It is not uncommon for a man in such a position to suddenly become concerned about things spiritual. Plehve himself explained his visit this way: "I understand and am fully aware that I am about to die."[10]

On Easter Sunday morning the absolved penitent left the monastery and, after a brief stopover in Moscow, headed south on the express train to Khar'kov. Arriving the next day, he held long meetings with the governor, Prince I. M. Obolenskii, and the procurator, A. A. Lopukhin. Not surprisingly, considering his own background, Plehve seems to have placed particular weight on the procurator's report, demanding of Lopukhin not just an account of events but a critique of the local administration. During the next several days he met with numerous other local dignitaries, and made a brief trip to Poltava, where he spent the day interviewing officials in his railway car.[11] From all these discussions, there began to emerge a rather disturbing picture.

The "black-earth" provinces of Khar'kov and Poltava were located in the midst of the Russian Empire's best farm country, an area known simply as the "Center." Ironically, the very richness of the soil had been part of the problem: peasants there had done little to improve their primitive farming methods and, unlike their counterparts in less fertile regions, had not developed alternative sources of income. To make matters worse, increasing indebtedness often forced many peasants to turn over a substantial portion of each year's harvest to their creditors. They were particularly vulnerable, therefore, to crop failure, and they had been hit especially hard by the poor harvest of 1901.[12]

As spring of 1902 approached, the dwindling peasant food supply had begun to run out in several locales. Nightly theft of bread and potatoes from the storehouses of local nobles increased, spurred on by rumors that the peasants had been authorized to seize the grain. Beginning in mid-March, in several counties of Poltava province, groups of peasants began appearing at the manor houses of local nobles, requesting food for themselves and fodder for their livestock. The requests soon turned to demands, and the demands were soon enforced by violence. Manor houses and warehouses were plundered, and large quantities of foodstuffs were removed. On March 30 the Poltava governor, slow to realize the severity of the problem, finally called out troops to quell the riots. The soldiers encountered resistance from peasant crowds armed with stakes and pitchforks, but by April 3 they were able to restore relative calm to the affected districts, although not without bloodshed.[13]

In the meantime, the violence had spread to Khar'kov province. Here it took on an even more unbridled character: several manor houses were wrecked and burnt. Responding quickly, Khar'kov governor Prince Obolenskii set out for the scene of the disorders on March 31 with an infantry battalion and a band of cossacks. In their effort to put down the disorders, Obolenskii and his troops made liberal use of corporal punishment, including wholesale and apparently indiscriminate flogging. These extreme measures evidently were effective: within several days the turmoil had ceased and order was restored. According to government figures, only twenty-six estates were ravaged in Khar'kov province, as compared with seventy-nine in Poltava.[14]

Obolenskii's actions created a good deal of controversy. It was widely felt that, in resorting to corporal punishment, he had overstepped the bounds of his authority.[15] The attention of government and society therefore focused on the new Minister of Interior. Plehve's response would provide the first solid evidence of what sort of course he intended to pursue.

The minister returned to Saint Petersburg on April 20 without making known his conclusions. Before long, however, it became clear to all where he stood. Following Plehve's report to the emperor, it was announced on April 28 that Obolenskii had been awarded the coveted Order of Saint Vladimir for his "outstanding zeal and earnest service in taking measures to quell the disorders." At the same time his Poltava counterpart, who had been relatively slow to respond, was dismissed from his post. On Plehve's initiative, the Law on Exceptional Measures was invoked to place much of Poltava province in a state of "strengthened security."[16] "Decisive measures" were the order of the day.

The agrarian disorders, and Plehve's response to them, had several important consequences. They served, of course, to focus government attention even more sharply on the peasant question, and to underscore the need for reform in this area. In addition, they brought the new minister into conflict with the zemstvos, at whose doorstep he lay much of the blame for stirring up the peasants.

THE PEASANT QUESTION

The largest problem facing the Russian government in 1902 was the peasant question. In spite of Witte's industrial revolution, Russia was still a peasant country: the vast majority of Nicholas's subjects were peasant farmers who survived by tilling the soil, much as their ancestors before them. They were, like their ancestors, an uneducated and simple folk, conservative and superstitious, with little awareness of anything beyond their own villages. Yet unlike their ancestors they were free: serfdom had been abolished in 1861, and roughly half the empire's privately owned land had been allotted to the peasants.

This had not made them independent landowners. In general, the land had been turned over, not to the individual peasant, but to the village commune as a whole. The commune, an indigenous institution of joint land tenure, had inherited some arbitrary powers, including the right to impose forced labor, to banish members, and to regulate their comings and goings. Its members were bound by collective liability (krugovaia poruka) for taxes and debts, and they could not sell their allotments, or leave the village, without approval from the village assembly. The commune even controlled the working of the land, since the allotment of each member normally consisted of separate strips of land in each of the open fields surrounding the village. Not only did the peasants have to sow and reap according to the commune schedule, in most villages the land was periodically "repartitioned," with each member receiving an entirely different set of strips every dozen years.

By 1902, it had become apparent that all was not well in the Russian village. Thanks partly to ignorance, partly to tradition, and partly to the restrictions imposed by the commune, farming methods had failed to keep pace with the growing population. Since 1861, the number of peasants had nearly doubled and thus, despite constant efforts to make more land available, the size of the average peasant allotment had shrunk by one-third. Direct and indirect taxes added a considerable burden to the peasants, especially since they also had to pay regular "redemption dues" to the government for lands received in 1861. Rising land prices, falling grain prices, and fluctuating pay for agricultural work often added to the problems of many peasants, and even threatened the nobility.

Paradoxically, these problems were most acute in areas where the soil was richest. In places where the soil was poor, peasants had learned to improve the land and to supplement their income from outside work. As consumers, they even tended to benefit from lower food prices. In the fertile Center region, however, the only way most peasants knew to increase their income was to cultivate a larger area. Increasing population thus had led to "land-hunger": more and more peasants could not support themselves from their own shrinking allotments. Meanwhile, some wealthier landowners who had turned to more advanced, intensive farming were producing bumper yields. As a result, overall production was actually increasing in the same areas where rural poverty was at its worst. These were the conditions that led to the Khar'kov and Poltava riots, and these were the factors behind the growing government concern about conditions in the Russian village. [17]

Within the government, there had emerged two main schools of thought on how to deal with this problem. The "tutelage" approach, identified mainly with the Ministry of Interior, was concerned primarily with keeping order in the villages. The peasants, it was felt, required special treatment, and the government had a duty to guide, supervise, and protect this class. Peasant problems could be dealt with effectively only if the administrative apparatus were expanded and perfected so as to bring local affairs more directly under state control. This approach had been embodied in measures such as the land captain law of 1889, the zemstvo statute of 1890, and the 1893 law against "alienation" of peasant land. Its main responses to peasant poverty were to make more land available, and to prevent the sale of peasant lands to outside persons. It sought, in general, to preserve the traditional institutions, including the peasant commune.[18]

The other school of thought, which might be called the "self-reliance" approach, felt the main concern should be increased agricultural productivity. From this viewpoint, government efforts to prop up the existing order merely perpetuated backwardness, and protection of the "weaker elements" merely encouraged weakness. The commune, in which the more industrious peasants were "held back" by their less productive comrades, was seen as particularly injurious. What was needed was "freedom": freedom for the sturdy and strong to grow and prosper at the expense of their weaker fellows. There was a certain harshness to this approach: it suggested that, left to their own devices, only the stronger peasants would survive. The weak would have to hire out as wage laborers, move to the city, or perish. In this way the Russian countryside would be transformed from a multitude of narrow strips to a smaller number of larger, productive farms. Agriculture would prosper, food production would increase, and cheap labor would be provided by industry. Proponents of this view admitted it would cause a certain amount of social upheaval, but insisted the alternative was continued backwardness, poverty, and increasing unrest.[19]

The lines of conflict, in reality, were by no means clearly drawn. The landowning nobility, traditionally conservative, tended to favor the preservation of time-honored institutions and oppose the growth of capitalism, implicit in the self-reliance approach. Some, seeing their own existence threatened by falling grain prices and American competition, demanded state support. Others, however, had begun to improve their lands, employ more advanced methods, and strive for an agricultural revolution based on individual entrepreneurship. They sought, like the British nobles of the eighteenth century, to consolidate and enclose their fields, and to put an end to things such as open-field cultivation, common grazing, and the intermingling of peasant and noble plots. These persons, many of whom were active in the zemstvos, increasingly emphasized self-reliance as the key to rural prosperity.[20]

Within the government, Sergei Witte—as he turned his attention to agriculture—was also coming to champion the self-reliance approach. The depression of the past few years had demonstrated dramatically how dependent Russian industry was on agriculture. High production and low grain prices were essential, both to secure loans and purchases abroad, and to feed the growing urban labor force. Perhaps the capitalist virtues of self-reliance and competition could also work for farming—or, as Witte preferred to call it, the "agricultural industry." Ironically, the views of the Minister of Finance and those of his enemies, the rural nobility, were beginning to converge.[21]

Viacheslav Plehve, an avowed supporter of the nobility, was closely identified with the tutelage approach. A firm advocate of increased social control, he had been one of the foremost proponents of the tutelage legislation of the 1880s and 1890s. Still, by 1902 even he was expressing private doubts about the traditional order. "In complete secret I must tell you that I am by no means a sectarian on theories of land-usage," he told a State Council member. "I recognize that collectivism and its expression—communal land ownership—is nonsense, leading only to confusion." Nevertheless, he concluded, any change-over must be gradual, and steps should be taken to prevent the growth of a landless rural proletariat.[22] Placed into context, these remarks are significant: they show that Plehve, at the beginning of his ministry, was not necessarily opposed to more freedom of action for individual peasants, nor was he unalterably committed to the preservation of the commune.

THE SPECIAL CONFERENCE ON THE NEEDS OF AGRICULTURAL INDUSTRY

Plehve's handling of the peasant question was conditioned by two events that had occurred in January 1902—three months before his appointment. One was the emperor's instruction to Minister of Interior Sipiagin to begin the process of revising peasant legislation. The other was the establishment of a "Special Conference" to study the agriculture question, under the chairmanship of Sergei Witte.

The work of revising peasant legislation was actually the resumption of an earlier project, begun by the Ministry of Interior in 1893, but suspended several years later. It was a careful, time-consuming program, typical of the legislative revisions undertaken by the Russian government. Various departments within the ministry were to draw up proposals and submit them to an "Editing Commission," directed by the assistant minister in charge of peasant affairs. The projects would then go to a special conference chaired by the minister himself. Its conclusions, finally, would be re-drafted by the ministry's Land Section, and submitted to the State Council. Semi-annual reports were to be made to the emperor on the progress of the work.[23]

The Special Conference, on the other hand, was a new attempt to deal with the agricultural problem. On January 18, 1902, four days after commissioning the Ministry of Interior's project, the emperor called in Sipiagin, Witte, and Minister of Agriculture Ermolov to announce the formation of an imperial conference on agriculture. It was to be chaired by Witte and include, besides the major state officials, any other knowledgeable person the chairman cared to invite. The choice of a chairman was in some ways odd: Witte had long been perceived as an enemy of agriculture, and he had consistently opposed additional appropriations for the agriculture department. But the situation was getting desperate, and Witte was Nicholas's most capable and most imaginative statesman. "I have appointed you chairman because if you cannot do this job, no one can," the emperor reportedly remarked. The Special Conference on the Needs of Agricultural Industry was established by imperial order on January 23, 1902.[24]

The simultaneous commissioning of these two efforts caused a good deal of confusion. Nicholas apparently intended that Witte's conference was to deal solely with agricultural production, while Sipiagin's project was to concern itself with the legal aspects of peasant life—as if it were somehow possible to treat the "peasant question" and the "agricultural question" as two separate issues. Witte at once recognized the futility of trying to cope with "the needs of agricultural industry" without addressing the legal organization of village life. He proposed, therefore, that the question of peasant legislation be included within the purview of his conference. Sipiagin, however, insisted upon the prerogatives of his department and refused to back down. In an attempt at compromise, the emperor suggested that the peasant question should be discussed in full in both the Special Conference and the Ministry of Interior, after which the conclusions would be presented to him for final decision.[25] But Nicholas' attempt to appease both ministers only made matters worse. The responsibilities of the conference and the ministry would now overlap—causing needless duplication, and making some sort of conflict almost inevitable.

Sipiagin's project never really got started: he had done little more than make application for funds by the time he was assassinated. Witte, however, attacked the problem with characteristic energy and speed. He quickly selected the members of his conference, got them approved by the emperor, and began holding meetings in early February. The first several meetings were devoted primarily to procedural questions; nevertheless, they produced an important development. At its second session, following a rather sudden turnabout by its chairman, the conference adopted a plan by which committees for preliminary discussion of local agricultural needs were to be established in every province and county. The information and recommendations presented by these committees would then be assembled and used as a basis for action by the Special Conference. The proposal was confirmed by the emperor on March 22, 1902.[26]

The idea of soliciting local opinion prior to the drafting of legislation was not uncommon in imperial Russia, and there was little reason to suspect that these new committees might present a threat to public order. Even V. K. Plehve, participating in the conference as Imperial Secretary, supported their formation. But the fact that the committees were established on the county level, as well as on the provincial, meant there would be more than six hundred of them: a rather large number from the standpoint of control. And the committees would contain a fairly large number of zemstvo officials, marshals of the nobility, and "knowledgeable local persons." It was almost certain, therefore, that at least a few of these committees would stray from purely agricultural concerns to an evaluation of government policy. And those that did, as Witte surely realized, were likely to be critical of the tutelage approach. Accordingly, when Plehve proposed that "certain guidelines" be placed on committee discussions, the conference chairman demurred: "I consider it essential to ask local leaders about all their needs, granting them the right to add to our program, and to consider all those questions they wish to."[27]

Such, then, was the situation when Plehve took over as minister. The local committees had been mandated, but had not yet been convened. In Saint Petersburg, the Special Conference itself was discussing the issue of small credits to help the peasants, and other technical questions. Within the Ministry of Interior, the work of revising peasant legislation had scarcely begun. All this was about to change. The commissioning of the Special Conference, by providing Witte with an opportunity to meddle in peasant affairs, had sown the seeds of a new conflict with the Ministry of Interior. As long as Sipiagin had been minister, his dilatoriness and friendship with Witte had postponed a major clash. Now both of these obstacles were gone, and the Khar'kov-Poltava riots were bringing an added measure of urgency to the question of peasant legislation. Plehve, anxious to assert his ascendancy, could be expected to revitalize his predecessor's project, and to tackle the problem with an intelligence and vigor that far exceeded

Sipiagin's. And he would scarcely be inhibited by any friendship for Witte.

THE MINISTRY OF INTERIOR'S PEASANT REFORM PROJECT

Plehve came to office in 1902 with an appreciation of the peasant question gained from his work on various committees, and with a reputation as a supporter of the tutelage approach. He had, however, no ready-made program for improving the situation. He inherited Sipiagin's mandate from the emperor to revise peasant legislation. Among his immediate concerns, after his hectic first few weeks in office, were the tailoring of the ministry staff to suit his style, the regeneration of his predecessor's slow-moving peasant project, and the formulation of plans to streamline and coordinate the workings of local government.

For reasons of continuity the new minister chose to retain Sipiagin's corps of assistant ministers almost intact. The most capable of these was P. N. Durnovo, who had been Plehve's assistant and then successor as Director of the Police Department in the 1880s. Despite their long acquaintance, however, relations between Plehve and Durnovo soon deteriorated, and the latter did not play a major role in the policy-making process. Assistant Minister A. S. Stishinskii, the resident expert on peasant legislation, had been Plehve's assistant Imperial Secretary before transferring back to the Ministry of Interior in 1899. He was a man of modest talent and perspective, but he was reliable, trustworthy, and unswervingly loyal to his past-and-present boss. N. A. Zinov'ev, a former governor and director of the ministry's Economy Department, was a man distinguished by thoroughness, consistency, and limited ability. The retention of these three seemed to indicate that there would be little change in the ministry's policies, and little hope for reform.[28]

The one change Plehve did make among his top assistants did nothing to change this impression. In September of 1902 Prince P. D. Sviatopolk-Mirskii, the most reform-minded of Sipiagin's assistants, was replaced as Commander of Gendarmes by V. K. von Wahl. In his service as governor in Saint Petersburg and Vilnius, von Wahl had acquired a reputation for harsh and repressive police measures. His appointment served mainly to highlight the minister's discontent with the police, and to stress his desire for greater control.[29] It may also have been a concession to Prince Meshcherskii, the outspoken conservative publisher who had the ear of the tsar.[30]

As it turned out, however, the assistant ministers were not destined to play a very significant role under Plehve. The minister, with his indefatigable energy, preferred to deal directly with the heads of the various departments and sections, and these became the centers of gravity within his administration. And here he did make a number of significant changes. A. A. Lopukhin, the young Khar'kov procurator who had reported on the peasant riots, was made Director of the Police Department. N. A. Zverev, a former professor and Assistant Minister of Education, was chosen to head the Main Office on Affairs of the Press. From within the ministry came A. V. Krivoshein, promoted to head the Resettlement Administration. From the Imperial Chancery came D. N. Liubimov, who took over the Chancery of the Minister of Interior, and V. I. Gurko, chosen to head the important Land Section.[31] With the exception of Zverev these were young men, men of talent, pragmatism, and innovation, men with moderate and flexible views. The safe, experienced bureaucrats were nominally in charge, but the young, pragmatic reformers did much of the real work. This made it possible to preserve an aura of continuity, while laying the groundwork for future change.

This practice was nowhere more in evidence than in the handling of the peasant question. Anxious to prevent Witte's Special Conference from wresting control of peasant affairs, Plehve wasted little time in revitalizing his own ministry's project. In June of 1902, he formally established the "Editing Commission on the Revision of Peasant Legislation" as the central agency for drafting a new peasant code. Its chairman was Assistant Minister Stishinskii, the peasant expert Plehve had inherited from Sipiagin. Stishinskii, a collaborator in the original land captain reform, possessed a great deal of expertise on prior peasant legislation, and a staunch dedication to the tutelage approach.[32] Plehve's decision to retain him and permit him to chair the Editing Commission seemed to insure that the coming revision would be based on this philosophy.

Stishinskii's actual role, however, was not a dominant one. So great was the importance Plehve attached to this project that before long he personally took an active interest. To expedite matters, the minister divided the project into three sections: one on peasant land usage, one on peasant courts, and a third on village government. The first section, under special counselor D. P. Semenov, soon came up with a far-reaching radical proposal for compulsory consolidation of all peasant strips into single unfragmented farmsteads. Plehve, however, rejected this plan on the grounds that it would be impossible to implement, especially in the face of probable peasant resistance. Semenov was replaced by A. I. Lykoshin, a peasant expert from the Ministry of Justice, who strove to work out a plan to achieve similar objectives through a more gradual and less disruptive process. Meanwhile the second section, directed by former Land Section Head G. G. Savich, worked on measures to streamline the peasant courts and bring them into conformity with the empire's civil and criminal codes. [33]

The third section, on peasant government, was the most productive of the three. It was directed by V. I. Gurko, one of Plehve's subordinates from the Imperial Chancery. Within a very short time, this section had worked out a series of proposals designed, among other things, to consolidate smaller villages and townships into larger ones, and to define more precisely the jurisdiction of peasant institutions. So impressed was Plehve with the speed and conciseness of this report, and with the apparent talent of its author, that he appointed Gurko to head the ministry's Land Section in September 1902. [34]

This appointment could not help but have a pronounced effect on the whole peasant project. The Land Section, besides being the central office for land captains, was responsible in general for peasant affairs. Because of Plehve's penchant for bypassing his assistant ministers, the director of this section was certain to be the de facto coordinator of peasant policies. But Gurko, a self-styled agrarian expert who had published a book and several articles on Russian agriculture, was an opponent of the tutelage approach. [35] In order to improve Russia's agricultural productivity, in his opinion, it was necessary for the government to concentrate its efforts on the most capable and advanced elements: the landed gentry and the wealthier peasants. It was folly, he felt, for the government to assist the transfer of land from the gentry to the poor peasants; instead it should be assisting the "culturally-advanced" classes in improving their land and buying better machinery. His outlook thus clashed with that of Assistant Minister Stishinskii, who was to be his nominal boss, and with the traditional viewpoint of the Ministry of Interior.

There is some question as to how familiar Plehve was with Gurko's views when he chose him. The minister had not read his appointee's earlier articles, and Gurko himself avoided a complete revelation of his opinions. Still, Plehve could not have been totally ignorant of his new subordinate's leanings, nor could he have been totally dissatisfied with them. As time went on and he became more familiar with the views of his new Land Section Head, the minister continued to allow Gurko considerable autonomy.[36]

By appointing men with such dissimilar views as Gurko and Stishinskii, Plehve might, on one hand, have been working against himself. On the other hand, however, these two appointments meshed well with his own views and intentions. Gurko would bring to the work an assurance of Plehve's desire for meaningful reform, especially in the wake of the peasant disorders, as well as a reflection of the minister's own misgivings about the traditional order. Stishinskii, as chairman, would give to the work that air of respectability, caution, and gradualism which best suited Plehve's own tastes, not to mention those of Nicholas II.

Meanwhile, in July of 1902, as the peasant project was just getting under way, Plehve decided to introduce a significant change in procedure. The project was so important for rural Russia, he told the tsar, that "to decide these questions without the participation of local persons who are close to the land would scarcely be desirable." Therefore, he proposed, once the Editing Commission had completed its work, the conclusions should be submitted to special provincial conferences for discussion. This would add an extra step to the process, and no doubt delay its completion, but it would also produce some important advantages. For one thing, it would certainly bring some useful suggestions, changes, and clarifications. For another, it would give the project some stamp of local approval, even though the committees would be carefully controlled and exist only on the provincial level. Finally, it would detract from the significance of Witte's local committees, deprive them of a justification for discussing peasant laws, and thus help protect the prerogatives of the Ministry of Interior. Needless to say, Plehve neglected to mention these latter considerations in his report to the tsar.[37]

THE MINISTER AND THE ZEMSTVOS

Plehve's proposal for provincial conferences, opportunistic as it was, contained a tacit recognition of his dependence on "society": that group of persons, outside the state bureaucracy, who were involved in public affairs. These were the activists—noblemen and professionals —who took part in the institutions of "local self-government." In order

to govern effectively, the minister realized he would need the cooperation of such persons. If these groups supported him, he would be
in a strong position to implement his policies, and he would have a
powerful weapon in his struggle against Witte. If they opposed him,
there was little he could accomplish, at least on the local level. [38]

The institutions of local self-government were a peculiar feature
of Russian state life. They were governing bodies not appointed by
the government, elective assemblies in the bosom of an autocracy.
The most active and ambitious were the zemstvos, which operated in
many Russian provinces, but not in the non-Russian borderlands. Their
basic units were the county zemstvo assemblies, which were elected
by the rural population through a complex, indirect process, and
which in turn elected a provincial zemstvo assembly. Each assembly
also chose a "zemstvo board" to conduct its day-to-day business. The
zemstvos collected a modest tax revenue, with which they built roads,
schools, and hospitals; hired teachers, doctors, and agronomists; supplied fire insurance and famine relief; and provided, in general, for the
health, education, and welfare of rural areas. Similar functions were
performed in most cities by town councils, elected by the upper ech-
elon of taxpayers, and responsible for choosing a mayor and municipal
board.

By 1902 many zemstvo members, elected to their positions, had
come to see themselves as spokesmen for the "people" against the
bureaucracy. [39] This was not really accurate: because of education,
resources, and weighted electoral laws, almost all zemstvo-men were
of the nobility. Furthermore, the zemstvos had been founded in 1864
to deal with local needs, not to represent local interests. They were
intended to conflict with neither bureaucracy nor estates. Their authority was limited to certain narrow spheres, and their concerns could
not extend beyond their county or province borders.

As time had passed, however, the zemstvos had begun to expand
their horizons and change their political views. Since their functions
were so similar, and since their programs often overlapped, they had
soon voiced a need to share ideas and coordinate activities. As the
economy grew more complex, and as rural welfare declined, they
began to talk of a national zemstvo assembly to coordinate their work.
Meanwhile, as Russia's problems increased, and the bureaucracy failed
to solve them, more and more zemstvo-men had become disillusioned
with government. Witte's industrialization drive, by slighting agriculture during a growing rural crisis, had severely compounded this disenchantment.

In terms of political outlook, there were two generally recognized groups, or "camps," among the zemstvo nobility. The "constitutionalists" were the smaller, but more vocal, of the two: they wanted to transform Russia into a limited constitutional monarchy complete with western-style freedoms and an elected national assembly. The larger group of "Slavophiles" were romantic traditionalists who, taking their cue from Russia's past, idealized a mystical, organic union between tsar and people. Neither had much use for the bureaucracy, which the former considered an impediment to democracy, and the latter saw as a "wall" between the monarch and his subjects.

In spite of this, Plehve had reason to hope that he could make common cause with the zemstvos, or at least with the Slavophiles therein. As a landowner himself, and as a supporter of the nobility, he felt he had the same class interests as most of the zemstvo-men. As a critic of rapid industrialization, and as an upholder of agricultural interests, his views corresponded with those of the zemstvos. Above all, as an enemy of Witte, the *bête-noire* of the noble class and the zemstvo movement, he might well expect some sympathy and support. Perhaps, if he played his hand well, he might be able to form an alliance with the more traditionalist element.[40]

There were other factors, however, which made any such hopes unrealistic. For one thing, although Plehve was technically a nobleman, his family was neither particularly distinguished nor particularly Russian. More importantly, his entire career had been spent in the bureaucracy: he had never participated in local self-government, and he had developed no real ties with the landowning class. Furthermore, as a result of his background, Plehve had a tendency to subordinate all considerations—even the needs of the landed nobility—to the political objectives of the Russian state bureaucracy. He was not opposed to the zemstvos *per se;* indeed, under the right conditions, he favored expanding their activities. But he insisted that they must act only under close state supervision, and he was strongly opposed to any national zemstvo organization. In his view, there already existed a national agency to coordinate zemstvo activities. This, not surprisingly, was the Ministry of Interior.[41]

As a result of the Khar'kov and Poltava disorders, Plehve got off on the wrong foot with the zemstvos almost from the beginning. His report on the disorders, submitted after his April tour, placed a large share of the blame on the statistical departments of the local zemstvos. These had been engaged, for several years, in gathering data on property values. During the summers, according to Plehve, they had hired large numbers of temporary workers, many of whom were "far from irreproachable in political attitude." Taking advantage of their "constant intercourse with the peasants," these "seditious" statisticians had spread rumors, proclamations, and propaganda calling upon the lower classes to seize the nobles' estates. Plehve's response was swift and stern; as a result of his activity, the Poltava statistical director was fired, and the gathering of statistics was suspended in a number of sensitive provinces.[42]

This served at once to damage relations between the minister and the zemstvos. Despite Plehve's reputation, his appointment had occasioned hopeful rumors in some zemstvo circles that a more cooperative approach was forthcoming.[43] After his reaction to the peasant riots, however, little was left of these hopes. The zemstvo-men, although themselves disquieted by the prospect of peasant revolt, resented the minister's interference in their affairs. The minister, meanwhile, had himself become quite hostile to the professional zemstvo employees. This so-called "third element" (neither nobles nor peasants) included not just statisticians, but doctors, teachers, surveyors, and others, hired by the zemstvos to care for local needs. They tended for the most part to be young, idealistic, and democratically inclined. They were far more radical than the nobility-dominated zemstvo assemblies and boards, and they outnumbered the elected representatives by as much as fifty to one. Needless to say, Plehve's attack upon the statisticians merely increased their antagonism toward the government, and damaged his hopes for accommodation with society.

Further damage, ironically, resulted from zemstvo displeasure toward Witte and his Special Conference. To many zemstvo-men, the formation of the local committees on agriculture appeared as a bureaucratic trick to bypass the zemstvos, which should have been the logical forum for discussion of local issues. Zemstvo-men, to be sure, would be included in the committees, but their influence would be seriously diluted. It was decided, therefore, that the zemstvo leaders should get together and work out a common approach to the committees.

As a result of this decision, an unauthorized conference of zemstvo-men took place on May 23–25 at the apartment of D. N. Shipov, the chairman of the Moscow provincial zemstvo board. It was attended by many prominent zemstvo leaders, including sixteen provincial zemstvo board chairmen. Some advocated a boycott of the local committees, but most felt this would disobey a direct imperial order, and would leave the zemstvos vulnerable to charges of sabotage. It was agreed, however, that the zemstvo-men should participate only in a personal capacity, not as zemstvo representatives, and that the questions raised should also be debated in the zemstvo assemblies. Further, those who did take part were each to submit memos condemning the government's circumvention of the zemstvos, and outlining fundamental changes necessary for agricultural progress. A program was drawn up as a basis for these memos. It called, among other things, for peasant equality with the other classes, the end of administrative tutelage, the abolition of class representation in the zemstvos, the lowering of indirect taxes on staples, and greater freedom of public discussion. [44]

Although the meetings took place in a private apartment, there was little attempt to keep them secret, and word of them quickly reached the Minister of Interior. Plehve in turn reported the matter to the emperor. His report cast the Moscow conference in a very unfavorable light: this was precisely the sort of zemstvo activity the new minister wished to avoid. The zemstvo-men had assembled without authorization from government authorities. They were attempting to act on a unified national basis, rather than restricting themselves to local issues. They were calling for political and administrative changes, thus encroaching on the domain of the central bureaucracy. Worst of all, they were setting up a mechanism which could conceivably be used to challenge the very existence of the autocratic regime. [45]

The emperor, according to Plehve's account, was indignant. He and the minister agreed that such actions could not be permitted to go unchecked. Consequently, in June of 1902 they issued reprimands to all who had participated in the Moscow meeting, accompanied by warnings that repetition of such activity would lead to dismissal from public life. [46] The reprimands, coming on top of the prohibition of statistical activity, served as further evidence of the new minister's hostility toward the zemstvos.

This was not, however, what Plehve intended. According to a close associate, one of the minister's strongest desires was to bring about greater cooperation between the central bureaucracy and the organs of local self-government. As he had made clear on several occasions, he realized his ministry could do little to solve Russia's problems without local assistance. In his investigation of the Khar'kov and Poltava disorders, he had made sure to consult with the local zemstvos. Even his report on these disturbances, so critical of the statistical workers, was careful not to blame the zemstvos themselves. [47] In fact, as events unfolded, it became apparent that Plehve's strategy was to win the cooperation of the zemstvo Slavophiles, and then use this support to incorporate the zemstvos more fully into the workings of his ministry.

PLEHVE'S BID FOR ZEMSTVO SUPPORT

The imperial reprimands to the participants of the May zemstvo conference were served, in most cases, by the local governor. In two cases, however, Plehve chose to communicate the censure himself. In mid-June he talked with Orel marshal of nobility M. A. Stakhovich, one of three participants who publicly professed innocence and blamed the whole thing on a slanted report from the minister.[48] A short time later he summoned to Saint Petersburg D. N. Shipov, the zemstvo board chairman at whose home the conference had taken place.

It is clear from his actions that Plehve placed great significance on this meeting with Shipov. Dmitri Shipov was a man of honesty and integrity, universally respected in zemstvo circles; he was also the unofficial head of the movement toward some sort of national zemstvo union. He was a bitter opponent of the policies of Sergei Witte, and a representative of the Slavophile nobility, the group to which Plehve looked for support. He was at the same time a sincere and loyal monarchist who could be expected to welcome a friendly gesture on the part of the government.[49] His cooperation was indispensable for any attempt to establish closer ties between bureaucracy and zemstvo. Accordingly, when he arrived in Saint Petersburg on July 2, Shipov was immediately invited to visit the minister's dacha on Aptekarsk Island.[50]

Plehve made every effort to make his guest at home and dispel any fears of hostility. He greeted Shipov cordially and engaged him in an informal, amicable discussion over tea. The official business—transmittal of the imperial reproach—was handled expeditiously: the minister listened politely to the zemstvo-man's explanation and objected only that the conference had been illegal, and therefore could not be tolerated. He then shifted the topic of conversation to the real purpose of the interview: the endeavor to bridge the gap between government and zemstvo. "I believe that you and I are very close together in our convictions," the minister began, "and I think we might both belong to the same camp. . . . I am in favor of zemstvo organizations, and I am convinced that no state order is possible unless society is drawn into local self-government. I do not consider it possible to govern a

Moscow Zemstvo Board Chairman D. N. Shipov.

country solely by means of an army of bureaucrats, and I do not consider zemstvo institutions incompatible with our political order. On the contrary, I believe that the broad development of local self-government is indispensable under an autocratic system."

The minister's cordiality and friendly attitude came as a pleasant surprise to his guest. Contrary to the impressions of the past few months, the Minister of Interior was not anti-zemstvo. All he asked was that the zemstvos act within their proper legal framework. "Although I recognize the necessity for public participation in matters of local administration," Plehve went on, "I cannot help but think that zemstvo institutions are often inclined to go beyond the limits of their work and pursue political aims." An example of this, he suggested, was the discussion of peasant legal status—which had "little connection" with "the needs of agricultural industry"—in the program drawn up by the Moscow conference. He also listed previous occasions when certain zemstvos, asked by the government to consider major issues, had called for alterations in the political order. This type of activity, he insisted, merely made it more difficult for the pro-zemstvo elements within the government to prevail. "As Minister of Interior," he explained, "I am obliged to consider the tendencies of those above me. . . . Among other things, the raising of political issues by zemstvo people strengthens the tendencies which are unfavorable towards the public institutions, and provides ammunition to those who are generally opposed to the principle of local self-government."

The minister's pose as a friend of the zemstvos was obviously self-serving, but his insinuation that "those above him" disliked the zemstvos was not without foundation. After all, the current tsar had begun his reign by denouncing "senseless dreams" of zemstvo participation in state affairs. In 1899, Minister of Interior Goremykin had lost his job after proposing an expansion of the zemstvos. More recently, Minister of Education Vannovsky had been fired for pushing a reform that smacked too much of "society opinion."[51] Although he was "prepared to assist in the establishment of the necessary cooperation between the government and society," Plehve had no intention of making a similar mistake.

Having made his point, Plehve offered his guest a surprising little treatise on the political future of Russia: "I daresay that no state order can remain unchanged forever, and it might well be that our political structure will have to be replaced by a different one in thirty, forty, or fifty years. (I beg you not to take these words of mine beyond these walls.) In any event, now is not an opportune time for the raising of this question. Historical events must unfold gradually."

Whether this was in truth a candid forecast of things to come, or merely an attempt to buy time and win support, it indicates that the minister's view of autocracy's future was far from sanguine. It also shows him to be a man dedicated not so much to the old order as to the concept of order, a man opposed not so much to change as to loss of control. It is significant that all he ventured to ask was that society refrain from premature attempts to alter the political order.

Plehve also tried to use this meeting to enlist support against Witte. Shipov, in relating his own views, was especially critical of the Minister of Finance, and Plehve could not resist the opportunity to undermine his rival. Employing a rather obvious double-standard, he encouraged the zemstvo-men to "pay special attention to the weak points of our financial and economic policies" in their memoranda to the local committees. Remarkably, the Minister of Interior—who had just finished warning against discussion of peasant policy—was now encouraging the zemstvos to criticize the government. Apparently he did not consider criticism of the Minister of Finance to be outside the limits of zemstvo activity!

In discussing the framework for government–zemstvo cooperation, Shipov and Plehve were not entirely in agreement. The zemstvo leader drew a Slavophilic distinction between "autocracy" and "absolutism," claiming that a true autocracy must carry out the will of the people, as ascertained through contact with the people's representatives. Plehve disagreed with the notion of representatives; instead he suggested that cooperation was possible through contact with knowledgeable public men such as the zemstvo board chairmen. What was needed at the moment was not "representation of various interests" but "enlightened men who are well acquainted with local conditions"—it would be "untimely" to raise the question of elected representation. "I want to bring the provincial board chairmen into joint conferences in the Ministry of Interior on various issues within the competence of the zemstvos," the minister promised Shipov, "and I shall try to do so."

The remainder of the long conversation dealt with a wide range of issues. Plehve once again voiced strong criticism of the "third element"—the professional zemstvo employees—whom he described as being devoted to "the destruction of the entire existing social order." He also requested Shipov's participation in the preparatory work for his proposed joint conferences, adding that he was counting on the zemstvo-man's close collaboration in the near future. The two men parted on friendly terms, Shipov's spirits buoyed by the fact that the new minister apparently recognized the usefulness of zemstvo work, and the necessity to consult with the opinion of society.

For a short time thereafter, Plehve's efforts at accommodation seemed to be bearing fruit. Shipov paid a visit to Witte, who also professed to be a supporter and a friend of the zemstvos, and then returned to Moscow. There he succeeded in convincing his colleagues to drop the controversial section of their May program which called for direct zemstvo participation in organs of the central government— a concession aimed at demonstrating the good will of the zemstvos. At the same time Shipov took pains to inform all the other provincial zemstvos of the content of his conversations in Saint Petersburg, hoping thereby to dissuade them from erecting any obstacles to improvement of government–zemstvo relations.[52]

The minister, for his part, began to take steps aimed at satisfying the zemstvos. Shortly after Shipov's visit it was announced that Plehve had obtained imperial consent to permit the zemstvos to borrow cash from the famine-relief fund, to be used for the purpose of "bettering peasant economy." On August 10, a month after the visit, Iaroslavl governor B. V. Sturmer—a former chairman of the Tver Provincial Zemstvo Board—was appointed Director of the Department of General Affairs of the Ministry of Interior. As a conservative zemstvo leader, Sturmer had acquired a reputation for the tactful ability to reconcile the opinion of society with governmental policy. Plehve evidently hoped his new appointee could likewise win zemstvo support for his new programs.[53]

In a further effort to conciliate society, and to dramatize the government's changing priorities, Plehve enlisted the services of the tsar. In late summer of 1902, Nicholas made a trip to the province of Kursk, in the agricultural Center, to observe some military maneuvers. Here, on August 30, he addressed a major speech to the local nobility and zemstvo leaders. With Plehve standing behind him, the emperor announced that he had ordered the minister to remove "the continuing defects in peasant life." "In due time," he went on, "we shall call upon provincial conferences, attended by members of the nobility and zemstvos, to take part in this work. As for noble landownership—the traditional bulwark of order and moral strength—its fortification will be my constant concern.[54]

The emperor's speech was rightly viewed, by the press and by the public, as a statement of the goals of the new internal administration.[55] The solution of the peasant problem, with the assistance of nobility and zemstvos, was clearly at the top of the list. After a decade of concentration on industrial growth, the government was returning its attention to rural Russia, and pledging its cooperation with local forces. The pledge was not without strings, however: nobles and zemstvo-men would be expected to behave themselves, avoid political questions, and limit their discussions to local economic needs. "Rural economy is a matter of utmost importance," the tsar told the zemstvo chairmen that same afternoon, "and I hope you shall devote your entire strength to it. I shall be glad to show you any assistance, for I wish to unify the actions of all local authorities. Remember that your primary obligation is to take care of local economic needs."[56]

Plehve, of course, attached great significance to these remarks, since they in effect constituted an announcement of his program. The tsar's speech was, among other things, the first public indication that the Ministry of Interior would submit its peasant reform project to provincial conferences. Hopefully, these "conciliatory" words and actions would ensure zemstvo support. In his own conversations with the Kursk zemstvo-men, the minister expanded on the emperor's comments, assuring them that the new policy would leave a wide range for zemstvo operation. He also expressed sorrow that the funds available to the zemstvos were so modest, and told those present that, as a landowner himself, he was not unfamiliar with the problems of rural Russia. At the same time he took the occasion to criticize the zemstvo statisticians and their role in the Khar'kov and Poltava disorders.[57]

As autumn of 1902 approached, Plehve could look back with some satisfaction on his first several months in office. He had shown authority in quickly taking control of his ministry, decisiveness in dealing with the Khar'kov and Poltava riots, and firmness in handling the illegal zemstvo congress. He had brought to his staff some promising young officials, while retaining the continuity and experience of older and wiser colleagues. He had set in motion the process of revising peasant legislation, and in so doing had reasserted his ministry's control over peasant policy. Most importantly, perhaps, he had apparently reached an agreement with the zemstvos—or at least with the zemstvo Slavophiles—providing an opening for potential cooperation between government and society. This latter "alliance," so tentative and fragile, would be severely tested in the months to come.

4

Plehve, Witte, and Society

BACKGROUND

The emperor's speech at Kursk, on August 30, 1902, was significant in several respects. For one thing, it marked a shift in government emphasis, from the industrial sector to the agricultural, a change already foreshadowed by Witte's Special Conference and Plehve's peasant project. Secondly, it served notice that the government wished to regain the support of society—support which had been seriously eroded in the previous decades. Thirdly, it mandated a reform of the bureaucracy—an attempt to "unify the activities of all local authorities." Finally, in a very real sense, it bore witness to the declining influence of Witte and the ascendancy of Plehve. The emphases on rural economy, social control, and bureaucratic reform all reflected the latter's views, and the speech itself may well have been written by him.[1]

The system of Witte, however, did not give way to the Russia of Plehve without a struggle. Plehve's star had risen, to be sure, but Witte's continued to shine, albeit less brightly, for another whole year. During that time Russia's two foremost statesmen, heading the two main departments of government, did battle. They battled in public and behind the scenes, they intrigued against each other, contradicted each other, undermined each other. They battled over dozens of issues, great and small. They battled for the affections of society, the direction of government, and above all for the support of the tsar.

The differences that separated Witte and Plehve were deep-seated and very real. They differed in temperament and they differed

62

in style. They differed in their ideals, and in their approach to Russia's problems. They differed on the peasant question, on the role of the nobility, on the worker issue, on the treatment of national minorities, on the Far Eastern problem, and on a host of lesser issues. Underlying all this was a fundamental conflict between the responsibilities, goals, and visions of the ministries they headed.

This is not to deny a certain similarity of background and ambition between the two men. Both had strange Germanic names, which called attention to the fact that neither was of solid Russian stock. Both had been raised in non-Russian borderlands: Plehve in Poland and Witte in the Caucasus. Both had a claim to hereditary nobility, but neither had been born into the landed class. Both had made their careers through ability more than influence, although Witte, whose maternal grandmother was a Russian princess, did benefit from court connections.[2] Both sought high office, not for status or wealth, but for power—and for a chance to make constructive use of their energies and abilities. Both had character traits which irritated their colleagues: Plehve was cool, imperious, and reserved; Witte was brusque, impatient, and direct. Both were regarded as egotistical, cynical, opportunistic, and unprincipled. Both, on the other hand, were widely respected as men of enormous energy, intellect, and talent.

Despite these similarities, the paths they had chosen to make their careers were by no means parallel. Plehve, as an outsider, had chosen to work within the system, in hopes of one day joining the establishment. Educated in Moscow at Russia's foremost university, he had joined the state service, worked hard to please his superiors, sided with the propertied classes, and striven for acceptance. Witte, on the other hand, had studied mathematics in Odessa, and had made his early career in private industry as well as state service. Unimpressed by the traditional order, he had made little attempt to ingratiate himself with society, he had openly associated with capitalists and Jews, and he had even risked his career by marrying a Jewish divorcée of scandalous repute.[3] Plehve's career was devoted to order and stability, Witte's to expansion and change. Plehve tended toward excessive caution, Witte toward impetuosity. Plehve was, above all, an administrator; Witte was a financier.

To some extent, these differences were dictated by the ministries in which they served. In simplest terms, Interior's job was to keep order, and Finance's was to raise revenue. Both goals were necessary; neither could be attained without the other. But a society based on peasant agriculture, at least according to Witte, could not produce enough revenue to keep Russia competitive and independent in the twentieth century. The old order of noble estates and peasant communes must therefore give way to a new order of industry and capital. This meant change, change involved dislocation, and dislocation led to disorder. And disorder was one thing no Minister of Interior could tolerate.[4]

During Plehve's previous sojourn in the Ministry of Interior (1881–94), great strides had been made toward bringing order to Russia. Revolutionary terrorism had been rooted out and destroyed. The press and universities, zemstvos and town councils had been brought under close state control. Measures to supervise peasant life, to secure peasant lands, to assist the landed nobility, and to protect the factory workers, had all been implemented or initiated. By 1894, it had seemed, the Ministry of Interior was beginning to get a handle on the internal situation in Russia. Plehve himself had been a major force in all this, and he was understandably proud.[5]

During Witte's nine years as Minister of Finance, however, much of this had seemed to come undone. Rapid industrialization had doubled government revenues, but it had been accompanied by disturbing developments. The revolutionary movement had revived, and terrorism had reappeared. The plight of the peasants, at least those in the Center, seemed to have worsened, and the conditions of the factory workers had shown little improvement. Worst of all, perhaps, the landed nobility—that traditional bulwark of the existing order—had become disenchanted with the government and its policies.

From Plehve's viewpoint, this was scarcely all a coincidence. Nor was it entirely coincidental that his own career, hitherto so successful, had seemed to languish during these years. Twice the post of Minister of Interior had become vacant; twice he had been passed over. Plehve was too intelligent to blame all his troubles—and all Russia's woes— on one man, and he readily admitted that Witte had done much for Russia's finances.[6] But neither was he ready to thank the Minister of Finance for his help, or to applaud his contributions to internal stability.

It is not surprising, then, that relations between the two men had been something less than cordial. In the late 1890s, especially, Plehve had come forth in conference and committee as the most outspoken critic of Witte and his policies. He had blamed the Finance Minister, above all, for an "excessive tax burden" that was ruining Russian agriculture. He had, at times, been vituperative, accusing Witte on one occasion of "socialism," and objecting on another to his "ridicule."[7] But the Minister of Finance had managed to parry Plehve's blows, and to prevent any major change in policy.

Now, at last, the tide had turned: Plehve had the initiative, and Witte was on the defensive. Nicholas II, however, had not made the break complete: Witte remained in office another whole year. The Minister of Interior, like a confident new pilot, wished to return the ship of state to its previous steady course. For his first sixteen months, though, he was obstructed by the interim helmsman, who refused to let go of the wheel.

WITTE, PLEHVE, AND THE LOCAL COMMITTEES

Despite the animosity between the two ministers, the first several months of Plehve's ministry were not marked by open warfare. The new Minister of Interior seems to have made a real effort to behave correctly toward his senior colleague. He took pains to consult Witte on a number of matters, and the two men even found several points of agreement. On one major issue—the abolition of collective tax liability among peasants—Plehve even withdrew his ministry's opposition to Witte's plans. As late as autumn of 1902, one observer could still write about a possible Witte–Plehve "duumvirate."[8] Given the background and ambitions of the two men, however, and the competitive situation of their ministries, it was only a matter of time before hostilities flared.

Although almost any issue could have served as a fuse, it was the peasant question, and Witte's local committees on agriculture, that touched off the fireworks. These local committees, formed under the aegis of the Special Conference, met throughout the summer and fall of 1902. Despite complaints from the zemstvos that they were being bypassed, the leaders of local society actually dominated the proceedings. The county committees, chaired by the marshals of the nobility, were composed largely of zemstvo board members and specially invited persons. The provincial committees, chaired by the governors, included marshals of the nobility, zemstvo board members, local officials of the central government, and anyone else the chairmen found helpful. In most cases, the county committees met first, discussed the issues, and forwarded their conclusions to the provincial committees. Needless to say, the whole affair engendered a good deal of curiosity, publicity, and excitement.[9]

It also engendered no end of controversy. Plehve, who hoped the committees would concentrate on economic issues—including criticism of Witte's financial policies—was anxious to limit their discussions to local economic needs. He felt the committees should consider no questions except those formally submitted by the Special Conference, and that these should be very narrow and specific. "By staying within certain guidelines," he argued, "they can better reveal the most urgent needs of local agriculture, and will give us answers strictly conforming to local needs."[10] The organization of peasant life, currently being studied within his own ministry, should clearly be off limits: this was the business of the central government. And no discussion of possible changes in Russia's form of government could ever be tolerated: this would be tantamount to "sedition."

Witte, on the other hand, insisted that the committees be given the widest possible latitude. He apparently calculated that, given a chance to express their views on the peasant question, many local leaders would call for an end to the Ministry of Interior's tutelage approach. "By narrowing the program of questions . . . and limiting the framework of discussion," he pointed out, "we open ourselves to the reproach that we do not touch on the major questions . . . and the most essential needs." Accordingly, in August 1902, when several local chairmen inquired about the boundaries of discussion, Witte replied that the questions submitted were meant only as suggestions, and were not intended to limit debate. "The provincial and county committees have been granted leeway to express their views . . ." he wrote, "depending on the actual needs of their locales."[11]

In many respects the results bore out Witte's expectations. Although the committees in general confined themselves to agricultural matters, there were a significant number who addressed themselves to administrative and organizational questions. The majority of these rejected the tutelage approach. Fewer than a third, for instance, discussed the peasant commune, but most of those that did favored its abolition. The number that concerned themselves with "non-alienation" of peasant lands was smaller still, but these almost all favored modification or removal of this policy.[12]

In some respects, however, Witte may have overplayed his hand. Certain committee chairmen, taking advantage of the latitude given them, allowed the discussions to get out of hand. Questions which so remotely concerned agriculture as freedom of speech and freedom of press, the abolition of corporal punishment, the cessation of government "oppression" against society, and the establishment of some form of popular representation, were discussed in various committees. Others tackled issues such as expanded powers for the zemstvos, full civil rights for the peasants, and broadened popular education. One committee had the gall to invite the entire county zemstvo assembly, while at the same time excluding all the local land captains; another went so far as to raise the question of "nationalization" of the land. A county committee in Novgorod province even passed a resolution calling for "the participation of the people in the affairs of the entire administration, not only the local, but even the central."[13]

It was not long before Plehve, disturbed by these developments, began to take actions to bring things under control. In July, he forced the resignation of acting Moscow governor Baratynskii for permitting zemstvo-men to raise "political" questions in his committee. The new governor, Kristi, eventually disposed of the problem by adding twenty-six "knowledgeable" men—including, it was rumored, several police agents—to the committee. This gave him an effective majority every time he needed it, allowing him to override the zemstvo-men and prevent discussion of "political" issues. In August, Plehve cracked down on the Sudzha county committee of Kursk province, where Marshal of Nobility A. V. Evreinov had encouraged discussion of "constitutional" issues and criticism of government policies. Following Plehve's report to the tsar, Evreinov was issued an imperial reprimand and ordered to restrict discussion to local issues. When he tried to do so, however, the zemstvo-men, led by board chairman Prince Peter Dolgorukov, quit the committee in protest. This in turn led to the termination of the committee, and brought a summons from Saint Petersburg for Evreinov and Dolgorukov. Plehve met personally with Evreinov and, in a stormy session, demanded the latter's resignation. Dolgorukov, a scion of one of Russia's oldest families, was interrogated by Assistant Minister von Wahl, forced out of his zemstvo position, and prohibited from further public activity.[14] Control, it seems, meant more to Plehve than friendship for the nobility.

Of all the local committees, the one in Voronezh county of Voronezh province was the most outspoken, and it in turn was dealt the most severe retribution. Following inflammatory speeches by zemstvo workers Bunakov, Martynov, and Shingarev—calling for freedom of speech, press, and assembly, and for an all-Russian "land assembly" (zemskii sobor)—a commission under F. A. Shcherbin was set up to study these suggestions. The commission report, which endorsed these proposals, was accepted by the committee as a whole, and subsequently even approved by the Voronezh provincial committee. Voronezh governor Slieptsov, fearful of the consequences, neglected to inform the Ministry of Interior of what was going on.

Plehve, however, did manage to learn of the Voronezh proceedings. In mid-October, while on his way to Crimea to attend the emperor, the minister was handed a stenographic protocol of the Voronezh meetings. He immediately reacted with harsh measures. On his orders, Martynov and Bunakov were arrested and sent to Saint Petersburg for police interrogation. On November 1, Assistant Minister Zinov'ev was dispatched to Voronezh to question others involved. By the time the affair was over, Bunakov and Shcherbin had been exiled to their birthplaces, Martynov had been banished to Arkhangelsk, provincial zemstvo board member Pereleshin had been removed from his post, and governor Slieptsov had been fired.[15]

Plehve's persecution of the local committees touched off a bitter dispute between him and the Minister of Finance. Witte, after all, was chairman of the Special Conference; control of its committees was his responsibility. The Minister of Interior, however, was responsible for internal security, and felt an obligation to respond to any attacks against the government—even those made by respectable persons in government-sponsored committees. The fact that he was simultaneously derailing his rival's agricultural program did not dampen his ardor. Nor did it hurt that the committees were providing Plehve with an opportunity to depict his opponent as a supporter of "sedition."

The inevitable confrontation finally came at Yalta in October of 1902. Witte, freshly returned from a trip to the Far East, had come to the Crimea to report to the emperor on his journey. Plehve, who had recently learned of the Voronezh problem, was already there. One evening, after an audience at the palace, Plehve invited Witte and several others to dinner at his hotel. Present also was the Director of the Minister of Interior's Chancery, D. N. Liubimov, who recorded the conversation which took place.[16]

Plehve incautiously began the dispute by mentioning his troubles with the local committees; Witte in turn blamed the entire affair on the Minister of Interior's policies. The movement now afoot in society, he went on, was deeper than most officials thought; it could no longer be controlled by police coercion and repression. This movement had not been caused by the local committees; indeed, it had its roots in the reforms of Alexander II. The longing for more freedom, self-government, and a national assembly was but a natural outgrowth of these reforms: a desire to complete the unfinished business by "putting a roof on the building." By depriving this movement of a legal outlet, the government was only forcing it to seek other means. The regime should therefore "place itself at the head" of the movement, and in this way "take possession" of it.

Witte finished his agitated tirade with a despondent wave of his hand. The imperturbable Plehve, a marked contrast to his colleague, coolly began his response. "I absolutely agree with you that the movement is deeper than many think," he said with an ironic smile, "but not I." He agreed that the turmoil was rooted in the past, and that it was certainly not caused by the committees; but he insisted that they provided a "favorable climate" for opposition, and thus could not be left unsupervised. He even admitted that Russia might be on the verge of a "great revolutionary shock" that would "jolt the state," but this only meant the government had to redouble its efforts to prevent, or at least contain, the explosion. It must not "swim with the current, striving always to be in front." For the Russian revolution, if it were to come, would be an artificial one; it would be a revolution made by "the educated classes, the public elements, and the intelligentsia," and not by the people.

Here Plehve revealed a basic anomaly: despite his support for the noble estate, and his desire to work with the zemstvos, he was deeply distrustful of society. To him, the "public elements" were good only at criticism; they lacked the tradition, custom, and ruling experience of the tsarist government. "All they have is the desire for power, even if it is inspired, in their opinion, by love of country. They could never take charge of the movement. Having begun in power at the head, they would soon find themselves at the tail"—and the movement would be taken over by "criminal elements" and "Jews." Pointing to the work of Alexander II, and to the reforms of Witte himself, he claimed that all of the careful, useful, and liberal reforms had been made at the initiative of the autocracy, and that "only on the shoulders of the autocracy" could Russia be renewed and survive its present crisis. "You yourself, Sergei Iul'evich," he artfully flattered his opponent, "are a clear example of what can be done for the country by a talented and energetic Russian minister without any constitution." Society, on the other hand, had usually *opposed* reforms. "Hence it seems," the minister concluded, "that everyone in Russia who thirsts for reform ought to be on the side of the autocracy, but in fact we have quite the contrary. The present campaign by the public elements against the bureaucracy has a battle slogan which cries for a different goal—the destruction of the autocracy. Here, in essence, is the whole meaning of the present movement. How can the Minister of Interior do anything but struggle against it? And how can Sergei Iul'evich say that he should place himself at its head?"

The debate between these two perceptive statesmen pointed up a basic dilemma facing the Russian government. In order to preserve the political system, they both realized, it was necessary to implement reforms and to solve Russia's problems. But the government could not do this on its own; it needed the expertise, human resources, and cooperation of society. Society, however, was increasingly unwilling to cooperate without a change in political system.

Witte's point was clear and direct. The government needed the support of society; it could not hope to function if society was totally opposed to it. And Plehve's repressive measures were needlessly driving society further and further into opposition. The course Witte advocated may have been fraught with danger, but it was the only real alternative: Plehve's approach led directly and inevitably toward disaster.

To Plehve, this argument must have sounded strange indeed. After all, had not Witte's financial policies played a major role in the alienation of rural society? And had not Witte himself authored a notorious diatribe against the zemstvos? Plehve, too, realized that change was necessary, indeed, that it was inevitable. But, as he repeatedly insisted, the change must be controlled and gradual, directed from above by the imperial government. His position made him as aware as anyone of the strength of the opposition movement, but the very fact that it was an opposition movement made him all the more determined to combat it. If these critics were really so selflessly concerned about Russia's problems, they would have been cooperating with the government. Instead, by their opposition, they were making it very difficult to implement reform. More than once Plehve would call for the assistance of society, emphasizing that the bureaucracy could accomplish little without strong public support.[17] But, apparently, these people were more concerned with obtaining a share of power for themselves: they refused to cooperate, and instead aimed at the overthrow of the existing order. And this no minister could permit. "The public element's passion for obtaining power—not through the normal means of being invited to counsel and advise the government, but by means of seizure and usurpation of authority—obviously cannot be tolerated, and any playing at a constitution must be cut off at the roots."[18]

Plehve himself realized that police measures alone could never be totally effective. The answer, he was convinced, was to enlist the support of those who were willing to work with the government, while relentlessly pursuing those who stood in opposition. The efforts to circumscribe committee discussions would therefore continue. "As long as you are concerned about your own local affairs," he told one committee member several weeks later, "you will receive from me every support. But bear in mind, if you cross this demarcation line you will meet me not as Minister of Interior, but as Chief of Gendarmes." [19]

It was not long before the interference of the Minister of Interior began to have its effect. By the end of 1902, almost all the county committees had completed their work, and the scene had shifted to the provincial level. Here, where the governors themselves were chairmen, Plehve had more control. He instructed them not to permit discussion of such "general questions" as education, peasant legal status, and zemstvo self-government. And, since the governors of Moscow, Voronezh, and Kursk had lost their jobs for too loose an attitude toward the committees, the others hastened to comply. By various devices—phony "summaries" of local committee work, the creation of new members to counterbalance the zemstvo-men, and simple parliamentary obstruction—they managed to restrict the scope of discussion. As a result of this bureaucratic pressure, the committees lost a great deal of significance in the eyes of society. [20]

At the same time, they were losing significance in the eyes of the emperor. The critical resolutions of some committees could not help but irritate Nicholas II. The conservative press, led by Prince V. P. Meshcherskii's *Citizen*, railed against the committees as "hotbeds of antigovernment chatter." In his private reports to the tsar, Plehve apparently made use of their activity to compromise Sergei Witte. The evidence that the Special Conference was indirectly aiding the government's opponents could only undermine the position of its chairman. [21]

In spite of this, the committees pressed on and completed their work, which was compiled during spring and summer of 1903 and published in autumn of that year. The resulting fifty-eight volume report offered a wealth of information on the problems of rural Russia, and a wide variety of possible solutions. [22] Armed with this information, the Special Conference should have been in a position to formulate a comprehensive program to deal with the needs of agricultural industry. But, as Witte's star declined, so did that of the conference he chaired. By 1903 it was becoming apparent that Plehve, not Witte, had the emperor's favor, and that the views of the local committees would have little impact on the government's peasant policy, at least for the time being.

THE THRUST FOR BUREAUCRATIC REFORM

Plehve's troubles with the local committees were but symptoms of deeper problems. The tsarist government, for all its vaunted power and authority, had little real contact with rural Russia and only tenuous control over what went on there. Government agents on the local level, including police and land captains, were often ill-trained, poorly paid, and overworked—and there were far too few of them to govern effectively. In order to learn the needs of local people, and to carry out any changes it wished to make, the central bureaucracy often had to rely on people—like the members of the local committees—in whom it had little trust, and over whom it had little control.[23]

The problems, at least from Plehve's perspective, were administrative ones. In his view, it was the bureaucracy's slowness in adapting to change that had generated the current crises, and it was the government's ability to control the people and meet their needs that would determine its survival.[24] But the imperial administration, by general consensus, was overcentralized, ill-informed, and uncoordinated. In the capital, overburdened officials were making too many decisions that could better and more efficiently be made on the local level. Even in formulating legislation, these officials were often poorly informed: there existed no regular system for obtaining local input, which had to either filter up through the bureaucracy or await *ad hoc* arrangements like Witte's local committees. In the provinces, meanwhile, authority was divided among various agencies of government and self-government, answering to different masters, and sometimes working at cross purposes. The state bureaucracy, as a result, was inadequate to the tasks at hand: it could hardly understand Russia's problems, let alone resolve them. It is little wonder, then, that bureaucratic reform was a cornerstone of Plehve's program.

The difficulties facing Plehve were by no means new ones. The ministerial system, established a century earlier, had lacked from the beginning a unifying, prime ministerial official. Although supervision of the governors and local officials had been vested in the Ministry of Interior, other ministries, anxious to increase their effectiveness, had soon created their own provincial agencies. Then, in 1861, the abolition of serfdom had removed the stratum of landlords who had hitherto "governed" the peasants, creating vast new responsibilities for the state administration. The peasant assemblies and soon-created zemstvos helped somewhat to fill the gap, but they also represented a type of local authority that was difficult to coordinate and even harder to control. "Collegial" bodies, organized under the governors to provide interaction among the various local agencies, had not proven effective; instead they only added to the plethora of provincial institutions. When faced with a new problem, it seemed, the government simply formed a new agency.[25]

Several of Plehve's predecessors had tried vainly to solve these problems. P. A. Valuev, Minister of Interior from 1861 to 1868, had advanced a plan to set up unified directories, under the governors, to coordinate the workings of all provincial agencies. It was opposed by other ministers, who were loath to place their agents under the Minister of Interior's governors, and emasculated by the State Council. Meanwhile, fearful that the new zemstvos might become a competitor state, he had sought both to control and to co-opt them. On one hand, he would strictly limit the scope of their activities; on the other, he proposed to let their provincial assemblies elect representatives to the State Council. He was ultimately successful at neither: his representation plan, criticized in conference as a threat to autocracy, was rejected by the tsar, and the zemstvos never fully complied with the intended bureaucratic constraints.[26]

M. T. Loris-Melikov, the man who first brought Plehve to the Ministry of Interior, had tried a slightly different tack. His solution to disunity was to concentrate in the person of the Minister of Interior all police and administrative authority, and even some judicial responsibilities. The minister would then be able to coordinate state policy on both the central and local levels. As for the zemstvos, their competence would be widened a bit, and they would be allowed to select local persons for a "General Council" which would comment on legislation before it went to the State Council. This way it would be possible to incorporate the ideas of local society without sacrificing state control. Loris did manage to consolidate direction of the police, but the rest of his program was abandoned soon after the murder of his patron, Tsar Alexander II, in 1881.[27]

Ministers Tolstoi and Durnovo, Plehve's supervisors and mentors from 1882 to 1894, had followed a third approach. They, too, wished to perfect the bureaucracy and make use of local persons, but they refused to consider any representative role, or any political input, from the zemstvos and town councils. Instead they had more carefully restricted these bodies, and brought them under close administrative control by the governors and the ministry. To better coordinate the workings of local government they had also created under their min-

istry a new type of official, the land captain, with extensive administrative and judicial authority to deal with local peasants. These
"reforms," although implemented, had not solved all the problems, but
they had certainly helped exacerbate the rift between bureaucracy and
self-government.[28]

The zemstvos, meanwhile, were developing their own approach.
In their efforts to meet rural Russia's economic needs, they too had
been frustrated both by lack of local control and lack of coordination.
With no organs below the county level, they found that they were not
always close enough to the villages to receive needed information and
provide needed services. Partly to meet this need, they had created
their own cadres of surveyors, statisticians, veterinarians, agronomists,
teachers, physicians, and the like—the "third element." Many also
called for the establishment of a local zemstvo unit, to supplement or
replace the peasant township assembly. At the same time, on the interprovincial level the zemstvos felt hampered by the absence of a body
to coordinate their actions and serve as a forum for exchange of ideas.
Zemstvo leaders proposed, therefore, that some sort of national zemstvo assembly be established, made up of delegates from the provincial
zemstvos.

Such an approach had widespread support among zemstvo activists—constitutionalists and Slavophiles alike. Whatever their differences, they shared a common interest in improving their programs,
offering better services, and preserving some measure of autonomy.
Contemptuous of Petersburg bureaucrats who tried to rule Russia from
behind chancery walls, they saw no reason to believe that these officials were any more capable or more loyal than they. They tended to
resent any extension of the bureaucracy—such as the land captain law
—as an attack against self-government. They differed in their views
toward autocracy, but they agreed in their opposition to bureaucracy.[29]

Plehve's task, then, was not an easy one. His goal, like those of
his precursors, was to find some way to synthesize the various compet-
ing elements and, in so doing, to coordinate and streamline the Russian state machinery. In spring of 1902, shortly after becoming
minister, he had quietly begun to consider ways to reform the bureaucracy and incorporate local society. He had summoned from the archives the various reform projects of Valuev, Loris-Melikov and
others, hoping, according to one associate, to gradually acquaint the
tsar with these ideas. Within his ministry, work was undertaken on

proposals to reorganize local administration, several drafts of which were completed by autumn of that year.[30]

Late in October, around the time of his Crimean confrontation with Witte, the Minister of Interior presented to the tsar his proposals on local reform. The concept was a simple one. Building upon the legacies of Valuev, Tolstoi, and Durnovo, Plehve proposed to unify state policy by bringing all organs of local and provincial government directly under the control of the governors. The provincial chiefs, it was foreseen, should be given extensive powers to regulate, assign, inspect, and instruct all agencies in their provinces, including the agents of the various ministries and the organs of local self-government. Even the marshals of the nobility would lose some of their power. The emperor's reaction was favorable and, in January 1903, he approved the formation of a special commission, under the auspices of the Ministry of Interior, to further discuss these suggestions.[31]

Meanwhile, in spite of his problems with the local committees, Plehve forged ahead with his plans to increase communication between bureaucracy and self-government. In November of 1902, on his way home from the Crimea, the minister stopped in the city of Kiev and paid a visit to the town council. Expressing his good will toward the concept of local self-government, Plehve reiterated his desire to co-operate with society. "I am convinced that we shall live with you in good harmony," he told the council members, "and that I will eventually have occasion to show favor to you." About this time, the Ministry of Interior made known that it was seriously considering the reduction of zemstvo electoral qualifications, so as to give more people a chance to participate in local self-government.[32]

On December 29, 1902, speaking at the centennial jubilee of the Ministry of Interior, Plehve more fully discussed his views and goals.[33] During the past half century, he asserted, the "gigantic growth of popular forces" had "complicated administrative activity" and "placed all sorts of new demands" upon the government. To meet this challenge, he reported, the ministry was already working on a reform of local government, whose goal would be to "strengthen the managerial authority in local areas" and to "simplify the procedure of this activity." This apparently referred to the ministry's proposals to increase the governors' powers.

The minister was a bit more explicit about his plans to improve interaction between government and society. "In the very near future," he announced, there would be held within the ministry conferences

V. K. Plehve with the officials of the Ministry of the Interior on the
occasion of the Ministry's centennial, 1902.

on "local economic needs" to which persons from local society would
be invited. These conferences would also include, it was hoped, "a
discussion of measures to more correctly combine the activities of
administration and society, and to more clearly define their mutual
relations. . . ." In an implicit recognition of the problem of overcentralization, he added that they should also seek ways "to bring local
persons into more active participation in the work of local administration."

In his discussion of peasant reform, which he termed "the foremost concern of all," Plehve also stressed the need for local input. "It
would be frivolous conceit," he admitted, "to suppose that the Ministry
of Interior can cope with these problems on its own." Nevertheless, he
made only passing reference to Witte's Special Conference, ignored
the local committees, and concentrated on his own peasant project.
He emphasized that "persons experienced in life and familiar with

village affairs" would be "brought into the current work on peasant reform." All this would not be easy. "At the outset of our second century," he concluded, "we are faced with difficult and complex tasks."[34]

By the end of 1902, then, the basic outlines of Plehve's approach were becoming increasingly clear. To unify state policy, he would bring all organs of local and provincial government under the direct control of the governors. To decentralize the administration, he would transfer more responsibility for local affairs to the shoulders of local persons. To better inform the bureaucracy—and to better communicate with society—he would seek to provide for regular local participation in the councils and conferences of the Ministry of Interior. Such a program, he hoped, would promote harmony, efficiency and strength. No less importantly, it would also increase the influence of the Minister of Interior.

THE ASCENDANCY OF PLEHVE'S PROGRAM

The minister's centennial speech was duly reported in the press, and subjected to cautious analysis by various persons. But circumstances may have robbed it of some of the attention it deserved. For one thing, the Committee of Ministers, and several other ministries, were also celebrating their centennials. For another thing, Witte's annual budget report, and his speech outlining Russia's financial picture, both attracted much attention. In addition, the beginning of the new year was marked by numerous proclamations and appointments, including a flattering Imperial rescript to Witte, praising his decade of service at the Ministry of Finance. This latter event seemed to belie recurrent rumors that Witte had lost favor, and even led to speculation that Witte and Plehve may have "buried the hatchet."[35]

Witte himself was by no means elated: the signs of his decline could not be effaced by the emperor's commendations. The Minister of Finance was being excluded from the decision-making process. His long report on the Far Eastern question, submitted after his recent journey, had been studiously ignored. In November 1902, the emperor had taken away one of the Finance Ministry's departments, and created a separate "Main Office of Commercial Navigation" under Grand Duke Alexander Mikhailovich. In December, when Witte presented his annual budget to the State Council, he was subjected to humiliating criticism from the State Controller, and forced to admit that all was not well with the Russian economy.[36] The imperial rescript, when viewed against this backdrop, was hardly reassuring. The most vehement professions of faith, as often as not, are those made when faith is lacking. A vote of confidence, coming from someone like Nicholas II, could well be a kiss of death.

Within a few months, in fact, Plehve was given a chance to show where the tsar's favor really lay. On February 25, 1903, at the time of his regular report, the emperor asked him to prepare a manifesto proclaiming the features of the new state program. It was to be issued on the tsar's late father's birthday—which was the following day! Anxious to "seal his plans by a state act from the throne," the minister agreed to draw up such a document. Bypassing, as usual, his assistant ministers, Plehve called in Police Director Lopukhin, Land Section Head Gurko, and Chancery Director Liubimov to help him. The four of them worked late into the night trying to hammer out a manifesto. Liubimov drafted the introduction and the section on local government, Gurko the parts on peasant reform. Finally it was finished, and the minister rushed off to get the tsar's signature in time for morning publication.[37]

The resulting Manifesto of February 26, 1903, was a curious and ambiguous document.[38] It revealed a government striving for change but hesitant to change too rapidly; a government seeking accommodation with society, but above all seeking control. It amounted, for the most part, to a confirmation of the course set forth in the emperor's remarks at Kursk, and in Plehve's centennial speech. Provincial and local administration were to be reorganized so that "the needs of rural life" could be satisfied "through the efforts of local persons. . . ." To insure coordination and unity, however, they were to be "guided by strong and just authorities responsible strictly to us." The Ministry of Interior's peasant reform project was to be transferred eventually to provincial conferences, which would include "deserving persons who enjoy the confidence of society." This was the heart of Plehve's program: decentralization, coordination, cooperation, and control.

The manifesto did contain at least one interesting departure in the area of local affairs. As a "next step," after the reform of local government, it wished to unite the activities of local self-government with the work of the Orthodox parishes. This was apparently a passing fancy of Plehve's; perhaps it was an attempt to respond to the call for the formation of township zemstvos. In a conversation with the War Minister six weeks later he reiterated the idea. In order to win the support of "the better elements of the population," he suggested, it was necessary to "raise the significance of the Church," and to "strengthen the significance of the parish." Nothing ever came of this concept, it seems, except further aggravation of zemstvo fears for their autonomy.[39]

The most substantive parts of the manifesto were those that dealt with the peasant question. Here the government served notice that it was beginning, ever so slowly, to respond to changing circumstances. One section called for "immediate measures to abolish the oppressive system of collective liability which burdens the peasants." Such a step, to be sure, came as no sudden surprise. Plehve, having privately expressed the view that collectivism was "nonsense," had abandoned his ministry's support for this system shortly after taking office. Subsequently, Witte's proposal to abolish collective liability had been approved within the State Council, and required only formal ratification. Within a few weeks after the manifesto, on March 12, 1903, the emperor confirmed it into law, thus formally ending a practice that dated back centuries—and removing an important obstacle to peasant individualism and mobility. The government, apparently, was finally willing to consider alternatives to collectivism.[40]

Further evidence of this came in the section of the manifesto dealing with the peasant commune. Abolition of the commune had become a *cause célèbre* for many members of society, and had been advocated by many of the local committees. The manifesto refused to go this far. The basis of peasant reform, it declared, would be "to preserve the inviolability of the communal structure . . . , while at the same time searching for ways to make it easier for individual peasants to leave the commune." This sentence, inserted at the insistence of Gurko, spoke volumes about the government's position. What was remarkable was not so much the tribute paid to the "inviolability" of the commune, which was only to be expected, but the fact that it was juxtaposed with a desire to facilitate peasant departure. This contained an implicit recognition that the commune was not necessarily sacrosanct, that it could at times serve as an obstacle to progress. The Russia of Plehve was not prepared to make a frontal assault on the commune —that would be too disruptive—but it was willing to open the way for future, gradual change.[41] It hoped, somewhat incongruously, to bring about a new order without disturbing the old one.

This paradox was reflected in the Ministry of Interior's work on peasant reform, accelerated in the wake of the manifesto. Although Assistant Minister Stishinskii, an advocate of collectivism, was still nominally in charge, the "Editing Commission" he chaired was for all intents a "fictitious" organization. According to Land Section Head Gurko, the bulk of the work was done by subordinate officials, many of whom, like Gurko himself, favored individualism. In spring of 1903, anxious to complete the project, Plehve temporarily relieved Gurko and his associates of all other duties, so they could concentrate on the task at hand. By summer, several legislative drafts and a summary "sketch" of the reform were nearing completion. In June, several meetings—attended by Plehve, Zinov'ev, Stishinskii, Gurko, and three outside "experts"—were held at the minister's dacha to discuss the preliminary project. By July, Plehve was able to report to the tsar that a draft would be ready for submission to provincial conferences toward the end of the current year. [42]

Meanwhile, the Minister of Interior was also trying to "direct the activity of the state credit institutions" so as to "strengthen rural economy." This promise, contained in the Manifesto of February 26, was an implicit criticism of Witte, under whose purview these institutions functioned. It applied in particular to the Peasant Land Bank which, according to Plehve, had not been used to the best advantage of the Russian state.

The Peasant Bank had been founded in 1883 to help peasants expand their properties: it lent them money to buy land, and acquired land for them to buy. As a rule, it made loans only to those who were good risks, helping prosperous peasants to purchase more land, often from the local nobility. From Plehve's standpoint this was contrary to state interests: land prices were rising, noble landownership was shrinking, and the poorer peasants—those most in need of assistance—were unable to procure loans. He wished to see procedures revised, so as to preserve the land balance between noble and peasant, to help colonize border areas that were politically unstable and, in so doing, to relieve the "land-shortage" in the Center. [43] But the bank came under the Ministry of Finance, where Plehve had no control.

This did not prevent him from doing his best to influence its work. In December of 1902, a commission had been formed to re-examine bank policy. Its chairman, Prince A. D. Obolenskii, was an Assistant Minister of Finance; twelve of its members came from Finance as against only four from Interior. Still, Plehve had sent a strong delegation, including Resettlement Director Krivoshein and Land Section Head Gurko. Then, on January 28, 1903, five days after the commission's first session, he had submitted to Witte a long official letter outlining his views on the bank. [44]

Plehve's letter, highly critical of current bank policy, had demanded a new approach. It proposed, in effect, that the bank be used as an instrument to promote internal stability and increase state control. Instead of helping wealthier peasants buy land from local nobles, it should be assisting poorer peasants moving from crowded areas. It should buy land mainly in regions, such as the western provinces and the Caucasus, where an increased proportion of native Russians might improve internal security. It should deal in smaller parcels, so that more plots would be available to poorer peasant families, and it should make available special loans to those who would resettle. Finally, the Ministry of Interior should be given a role in determining bank procedures, and handling the new loans.[45]

The commission, dominated as it was by the Ministry of Finance, did not take kindly to these proposals. It met seven times in the first three months of 1903, then twice more in April to consider Plehve's letter. According to one participant, the meetings were filled with violent debates between Witte's people and Plehve's. The vote on almost every issue split along ministerial lines. The commission's majority, led by chairman Obolenskii, voted time after time to preserve the Peasant Bank as a purely financial institution, and to reject efforts to make it a tool of social regulation. Only token concessions were made: the Ministry of Interior, for instance, was granted the right to "make comments" on the bank's annual report.[46] Other than that, the commission accomplished little, except to exacerbate the Witte–Plehve feud. In this instance, at least, the Minister of Finance was able to block the meddling of his colleague.

Be that as it may, the Imperial Manifesto of February 26, 1903, might well be seen as a confirmation of Plehve's ascendancy. Witte had no hand in drafting this document, nor could he derive any satisfaction from it. The industrial growth of Russia, judging from its text, was no longer the top priority. And the Special Conference on the Needs of Agricultural Industry, whose local committees had been the focus of so much attention and energy in the previous eight months, was not even mentioned.

The manifesto also might be viewed as an official presentation of the program of Plehve. It was certainly no drastic reform program; indeed, it was essentially a cautious program aimed at perfecting, rather than altering, the state apparatus. Yet it did foresee some important changes: increasing government control was to be combined with coordination of local government, cooperation with local society, and decreasing peasant collectivism. With this formula, Plehve hoped

to relieve rural poverty and social discontent, and provide a solid base
of support for the Russian autocracy.

THE REFORM OF LOCAL GOVERNMENT

The publication of the Manifesto of February 26, 1903, corresponded
with a series of efforts on the part of the Ministry of Interior to reform
the state machinery. This work had three main objectives: to coordinate the workings of local government, to decentralize the administration, and to involve local society in the decision-making process. The
first goal was addressed by a special commission on provincial administration, and by several measures enacted toward this end. The second
was considered in an interministerial decentralization conference
which began its work in May of 1903. And the third was dealt with
by a succession of conferences within the Ministry of Interior, to
which various members of local society were invited.

The imperial commission on provincial administration, authorized by the tsar at Plehve's behest in January of 1903, held its first
meeting on February 27, the day after the manifesto's publication.
Plehve himself was the chairman, while the membership included a
number of governors and most of the high officials of the Ministry of
Interior. In this group, at least, there would be little obstruction: no
representatives from other ministries were invited to attend.[47]

The formal meetings, nonetheless, produced some disagreement.
Chairman Plehve, outlining the commission's goals, called for proposals to increase the governors' powers, so as to restore the rightful status
as "masters of the provinces" they had been given by Catherine the
Great. Some of the governors wished to strengthen all aspects of their
authority, including the direction of zemstvos, town councils, and
agencies of the various ministries. This view, in general, was supported
by the ministry. A few governors, although seeking more control over
administrative organs, felt that further subordination of local self-government would needlessly antagonize society. One, Prince B. A. Vasil'chikov, insisted that the governors must be free to act as
representatives of the tsar and Ruling Senate, and not just as officials
of the Ministry of Interior. Another, Count F. E. Keller, created a stir
by asserting that his current powers would be more than adequate, if
only the bureaucrats in the Ministry of Interior would stop interfering.

These latter views, needless to say, aroused no sympathy from Plehve. [48]

At any rate, the various statements were recorded and, after a total of seven meetings, the work was turned over to the Minister's Chancery to draft a commission report. That summer, as a follow-up, the minister sent a detailed questionnaire to all the governors, asking their opinions on the issues which had been raised. The majority, out of either conviction or expediency, supported the ministry's views. Almost all wanted greater authority in their provinces; only a few called for more independence from the ministry. The material thus gathered was included in the commission journal, which was completed by the chancery toward the end of the summer. [49]

In general, the commission's proposals on local reform reflected the ministry's earlier recommendations. Most ministries were to communicate instructions to their local agents only through the governor. Heads of local bodies such as the fiscal chamber, gendarmerie, and factory inspectorate were to make regular reports to the governor. The governor was to be given direct supervisory authority over all primary and secondary education, and the power to inspect all other administrative institutions. With regard to the zemstvos and town councils, he was to be given the right to dismiss their elected officials in cases of "unreliability," and to remove from their agendas any item he felt was "unbecoming." Furthermore, in instances where such institutions refused to carry out their "assigned duties," the governor was to undertake these measures himself, charging all costs to the zemstvo or town council. All governors were to be given the right to issue "binding resolutions" for prevention of disorder, a right previously enjoyed only in provinces under "strengthened security." Finally, a new "provincial council" was to be established, under the governor's control, to help coordinate the various collegial bodies. [50]

On the surface, the thrust of the provincial reform program was clear: the work of the various local institutions was to be unified by making all these bodies directly responsible to the governor. Just beneath the surface, however, there were several additional ramifications. For one thing, the reform would have deprived the zemstvos and town councils of the last vestiges of their autonomy, making them little more than branches of the provincial administration. The governors would be able to dismiss their officials, carry out their work, and decide what topics they could discuss. For another thing, these proposals would have added to the power of the Minister of Interior, giving him a clear supremacy over his ministerial colleagues. The governors were still, in effect, local officials of the Ministry of Interior, only now it was proposed that the local officials of all other ministries should be subordinated to them.

Although such a reform would never actually become law, a series of measures in its same spirit were in fact enacted in the wake of the manifesto. One of these was a May 1903 statute that placed the factory inspectors, officials of the Ministry of Finance, under the supervision of the governors. Making use of the tsar's support, Plehve was able both to overcome Witte's objections and to circumvent the legislative process. Another was a law of April 1903 which extended the "zemstvo" system into six Baltic and western border provinces. This action, initiated under Sipiagin, caused a great deal of dismay in zemstvo circles. It provided them with a clear picture of the type of "local self-government" the regime preferred. The "zemstvos" set up by the new law were so truncated they were hardly recognizable. Members of the assemblies and boards in these provinces would not be elected; instead they were to be appointed by the governors from among the propertied classes. These bodies were obviously intended to operate as local branches of the imperial administration, under the direct control of the governors.[51]

The spring of 1903 also witnessed the enactment of an important reorganization of the local police system. Prior to this, police work in rural locales was in the hands of certain unpaid and untrained peasants, elected by the villagers for a definite term. These were known as "teners" (desiatskie) and "hundreders" (sotskie), based roughly on the number of households that selected them. In general, the quality of their work was very poor: many peasants tried to avoid this uncompensated burden, and those who did get elected were often incompetent, corrupt, or unwilling to do their duties. This had become very clear during the Khar'kov and Poltava riots, when the local police failed to provide any forewarning of trouble. A law of May 5, 1903, initiated by the Ministry of Interior, set out to change all this. Over a period of five and a half years, it declared, the empire's 67,500 hundreders were to be replaced by a system of paid police guards (strazhniki), at a rate of one for every 2500 persons. The teners would remain, a concession to fiscal realities.[52]

In defending this project before the State Council, Plehve had given two major reasons for it. It was necessary, he asserted, to staff the local police with persons selected and paid by the government, and at the same time to lighten the burden of police service on the peasantry. Implicit in this law, however, was the strengthening of the power of the governor, whose major source of control was the police. By vastly increasing the size of the police force at his disposal, it would eventually give the governor a greater opportunity to extend his control into rural areas. Incidentally, it would also increase the power of the Minister of Interior, who was given the authority to move these "guards" from province to province to cope with "emergencies."[53]

Plehve's efforts to decentralize the state bureaucracy were manifested in a special conference on this subject, convened in May of 1903 and chaired by the emperor himself. Also present, along with Plehve, were the Ministers of Agriculture, Justice, and Finance, and State Council member S. F. Platonov. The discussion, judging from the conference journal, must have been an interesting one. Although all the participants expressed concern about overcentralization, they were not particularly anxious to transfer much authority to the Ministry of Interior's governors. Witte, as might have been expected, took the lead, arguing that only insignificant matters could be transferred to the governors unless and until an administrative reform made them full representatives of the emperor, and not just officials of the Ministry of Interior. Although he could not openly oppose such a view, Plehve countered by pointing out that a special commission within his ministry was already working on provincial reform. Its goal, he added, was to unify all local agencies of both state and society under control of the governor, who would once more become the "master of the province." The tsar himself then seconded these remarks with a strong expression of support for Plehve's reform.[54]

After a bit more discussion, the emperor directed that all ministries and main offices must compile lists of items to be transferred "from the central institutions to the final decision of local authorities." They were to indicate, in addition, which of these could be transmitted immediately, and which must await the reform of local government. The lists were then to be submitted, for correlation and review, to a commission chaired by Platonov, which began its work in August of 1903.[55] Plehve had again prevailed, at least for the time being.

In pursuing his third objective, that of consultation with local society, the Minister of Interior had several different goals. On one hand, he was anxious to make better use of their extensive knowledge of local affairs, knowledge that was largely lacking among Petersburg bureaucrats. On the other hand, he hoped to forge a link between state and society by co-opting those who were willing to work with the government—he would make them part of the system they were so critical of. In so doing, he intended to split the opposition move-

ment: to draw the "loyal" zemstvo-men into "useful government work,"
thus isolating the "unreliable" elements.[56]

The first of his promised conferences combining ministry officials
and zemstvo-men was a January 1903 discussion of a new veterinary
law. Similar conferences were held in March, on emergency local food
provisioning, and in April, on zemstvo fire insurance. On each occasion, the minister met with the zemstvo-men, expressed his good will,
and discussed the need for further cooperation.

The veterinary conference in January had been called to reconsi-
der provisions of a newly-enacted law that had been widely criticized
by the zemstvos. To this conference, chaired by Assistant Minister
Zinov'ev, were invited eleven zemstvo board representatives and three
zemstvo veterinarians. In a private meeting with Moscow zemstvo-
man M. V. Chelnikov, Plehve admitted that the law was "not free of
. . . deficiencies," and agreed that it would be necessary "to introduce
several legislative corrections" so as to satisfy the concerns of the
zemstvos. He also seemed to recognize the legitimacy of some other
zemstvo complaints. "There should be no talk of decreasing the rights
of the zemstvos," he told Chelnikov. "There are so many sins on our
souls in this regard. . . ." However, he insisted that much of the blame
for poor government–zemstvo relations rested with the institutions of
local self-government, which had a "marked tendency" to "see everything as an attempt to restrict their independence."[57]

In March, Plehve held a private conversation with the nine zemstvo-men, and five marshals of the nobility, who had come to Saint
Petersburg for the conference on provisioning. A broad array of issues
was discussed, including zemstvo representation, public education,
inter-zemstvo cooperation, the status of the nobility, the third element, and the Peasant Land Bank. The minister, who moderated the
informal discussion, did not hesitate to express his views. On one
hand, he was sharply critical of zemstvo attempts to hold unauthorized
congresses, and he defended his refusal to confirm the elections of
troublesome zemstvo officials. At the same time, he stressed his willingness to consult and cooperate. He told those present that he intended "to reorganize the Economy Department of the ministry and
set up a special council where the chairmen of the [zemstvo] boards
would periodically get together." And, in concluding the discussion,
he remarked that although he "might not agree with the opinions of
the zemstvo-men on every issue," he hoped that at least their "differences would not be too pronounced."[58]

On April 7, while spending the Easter season in the Moscow

area, Plehve took the time to receive the members of the Moscow provincial zemstvo board. He greeted the board members in a friendly manner, and displayed an active interest in their work.[59]

Then, back in Saint Petersburg that same month, he held a reception for twenty-eight zemstvo-men who had assembled for the conference on fire insurance. He made use of the occasion to deliver a short speech. "I am very glad to see you here," he told the zemstvomen.

> Your conferences within the ministry are bringing you together with the representatives of the ministry on the ground of practical business, facilitating common work and mutual relations. At the same time this sort of conference gives you an opportunity for intercourse among yourselves on the various other questions of zemstvo life. I strongly sympathize with this intercourse; I consider it necessary and desirable. At any rate, these meetings are more proper than secret assemblies. Persons invested with public confidence should not act behind drawn shades.

He concluded by stressing the importance of practical activity. "I attach great significance to the participation of zemstvo workers in preparatory work within the ministry," he proclaimed. "I consider your activity on the ground of practical issues very helpful; it is better than abstract philosophizing."[60]

Thus, in his speeches, conversations, and initiatives, did Plehve reveal his attitudes toward the working of local government. He was concerned about disunity, and he wished to give the governors real authority to coordinate the actions of all agencies in their provinces. He was concerned with centralization: he realized that people in the provinces were better acquainted with local affairs than Petersburg bureaucrats, and he wanted their input and support. But he was concerned, above all, with control. For the governors he sought power, but not independence: they were to remain under the bureaucratic supervision of his own ministry. To the zemstvos, he extended the hand of cooperation, but he insisted that they work within the government, rather than outside it, and that they concern themselves with "practical," not "political" or "philosophical" questions. His efforts, however, were doomed to failure: while he was winning the battle for the emperor's favor, Plehve had been losing the contest for public support.

PLEHVE'S BREAK WITH THE ZEMSTVOS

Early in 1903, as Plehve's new programs were coming to light, his agreements with zemstvo leader Shipov broke down. The reasons for this were several. Prominent among them was the minister's insistence that zemstvos act only on the local level. As early as May 1902, he had refused to permit the Moscow provincial zemstvo to begin publication of an empire-wide zemstvo newspaper. In August his ministry had put forth a reform designed to make the county zemstvos' more independent of the provincial—a clear attempt to decrease the power of the provincial zemstvos. Not long thereafter, he apparently had the governors instruct the marshals of the nobility to prohibit all discussion of the issues raised at the May zemstvo conference in Moscow. Then, at the January 1903 veterinary conference, all participants of that May zemstvo meeting were purposely excluded, and efforts were made to prevent those who did come from consulting beforehand among themselves.[61]

Another factor was the refusal of zemstvo-men to stay away from political issues. Many saw the government as the main obstacle to progress, and felt that no real improvement could occur without basic changes in the political structure. Shipov himself made an effort to cooperate, but many of his colleagues denounced the "deal" with Plehve, and refused to abide by it. Furthermore, in June of 1902 the first issue of a constitutionalist émigré journal called *Liberation (Osvobozhdenie)* was published in Stuttgart, with the apparent collaboration of a large group of zemstvo-men. In this and subsequent issues *Liberation* called for sweeping political changes aimed at the establishment of a system of popular representation in Russia.[62] Although most zemstvo activists still wished to achieve their goals by "legal" and peaceful means, they were obviously unwilling to confine themselves to local and technical problems.

A third factor was the conflict between the minister and the local committees on agriculture. Despite Shipov's agreement to avoid raising "obstacles" to government–zemstvo cooperation, a number of zemstvo-men in the committees had raised "constitutional" questions. Shipov, of course, had had little control over this, but Plehve had seen it as evidence of bad faith. The outspoken radicalism of some committees had caught him by surprise, and he had reacted in a very harsh fashion. In turn, his response—the use of banishment, reprimand, and forced retirement—had antagonized the nobility, who felt their "privileges" threatened, and had persuaded even the Slavophiles that the minister was simply deceiving Shipov to acquire a temporary advantage. Shipov himself, by the end of 1902, had become convinced of this.[63]

The extent of Plehve's sincerity is certainly open to question. He was trying, no doubt, to "take advantage" of Shipov—to encourage criticism of Witte, and to open up a split between zemstvo Slavophiles and zemstvo constitutionalists. In the latter, at least, he achieved some early success: the constitutionalists responded to the Plehve–Shipov agreement with anguished cries and personal attacks upon the Moscow zemstvo board chairman. To them and to others, the lesson was clear: the Minister of Interior was a conniving, unscrupulous politician, making use of personal charm, misrepresentation, and outright lies for his own political purposes.[64]

This, however, was not necessarily the case. Surely Plehve sought political advantage in wooing Shipov, but that did not make him unscrupulous or deceptive. It was only natural that someone entrusted with preserving the autocracy should attempt to ally himself with the monarchists and loyalists, and to isolate the constitutionals. Shipov was, after all, sincerely interested in preserving the monarchy, opposing Witte, and reconciling the government with society. In these areas, at least, his goals were at one with Plehve's. Nor was the minister deceitful: he had quite frankly informed the zemstvo-man of his opposition to the raising of "political" questions, his hostility toward the third element, and even his unwillingness to permit any sort of elected representation. In short, the program which Plehve outlined to Shipov in July 1902 was quite similar to the one he actually would pursue over the next two years. No doubt the minister exaggerated his "friendship" for the zemstvos; no doubt he was "using" the Moscow zemstvo leader. But then, so were the constitutionalists, who were striving to push Shipov and the zemstvos into the very sort of confrontation with the government that the Moscow board chairman was seeking to avert.[65]

Plehve, of course, had his own reasons for feeling betrayed. After all, had he not tried to keep his end of the bargain? Had not he and the emperor displayed favor to the zemstvos on several occasions? Did not the conferences in the ministry represent an honest fulfillment of his promise to Shipov? True, Shipov was not included, but whose fault was that? Did not the zemstvo sabotage of the agricultural committees, and continued efforts to form a national organization, show evidence of bad faith? "Does not the guilt in this case lie with your friend Shipov," he asked one zemstvo-man, "who has created for himself the position of some sort of zemstvo executive?"[66]

The "guilt," in fact, lay with neither. Underlying their conflicts and antagonisms was a fundamental difference in perspective and approach that could not readily be reconciled. Zemstvo leaders—indeed, most thoughtful Russians—could have no quarrel with Plehve's objectives: coordination, decentralization, and state-society cooperation were widely-recognized needs. But the issue of central control *versus* local initiative prevented any meeting of the minds. The crux of Plehve's solution was bureaucratic expansionism: he would "decentralize" the administration by increasing the influence of its provincial and local branches, and by incorporating into it the organs of self-government. But the bureaucracy itself was anathema to the zemstvo-men, and many resented the Minister of Interior's efforts to "buy" zemstvo support and co-opt them into his system. They argued—and here they stood on common ground with Witte—that Russia's creative and productive forces were being stifled by the bureaucracy, and that they could only be unleashed through local and individual intitiative. Society itself, they felt, could resolve Russia's problems, if only it were given the freedom to do so.[67]

Zemstvo activists—monarchists and constitutionalists alike—wanted more autonomy and broader jurisdiction. Plehve's formula, in essence, offered them neither. He promised to treat them well, to consult them often, to increase their funding, and to make good use of their talents, but he would neither ease up on their reins nor loosen their harnesses—at least until they had proven themselves "reliable." His notion of "cooperation," it seemed, was that they must work for him.

The final break between Shipov and Plehve came as the result of events in late 1902 and early 1903. In November, disturbed by provisions of the new veterinary law, Shipov wrote a letter to his counterparts in other provinces asking them each to request its repeal. Plehve, when he learned of this, was displeased: here was Shipov once again acting as a national zemstvo coordinator. Then, in January, an unauthorized congress of zemstvo teachers was held in Moscow. Shipov was not directly involved, but he could scarcely have been unaware of it. Plehve reacted with punitive measures: when the teachers returned to their homes, many were subjected to search or arrest. This incident, of course, helped increase the ill will between Plehve and society.[68]

In February, during the meetings of the Moscow provincial committee on agriculture, came the final blow. When it became clear that governor Kristi meant to use his artificial majority to vote down any "political" resolutions, Shipov led the zemstvo-men in a walkout. Several days later, in a "letter to the editor" in the *Russian Gazette*, the zemstvo board chairman explained that they had quit because the committee represented the "administration," and not the "people." Plehve replied with an order forbidding any discussion of Shipov's letter. In addition, the name of Shipov was conspicuous by its absence on the lists of those invited to the ministry's conferences on local affairs.[69]

On March 17 the zemstvo leader happened to be in Saint Petersburg, and he took the occasion to pay a visit to the Minister of Interior. This gave the two men a chance to discuss the deterioration of their mutual understanding.[70] Plehve began by accusing his visitor of bad faith. "Today is our first meeting since last summer on Aptekarsk Island. . . . It is a shame that the wish I then expressed—to organize cooperation between us—has not been realized, and that I was unable to bring you to participate in the conferences which have occurred within the ministry. I cannot do this alone; you have not cooperated with me. You continue to lead a dissident social group whose purpose is constant opposition to the government." When Shipov demanded clarification, the minister enumerated his complaints, including the May congress of the preceding year, a summer convention of county board chairmen in Moscow, the liberal program of the Sudzha agricultural committee, and, in general, an attempt to sabotage the local committees on agricultural industry: "You and your supporters strove to convey to the committees an indication of how the government should reorganize the state administration."

Shipov, of course, denied the allegations, insisting he had done nothing illegal. With some justification, he argued that he had little control over agricultural committees in other provinces. But Plehve's main accusation did not involve any specific wrongdoing; it centered around the zemstvo-man's position as unofficial leader of a national zemstvo union and spokesman for the oppositional elements of society: "The people who are grouped around you in Moscow oppose the current direction of the government, and information flows to you from all points about the activities of the committees and public institutions." This activity, the minister insisted, was "intolerable," especially on the part of "official persons." From his standpoint, "even though the board chairmen are elected by the zemstvo assemblies, they are nevertheless officials in state service like all of the others."

Here, indeed, was the root of the misunderstanding between
Plehve and the zemstvos. The minister, for all his talk of cooperation,
refused to see the zemstvos as anything more than a peculiar branch
of the administration. Zemstvo officials, therefore, were government
officials; they were directly responsible to provincial administration,
and owed their first allegiance to the imperial government. The zemstvo leaders, however, tended to view themselves as elected representatives of autonomous public institutions. ". . . [E]ven though I am an
official in state service," was Shipov's reply, "I consider myself above
all an elected representative of that society that has placed its confidence in me, and I consider it my sacred obligation to defend the
freedom and independence of the public institutions."

The meeting ended on a note of resignation. After expressing
wonder that zemstvo-men could still doubt the government's goodwill after the emperor's speech at Kursk, the minister rose and shook
his visitor's hand. "I know, Dmitri Nikolaevich, that you are steadfast
in your convictions and will not retreat from them," he said. "Apparently we are not going to get together."

Several weeks later, during Plehve's Easter visit to Moscow, Director of the General Affairs Department B. V. Sturmer made a con-
certed effort to arrange another meeting between the two men, in the
hope that their differences could be smoothed over. Whether Sturmer
realized that Shipov's defection spelt ultimate doom for his boss's program, or whether he was merely acting at the minister's behest, his
efforts were in vain. Both men were adamant in their positions, and
each felt he had been betrayed by the other.[71]

The dissolution of Plehve's agreement with Shipov was of great
significance, both symbolic and practical. It was, in fact, a signal
victory for the zemstvo constitutionalists. Plehve's attempt to split the
zemstvo movement, to isolate the constitutionalists from the monarchists, had ended in failure. This cost the minister his only chance of
accommodation with society, and earned for him the opprobrium of
Slavophiles as well as constitutionalists. Plehve nevertheless went
ahead with his programs, still intent on drawing "enlightened local
persons" into the governmental process.[72] But no longer could he hope
for support from the "loyal" zemstvo element: his reforms would have
to be forced into effect against the hostility of almost every segment
of society.

5

The Jewish, Finnish, and Armenian Questions

THE KISHINEV POGROM

On April 4, 1903, the first anniversary of his appointment, Minister of Interior Plehve traveled to Moscow to celebrate the Easter holidays. As he had done the previous year, he managed to mix business with piety, taking the opportunity to meet with zemstvo and worker groups, and to accompany the emperor to religious and social functions.[1] During his first year in office, Plehve had become a well-known and controversial figure within the tsarist empire, but outside of Russia he was still relatively unknown. This was soon to change. For, while the minister prayed and politicked in Moscow, events were taking place in a distant and obscure corner of the empire that were to bring him notoriety throughout the Western world.

On Easter Sunday, April 6, 1903, a riot broke out in Kishinev, the capital city of the far southwestern province of Bessarabia. Accounts vary as to how the tumult started, but it is clear that by mid-afternoon unruly bands of Christian townsfolk had assembled in the streets of the Jewish sector and, aroused by some minor incident or by pre-conceived plan, had begun throwing rocks through the windows of the Jewish shops. Unhampered by the local police, who were either unwilling or unable to restore order, the mob soon turned to looting and violence. Jews, even though they made little effort to resist, were severely beaten, many of them to death. This was the beginning of the infamous Kishinev "pogrom," the largest and bloodiest of these anti-Jewish riots.

The violence ceased shortly after nightfall, but resumed the following morning. By this time the alarmed Bessarabian governor, Lieutenant General von Raaben, had appealed to the local military commander to help put down the disorders. Inexplicably, however, the soldiers took no action until early evening. As soon as they did the situation was brought under control. But the bloodshed had already reached disastrous proportions: forty-five to fifty Jews had been killed, hundreds of others had been wounded or maimed, and vast numbers of shops and homes had been damaged or destroyed.[2]

The Kishinev pogrom aroused an international wave of anger and revulsion. Despite the Russian censorship, lurid eyewitness accounts soon reached the Western press. These described, among other things, the inactivity of the authorities, and the apparent sympathy of the police and soldiers toward the Christian mob. They also indicated that many among the local populace felt they were carrying out the emperor's will. The conclusion was quickly drawn that the massacre had occurred with the connivance of local officials—and accusing fingers soon pointed at the head of the ministry to which the police and local authorities were responsible.[3]

The Minister of Interior seemed a logical person on whom to pin the blame: throughout his career, Plehve had acquired a reputation as a rabid anti-Semite. In the early 1880s, while he was Director of Police, there had occurred a series of anti-Jewish pogroms rumored to have been instigated by the police. During the same period, with Plehve's support, a number of repressive regulations had been enacted against the Jews. In 1890, as chairman of a commission on anti-Jewish laws, he had helped devise a program for further restrictive measures. And, although these had never been implemented, the town council reform of 1892, drawn up by a Plehve commission, had restricted Jewish participation in municipal self-government. According to Witte, in fact, "the guiding spirit and real author of all the anti-Jewish laws under Ignat'ev and Durnovo was Plehve."[4]

The events preceding the Kishinev riot also seemed to implicate Plehve. The stage had been set for the pogrom by three prominent local persons, each of whom had some connection with the Minister of Interior. One of these was P. A. Krushevan, owner of the town newspaper, who had stirred up the populace with reports blaming Jews for the "ritual murder" of a local Christian boy. A notorious anti-Semite, Krushevan had recently received a subsidy to begin a Saint Petersburg daily, reportedly arranged by the Minister of Interior. Another key figure was Pronin, a wealthy local contractor and extreme Judophobe who had spread spurious rumors and anti-Jewish propa-

Bodies of those slain in Kishinev pogrom, 1903

ganda, and had written demagogic articles in Krushevan's newspaper. Pronin liked to brag about his close relationship and frequent meetings with the Minister of Interior. Furthermore, he was known to be an intimate friend of a third instigator, Levendal, the chief of the local Okhrana. On the first day of the pogrom, according to later testimony, Levendal had gone to the governor's home and dissuaded von Raaben from going to the scene of the disorders. This, it seemed, was strange activity indeed for a high official of Plehve's security police.[5]

Plehve's own actions during and after the pogrom hardly allayed suspicions. Although Levendal apparently had warned the Police Department of possible disturbances, no preventive steps were ordered from Saint Petersburg. Although the minister learned of the riots on Easter Sunday evening, he did not demand "decisive measures" until the following day. After the massacre, although the Jews had been the victims, Plehve almost seemed to justify what had taken place. The Jews needed to be "taught a lesson," he explained to the Minister of

War, because they were "conceited" and stood "in the forefront of the revolutionary movement."[6]

The impression of Plehve's complicity was further enhanced by an article appearing in the *Times* of London a month after the pogrom. In it was cited a document purported to be a dispatch sent from the Minister of Interior to the governor of Bessarabia two weeks before the riots. It read, in part: "It has come to my knowledge that in the region entrusted to you wide disturbances are being prepared against the Jews, who chiefly exploit the local population. In view of . . . the unquestionable undesirability of instilling, by too severe measures, anti-government feelings into the population . . . your Excellency will not fail to contribute to the immediate stopping of disorders which may arise, by means of admonitions, without at all having recourse, however, to the use of arms."[7] If this dispatch was authentic, its implications were clear: Plehve had known beforehand of the disorders and had advised the governor to refrain from taking strong action.

The Russian government made no immediate response, thus reinforcing the perception that the report was accurate. Only on May 13, eight days after the article appeared, was its authenticity denied. By this time much of Europe and America had come to accept it as genuine, and had come to credit Plehve as the author of the pogrom. Even the firing of Governor von Raaben, on the grounds of his inactivity, did not serve to shift the blame.[8]

If the minister was guilty, he hardly seemed repentant. Not long after the pogrom, he instructed the governors to prevent the formation of Jewish defense societies. He had his censorship department preclude dissemination of stories about the tragedy, and he censured several journals which dared to print articles critical of the government's role. He refused to provide financial relief to the Jewish victims and their survivors, yet he intervened to have arrested Christians released from jail so they could tend their fields. He insisted that the trial of the perpetrators be held behind closed doors, to prevent the airing of charges against the government. He even threatened a delegation of Jewish merchants in July 1903: ". . . if you do not keep your young people out of the revolutionary movement, we will make your situation so unbearable that you will all be compelled to leave Russia."[9]

All these acts and statements merely reinforced the impression of Plehve's guilt. Further damaging evidence was added several years later, when it became known that there existed during 1905 a special secret printing press for publishing anti-Jewish proclamations within the Department of Police. Was it not probable that this practice had been instituted during Plehve's time? Then, when Sergei Witte finally wrote his memoirs, he too implicated his former rival. He charged that Plehve, "looking for a psychological turning point in the revolutionary mood of the masses," had "sought it in Jewish pogroms," and that the Kishinev pogrom was "arranged with the connivance of Plehve." [10]

These factors, taken together, present an impressive case against the minister. His history of anti-Semitic activity, and reputation as a Jew-hater, made him appear a person capable of instigating pogroms. The growing revolutionary mood in Russia, and the large number of Jews involved in revolutionary activity, provided his probable motive. His links with local agitators gave him the implements necessary to carry out such a crime. And his behavior during and after the massacre befitted that of an unrepentant criminal trying to cover up his involvement. The verdict, to many, seemed inescapable: the plot had been hatched in Saint Petersburg by Plehve, transmitted through the police apparatus by Assistant Minister von Wahl, orchestrated by local Okhrana chief Levendal, and carried out by Pronin and Krushevan. Then, in order to appease public opinion in Russia and the West, a scapegoat was made of Governor von Raaben, who was ingloriously dismissed. [11]

The evidence, however, is not entirely conclusive. It demonstrates that Plehve was anti-Semitic, that he advocated and pursued anti-Jewish policies, and that he was sympathetic in his treatment of local Jew-baiters. It indicates that he tended to blame the Jews in large measure for the growth of the revolutionary movement. It also shows that he was less than heartbroken about the tragedy, and that he used his authority to silence his critics and accusers. But it falls short of proving that he consciously planned and orchestrated the Kishinev massacre.

Many links in the chain of evidence are, in fact, rather weak. There was no clear connection, for instance, between Plehve and the pogroms of 1881–82. The first wave of riots, in fact, occurred while the "liberal" Loris-Melikov was still Minister of Interior, before the new Police Director had settled into his job. Later waves, although accompanied perhaps by official negligence, do not seem to have been instigated by the police. And Minister Tolstoi, who ended the pogroms, did so with the assistance of Plehve, whom he retained as Police Director for two more years. [12]

Plehve's views, furthermore, were far more complex than those of a simple Jew-hater. Having been raised among Jews, he claimed a certain understanding and admiration of them. He was aware, moreover, that the oppressive misery of many Jews was pushing them toward revolution. As minister, he used anti-Jewish restrictions to "protect" the Russian populace, but he also strove to relieve Jewish poverty and remove "unjustified" restraints. He even showed some sympathy and support for the Russian Zionist movement. While these steps hardly qualified him as a "Judophile," they did show a sensitivity that is difficult to reconcile with his pogrom-maker image. Even Witte admitted that his rival "personally had nothing against the Jews."[13]

As for Plehve's alleged connections with the Kishinev agitators, these were tenuous at best. Pronin's boasting of intimacy with the minister must be regarded as exaggerated and suspect. Plehve's support for Krushevan's Saint Petersburg newspaper had nothing to do with Kishinev, and it did not prevent his ministry from censuring this gazette shortly after the pogrom. The normal channel from the minister to Levendal would have run through Police Director Lopukhin and Special Section Head Zubatov. These two officials, whatever their faults, were in no sense considered anti-Semites.[14]

Other aspects of the case are no more convincing. The clandestine police printing press, according to Lopukhin, was not established until well after Plehve's death. Witte's accusations, whatever their merit, were contradicted by their author, who at one point wrote: "I would not go so far as to say that Plehve engineered these pogroms personally."[15] Even Plehve's remarks to Kuropatkin about "teaching the Jews a lesson," damning as they were to the minister's character, were not sufficient to show that he was personally involved.

Furthermore, the minister did have his defenders. Several persons, in a position to know whether Plehve was involved, unequivocally denied his complicity. One of these was Land Section Head Gurko, who was among the minister's closest collaborators. Another was D. N. Liubimov, Director of the Minister's Chancery, who handled Plehve's correspondence. Most important, perhaps, was A. A. Lopukhin who, as Director of Police, would have been aware of any pogrom-making activities conducted through his department. In the days following the massacre, Lopukhin made an on-the-spot investigation of the riot and its causes. "Whatever the political sins of Plehve," he would later write, "I am deeply convinced that it is unjust to attribute the organization of the Kishinev pogrom to him. His anti-Semitism is not subject to doubt, but this one fact is not enough to attribute to an intelligent man a measure which is not only vile, but also politically stupid."[16]

Plehve's defenders, in general, saw the "von Raaben dispatch" as the main incriminating evidence, and hastened to refute it. "Obviously there never was any such letter," asserted Liubimov, whose department was alleged to have sent it. Gurko wrote that Plehve at first thought it might be authentic, but was convinced of its fraudulence by Lopukhin. The latter, in an even better position to comment, stated categorically that ". . . as a result of my painstakingly conducted investigation, this letter was shown to be a forgery." Even the new Bessarabian governor, who was not a defender of Plehve, was "deeply convinced of its spurious character."[17]

The inactivity of the local authorities, according to these defenders, was not the fault of Plehve. In situations of public unrest, it was the governor's duty to call out the troops and give them their orders. But Governor von Raaben took no such action: he summoned the troops, but gave them no further instructions. On the morning of the second day, according to Liubimov, Plehve sent the governor a strong telegram calling for "decisive measures to restore order with the aid of the troops." But even then von Raaben did nothing. The military commanders, having no authority to act, merely deployed their forces and allowed the slaughter to go on. This, at least, was the version of the local military commander. It was confirmed by Lopukhin's investigation and repeated in Plehve's report to the emperor, which in turn led to the dismissal of von Raaben.[18]

The firing of von Raaben was cited by these persons as proof of the minister's innocence. It was inconceivable, they contended, that Plehve would have fired the governor if he was himself involved—otherwise von Raaben could have implicated the minister in self-defense.[19] There appears to be some merit to this. The former governor suffered greatly as a result of the pogrom, in terms of ruined career and lost prestige. In an effort to rehabilitate himself, he wrote several confidential letters to Plehve and, after the minister's death, he defended his actions in testimony before the Ruling Senate. In none of these contexts did he justify his actions by asserting that he was merely following instructions from his superiors. If the "dispatch" were genuine, it would seem, this would have been his most logical and effective defense.[20]

Von Raaben's successor, Prince S. D. Urusov, was no doubt the least partial observer. The prince did not personally witness the pogrom or the events leading up to it—he did not arrive in Kishinev until two months afterwards. But he did become familiar with the details of the case, he did come to know most of the principals, he did study the relevant documents in the police files, and he did have a close relationship with Police Director Lopukhin. Most important of all, he was present at the closed trial of the rioters, where capable lawyers for the accused peasants and townsfolk tried to prove the guilt of the government. An honest and fair man, Urusov won high praise for his conduct, especially from the Jews. He did indeed blame the government for the massacre, and he also attested to Plehve's anti-Semitism.[21] But at the same time he absolved the minister of direct complicity. ". . . I think that with all his hatred towards the Jews," he wrote, "Plehve was too shrewd and experienced to adopt such an expedient in his fight against them." In examining the secret police files on the Kishinev case, Urusov reportedly found "not a thing to justify the assumption that the Ministry of Interior thought it expedient to permit a Jewish massacre, or even an anti-Jewish demonstration, in Kishinev."[22]

Perhaps the most telling argument against Plehve's involvement was the character of the minister himself. Plehve's entire career had been dedicated, in one form or another, to the preservation of public order. As Minister of Interior, social control was his primary concern: any manifestation of disorder, no matter what the reason, reflected badly on his competence. His reaction to the Khar'kov–Poltava rebellions, and his constant advocacy of "decisive measures," make it seem rather unlikely that he would purposely instigate a riot, or that he would advise the authorities to refrain from force in the face of violent disorders.

In one respect, however, the whole issue is academic. For, whether or not Plehve actually planned the pogrom, much of the responsibility still rests upon him. Clearly, a major cause of the pogrom was official anti-Semitism: this provided both the setting and the impetus for the action of the mob. The bureaucracy, from the emperor on down, was rife with unabashed Judophobes; and the government, as was apparent from its policies, favored repression of the Jews. Plehve, the most influential man in government at the time, not only failed to oppose this trend, he even tolerated and encouraged anti-Jewish activities. His actions and reputation made it appear to lesser bureaucrats that maltreatment of the Jews was condoned and rewarded. It is little wonder that ambitious officials could hope to advance their careers by repressing the Jews, or that ignorant peasants and townsfolk could feel they were obeying the emperor's will by beating and plundering their Semitic neighbors.

A. A. Lopukhin himself later admitted that "government anti-Semitism," moving down the "hierarchic staircase" and reaching the lower strata as a "direct appeal to acts of violence against the Jews," was the primary cause of pogroms.[23] Governor Prince Urusov, after much experience, study, and reflection, concluded that the predominant motive activating the Kishinev rioters was "neither hatred nor revenge, but the enforcement of such measures as, in the opinion of some, promoted the aims and intentions of the government." The local police, he noted, had come to regard "a hostile attitude toward the Jews" as "sort of a government watchword." In this atmosphere, he added, it was quite possible that Plehve's anti-Semitism, "rolling down the hierarchic incline of the gendarmerie corps, reached Levendal in the guise of a *wish* on the part of the higher authorities, reached Pronin and Krushevan as a *call* for patriotic exploit, and reached the Moldavian rioters as an *order* of the Czar."[24]

Regardless of Urusov's suppositions, the fact remains that Plehve, responsible above all for law and order in Russia, had failed in his duties. He was aware of the dangerous anti-Semitism of the masses but, rather than combatting it, supported and continued the policies that encouraged it. When this finally led to violence, he did not act quickly enough to keep the peace or to protect life and property in Kishinev. The situation was hardly beyond his control: a year later, amid rumors of a new Easter massacre in Kishinev, his strongly worded message was sufficient to galvanize the police into preventing fresh disorders.[25] So the minister's condoning of anti-Semitic activity, and his failure to act decisively to prevent or confine the riot, must both be held against him. The evidence might not be enough to convict Plehve of first-degree murder, but it presents a strong case for negligent homicide.

THE NATIONALITIES QUESTION

The Kishinev pogrom was, in several respects, an important setback for Plehve. The rumors of his complicity helped destroy whatever credibility he had left with society, and increased the hatred and fear of him among the government's opponents. They also, of course, won for him the undying enmity of thousands of Jews, including the man who was to plot his assassination.[26] And they undermined his chances for dealing effectively with the nationalities question in general, and the Jewish question in particular.

The empire of Nicholas II, although called the *Russian* Empire, was in fact a comglomeration of peoples, races, creeds, and tongues. Over the centuries, it had come to include substantial numbers of Ukrainians and Poles, Georgians and Armenians, Finns, Jews, Germans, and others. Most of these peoples had their own languages, customs, traditions, and laws—and often their own religions. This complicated the task of government, and it also led to conflict. As the spirit of nationalism spread, many of these groups came to hope for their own autonomous institutions, and even their independence. The Russians, understandably, tended to perceive such aspirations as threats to the integrity of their empire, and they often responded to requests for more autonomy with demands for more conformity.

During the nineteenth century, as the Russians had expanded and systematized their administrative structure, they had naturally sought to incorporate the non-Russian nationalities into the larger system. At first this "russification" had been confined primarily to administrative functions: the entire populace was to be made subject to Russian law and Russian institutions. Beginning in the 1880s however, at the urging of Slavophile theorists and conservative officials like Pobedonostsev, the government had embarked on a conscious effort to inculcate Russian language, religion, and culture into some of the border areas. This attempt had encountered resistance: many of the "alien" nationalities considered their own cultures and religions superior to those of the Russians, and were disposed neither to adopt Russian ways nor to think of themselves as Russians. Some, like the Finns and Baltic Germans, could even point to rights and privileges which had been "guaranteed" by previous tsars and were now, in their view, being violated.[27]

V. K. Plehve, as a prominent statesman of this era and an assistant of Count Tolstoi, supported the russification policies. Officially he advocated "the combination of imperial unity with local autonomy." On one hand, he wrote, "the people should recognize the unity of the state principle and policy, and the binding character of its aims;" at the same time he felt that "the government should acknowledge the benefit accruing to the state from public activity, along the lines of individual development, of its component elements."[28]

At the same time, however, he insisted that the overriding concern must always be the overall interests of the Russian empire. And these interests, in his view, were best served by emphasizing unity, homogeneity of population, and assimilation of alien elements. "Of course, we know that we cannot do away with all the differences in language and creed. . . . But we are obliged to demand of all the peoples which compose our Empire . . . that they look patriotically upon the Russian state as an integral part of their lives. We want to assimilate them."[29]

Plehve's objectives in this area—imperial unity, local autonomy, and assimilation of nationalities—parallelled his overall administrative aims of coordination, decentralization, and cooperation.[30] The overriding concern, in either case, was "the unity of state principle and policy"; all else was subordinate to the need for coordination and control. Within this context he favored local autonomy, but only in the sense that local persons should take more responsibility for matters of *purely local concern*. "Political" affairs, and matters of "empire-wide" concern, must be left to the central authorities. Those who were willing to work within these confines would get every assistance and support; those who would not could expect only retribution and repression.

The goal of "assimilation" caused the greatest difficulty for nationality groups. Just as he wished to co-opt local society, and make it part of his bureaucratic system, so too Plehve desired to absorb the various alien elements into a unified Russian polity. The Russian empire, unlike the British or French, was a territorial unit: like the Americans, the Russians had expanded by annexing contiguous lands. For people like Plehve, then, the conquered lands were not simply colonies, supporting a "mother country," but part and parcel of that mother country itself. The inhabitants of these lands, it followed, must not just be subjugated as colonials, they must eventually be incorporated as Russian subjects and citizens. Once they had abandoned all aspirations to national independence, and had come to "look patriotically on the Russian state as an integral part of their lives," they could look forward to the rights and benefits of citizenship. In this way, the empire, despite its wide diversity of peoples, could function as a united, harmonious whole.

In dealing with non-Russian nationalities, as in dealing with Russian society, Plehve's instincts were to "split the opposition" by conciliating the "loyal" and repressing the "unreliable." In the late 1880s, for example, he had called for efforts to win the support of Latvians and Estonians by reducing the power of the Baltic German nobility. Later, as State-Secretary for Finland, he had sought to work with the "Finnish" party by opposing the dominant "Swedes."[31] In both cases, however, his emphasis was on political reliability and Russian imperial interests; in neither case was he successful.

By the time he became minister, Plehve had had considerable experience in dealing with the nationalities question. Under Alexander

III he had chaired commissions on the Baltic Provinces and the Jews; more recently he had been active as State-Secretary for Finland. As minister, too, he would confront the nationalities problem, primarily in relation to the Jews, the Finns, and the Armenians.

PLEHVE AND THE JEWS

The Jews, of all the empire's nationalities, were the most widely respected—and the most widely feared. Although they were centuries removed from their homeland, they had managed to preserve their unique religious and cultural identity. Furthermore, they had gained a reputation for being more ambitious, more industrious, and more clever than other groups. As a result, they were often feared and suspected by their superstitious Christian neighbors, and subjected to all sorts of inequities, disabilities, and persecutions. The government, rather than valuing their skills, treated them as an undesirable alien element from which the rest of the population had to be protected.

Many Russian officials, V. K. Plehve included, were convinced of the Jewish peril. They saw the Jews, not so much as an inferior, sub-human species, nor as an errant religious group, but as a superior race with talents and abilities far beyond those of the average Russian. It was their very intelligence, their drive, their competence, and their tenacity that made the Jews such a threat. If something were not done to hold them back, it was feared, they would come to dominate schools and hospitals, villages and cities, society and government. As a result, any action taken against the Jews was seen as self-defense— defense against a powerful and sinister alien threat—and need not be justified under the normal canons of Christian morality. It was their reputed superiority, more than their religion, customs, or language, that set the Jews apart. Jews might change religion, learn Russian language, adopt Russian ways, but unless they could be made ignorant, poor, unambitious, and illiterate, they could not be fully assimilated. In a state that strove to be monolithic, the Jews represented a cancer; to a people that felt inferior, they were a dangerous foe.[32]

Over the years, in accordance with this perception, the Russian government had taken a series of steps to repress them. For many years Jews had officially been permitted to live only in the western borderlands, in fifteen provinces which made up the "Pale of Settlement." Since 1882, they had been restricted also to the cities and towns in the Pale, and prohibited from owning or managing land outside the fifteen provinces. Quotas had been established, limiting the number of Jews in government, schools, and the professions; and governors of provinces outside the Pale had been encouraged to hunt down and expel illegal Jewish residents. Only Russia's need for foreign loans, financed in part by Jewish banking houses, seems to have forestalled further restrictions.[33]

Meanwhile, the Jews had begun to fight back. Some—especially those who wished to remain outside the Pale—decided to go through the motions of russifying themselves and renouncing their religious heritage. A large group of others, seeking freer and greener pastures, migrated to foreign lands. Still others, determined to stay on and fight, joined the revolutionary movement: Plehve himself claimed that forty percent of all Russian revolutionaries were Jews. A fourth group, the so-called "Zionists," reasoned that they must always remain an alien and oppressed race until they could establish a homeland of their own, preferably in Palestine. This movement made rapid progress among Russian Jews in the aftermath of the World Zionist Congress in Basel, Switzerland in 1897.

By 1902, when Plehve became minister, the Jewish situation had reached crisis proportions. The Jews, huddled in the crowded ghettoes of the cities and market-towns of the Pale, were a desperate lot. The Zionist movement was spreading rapidly, while Jewish youth were joining the revolutionary cadres in large numbers. Any loyalty to the Russian government, the source of oppressions and deprivations, had long since vanished.

Plehve himself was well aware of this. In May of 1902, he concurred with a friend's assessment that anti-Jewish legislation, set up to "protect" the Russian peasants, had actually been detrimental to the country as a whole. He even seemed to disavow his own role in this repression, claiming that he had merely been "carrying out the instructions of others."[34] In January 1903, in a debate over the establishment of a workhouse for poor Jews in Vilnius, he set forth his views more clearly. "I consider Jewry to be a phenomenon that is hostile to the . . . welfare of Russia," he began, adding that, in his view, the government had a "duty to impose oppressive measures" upon the Jews. At the same time, he pointed out that there were over three and a half million Jews in the Pale, most of them "huddled in the most startling and abject squalor" in the cities. Their increasingly difficult plight had brought "a marked weakening of religious principles and family authority," while "starvation-inspired bitterness" was driving many young

Jews into revolutionary activity. "Therefore," he concluded, ". . . any steps toward relief of the Jews . . . so as to alleviate their difficult economic situation, must be supported."[35] Once again he was proposing to offer repression with one hand and assistance with the other.

Indeed the record shows that Plehve, as Minister of Interior, was more reasonable than his reputation would indicate: in order to solve the Jewish problem he was willing to improve Jewish welfare, modify Jewish restrictions, and assist Jewish emigration. Late in 1902, for example, it became known that his ministry was considering measures to liberalize Jewish residence rules, and to allow Jews a limited right to purchase farmland. Early the next year, at a conference called to study such questions, the minister warned against any new restrictions. He even implied that the current regulations, confining Jews to certain cities and towns, had backfired: ". . . the Jewish population, crowded into the cities, does not have sufficient wages. Impoverished Jews, living in unsanitary conditions, present a danger for public health and order, while young Jews, raised without proper supervision, are always open to revolutionary propaganda. . . . New restrictive measures could make matters still worse." In May of 1903, as a result of his concerns, a hundred new areas in the Pale were opened to Jewish residence.[36]

Plehve's most creative approach to the Jewish question was his support of the Zionist movement. Although Zionism, as a manifestation of Jewish nationalism, was a potentially dangerous force, the minister was intrigued by the prospect of wholesale Jewish emigration. Such a mass departure, needless to say, would have gone a long way toward solving one of his most pressing concerns. Therefore, he went out of his way to encourage and endorse the activity of Zionist worker groups in Vilnius and Minsk. And, in September of 1902, he even permitted a Conference of Russian Zionists in the city of Minsk—the only such conference ever permitted by the imperial government.[37]

Plehve's hopes for cooperation with Zionism, however, like his attempts to win zemstvo support, were doomed to failure. There were two basic reasons for this. One was the minister's penchant for repression, symbolized in this case by the Kishinev pogrom. What Russian Zionist could be expected to cooperate with a government that condoned the slaughter of Jews? The other was the fact that the Zionists, like the zemstvo-men, refused to stay away from "political questions." At their Minsk Conference, for instance, the Zionists had spent precious little time discussing the search for a Jewish homeland. Instead, they focused their attention on such things as solidarity among Russian

Jews, the preservation of their ancient language and customs, the growth of education and culture, and the raising of money for Jewish activities.[38]

Perceiving a new and dangerous tendency, Plehve finally decided to instruct the governors to take steps to counteract it. In a secret circular of June 24, 1903, he let it be known that "from information in the Department of Police concerning the so-called Zionist societies," it had become apparent that they had "put off into the distant future" their "primary goal" of emigration to Palestine. Instead they were now "directing their activity toward the development and strengthening of the national Jewish idea, and preaching solidarity in exclusive organizations of Jews in their current places of residence." This being "contrary to the principles of the Russian state idea," Plehve warned the governors to prevent "the development of the Zionist movement in a harmful direction." He therefore ordered them to prohibit Zionist propaganda and Zionist meetings, and to prevent the collection of money for Zionist causes.[39]

Although this circular was confidential, its contents soon became common knowledge among Russian Jews. Coming close on the heels of the Kishinev pogrom, it intensified the bitterness toward Plehve, who was by now an internationally-despised symbol of anti-Jewish repression. Worse still, it further alienated those moderate Jews who had not wished to become involved in revolutionary activity. Meanwhile, conveniently for Plehve, an opportunity had presented itself to counter some of this hatred.

Just as the local authorities were beginning to implement his anti-Zionist instructions, the minister received word that Doctor Theodor Herzl desired a private meeting with him. Herzl, an Austrian subject, had been the originator of political Zionism and the organizer of the Basel Zionist Congress of 1897. An eloquent, dedicated, and charismatic individual, he had become a legendary figure among Russian Jews. An idealist with a practical bent, he had worked indefatigably for a Jewish state, negotiating with world leaders on one hand, and encouraging the Jewish masses on the other. Considering himself a "statesman" rather than a "historian or moralist," he had chosen to ignore Plehve's reputation and approach him as a man who was in a position to help the Zionist cause.[40]

On the morning of July 26, 1903, and again on July 31, Plehve received the Zionist leader. Despite the minister's alleged connection with the Kishinev pogrom, the two got on rather well. Herzl was at once impressed with Plehve's congenial hospitality, his self-confidence, and his firm grasp of the details. The minister, for his part, was heard to remark that he could use men of Herzl's calibre in his own departments. Their discussions were cordial, even friendly; and they parted on the best of terms. In between their meetings, Herzl also had an audience with Witte, and the contrast was vivid. The Zionist leader was immediately repulsed by Witte's coarse manner and crude allusions to the Jews, and by his concern that any Jewish settlement in Palestine should be a considerable distance away from the "Holy Places."[41]

The reason for the cordiality between Herzl and Plehve was simple: each had something to offer the other. Herzl wanted three things of the Russian minister: intervention with the Turks to obtain a charter for Jewish colonization of Palestine, financial aid for Jewish emigration, and non-interference with Zionist organizational work. Plehve was seeking a solution to the Jewish question, and was therefore interested in any scheme that called for mass emigration of the people who were causing him so much concern. More immediately, Plehve was trying to divert the world's attention from Kishinev: the furor over the pogrom might hamper his policies and weaken his position. There was to be a new World Zionist Congress at Basel the following month, and Herzl could perform a considerable service by steering the discussion away from the Bessarabian riot. Witte, on the other hand, had little to gain from the Zionist leader's visit and, at least in Doctor Herzl's estimation, was "bent on exploiting Plehve's embarrassment over Kishinev."[42]

In general, Plehve and Herzl found a wide basis for agreement. The minister quite readily accepted the Zionist leader's proposals to aid emigration, insisting only that the money to finance this operation must come from the pockets of wealthy Jews. He provided his visitor with a letter to this effect, assuring him that the Zionist movement could count on Russia's "moral and material assistance" in any efforts which would "lead to the diminution of the Jewish population in Russia." He also agreed to work with Russian Jews on plans to improve their lot, citing "assimilation" and economic improvement as parts of his Jewish policy. Most importantly, at least in Herzl's eyes, he promised to press for diplomatic action to secure a Jewish settlement in Turkish-controlled Palestine. In return, he asked the Zionist leader to restrain criticism of Russia at the forthcoming Basel Conference, and to keep him informed of what transpired.[43]

Herzl's visit, unfortunately, had few concrete results. The Zionist Congress in Basel turned out to be a disappointment: Russian delegates, disturbed by his visit to Plehve and unnerved by his promotion of British Uganda as an alternative colony site, opposed Herzl at every turn. "The opposition was composed almost exclusively of Russian Zionists," he wrote Plehve in August 1903. "And at a private caucus of the Russian Zionists, they even started accusing me of treason." The split thus occasioned in the Zionist movement lasted many months, robbing Herzl of much of his prestige.[44]

Meanwhile, Plehve himself was further discredited in the eyes of the Jews by events in Russia. On September 1, 1903, a new pogrom broke out in the Belorussian city of Gomel. This time, however, the Jews banded together to defend themselves, preventing a Kishinev-style massacre and exacting a heavy toll on their attackers. All told, about twenty persons perished in the short-lived pogrom, eight of whom were Christians. Reports of this riot did not directly implicate Plehve, as they had after Kishinev; nevertheless, the "pogrom-policy" had become closely linked with the minister's name. Plehve's efforts to prohibit Jewish self-defense societies were cited as evidence of tacit involvement, as were the attempts by the local authorities to blame the riot on the Jews. Shortly thereafter, when the Kishinev rioters came to trial, the minister aroused further distrust by insisting that the trial be closed to the public. Many Jewish leaders had been critical of Herzl for even meeting with the infamous Mr. Plehve; now events seemed to confirm their fears that the Zionist leader had been used.[45]

This was not necessarily the case. The minister does seem to have made a conscious effort to live up to his part of the agreement. In August of 1903, for instance, he solicited the views of governors, mayors, and police chiefs concerning the revision of anti-Jewish regulations, and he eventually formed a commission to deal with this issue. Later that year, the minister met with Russian Jews, as promised, to discuss efforts to improve their situation. He considered it possible to let educated Jews live outside the Pale, and to legalize the purchase of small farmsteads by Jews. He also agreed to assist the operations of the Russian branch of the Jewish Colonial Trust, which was intended to be the financial instrument of emigration. Finally, in December, he and the Foreign Minister requested I. A. Zinov'ev, the Russian ambassador to Turkey, to intercede with the Turkish government on behalf of the Zionist movement. The Sultan was to be asked to grant a parcel of territory around Acre, in return for which the Russian government would pay "an annual tribute of one hundred thousand Turkish pounds."[46]

Plehve's intercession, however, accomplished nothing. All along, Herzl had felt that an approach through normal channels would be fruitless, and had pressed for personal intervention by the Russian Emperor. No such intervention ever came. It is doubtful whether ambassador Zinov'ev even attempted the requested *démarche*. On December 22, 1903, a dejected and disappointed Theodor Herzl relayed the following information to Plehve in a letter: "The confidential representative whom I charged with transmitting my letter to H. E. M. Sinoviev, the Russian ambassador, received this reply: 'They have written me about it from St. Petersburg; but up to now I have not done anything, and it will not be easy to do anything.' Under these circumstances, and despite my good will, I cannot do anything on behalf of the emigration, and the situations of the Jews will remain as sad and distressing as it has been up to now."[47] Herzl's mission to Russia had ended in failure. A month later Russia would go to war with Japan, and the attentions of the Imperial Government would be concentrated on the Far East. The establishment of a Jewish state, and the mass emigration of Russian Jews thereto, remained an unrealized dream.

The question remains of Plehve's sincerity in dealing with the Zionist leader. It is possible, as many Jews would insist, that he never really did intend to help Zionism, and that he was merely taking advantage of this "noble-minded dreamer." In so doing he might distract world attention from Kishinev, and perhaps briefly curtail the activities of Jewish revolutionaries in Russia. There is little doubt that the minister had such considerations in mind, or that he still intended to pursue a "no compromise" policy toward dissident Jews.[48] But Herzl, for one, was convinced of the minister's sincerity, and Plehve's later actions, however cautious and timid, show that there was at least a modicum of substance to his promises. After all, the Jewish question was of great concern to him, and Herzl's proposals did offer a chance for its solution. Why should he not cooperate with efforts to pacify or remove the majority of Russian Jews?

PLEHVE, BOBRIKOV, AND THE FINNS

The "Finnish question," which had come to a head at the turn of the century, involved a clash among three different brands of nationalism. During the nineteenth century, two national groups had arisen in Finland: a Finnish party (Fennomen), and a Swedish one (Svecomen). The Fennomen advocated throwing off the Swedish language, culture, law, and institutions which had dominated the land since the days of

Swedish rule, and forming a new culture, based on the native Finnish language spoken by the majority of the population. The Svecomen, composed of the old Swedish-speaking nobility and a segment of the liberal, educated class, felt it would be folly to destroy the relatively advanced Swedish culture and replace it with an inferior Finnish model. They also feared that the removal of Swedish would pave the way not for Finnish, but for Russian.

Russian nationalists, meanwhile, had begun to be concerned about the growing trend toward Finnish independence. As recently as the 1860s, Tsar Alexander II had reaffirmed Finland's "constitutional" rights—partly to preclude the formation of a Polish-style revolutionary movement. But Alexander III and his advisors came to have second thoughts: increasing Finnish separatism seemed to them to conflict with the empire's need to modernize and unify its economic, military, and administrative structure. By the late 1890s the Russians were actively seeking to reverse this trend, and to incorporate such things as the Finnish postal service and the Finnish military into the imperial system. They sought, in addition, to restrict Finnish autonomy to purely local concerns. These russification measures were relatively mild, at least from the perspective of Saint Petersburg, but they did seem to violate the Finnish "constitution," and they were accompanied after 1898 by the harsh and unyielding policies of Governor-General Bobrikov. The Svecomen, and a large segment of the Finnish party, soon joined in opposition to the Russian threat. [49]

Plehve, of course, had been closely involved with the Finnish question for several years. He had been instrumental in drafting the documents which deprived the Finns of their legislative autonomy in 1899. He had been Minister State Secretary for Finland since 1899, and chancellor of Helsingfors University since 1900. In these posts, he had supported most of the repressive measures implemented by Bobrikov. In 1901 he had argued in the State Council for the military conscription of Finns, and he had helped in the push for abolition of the separate Finnish army. All this apparently met with the tsar's approval: on April 7, 1902—three days after his appointment as Minister of Interior—V. K. Plehve was ordered to remain Minister State Secretary for Finland "until further notice." [50]

Finland, by this time, was in a state of turmoil. The Conscription Act of 1901, which called for the drafting of Finns into the Russian army, had produced wholesale discontent. The first attempted levy, beginning April 2, 1902, was met by almost total noncompliance. Nine out of ten prospective recruits failed to appear, and most of those that did were unfit for military service. In addition there occurred several major disorders, the most important being the Helsingfors riots of April 4 and 5. On his very first day as Minister of Interior, portentously enough, Plehve was confronted with trouble in Finland.[51]

Meanwhile, the force of Finnish resistance had occasioned a split between Plehve and Bobrikov. Although the minister agreed with the governor-general's aims, he felt they should be pursued with a bit more tact and moderation. He had opposed Bobrikov's efforts to accelerate the forced introduction of the Russian language, and to carry out an immediate reform of the Finnish judicial system. He favored working closely with the so-called "Compliants": that segment of the Finnish party willing to accept Russian authority. He even strove to attract native Finns to work for him in the State-Secretariat. He was anxious, above all, to preserve peace and order in the Grand Duchy, and for this reason he was not unwilling to proceed slowly and to make concessions. For Bobrikov, however, russification was an end in itself. His extreme nationalism would permit no compromise with any sector of the population. He would settle for nothing less than total submission to Russian authority, Russian institutions, Russian language, and Russian ways.[52]

In spring of 1902, Plehve presented the governor-general with his prescription for calming Finland. In a long memorandum, which was in fact a *résumé* of three separate reports to the emperor, the minister advanced his opinions as to the causes of the unrest, and enumerated specific measures to deal with it. By an odd coincidence this letter was dated April 4, 1902—the same day as the outbreak of disorders in Helsingfors, and the day of Plehve's appointment as Minister of Interior.

The minister began his memo by reasserting his philosophy of firmness. "Any wavering in the taking of decisive measures," he wrote, ". . . would make it impossible to accomplish the work which has recently been begun." At the same time, however, he saw a need to reassure the Finns of Russian intentions. Unfounded rumors of new russification measures were spreading throughout the land—rumors which only aided the cause of the opposition. In order to reverse the trend of Finnish disaffection, Plehve felt, it was necessary to postpone any new "unification" measures, to be "prudent and consistent" in implementing those already begun, and to increase cooperation between the governor-general and the Finnish authorities. Steps should be taken to preserve the basic features of Finnish administration, and to establish a clear boundary between subjects for imperial legislation and matters of local decision. It also might be helpful, he went on, to publish a senate enactment allowing the use of the Finnish language in local Finnish affairs, and even to "add several members of the Swedish party to the government."[53]

Plehve's approach to Finland thus exhibited that same combination of repression and reform he was to use in dealing with Russian society. Any and all manifestations of "seditious" activity were to be met with firm, repressive measures. At the same time, an effort was to be made to win the support and cooperation of "responsible" and "moderate" elements—in this instance the Compliants. The strategy, likewise, was to split the opposition: the authorization of the Finnish language, it was hoped, might reopen the split between Fennomen and Svecomen.

In the case of Finland, however, Plehve's "conciliatory" proposals were never even attempted. After reading the minister's memo, Bobrikov objected vehemently to its "internal contradictions." In the beginning, he pointed out, it asked the governor-general to get the troublemakers out of government, yet later on it sought to bring the Svecomen back in. In one place it denounced "wavering" in the face of disorders, but throughout it proposed measures that seemed to yield to the demands of the agitators. Above all, although Plehve's intent was to pacify Finland, there was no reason to expect that these policies would work. On the contrary, wrote Bobrikov, any delay in applying the unification reforms would only convince the Finns that their resistance was worthwhile. The Finns tended to view themselves as a separate, autonomous nation, responsible for their own destiny; any compromise measures put forth by the Russians were bound to be inadequate in their eyes.[54]

In this instance, at least, it appears that the analysis of the rabid militarist and super-nationalist governor-general was as insightful as that of the sane, shrewd, and intelligent minister. Finland, Bobrikov recognized, did not see itself as just another Russian province, despite what they thought in Saint Petersburg. Plehve's programs, both in Finland and in Russia, were based on the assumption that the people would willingly accept government by the Russian bureaucracy, as long as it was good government—that is, as long as it satisfied their real needs. The error in this premise was that most of the Finns—and a growing number of Russians—did not care to be governed by the imperial bureaucracy at all.

At any rate, Plehve's suggestions had little practical effect. Only one area of the program was actually put into practice—the publication of an edict allowing the use of Finnish in the lower administration. This edict, drafted by a Finnish senator the preceding winter, was confirmed by the emperor in May and published in Helsingfors on June 7, 1902. It strove to raise the significance of Finnish over Swedish by providing that local judicial and administrative affairs be conducted in the majority language of each locale. Since eighty-five percent of the population spoke Finnish, this would insure the predominance of that language.[55] It was a clear attempt to play upon the divisions in the Finnish body politic, and to restore some prestige to the Finnish Senate, which at this time was dominated by Compliants.

There is some evidence that Plehve, in the aftermath of his exchange with the governor-general, considered the removal of Bobrikov as a means of calming Finland. On October 1, 1902, the emperor's mother, Empress Marie Fedorovna, wrote her son: "For God's sake do think it all over again and try to put a stop to all those horrible actions of Bobrikov's. The only way out I can see is to recall him at once—his very name has become *odious* to the whole population. Plehve told me before I left that even he had advised you to the same effect, so you see I am not alone in finding this necessary."[56] If Plehve did so advise Nicholas II, his advice was not heeded. Bobrikov remained in his post and continued, on occasion, to clash with the proposals of the minister. "In policy, of course, I will not give in," he wrote Plehve in December 1902, "but, if you please, I am prepared to yield the post to someone else."[57]

Too much, however, can be made of the rift between Plehve and Bobrikov. In general, they supported the same policy: their disagreements were over the manner and speed of its implementation. In mid-1902, when it became apparent to Plehve that as Minister of Interior he would have little time for Finland, he considered giving up his post as Minister for Finland. Bobrikov, in spite of previous disagreements, hastened to protest. "I have long thought about the possibility of your replacement," he wrote to the minister, "and I have come to the conclusion that you are irreplaceable."[58] By this time Plehve, despite his tactical differences with Bobrikov, was working to secure more power for Finland's governor-general.

As time went on, the situation in Finland had continued to deteriorate. During the course of 1902, in response to Russian conscription efforts, the opposition movement grew to include almost every element of the population. Preachers, doctors, draft-age youths, and average citizens all participated in the nation-wide resistance, putting aside for the moment any differences in outlook. Their efforts included riots, demonstrations, petition drives, and simple non-compliance; one Finnish court even attempted to try a Russian governor for illegal use of cossacks during the Helsingfors riots. All this was accompanied by a sharp increase in hostility to both Russians and Compliants. In August, finally, with Plehve's assistance, Bobrikov obtained the rights to dismiss public officials—and even judges—on his own authority, to bring Russian nationals into the Finnish civil service, and to control the actions of the Finnish Senate. Even these measures, however, proved insufficient.[59]

At the end of 1902, disturbed by the continuing unrest, Plehve began to seek "extraordinary powers" for Governor-General Bobrikov. On December 22, in his report to the tsar, the minister declared that it was "senseless to struggle against Svecomen agitation without severe measures." Then, on March 20, 1903, he formally asked the emperor to declare a state of "strengthened security" for all of Finland, to grant the governor-general the power to close down hotels, bookstores, trade shops, and private societies, and to permit him to exile persons recognized as "harmful to state order and public tranquility." Nicholas confirmed this proposal immediately, and seven days later issued a formal rescript to this effect.[60]

It did not take Bobrikov long to make use of his new powers. Within a month, the foremost leaders of the opposition movement were exiled from Finland. In the meantime, large numbers of Finnish officials were either dismissed or resigned, only to be replaced by Compliants or Russians. Edicts were issued prohibiting the use and sale of firearms in the Grand Duchy, and setting up an internal passport system to stem the tide of emigration. All vestiges of the old Finnish army were utterly abolished.[61]

The granting of extraordinary powers to Bobrikov aroused a storm of indignation both in Finland and throughout Europe. The Finns themselves no longer saw Bobrikov as a "governor-general," but as a "dictator." Their entire constitution had been abrogated by the Russians. In other European countries, where there had been strong reaction against Russia's Finnish policy since 1899, the outrage only intensified. Even defenders of Russia, such as British journalist W. T. Stead, denounced the latest moves of the imperial government. Stead, who earlier had argued that Russia's policy toward Finland was more humane than British treatment of Ireland, now, in an "open letter" to Plehve, voiced strong criticism of the February manifesto, the military conscription act, and the conferring of extraordinary powers on the governor-general.[62]

Stead's article, published in August 1903, brought an unexpected response from the Russian Minister of Interior. In an effort to explain and vindicate his government's actions, Plehve released a long letter, subsequently published in England and the United States. In it he drew a distinction between the *means* and the *ends* of Russian policy: the means, he wrote, were constantly changing, but the ends remained unalterable. The end being pursued in Finland was the "combination of imperial unity with local autonomy." The guidelines for this, he insisted, had been set in 1899 by the tsar's manifesto: questions of empire-wide concern were to be decided by the imperial government, while local matters were to be handled by the Finnish authorities. All of the steps taken since that time, he argued, were consistent with these guidelines. Even the military conscription act, which actually decreased the service burden on the Finns, should be viewed within this context. [63]

The extraordinary powers recently granted the governor-general, however, had nothing to do with the overall Russian program. They were but an "incidental and temporary" expression of imperial policy, "necessitated by an open mutiny against the government in Finland." This temporary policy, he admitted, was "distinguished by its severity. . . ." However, he concluded, as soon as "peace is finally restored," and life in Finland "assumes its normal course," all repressive measures would be repealed. [64]

In Finland and abroad, with very few exceptions, the general reaction to Plehve's letter was negative and hostile. A group of notable Finns drafted a letter of protest, accusing Plehve of "distortions" and "erroneous interpretations of history," and sent a deputation to Darmstadt to present it to Nicholas II. Stead himself responded with a new "open letter" stating that Plehve had only confirmed the worst fears of Europeans and Americans, since it was apparent from his "defense" that the Russian government recognized no obligations at all toward the Finns. [65]

The Russian policy, all things considered, was a failure: it succeeded neither in reversing the trend toward separatism nor in strengthening the Russian state. Few Finns could be found to cooperate with imperial authorities; those who did were branded as "traitors" by their fellows. Accustomed to thinking of themselves as an autonomous nation, the Finns could not be made to view their land as merely a Russian province. Later, Plehve himself would tacitly admit this fact by suggesting that Russia annex the Finnish province closest to Saint

Petersburg, and then grant broad autonomy to the rest of the country.[66]

In fairness to the Russians, however, it must be remembered that this was the age of imperialism, and Russia's treatment of Finland was certainly no harsher than the western nations' treatment of *their* colonies. The principle of national self-determination had not yet been established; the principle of imperial aggrandizement ruled the day. Unfortunately for Russia, the Finns, under the shelter of autonomy within the Russian empire, had gradually been developing toward an independent national entity for many years before Saint Petersburg decided to assert its superiority. But the Russians, measuring themselves by the imperialistic actions of Western Europe, nevertheless felt that their Finnish policy was reasonable and just. "Not one government, not one state in the world," Plehve told a German correspondent, "would tolerate anything like" the situation in Finland, where an "insignificant minority" was striving "to attain the conscious goal of separation of Finland from Russia."[67]

THE ARMENIAN QUESTION

As if his problems with the Jews and Finns were not enough, Plehve decided in 1903 to extend the policy of forced assimilation to the Armenian peoples of Russia. This decision took the form of a decree confiscating the property of the Armenian-Gregorian Church, the center of religious and cultural life for Russian Armenians.

The situation of the Armenians was, in several respects, similar to that of the Finns.[68] Russian conquests in the Caucasus, combined with immigration of Armenians from territories under Turkish rule, had resulted in the absorption of a fairly large colony of Armenians. By the end of the nineteenth century there were over a million Armenians living within the empire, distributed throughout several southern provinces. These talented and industrious people had enjoyed considerable autonomy, especially in religious affairs, under their spiritual leader, the Catholicos of All Armenia, who resided at Echmiadzin. In 1836 a Russian ordinance had increased imperial control over Armenian religious affairs; nevertheless the Armenian church continued to control its own property, and to operate its separate parochial school system.

The Armenians, for the most part, had been peaceful and loyal subjects, appreciative of the relatively beneficent rule of the Russians, as contrasted with the brutal treatment accorded their kinsmen under Turkish sway. But, as in Finland, the spirit of nationalism also took hold in Armenia, and there arose in the late nineteenth century a movement for greater autonomy. At first it was aimed mainly at freedom from Turkish rule, but it also came to favor greater independence from Russia. This nationalist movement was fostered, to a certain extent, by the clergy of the Armenian Church.

In the 1890s the Russian government, motivated by its own nationalist tendencies, began to take steps to restrict the Armenians. The Armenian church schools bore the brunt of the attack: the higher grades were abolished, and many whole schools were closed. In 1897, all Armenian schools were placed under the Russian Ministry of Education. That same year Prince G. S. Golitsyn was appointed "Commander-in-Chief" of the Caucasus, a post akin to governor-general. He immediately began to russify the area: Golitsyn was to the Caucasus what Bobrikov was to Finland. In 1898, it was decided that even the property of the Armenian schools should be transferred to the Ministry of Education. Finally, in 1899 it was announced that all classes in these schools must thenceforth be conducted in Russian.

In spite of these moves, or perhaps because of them, the nationalist movement in Armenia continued to grow. The Armenian Revolutionary Union, or *Dashnak*, founded in 1890, attracted a large membership and a good deal of influence. It preached brotherhood and solidarity among Armenians, and it strove toward the goal of an autonomous Armenian state. Marxist circles began to form in the late nineties, and by 1902 these had grown strong enough for the formation of a "Union of Armenian Social Democrats." Meanwhile the Armenian clergy, in a series of legal actions, were able to regain the property taken over by the Ministry of Education. This property, they managed to show, belonged not to the schools, but to the churches and monasteries.

This was to prove a hollow victory. Alarmed by the growing revolutionary movement, Prince Golitsyn proposed in 1899 that the entire properties and funds of the Armenian Church be transferred to the Russian government. The proposal met with opposition from Witte and others, so it was submitted, in slightly watered-down form, to a special commission. The commission eventually rejected it, fearing the hostility and unrest it would cause among the Armenian people. Golitsyn did manage to persuade Minister of Interior Sipiagin to re-introduce his proposal to the Committee of Ministers in 1901, but no further action was taken until 1903.

Thus it fell to Plehve's lot to carry out the attack on the Armenian Church. Although V. I. Gurko later claimed the measure was "against Plehve's better judgment," the policy could not have been adopted without his support. In advocating Golitsyn's proposal before the Committee of Ministers, Plehve stressed the need, for the good of the government, to supervise the activities of the Armenian Church. He also pointed out that the church property had been badly mismanaged by the Armenian clergy, implying that it would be to the benefit of the Armenians themselves to have the Russian government administer it.[69] The argument from Plehve was a familiar one: both state and people would benefit from unity, coordination, and strengthened bureaucratic control.

According to Witte, the majority of the Committee of Ministers still rejected Golitsyn's proposal. Nevertheless, the measure was confirmed into law by Nicholas II on June 12, 1903, and published later that month. It ordained that all the property and capital of the Armenian-Gregorian Church was to be distributed between the Ministries of Agriculture and Interior. The property connected with the church schools was again to be placed under the Ministry of Education.[70]

The transfer was not accomplished without great difficulty. The Armenians, outraged by this attack upon their church, determined to resist. Anti-government activity became the order of the day. On June 29 a large crowd demonstrated before the Catholicos in Aleksandropol, demanding that he refuse to submit to the decree. A similar demonstration occurred at Echmiadzin on August 3, this one accompanied by some bloodshed resulting from clashes with local troops. The Catholicos finally issued a formal instruction that no Church property was to be turned over to the Russians. On August 6, taking note of this instruction, Plehve sent a sharp telegram to the Catholicos, commanding him immediately to issue directives for the orderly transfer of the property. "Any delay," the minister warned, "as an act of disobedience to the Tsarist Will," will bring harsh consequences."[71]

The aged Catholicos Mkrtich rejected this demand. He replied instead with telegrams to Plehve and the tsar, requesting that the implementation of the edict be delayed until he could obtain an imperial audience. This, he felt, would give him a chance to explain the Armenian position. On August 14, however, Plehve responded with a telegram stating that Nicholas had decided to refuse both the petition for an audience and the request for delay.[72]

The enforcement of the decree was handled through the local governors. To spur them on, Plehve sent out detailed instructions, ordering them to use non-Armenians for the seizure, and warning them that they must carry out the decree at all costs, even if it meant resorting to "extreme measures." Some of them, such as Prince Nakash-idze of Erevan, took this to heart. Troops and police were called out, and the transfer was accomplished by force. The Church's title deeds were taken by force even from Catholicos Mkrtich, who had incurred Russian hostility by ordering his clerics to refuse to hand over property or money. In Bessarabia, on the other hand, Governor Prince Urusov managed to avoid trouble simply by ignoring the minister's instruc-tions. After contriving to have the local bishop leave the province, he sent an influential Armenian around to the churches. At each church a formal "seizure" was made merely by listing the deeds and securities in the book of confiscation.[73]

In general, however, the expropriation was conducted rather bru-tally, and the Armenians reacted with anger. On August 29 there occurred a bloody encounter between Armenian demonstrators and Cossack troops at Elizavetpol; ten persons were killed and many others wounded. Similar demonstrations followed in Tiflis, Baku, and throughout the Caucasus. In addition, the Armenian revolutionaries turned to terror, assassinating several officials and seriously wounding Prince Golitsyn himself in October 1903. Plehve's attempts to control the situation by granting special powers to Caucasian officials had little effect. By the end of 1903, according to one high official, the entire Caucasus was on the brink of revolt. Government force prevailed nonetheless: numerous arrests were made, and the property seizure was accomplished.[74]

The results were of doubtful benefit to the Russia of Plehve. The confiscation, coming so soon after the establishment of a "dictatorship" in Finland and the Kishinev pogrom, merely added to the minister's unsavory reputation at home and abroad. His decisive action, it is true, may have convinced Armenian nationalists and revolutionists that they could not work against the government without suffering retri-bution. But it also increased greatly the prestige of the opposition, and turned many relatively loyal subjects against the regime.[75]

In sum, Plehve's nationalities policies caused considerably more harm than they did good. It took far more troops to keep order in Finland—and to restore order in the Caucasus—than were actually drafted from among the Finns and Armenians. The government's mon-etary gain in expropriating Armenian Church property was more than offset by the revenues lost on account of the resulting unrest.[76] And the repression of the Jews only perpetuated a fatal cycle: government restrictions, justified by the active participation of many Jews in anti-government activity, led more and more young Jews to join the revolutionary movement.

It is, no doubt, unlikely that a policy of accommodation could have stemmed the nationalist tide: the yearning for autonomy had not been caused solely by Russian repression, and it was probably too deeply rooted to be effaced by compromise measures. Perhaps some sort of conflict was eventually inevitable. But the problems facing Russia were by no means few or minor: it is hard to see how policies which precipitated internal conflict could have helped to make things better. It was Plehve's stated desire to instill patriotism and loyalty in all the nationality groups, and to assimilate them into an orderly, harmonious, and well-run Russian state. But, at least partly as a result of his policies and reputation, disunity and conflict prevailed, and loyalty to Russia became virtually non-existent among the Finns, Armenians, and Jews.

6

The Worker Question and the Police

THE WORKER QUESTION IN RUSSIA

As the summer of 1903 approached, according to Sergei Witte, Plehve decided to get away from the capital and spend some time at his country estate. There seemed to be little that demanded his presence: the work on his peasant and administrative reforms was nearing completion, the countryside was relatively quiet, and the furor over the Kishinev pogrom hopefully soon would die down. Sporadic labor unrest and acts of revolutionary terrorism had surfaced in several areas, but the police seemed to have things well under control. As fate would have it, however, the summer of 1903 would prove to be perhaps the most tumultuous period of Plehve's ministry. Early in July, a strike began among railway and steamship workers in the Black Sea port of Odessa; by mid-month much of Southern Russia was engulfed in crippling and violent strikes. The worker question, which had concerned Plehve less than the peasant and Jewish problems, suddenly occupied center stage. [1]

The worker question was of relatively recent vintage in Russia. Not until the late nineteenth century had there been enough factory workers to arouse government concern, and even then the industrial proletariat still comprised less than ten percent of the population. Its size was increasing steadily, however, as the growth of Russian industry combined with rural poverty to compel more and more peasants to leave for the cities. For some this was merely a temporary move to supplement their agricultural income, but many others came to the city to stay. And, unlike their peasant cousins, these workers were

122

concentrated in vital urban areas, giving them political clout far out of proportion to their modest numbers.[2]

Russian worker families, like those in other newly industrialized lands, lived and worked in conditions of almost unbelievable squalor. Their flats and hovels were small, poorly-lighted, and poorly ventilated; toilet facilities were crude, and privacy was unheard of. Hygiene was atrocious, disease was rampant, and industrial accidents were commonplace. Wages were low—in many cases barely subsistence level—and the workers were subject to the arbitrary caprice of their employers when it came to pay, working hours, hiring, firing, and working conditions.

The autocratic government had every reason to be fearful of the growing worker population, and the rising tide of worker discontent. Events in Western Europe had shown that poor factory workers constituted a potent force for social-political change, and that the industrial proletariat provided a ready audience for radical democratic and socialist theories. In order to prevent social disruption—and in the long run to preserve the monarchy itself—many Russian statesmen saw the need to keep worker discontent to a minimum. Therefore, there had arisen a sort of tutelage approach toward the factory population. On one hand, any worker disorders were to be repressed by prompt, firm police measures, while decisive steps were being taken to combat revolutionary agitation. On the other hand, the government was to champion the interests of the proletariat, providing the factory workers with aid and protection against their employers. This way, it was hoped, the workers would look to the autocratic government, and not to its enemies, as the best means to secure their rights and redress their grievances.[3]

Plehve himself, as chairman of the Special Commission on Factory Legislation of 1885, had been instrumental in formulating this approach. Working closely with labor expert I. I. Ianzhul, who was also a member of the commission, he managed to overcome industrialist opposition and draft several progressive labor laws. The first, enacted in 1885, banned night labor for women and children. The second, confirmed on June 3, 1886, set out to regulate the contractual relationship between worker and employer. Wages were to be paid in cash, on a fixed schedule, with no deductions for things such as medical aid and the use of tools. Arbitrary fines and reductions in pay were prohibited. To enforce these laws, a system of "factory inspectors," first established in 1882, was greatly expanded: its duties were to include observing the factory situation, investigating labor disputes, and reporting violations of the law. ". . . Plehve was an excellent chairman," Ianzhul later recalled, "more inclined to side with the interests of the workers than those of the factory owners."[4]

Although the law of 1886 did serve to correct some abuses, its effect in practice was rather limited. At the same time as it was protecting the workers, it also increased penalties against strikers, prohibited trade unions, and forbade worker assemblies of any sort. Furthermore, most workers were unaware of the existence of any laws protecting their rights and, even when they were aware, they could do little to make their employers conform. The procedure for bringing civil suit against the factory owners involved time and expense beyond the resources of the average laborer. The workers alone were powerless to compel redress of their grievances, and the factory inspectors were not always able or willing to help them.[5]

These problems were compounded by the protracted struggle which occurred between Interior and Finance. Ministers of Finance, anxious to further the development of industry, tended to support the factory owners at every turn, and to oppose government attempts to "protect" the workers. Ivan Vishnegradski (1886–92) was openly hostile to the factory inspectorate, and Sergei Witte (1892–1903) used it more as a tool to keep the workers in line than as an agency to secure their rights. Meanwhile, factory conditions remained deplorable, worker strikes increased, revolutionary socialism made serious gains, and the Ministry of Interior, faced with a new threat to internal stability, began to interfere in factory affairs. In 1897, while pushing a new law for a shorter workday, this ministry ordered its police to crack down on illegal worker activity, and to eliminate "oppression or injustice on the part of the factory owners." This outraged the Minister of Finance, who used an interministerial conference in 1898 to restrict police meddling in industrial concerns. His victory, however, was brief: in 1899 the Ministry of Interior obtained permission to set up, under its control, a special corps of factory police. Then, in the following two years, this ministry conducted several investigations, each of which concluded that the conditions of factory life were largely responsible for worker unrest and revolutionary advances.[6]

Out of these studies came several proposals for increasing government tutelage over the working class. Along with specific suggestions for housing and insurance programs, the Ministry of Interior made two broad recommendations. On one hand, it advocated the establishment of a delegate-representative system through which the workers could legally air their grievances. On the other, it suggested that factory inspectors be given greater power to intervene in labor-management disputes on the side of the workers. The former proposal met with the approval of the Ministry of Finance, which agreed in 1901 to draft legislation to this effect. The latter, however, was successfully quashed by Witte in March of 1902.[7]

It was at this juncture that Plehve replaced Sipiagin as Minister of Interior. This change did not bode well for a quick resolution of the dispute over labor policy. The new minister, besides being a bitter foe of Witte, had earlier shown himself to be a proponent of government tutelage and state protection of the workers. At the same time, by virtue of his police orientation, he was strongly disposed to use "decisive" measures in dealing with discontent among the workers. The ministry's policy of combining reform and repression was quite consistent with the predilections of its new head.

Shortly after his appointment, Plehve had occasion to discuss the worker question with his old friend and collaborator I. I. Ianzhul. Much had changed, Ianzhul argued, since their joint legislative work of the middle 1880s. The work force had grown in size and awareness, and the workers were anxious to test the strength of their new bosses. The time had come for the state to heed their legitimate demands. The labor expert therefore urged a three point program: workers should be allowed to form their own unions, they should be given the right to strike, and the factory inspectorate should be transferred from Finance, which was predisposed to favor the industrialists, to Interior. The minister cautiously concurred. "I am in complete agreement with the substance of everything you have said," he told his friend. ". . . I only ask that you do not refuse to help me when I need it."[8]

As it turned out, Plehve was to have little success in achieving any of these goals. He did manage to gain some control over the factory inspectors, but his bid to have the inspectorate transferred to the Ministry of Interior was eventually rebuffed. And his efforts to improve the lot of the working class became entangled with the work of the Police Department in one of the oddest experiments ever conducted by the imperial Russian government.

PLEHVE'S WORKER PROGRAM

Plehve's handling of the worker problem was consistent with the policy developed by Goremykin and Sipiagin before him, and with his own inclinations for cooperation, control, and coordination. It had three basic elements: the promotion of legislation designed to help the workers, the prompt and firm suppression of worker disorders, and the advancement of efforts to secure greater power for the Ministry of Interior in this area.

In the first category, the promotion of labor legislation, Plehve managed a degree of cooperation with his nemesis at Finance. In recent years, under the influence of increasing labor unrest and changing views of the factory owners, Witte had become more supportive of factory legislation. Many industrialists, it was clear, were willing to make concessions to the workers only if the government would force these same concessions on their competitors. As a result, Witte himself had introduced legislation dealing with worker representation and accident compensation.[9] In both cases he was supported by Plehve; in both cases the measures became law.

The bill to establish worker representatives, first put forth by Witte and Sipiagin in 1901, was embraced by Plehve as a consistent outgrowth of his earlier factory laws. When the measure reached the State Council, he spoke strongly in its favor, arguing that the proposed legislation would ease "the difficulty of dealing with undisciplined and disunited masses of workers." He pointed out that the fears of the Moscow industrialists with respect to the Factory Law of 1886 had proven groundless, and that now these same industrialists were asking the government to give a legal basis to worker organizations. He applauded the provisions which called for employer participation in the establishment and selection of the representatives. And he expressed the hope that this move would be followed quickly by other government measures designed to prevent the kind of problems which accompanied industrialization in the West.[10]

Backed by both Witte and Plehve, this project was passed easily by the State Council, and was confirmed by the emperor on June 10, 1903. The Law on Factory Elders provided that factory workers, with the permission of their employers, could elect "elders" to represent their needs and requests to the factory owners. Actually, the elders were to be selected by the factory officials from among those nominated by the workers. Once chosen, they would have the right to assemble the workers to find out their grievances and desires, and to discuss these with the owners and factory inspectors. It was a step forward for the workers, but not a very big one: the elders would have no authority save that of spokesmen, and they would largely be dependent upon the good will of the factory owners and government authorities. [11]

That same month there was confirmed another labor law, also introduced by Witte and supported by Plehve, which decreed that compensation must be paid when a worker was injured or killed in an industrial accident. Disabled workers, and widows of those who were killed, were to receive pensions based on a percentage of their previous income—as long as the accident was not the clear fault of the worker. The legal burden of proving worker negligence was now placed upon the factory management. [12]

These two laws, and a third measure regulating overtime, brightened the picture somewhat for the Russian laborer. [13] They were consistent with the long-standing desire of the Ministry of Interior to provide tutelage for the workers. But, like so many of the programs sponsored by Plehve, they were so cautious and timid as to have little real effect on the existing situation. They also fell far short of the program which Ianzhul and Plehve had discussed a year earlier: the granting to the workers of the right to unionize and strike.

The second aspect of Plehve's program, the suppression of worker disorders, had several unfortunate results. In November 1902, a score of workers were killed or wounded in Rostov-on-Don when striking railway employees, holding a mass rally in defiance of state orders, were forcibly dispersed by cossacks. Several days later, a similar bloody incident occurred in the neighboring town of Tikhoretsk. Then, in March 1903, came a full-scale disaster at the government iron foundry in Zlatoust, Ufa Province. The Ufa governor, unnerved by an unruly mob of striking workers, ordered the local military commander to have his soldiers fire. When the dust had settled forty-five workers lay dead and scores of others were injured. [14]

Plehve was disturbed greatly by these events, especially the latter. The government, he realized, could scarcely hope to win the allegiance of the workers by shooting them: such incidents only drove them into the arms of the revolutionaries. On one hand, the Minister of Interior was in debt to the military for helping preserve order, but on the other, as he told the Minister of War, he wished the troops would not use "such deadly bullets." [15] At the same time, it had become apparent that the government's labor laws, and the system of factory inspection, had served neither to win worker confidence nor to prevent violent disorders. What was needed was a new approach—and more power for the Ministry of Interior.

In reality, it was the third portion of his three-part program—the transfer of authority to the Ministry of Interior—which interested Plehve the most. Only after he had acquired sufficient jurisdiction over factory affairs could he hope to make significant changes. "It is impossible to do any of the things you have proposed while all the workers are not in my department," he had told Ianzhul; "therefore, I shall immediately commence with efforts to transfer the factory inspectorate from the jurisdiction of the Ministry of Finance to that of the Ministry of Interior."[16] In order to reform, he must first have control.

Any attempt to transfer the inspectorate, however, faced several important obstacles. Minister of Finance Witte, understandably, was adamantly opposed. He was supported by major industrialists, who recalled Plehve's pro-worker role in the 1880s, and who were disturbed by the prospect of increased interference in their affairs. Confronted with this opposition, Plehve opted for a gradual, indirect approach. On one hand, he promoted a plan to give the local governors more control over the factory inspectors. On the other, within his own ministry he laid plans to establish a department of labor.[17]

The first plan met with considerable success. The tsar, anxious to enhance the powers of the governors and to "unify the activities of local government," was readily supportive. And Witte, mindful of his declining influence, was compelled to make concessions. On May 3, 1903, bypassing the legislative order, Nicholas confirmed into law a "compromise" measure. Supervision of the factory inspectorate, and the right to appoint inspectors, would remain with the Minister of Finance, but he must consult the governors about assignment and allocation. Furthermore, the governors were given the right to demand regular reports from the local inspectors, and to countermand their instructions, if necessary, to preserve order. Despite the fact that this decree was based on an agreement between Finance and Interior, it was clearly a defeat for Witte. By working through the governors, Plehve would now be able to exercise a good deal of influence over the factory inspectors. Witte himself was bitterly critical of this measure.[18]

Plehve, however, was not completely satisfied. By this time, he was sponsoring a full-scale review of the worker question, with a view toward establishing a labor department within his own ministry. In January of 1903, on Ianzhul's recommendation, he had hired labor expert A. V. Pogozhev to draw up an extensive report on "the number of workers in Russia, their living conditions, and those needs . . . which can be met while preserving the autocratic regime." Pogozhev, a one-time zemstvo-man who traveled in liberal circles, had been impressed nonetheless with the minister's openness, friendliness and unpretentiousness. When he had asked whether he might express his feelings with total candor, the minister had replied: "I strongly beg you to do so. People like yourself who have long studied an important question, and have given it much thought, always can express considerations which are useful, even if they hold opposing points of view."[19]

Over the next year and a half, the liberal scholar, his work facilitated at every turn by the "reactionary" minister, made a thorough and exhausting study of the factory situation. During this time he made frequent and regular reports to Plehve, and the two men, despite the hostility between groups they represented, developed a profound mutual respect. "My very close relations with him at times left a favorable impression on me," wrote Pogozhev in retrospect. And the esteem was returned: Plehve allowed the scholar a free rein in his work, remarking on one occasion that for him to impose a set of orders or instructions ". . . would be equivalent to me giving orders to a famous sculptor, arriving at his place of business and starting to tell him how to hold the chisel in his hands." Pogozhev remained a bit nonplussed: "It is still an unexplainable riddle for me," he reminisced, "how the esteem, trust, and, if you will, even sympathy which I somehow managed to arouse in him . . . were maintained almost until the day of his death, despite the absence of any common ground between us."[20] But this was quite consistent with Plehve's ideal: activists and intellectuals should use their talent and expertise, not to oppose the government, but to assist it in solving Russia's problems.

In his reports to the Minister of Interior, Pogozhev painted a rather gloomy picture. Among the illnesses afflicting Russia he numbered the "threatening cloud of heavy industrial unemployment," the impoverishment of the peasants, the rapidly increasing size of the urban proletariat, and the progressive breakdown of the "nervous-psychic foundations" of the working class. His practical suggestions were similar to those which Ianzhul had advanced: the need to let the workers form organizations, the cessation of police interference in strikes and walkouts, and "the reform of the statistical and inspection apparatus." He feared, however, that any effective program would take two or three years to implement, and that "things in the worker movement were moving so fast that there would never be enough time."[21]

Plehve took a great deal of interest in Pogozhev's work, and listened intently to his dire prognostications. What effect they had on him is uncertain: he was an acknowledged expert at concealing his feelings. No doubt, however, the suggestions and reports of Ianzhul and Pogozhev served to re-enforce his determination to consolidate control of the worker question within the Ministry of Interior. At any rate, as fall of 1903 approached, he was actively making plans to transform his ministry's Central Statistics Committee into a "Department of Labor" which would include, among other things, the factory inspectorate.[22] By this time, however, the course of his worker policy had taken several unexpected turns.

S. V. ZUBATOV AND THE OKHRANA

Plehve's lack of control over the factory inspectorate did not prevent his ministry from meddling in labor affairs. There was, in fact, one section of the ministry that devised and implemented its own labor policy, much to the horror of Witte and the industrialists. Although it did not actually permit the workers to unionize and to strike, as Ianzhul had suggested, it did surreptitiously sponsor a number of worker organizations, and it did take the side of certain workers in their struggles against the industrialists. This section, remarkably, was the Okhrana—the counterrevolutionary arm of the Department of Police.

The Okhrana was a direct outgrowth of innovations made by Plehve himself when he had been Director of Police. In the early 1880s, to more effectively combat revolutionary activity, special "security sections," or "Okhranas," had been established in Moscow, Saint Petersburg, and Warsaw. To a certain extent, their official duties duplicated those of the gendarmes: the investigation and prevention of student disorders, worker strikes, and unauthorized meetings or demonstrations. Unlike the gendarmes, however, who were concerned mainly with formal investigations, the Okhranas were covert operations, acting primarily through spies, informers, and undercover agents. The Okhranas normally operated under the authority of local officials—in Saint Petersburg the city-governor and in Moscow the chief of police—but their work was scarcely restrained by provincial boundaries. After 1898, their activities were coordinated through the "Special Section" of the Department of Police, giving rise to the spectre of an "all-Russian Okhrana."[23]

After the demise of the People's Will in the mid-1880s, there had been an interlude of relative quiet on the revolutionary front. The Okhranas during this period, consisting of only a handful of officials, did not achieve particular distinction. It was only during the following decade, with the appearance of a new revolutionary threat, that they began to expand and systematize their operations. It was in this period that the Moscow Okhrana came to the fore as the most successful deterrent to revolutionary activity. And its success was due primarily to the work of a police official named Sergei Zubatov.

As a young man, Zubatov had been associated with Moscow revolutionary circles, but in 1886 he had gone over to the police. Here he had displayed such great energy and ability, and such genius at combatting revolution, that within ten years he had become Chief of the Moscow Okhrana.[24] Zubatov systematically collected information, he founded a school to familiarize agents with revolutionary ideology, and he even formed a "flying squadron" of highly trained agents willing to go anywhere to investigate "sedition." He also took the notion of "collaboration," employed with some success by Plehve and Sudeikin, and developed it into a science. Using his keen understanding of the radical mentality, and his formidable powers of persuasion, he was able to convince many young suspects that their best hope was to cooperate with the authorities. Once converted, the erstwhile revolutionaries were sent back out as double agents and informers. Zubatov soon established a constant flow of information, which he used to decimate the ranks of the Moscow revolutionaries. The Moscow Okhrana became the envy of the Russian police.

Zubatov's greatest fame, however, came from his interest in the worker question. In interviewing arrested factory workers, the Okhrana Chief had come to sympathize with many of their problems. He had also become convinced that, in order to stem the tide of revolutionary success, it was necessary for the government to win the workers to its side. He was joined in his conviction by D. F. Trepov, the Moscow Chief of Police. Before long, the police were conducting independent investigations of factory conditions, interfering with the factory inspectors, and, on occasion, ordering employer compliance with worker demands. Witte and the industrialists were furious at these tactics, but they could do little to stop them: Trepov and Zubatov had won the solid support of the governor-general of Moscow, Grand Duke Sergei, who was the emperor's uncle and brother-in-law.[25]

Sheltered by this support, Zubatov and Trepov eventually began to expand their pro-worker policies. Impressed by the schools and mutual self-help funds established by certain laborer groups, Zubatov decided that the government should encourage this type of activity. In 1900 he made an unsuccessful bid to get government sanction for a mutual help fund among the Moscow engravers. The following year, taking matters into his own hands, he combined with law professor I. Kh. Ozerov to initiate a self-help society among the city's mechanical workers. Trepov approved the charter of this body in March 1901.[26]

The society, its way cleared by police support, made rapid progress. Its well-attended Saturday meetings were soon supplemented by Sunday lectures, delivered by members of the liberal intelligentsia. By August a city-wide directorate—the Council of Workers in Mechanical Production of the City of Moscow—had been established, providing both coordination for worker activities and a control mechanism for the police. Although most of the liberals soon withdrew, as they learned of the police sponsorship, the "Council" continued to function and to expand. Ambitious plans were made for a newspaper, a "consumer's society," and other cooperative ventures. Meanwhile, the number of district branches under the Council grew, and it came to include other groups besides the mechanical workers. Textile workers, confectioners, tobacco workers, perfumers, and button-workers all began to organize their own mutual aid societies.[27]

Although Zubatov himself played down his own role, he was much more than a passive onlooker. He personally chose the workers who would lead the movement, introduced them to the authorities, intervened for them with Trepov and the Grand Duke, and gave them advice, assistance, and financial support. The Okhrana provided equipment and funds, as well as some of the membership, for the Council. "We have organized a 'Worker's Council' of 17 men," he wrote to Police Director Zvolianskii in 1901, "which is entirely infiltrated by our agents. . . . In a word, having taken possession of this Council, we control the focal point of the entire mass of workingmen." The following April, in a report to the newly appointed Plehve, Zvolianskii explained: "In spite of the seeming spontaneity of its development, the organization of a trade union workers' movement in Moscow . . . was conducted all along in accordance with a well thought-out plan. It was necessary to foresee every detail, and to direct every step of the workers who initiated it." Zubatov's behind-the-scenes role fooled few: the worker-police connection was widely recognized. The experiment even came to be known as the "Zubatov movement," or *Zubatovshchina*.[28]

It was not long before this idea spread to other areas. In the northwestern provinces, where the Moscow Okhrana had been called in to combat the growing Jewish Social Democratic movement (the *Bund*), there were several ardent youths who had been won over by

Zubatov during earlier arrests. The most notable of these was Mania Vil'bushevich, who was instrumental in founding the Jewish Independent Labor Party in Minsk in 1901. Unlike the Moscow Zubatov societies, the "Independents" were actually an illegal political party. They operated a secret printing press, distributed inflammatory handbills, and, much to the chagrin of Zubatov, organized several strikes. The authorities tolerated them, however, as the Independents were achieving some success in counteracting the militant, revolutionary *Bund* with their moderate "economist" and "Zionist" program. The imperial police, in effect, were breaking the law: they were sponsoring and funding an illegal trade union movement.[29]

During February and March of 1902, several events occurred in Moscow which brought empire-wide notoriety to the *Zubatovshchina*. On February 19, the anniversary of the emancipation of the serfs, more than thirty thousand workers marched in a huge patriotic procession to the statue of Alexander II in the Kremlin. The incident was peaceful—indeed, it was even moving—but the size of the throng was enough to strike fear in the hearts of the imperial authorities. The following month Trepov and Zubatov openly supported the workers during a strike at the silk mills of the French capitalist Goujon. The influential industrialist enlisted the aid of both Witte and the French ambassador, complaining that Zubatov had actually arranged for the formation of a strike fund. Minister of Interior Sipiagin responded to the pressure by demanding an explanation from Trepov, and followed this on March 26 with a letter to Grand Duke Sergei urging the suspension of the workers' council.[30]

A week later Sipiagin lay dead, and soon a new minister found himself faced with the knotty controversy of the Zubatov movement. At first, impressed by the threat to public order which worker organizations could cause, Plehve was opposed to the "harmful and stupid experiment." Shortly after assuming office, he took counsel with Witte, who advised him against allowing the *Zubatovshchina* to continue. Plehve agreed, and promised that he himself would go to Moscow to settle the question.[31]

Plehve's visit, however, accomplished little. In a series of meetings with Zubatov, Trepov, and Grand Duke Sergei, he expressed his reservations about the police-sponsored worker movement. Zubatov tried to convince the new minister of the inadequacy of repression, the need for reform, and the desirability of providing an outlet for potentially revolutionary forces. But Plehve denied the existence of revolutionary social forces, insisting that there existed only groups and circles which could be rooted out by good police work. Try as he might, the Okhrana Chief was unable to shake the minister's conviction. On the other hand, Trepov and the Grand Duke apparently were adamant in their support of Zubatov, and Plehve returned from his trip without taking any action.[32]

Shortly after his return, it is true, the new minister did manage to shame S. E. Zvolianskii, the Police Director who had defended Zubatov, into resignation. But if Witte and the factory owners expected a replacement who would take a stronger stand, they were in for a disappointment. A. A. Lopukhin had received his Candidate of Laws degree from Moscow University, and then had risen rapidly through the procuracy to become Procurator of the Khar'kov Chamber of Justice early in 1902. It was here, several months later, that he caught the eye of the new minister with his investigation of the peasant disorders. Plehve, who surely must have been struck by the parallel between Lopukhin's career and his own, convinced the liberal-minded young procurator that his ministry was about to embark on a program of serious and far-reaching reform. He talked about such things as reorganization of the police, revamping of the investigative procedure, the restoration of legality, and the abolition of the Okhranas. Lopukhin, who was already an acquaintance and admirer of Zubatov, accepted the job on these premises.[33]

The *Zubatovshchina*, therefore, continued. Plehve himself seems to have softened his opposition: in May of 1902 he met with Mania Vil'bushevich, leader of the Minsk "Independents," and authorized her to seek to expand her party's operations. That summer, as a result, branches were established in Vilnius and Odessa, both Social Democratic strongholds. In Vilnius, despite Lopukhin's request that the local gendarmes give them every possible assistance, the Independents could not dent the support of the Jewish-socialist Bund. In Odessa, however, they met immediate success. Many workers, disturbed at attempts by the Social Democratic leadership to "politicize" their economic demands, turned to the apolitical, non-revolutionary Independents. By mid-August it was reported back to Zubatov that an Independent Labor Group had been formed, and that unions had been organized in several professions.[34]

In Moscow, the controversy never did die down. A new lecture series was begun, this one backed by religious forces and much more conservative in tone. In spring and summer, as the Zubatov movement spread, there occurred several strikes. Again the police supported the strikers, freeing worker-agitators who had been arrested by gendarmes.

Director of Police A. A. Lopukhin.

Again the industrialists were outraged, and demanded an explanation. In July, they met with Zubatov, but the Okhrana Chief's overbearing manner did less to mollify them than to increase their irritation. The industrialists complained to Witte, Zubatov explained his side to Lopukhin, and the stage was set for confrontation.[35] But at this point Plehve made a surprising move that changed the situation entirely.

Plehve's move was facilitated by the departure of P. I. Rachkovskii from his post as chief of the Russian police agency abroad. Rachkovskii, who had held this Paris-based post since 1885, had been to the foreign secret police what Zubatov was to the domestic Okhrana. It was not poor performance, then, but excessive zeal that cost Rachkovskii his job. Early in 1902, the Russian court was touched by scandal: a French hypnotist and fortune teller named Philippe had somehow won the confidence of the imperial family. Philippe's prognostications on the birth of a male heir were taken so seriously that the empress went into false pregnancy. Rachkovskii, ignoring Sipiagin's warnings to the contrary, submitted a report proving Philippe was a semi-literate charlatan. The report so enraged the emperor that he threw it on the floor; this led, in turn, to Rachkovskii's dismissal in summer of 1902. Plehve himself was scarcely distraught: he had reason to suspect Rachkovskii of covert ties with Witte.[36]

L. A. Rataev, the Head of the Special Section of the Department of Police, was chosen by Plehve to fill the vacant post. This left an opening in Saint Petersburg, and it allowed the minister to make one of his most controversial appointments. On August 17, 1902, S. V. Zubatov was named Head of the Special Section. Now Zubatov could supervise the actions of all the Russian Okhranas.

There were several possible reasons why Plehve made this move. Perhaps he was impressed with Zubatov's counterrevolutionary expertise, and wished to employ his methods on a wider scale. Perhaps he was influenced here by Ianzhul and Lopukhin. Perhaps he had changed his mind about the worker organizations, and saw them as a counterforce to revolutionary Marxism. Perhaps his move was intended somehow to help him wrest control of worker affairs away from Witte's ministry. Perhaps it was a ploy to get Zubatov away from Moscow, and out from under the protection of the Grand Duke Sergei.[37]

Whatever his reasons, it is apparent that Plehve had not entirely abandoned his original reservations. As Zubatov himself later admitted, for all his persuasive powers, he was never able to convert the minister to his way of thinking. The minister's misgivings were reflected, a month after Zubatov's promotion, in the appointment of

Viktor von Wahl as Assistant Minister and Commander of Gendarmes. Von Wahl, as Governor of Vilnius, had been an outspoken critic of the worker organizations, which he continued to regard as a "fantastic" and "harmful" experiment.[38] The experiment, however, was far from over.

V. K. PLEHVE AND THE ZUBATOVSHCHINA

With the appointments of Lopukhin, Zubatov, and von Wahl, Plehve had set the stage for his reorganization of the police system. As he had done with Stishinskii and Gurko in the peasant department, he placed the reliable and cautious von Wahl in a position of nominal superintendence over the more innovative officials. And, as with so many of his other programs, his police reform turned out to be different in practice than it had been in promise.

One of Plehve's early promises had been to abolish the Okhranas, and turn political cases over to the courts. In practice, the exact opposite occurred. With Zubatov as Head of the Special Section, the Okhranas grew in size and importance. The former Okhrana Chief brought with him his cohorts from Moscow, and under Plehve's direction he began to implement his successful counter-revolutionary methods on an empire-wide basis. In addition to the ones in Moscow, Saint Petersburg, and Warsaw, "security sections" were established in many provincial cities, including Odessa, Vilnius, Kishinev, and Kiev. The system of spies and collaborators was expanded, the "flying squadron" was brought to Saint Petersburg, and the Special Section was made over in the image of the Moscow Okhrana. "On the initiative of Zubatov," wrote one police official, "all of Russia was placed under the net of the security sections, at the head of which were put young gendarme officers who, in the words of Zubatov, had not yet been ruined by the routine of the gendarme administration, and were more receptive to the new methods of political struggle."[39]

At the same time, the separate Corps of Gendarmes was being downgraded. In 1902, according to Lopukhin, it was decided that the gendarmerie should be placed under the Department of Police, with a view toward its eventual abolition. "There were even taken several measures aimed at weakening the authority of the chiefs of the gendarme corps over their staffs," he later recalled, "in order to strengthen the directorship role of the Department of Police. . . . " In the long

Commander of Gendarmes General V. K. Von Wahl.

run the attempt was to prove a failure: the new measures did not improve the situation, and the gendarmes continued their "ruinous ways." All that was accomplished was to create hard feelings among the gendarme administrators, who were reduced, according to one disgruntled officer, to the status of signing statements about persons confined by the Okhranas.[40]

Plehve's police reorganization represented a decided shift on the part of the minister. In spite of his denunciation of Zvolianskii's excessive surveillance, Plehve instituted an even broader program of observation and detention. In spite of his promise to Lopukhin to restore legality, Plehve's Okhranas conducted searches without warrants, made arrests without charges, and detained suspects without filing reports. In spite of his criticism of Zubatov, he came to employ the latter's tactics, designed to combat the widespread revolutionary movement whose existence Plehve had denied.[41] For all his vaunted firmness and decisiveness, it is apparent that Plehve had neither the political courage to defy Grand Duke Sergei, nor an effective program of his own for dealing with "sedition." In his first year as minister, both in police activity and worker affairs, he came to follow the lead of Zubatov.

Consequently, although the transfer of Zubatov to Saint Petersburg did avert a confrontation with the Moscow industrialists, it did not end his involvement in worker affairs. Not only in Moscow, but also in Minsk, Vilnius, Odessa, and Saint Petersburg, his partisans were active during the following twelve months. The Police Department, despite Plehve's original reluctance, did go along with these experiments, although it formally limited its support to:

1. non-opposition to the attempts of workers to organize themselves into mutual help societies with purely economic aims. . . .
2. rendering assistance to certain individuals, personally known to Zubatov, in the carrying out of such attempts.[42]

In Moscow, the absence of Zubatov did not spell the end of the movement, but the worker societies did get channeled along patriotic and religious lines. With Zubatov gone, Trepov began to change his tune: he refused to allow the "Council" to negotiate for the workers, and he actively supported the factory owners during several 1903 strikes. In the northwest provinces, meanwhile, the success of the Jewish Independent Labor Party was mixed. In Vilnius, the Independents were unable to make any inroads, and finally had to withdraw. In Minsk, however, led by the irrepressible Vil'bushevich, the party spread throughout the city, organizing unions among the Jewish workers in most of the important trades. A central committee was set up, composed of representatives from each union, and the beginnings of a national organization were established.[43]

In the south, the success of the Independents was even more conspicuous. The Odessa branch of the party found a charismatic leader in young Doctor G. I. Shaevich, an Odessa native won over by Vil'bushevich at the Zionist congress in Minsk. Its way cleared by police support, the Odessa branch grew rapidly, attracting workers away from the Social Democrats, and organizing unions among several labor groups. Not only Jewish workers, but many of Russian and Ukrainian origins, joined. Shaevich, who became the recognized leader of the Odessa Independents early in 1903, attained hero status among the workers, many of whom saw him as a direct emissary from the tsar. Like his mentors in Minsk he was a firm believer in strikes: in April 1903, in an effort to consolidate his following, he led the ironworkers of the Restel' foundry in a walkout. This strike was to last three months.[44]

While the older branches of the Zubatov movement were consolidating and expanding, a new offshoot was appearing in Saint Petersburg. This was a direct result of Zubatov's presence in the imperial capital. Shortly after his arrival, the new Head of the Special Section enlisted a worker named Pikunov to help him organize a workers' society like those active in Moscow. At first Pikunov and Zubatov were cautious, but by the end of 1902, having elicited the support of the authorities, they began openly to implement their plans. A skeleton organization was set up, Pikunov was chosen to head the society, and by 1903 regular meetings were being held. Success, however, was slow in coming: the capital's intellectual community refused to cooperate and the workers, influenced by Social Democratic warnings about police involvement, stayed away from the meetings in droves. Only after Zubatov's departure in August 1903, when leadership passed to Father G. A. Gapon, did the Saint Petersburg *Zubatovshchina* make any significant progress.[45]

Plehve's role in all of this was rather ambiguous. It is impossible, though, to escape the conclusion that he personally permitted the formation and spread of these worker societies. Zubatov himself guided and directed their activities, meeting frequently with the leaders from Minsk, Odessa, and Saint Petersburg. His actions were re-ported to Police Director Lopukhin, who appears to have given him every possible support. Lopukhin at this time enjoyed a close relation-ship with Plehve, and he certainly would have kept the minister in-formed of what Zubatov was up to. As Lopukhin later remarked to Witte, ". . . all these organizations were formed with the knowledge and approval of Plehve. I possess official resolutions on this subject."[46] The fact that the minister knew of these activities, and did not move to stop them, is evidence of at least tacit approval on his part.

Several actions by Plehve would seem to indicate that his ap-proval was more than tacit. In Vilnius, he personally commissioned the Independents to expand their operations, and supported the right of the Jewish workers to set up mutual aid societies. In Minsk, he reportedly agreed to grant subsidies to Vil'bushevich, but was pre-vented from doing so by Witte. In Petersburg, he met with the work-ers' circles and offered his support, as long as they conducted their movement along peaceful and legal lines. In Odessa, too, he was involved, although here it was Lopukhin who pressured authorities to encourage and assist the Independents. The Police Director took ac-tion to insure that their meetings could go on undisturbed, and to release certain party leaders from jail. Plehve himself sent a letter to the city-governor, asking him not to interfere with the activities of Independent leader Shaevich.[47]

The spring of 1903 seems to have been the high-point of Plehve's backing of Zubatov. The most striking expression of governmental support came on April 7, when the Minister of Interior and the em-peror himself, in Moscow to celebrate Easter, met with representatives of the various worker societies. A further sign came several months later when Plehve dismissed Kiev gendarme chief Novitskii for oppos-ing and interfering with Zubatov's policies.[48]

And yet, the impression persists that Plehve never fully overcame his qualms about the movement. For all of the ministry's encourage-ment, very few of the worker societies ever received official sanction, and these only after extensive delays. None of the various branches of the Jewish Independent Labor Party were ever legalized, while the statutes of the mutual aid societies of the Moscow confectioners, per-fumers, tobacco workers, and buttonmakers were not approved until January 1904, a full year after they were submitted. In Saint Peters-burg, no worker societies of any sort received official sanction until February 1904—a half year after Zubatov had retired from the police.[49] It stands to reason that, if the Minister of Interior had unreservedly supported the Zubatov movement, it would have obtained quicker approval and enjoyed greater success than it actually did.

Plehve's ambivalent attitude toward the *Zubatovshchina* was understandable. On one hand, the experiment fit in with his desire to have the government secure the interests of the workers, and to have the workers look first to the government for support. It also gave the police a certain amount of control over worker activities, and provided them with a potent new weapon against the revolutionaries. On the other hand, it encouraged the workers to band together into groups which, if the police were to lose control, could easily be transformed into illegal, and even oppositional societies. Once the workers had gained experience at organizing themselves, there was little to stop them from engaging in demonstrations, strikes, and even revolution.

This attitude, however, was symptomatic of a deeper ambivalence in Plehve's approach. Intelligent enough to recognize the need for meaningful reform in many areas, he was nevertheless unwilling to sponsor any program which might lead to disturbances, or to tolerate even a mild threat to the imperial order. He was anxious to cooperate with zemstvo-men, Zionists, peasants, and workers, but only on his own terms. Let any among these groups get out of line, and the smile of accommodation was quickly replaced by the stern frown of police repression.

THE END OF AN EXPERIMENT

Plehve's ambivalence toward the worker experiment, and his penchant for repression, were both instrumental in the demise of the *Zubatovshchina*. They led him, in June of 1903, to move against the Russian Zionist movement, thus alienating the moderate Jews and discrediting the Independents. They caused him, at the height of the Odessa strike the following month, to demand that order be restored by force and that Odessa Independents be arrested. And they motivated Zubatov, dismayed at the results of this repression, to plot to remove Plehve from power.

The sudden dissolution of the Jewish Independent Labor Party was a direct reaction to Plehve's repressive policies. By spring of 1903, the Minsk Independents had achieved considerable success in organizing local workers, and had proven themselves an effective obstacle to revolutionary agitation. There was little reason to suspect that their success, and the government's support of them, would not continue. There were, however, several problems that unexpectedly loomed important: the Independents had organized illegal strikes, and they had become closely identified with the Zionist movement. In April came the Kishinev pogrom, and widespread rumors of Plehve's complicity: suddenly, the ties with the police became an acute embarrassment to the Independents. That same month came a crackdown from Saint Petersburg: Party leaders were called in by Lopukhin and warned to stop promoting strikes and unlawful activity. In June, finally, came Plehve's secret circular attacking the Zionist movement, and banning Zionist activities. As the contents of this interdict became known, Plehve's Independent "collaborators" were thoroughly discredited. Early in July, in the wake of these developments, they held a congress and voted to disband their party.[50]

The end of the Odessa Independents was far more spectacular, and far more dangerous to Plehve. As mentioned above, Independent leader Shaevich had been responsible for a strike in April 1903 against the Restel' iron works. Since neither side proved flexible, and the Independents had enough cash to pay strike benefits, this strike dragged on through May and June. In May Restel' enlisted the support of Witte, who in turn complained to the Ministry of Interior.[51] Shortly thereafter Shaevich was summoned to Saint Petersburg by Lopukhin, and warned that any illegal activity by the Independents would lead to mass arrests. Disturbed by this lack of support, Shaevich announced that he would dissolve the Odessa Independents—but he did not carry out his threat. He returned to Odessa, and the Restel' strike went on, finally merging into the massive general strike that broke out in July.

The Odessa strike began on July 1, 1903, when the boilerworkers of a local railroad walked out, apparently in response to the firing of one of their fellows.[52] A few days later, they were joined by the stevedores at one of the steamship companies. Although the railway strike was soon settled, the stevedore strike spread to other lines and eventually to other occupations. On July 11, the sailors and stokers also walked out, effectively shutting down the entire port.

Plehve, kept well-informed by the city-governor, decided that the time had come for decisive action. He arranged to have the Russian merchant fleet send sailors and stokers to break the strike. From Petersburg, he also ordered that precautions be taken to prevent contact between these seamen and the strikers. By July 16 the port was open again, and the strikers had little choice but to return to work empty-handed.

This was, however, only the beginning. On July 15 the city's streetcar conductors and coachmen, buoyed by the closing of the port, took advantage of the situation to start their own strike. This act, which shut off Odessa's transportation, set in motion a rapid series of events. At one workshop after another the workers walked off their jobs, either as a result of persuasion by agitators, or because they were caught up in the spontaneous, elemental mood that swept the city. By July 17 the entire city was shut down, and actual control of Odessa rested with the bands of strikers who roamed the streets, pressuring others to join them.

Finally on July 18, under heavy pressure from Plehve, the Odessa authorities decided to restore order by force. The strikers, it seems, had taken to holding large open-air rallies at several fields near town. Soldiers and cossacks now moved in to break up these meetings, dispersing the workers with a minimum of violence. The striking workers were allowed to return to their homes unpursued, and relatively few arrests were made. That evening, the city-governor issued a statement that any new disorders would be met by force, and had copies distributed throughout the city. By the next day, city officials were again in control, and within a few days the city had returned to normal. The workers returned to their jobs without much resistance, and without having achieved their goals.

What was the role of Shaevich and the Independents in all this? Most observers agreed that the strike was economically-oriented and spontaneous, and that it was organized by neither the Independents nor the local Social Democrats. The strike, in fact, seems to have caught the Independents somewhat by surprise. In the early stages, Shaevich apparently tried unsuccessfully to persuade the sailors and stokers to return to work. When the streetcar operators decided to go on strike, however, he seems to have accepted the inevitable and switched his tactics from opposition to support. Disturbed by Plehve's attack on Zionism, and by the demise of the Minsk Independents, he may have decided to take "revenge" upon the government. But on the 17th and 18th, while his party struggled with the Social Democrats for control of the movement, the Independent leader claimed "illness" and refused to participate at party meetings.[53] Perhaps he realized that the halcyon days of the Odessa Independents were over.

The Independents, on the whole, seem to have had a moderating influence. They were generally able to restrain the workers from violence, and to insure that their demands were based on reasonable, economic needs. If they were not entirely successful in taking over leadership of the strike, they were at least able to prevent the Social Democrats from doing so.[54]

This moderating influence, in the end, was not enough to save the Independents. Even if the general strike had been spontaneous and unplanned, the Independents were not without guilt in the eyes of Plehve. They had started a movement and then lost control of it; they had countenanced, and even supported, illegal activities by the workers. Shaevich himself was arrested a few days after the strike ended; other Independents were held subject to prosecution. Discredited in the eyes of the workers, who never did receive the promised concessions or government support, the Odessa branch of the Independent Party ceased to exist.[55]

Despite the fact that his ministry had been responsible for the *Zubatovshchina*, Viacheslav Plehve assumed a hard-line stance from the very beginning of the strike. On the eve of the strike, in fact, he had replaced the worker-oriented city-governor with a more neutral figure. It was Plehve who arranged to have the merchant marine send in men to break the sailors' and stokers' strike. At about the same time, he had ordered an end to official protection for the Independents. "If there exists factual data that the strike was the result of agitation by the Independents," Lopukhin wired the new city-governor on July 14, "then the agitators, on the orders of the minister, must be arrested and exiled."[56]

As the strike spread throughout the city, the minister became even more vehement in his exhortations to "decisive action." On July 17 he wired the city-governor: "I propose that you take the most energetic measures against those persons who instituted the strike, including the Independents, and restore order to the streets even if it requires the force of arms." On another occasion, Plehve sent the following telegram: "Your negotiations with the streetcar strikers I consider to be an erroneous action, since in the presence of an unruly crowd it is necessary to be concerned not about the workers, but about the maintenance of order. In general, I continue to find that the necessary energy has not been shown. I approve beforehand any decisive measures." Finally, when the authorities wired for permission to arrest Shaevich, the minister's reply was quick and conclusive. "You may arrest Shaevich," he telegraphed, "and raise the issue with the Department of Police of having him banished."[57]

Plehve thus was directly responsible for the end of the Odessa Independents. He made no effort to help the workers achieve their goals, or even to give the Independents the benefit of the doubt. There are several explanations for the minister's harsh reaction. One was the fact that he received his information from the city-governor, who placed the entire blame on the Independents. Another reason was his need to protect himself against the machinations of Witte. The Finance Minister had kept on top of the Odessa situation through the local factory inspector. This man wrote about Shaevich and the Independents in the most derogatory terms, accusing them of fomenting the entire walkout.[58] Witte, of course, could not be expected to hide this knowledge from the tsar.

A third reason for Plehve's response was the internal situation in Russia. The Odessa strike was only one in a series of worker disorders that rocked southern Russia, the Caucasus, and the Ukraine in the summer of 1903. Strikes had broken out almost simultaneously in early July in several major cities, and then spread to nearby towns. By mid-July tens of thousands of workers were off the job, and the movement threatened to assume even greater proportion. Later investigation showed that the strikes were economic in character, and that the Social Democrats—although active in most of these cities—exercised little real control. This, however, was not known in July. The Minister of Interior, charged with the maintenance of internal tranquility, had scant time to worry about the justice of the workers' demands. The immediate and pressing need was to restore order, no matter what the cost, and prevent the further spread of the strike movement.[59]

It was not just in Odessa, therefore, that the authorities responded in force. In Baku, a late June walkout at several oil companies had triggered a massive general strike that shut down the city by July 10. The local officials and industrialists, acting on Plehve's instructions, refused to satisfy the workers' demands; instead troops were called out, curfews were enforced, and mass arrests were made. Plehve himself at one point wired the local military commander to urge more decisive action. In Tiflis, the general strike which broke out on July 14 was brought to an end by cossacks and the police. The suppression was accompanied by bloodshed, especially at the nearby Mikhailovo railroad station. In Batum, also, a brief three-day strike was ended with the help of the military, as was a Social Democrat sponsored walkout in Nikolaev. In Kiev, cossacks were called out to restore order during the widespread strikes of late July. They succeeded in doing so, but not without killing or wounding a number of workers.[60]

Only after the strikes were over did Plehve make an attempt to determine the causes of the walkouts and the nature of the workers' grievances. Late in July 1903, he dispatched his two top police officials to visit the affected areas. Assistant Minister von Wahl was sent to the Caucasus, while Police Director Lopukhin traveled to Odessa, Nikolaev, and Kiev. The former conferred with the authorities and industrialists of Baku, visited the various factories and workshops, and even talked to some of the workers. The latter made similar investigations in the cities he journeyed to, and submitted a report on them to the minister. Lopukhin's report, highly critical of the early inaction of the Odessa authorities, was followed by the dismissal of the city-governor.[61]

There were few other direct results of the minister's inquiry. Although Lopukhin's report tended to blame the strike movement on long hours, low pay, and poor working conditions,[62] little was done to correct the situation. Instead, the government's harshness in quelling the strikes had helped the revolutionary cause. The economically-oriented Independents were driven from the scene, and the Social Democratic point that the state could not be trusted was proven to the workers. Once again, Plehve had damaged his own cause with his harsh and repressive actions. For all his desire to help the workers, and to win their allegiance for the government, he did not hesitate to use "deadly bullets" to keep them in their place.

Zubatov, too, was disgusted and alarmed by Plehve's harsh reaction. "I could not refrain from expressing aloud my views on his internal policy," the Okhrana man later admitted. "The sooner he would leave or be dismissed, the better it would be . . . for Russia. . . ." At one point, early in July, Zubatov submitted his resignation, but this apparently was rejected. His next step was to enlist the support of Witte, hoping to find the Finance Minister more amenable to his views. Accordingly, he paid a visit to Plehve's arch-rival, bringing along Okhrana reports that "all of Russia was seething" and that the policies of the Minister of Interior were merely "driving the illness beneath the surface."[63]

What actually happened next is not entirely clear. According to Witte, he advised Zubatov to repeat his complaint to Plehve, but the Okhrana-man went instead to Prince V. P. Meshcherskii. The prince in turn told the Minister of Interior that Zubatov was intriguing against him. According to Plehve, Witte, Meshcherskii, and Zubatov had hatched a plot to make Witte Minister of Interior. The plot involved an "intercepted" letter—supposedly between two loyal subjects but actually forged by Zubatov—which Meshcherskii was to deliver to the tsar. The letter denounced Plehve and mentioned Witte as the only man capable of straightening out the empire's internal policy. The Minister of Interior supposedly learned of this intrigue from an Okhrana agent to whom Zubatov had confided. [64]

Since neither of these sources is entirely reliable, the true nature of Zubatov's betrayal probably will never be known. What is clear, from these and other sources, is that Zubatov tried to intrigue with Witte, and that Plehve somehow found out about it. What is also clear is that Plehve was thoroughly enraged.

On August 19, 1903, barely a year since Zubatov had taken over the Special Section, the police official was summoned to the minister's dacha. There he was received by Plehve and von Wahl. The presence of von Wahl had unfavorable overtones: the assistant minister had long been a critic of Zubatov's labor policies. Plehve's explanation of von Wahl's presence was even more ominous: the minister "was not in the habit of speaking alone with persons he did not trust." [65]

Zubatov was then asked to relate the history of the Jewish Independent Labor Party. He did so, but only after pointing out that he had kept nothing secret, and that the history of the party was readily available in Police Department documents. When he reached the point where the Independents moved into Odessa, Plehve took up the story and remarked to von Wahl: "In particular . . . the Jewess Vil'bushevich traveled to Odessa, where she placed the *Zhid* Shaevich in charge, issuing, with the approval of Mr. Zubatov, very stupid proclamations, fomenting strikes, etc." Zubatov admitted receiving the proclamations, but insisted he had no part in drafting or editing them. Under further questioning, he also admitted having supplied Shaevich with funds from the Police Department. Plehve then produced several documents intended to compromise Zubatov, and finally said to von Wahl: "It is obvious that Mr. Zubatov cannot continue in service after all this. His ultimate fate will be decided when the Director of the Department returns. . . . Now he must immediately relinquish his post." Zubatov then departed, slamming the door behind him. [66]

The dismissal of Zubatov did not necessarily mean the end of all he had started. The worker organizations in Moscow and Petersburg continued to operate, with the knowledge and consent of Plehve, for several more years. But it did mark the end of the systematic attempt to deal with the worker question by means of quasi-legal, police-sponsored worker organizations.

The *Zubatovshchina* was the most imaginative, as well as the most bizarre, of the programs sponsored by Plehve. The minister, who at first looked upon it as a "stupid experiment," had gradually come to countenance, and even to encourage, its operation. But his approval was not without misgivings, and as soon as it appeared that one of the Zubatov societies was engaged in illegal and disruptive activity, he hastily withdrew his support. In his view, as he had informed the Odessa authorities, strikes and unlawful force did not lose their illegal character simply because the instigators' goals were desirable to the government. Much later, Plehve asked A. V. Pogozhev for his views on the *Zubatovshchina*. The labor expert replied that it had created "frightful demoralization," and had dragged the worker question "out into the streets." The minister reflected somberly, and then replied: "Yes, you are right. I myself now see that it was premature to introduce such a movement among the Russian workers."[67]

Not only was it premature, it was also nearly disastrous for Plehve. The Odessa general strike, aided and abetted by a police-sponsored union, had presented Sergei Witte with a sudden opportunity to discredit his main rival and reverse his declining fortunes. In the wake of the strike, armed with reports from Odessa, Witte had hastened to point out to the tsar the harm that had been caused, expediently linking Shaevich's Independents with the Minister of Interior. His words, however, were greeted with skepticism, and Plehve soon managed to place the blame entirely on Zubatov.[68] Furthermore, it seems, the emperor had already arrived at a different sort of decision: the time had come for him to replace his volatile Minister of Finance.

7

The Fall of Witte and the Far Eastern Question

THE "PROMOTION" AND DISMISSAL OF WITTE

On Friday, August 15, 1903, at two o'clock in the afternoon, Minister of Finance Sergei Witte arrived at Peterhof for his regular report to the emperor. At the tsar's request he brought with him State Bank Director E. D. Pleske, a career bureaucrat in the Ministry of Finance. Leaving Pleske in the anteroom, Witte entered Nicholas's office and proceeded to deliver his report. The interview was cordial, and the emperor unusually lavish with his praise.

As Witte prepared to leave, however, the tone of the meeting changed. Nicholas, suddenly ill at ease, began asking questions about Pleske's character and abilities. Finally he came to the point: "Sergei Iul'evich, I am asking you to accept the post of Chairman of the Committee of Ministers, and I wish to appoint Pleske to the post of Minister of Finance."[1]

Witte, by his own account, was taken aback. The Chairmanship of the Committee of Ministers, as the emperor quickly pointed out, was "the very highest position which exists in the empire." But it was one usually reserved for venerable officials who had outlived their usefulness as full-time administrators. It provided its holder with plenty of prestige and honor, but with very little real power or solid authority. Some observers were soon speculating that Nicholas was finally taking steps to unify his government; that a forceful figure like Witte could turn this "new sign of trust" in to a *de facto* premiership. The erstwhile Finance Minister had no such delusions. "You perceive," he later remarked to Pleske, "that I was simply discharged. I had become tiresome. I was being pushed aside."[2]

Witte's dismissal, it goes without saying, was a victory for Viacheslav Plehve. It was not, to be sure, a total victory: the new Chairman of the Committee of Ministers retained his chairmanship of the Special Conference on Agriculture and his membership in the Siberian Railway Committee. Moreover Pleske, the new Finance Minister, was an admirer and disciple of Witte, and thus no friend of the Minister of Interior. But the outcome of the power struggle between Russia's two most prominent statesmen was no longer in doubt. Plehve had prevailed. He, more than anyone else, was responsible for undermining Witte's position; and he, more than anyone else, stood to gain from Witte's fall.

How Plehve managed to defeat his rival is apparent only in general outline. The reason for this is that, although their rivalry and their opposing views were readily apparent, the real power struggle took place behind the scenes. Plehve did not prevail because he devised a better program than Witte, because he was a more efficient administrator or a more capable statesman, or because he managed to convince a larger segment of society—or even a larger number of ministers—of the correctness of his views. He prevailed because he managed to discredit Witte in the eyes of his sovereign, while at the same time convincing one man, Nicholas II, that his, Plehve's, course was the best one for Russia.

Plehve had begun the contention for imperial favor with several advantages. Nicholas, although well aware of Witte's ability, disliked and resented his Minister of Finance. Witte had dominated the young monarch in Nicholas's first years and this fact, along with the Finance Minister's crude, blunt, and outspoken ways, could not but irritate the emperor. Witte himself, although sincerely devoted to his monarch, held Nicholas in rather low esteem, a fact which could only further strain their relationship.[3] Plehve, on the other hand was a model of courtesy and correctness. He himself may not have had the highest opinion of Nicholas, but he was much better at concealing his feelings than his outspoken rival.

Furthermore, the views and policies put forth by Plehve meshed better with the emperor's predilections than did Witte's bold and complex programs. In Witte's telling this was but rank opportunism on Plehve's part: patriots like the Finance Minister had the courage to tell Nicholas the truth, while careerists like Plehve tailored their opinions to those of the monarch, and told his majesty only what he wanted to hear. This charge, perhaps, was not entirely unjustified. But Plehve was indeed the more cautious of the two, and the one more concerned with harmony and order. It was his duty, he contended, to preserve and protect the monarchy, and obediently to carry out the wishes of the tsar, even if he were not always in full accord with them. More importantly, Plehve realized that he could accomplish little without the emperor's support. Ideas, policies, programs, reforms—all of these were meaningless without the authority to implement them. Witte was not just a rival, he was an obstacle to effective government and unified policy.[4] The very logic of Plehve's position compelled him to undermine Witte.

What Plehve actually told the tsar in private audience is unknown, but the fact that he tried to discredit Witte was recognized by all. After Plehve's death, in fact, an investigation of his papers revealed that he was trying to link Witte with the radical left in the mind of the emperor. On a later occasion, when Witte complained of this attempt to connect him with the revolution, Nicholas replied that he had "never believed those slanders." He did not, if Witte's account can be believed, deny that the slanders had been made.[5]

Plehve also strove to influence the emperor through the backstage "advisors" and favorites who surrounded Nicholas II. These advisors included men like Philippe, the French hypnotist and charlatan, Gesse, the ever-present commander of the Palace Guard, Bezobrazov, the Far Eastern adventurer and entrepreneur, and Prince Meshcherskii, the publisher of the conservative newspaper, *Citizen*. The last, a former favorite of Alexander III reintroduced into court circles by Sipiagin, was particularly influential. Plehve, seeing the existence of such persons as something inherent in autocracy, worked to take advantage of the situation. He rejected the argument that these persons would have no influence if they were not patronized by the ministers: "Autocrats outwardly listen to their ministers," he once remarked, ". . . but almost always people on the side find easy access to their hearts." He especially defended his patronage of Meshcherskii: "Personally speaking, I think Meshcherskii is worthless as an individual . . . but it is absolutely necessary to listen to his voice, as representative of a certain segment of society."[6]

Witte's distaste for Plehve's methods did not prevent him from using the same devices. He, too, tried to discredit his rival with the emperor, rushing to Nicholas with stories that Plehve's police were behind the anti-government activity in south Russia in the summer of

1903. He, too, patronized Meshcherskii: he seems, in fact, to have had better relations with the publisher-prince than Plehve. For the latter, despite his purported lack of scruple, did not hesitate to censure Meshcherskii's paper when the prince used it to criticize government officials.[7]

Another way to influence the emperor was through members of the imperial family. This tactic, too, was used by both Witte and Plehve. Plehve, in general, aligned with Grand Duke Alexander Mikhailovich, head of the merchant marine, who also stood to profit from Witte's demise. Witte had a powerful protectress in Empress Marie Feodorovna, the tsar's mother, who hated Plehve for his treatment of the Finns. Nicholas may have dismissed Witte as early as January 1, 1903, were it not for his mother's intervention.[8]

Apparently, all this backstage maneuvering had the desired impact. A few days after Witte's dismissal, Minister of War A. N. Kuropatkin wrote in his diary that three "mines" had destroyed Witte's position. The first had been laid by Grand Duke Alexander Mikhailovich, who complained to Nicholas that the Minister of Finance had acquired too much power, and that he was actually usurping the authority of the emperor. Another had been planted by Plehve, along with several other ministers, who managed to convince the tsar that Witte's activity aided the revolutionaries. They told Nicholas that all the anti-government forces—Finns, students, Armenians, and Jews—found support from Witte.[9] Plehve, in fact, had clashed with Witte in three major areas. In the first, the dispute over the peasant question, he had been victorious: he had used the local agriculture committees to show the tsar that Witte was sponsoring discussions of radical programs. In the second, involving the worker question, the roles had been reversed—but Plehve had deftly managed to parry Witte's attacks and shift all blame to Zubatov.

The third major area of confrontation—the clash over Far Eastern policy—was also the third of Kuropatkin's alleged "mines." This dispute was the most immediate and, in Witte's opinion, the most important cause of the Finance Minister's fall. According to Kuropatkin, this mine was planted by entrepreneur–adventurer A. M. Bezobrazov, who complained to Nicholas that Witte stood in the way of a correct Russian policy in Manchuria and Korea.[10] Bezobrazov, as might have been expected, was supported by V. K. Plehve.

THE FAR EASTERN QUESTION

The Far East had been a major concern well before Plehve became Minister of Interior.[11] Attention had been focused eastward during the 1890s, with the construction of the Trans-Siberian Railway. The major architects of imperial policy had been Witte and Nicholas II. Witte was interested in economic exploitation: he dreamed of opening up vast oriental markets to Russian goods. Nicholas's aims were political and dynastic: he had traveled in the Far East while still heir apparent, and he had come to regard Russian expansion in this region as a major objective in his reign. He therefore took a special, personal interest in Far Eastern affairs. For the most part, however, he had supported Witte's policy of peaceful economic penetration, and the Finance Minister had been given a relatively free hand.

The major obstacle to Russian expansion was not the decaying Chinese Empire, which could offer little resistance, but Japan. After a surprisingly easy victory in the Sino-Japanese War of 1894–95, Japan had demanded and received the Liaotung peninsula, between Korea and the Chinese mainland, as one of the fruits of its triumph. But the Russians, in conjunction with France and Germany, had forced the Japanese to give up their victory claim. Then, in 1896, by means of loans, bribes, cajolery, and financial manipulations, Witte extracted from the Chinese a secret treaty which provided, among other things, for a railway concession through the Chinese province of Manchuria. This meant that the last link of the Siberian railway, from Chita to Vladivostok, would not have to follow the circuitous route through strictly Russian territory. The actual concession was given not to the Russian government, but to a "private" concern, set up for this purpose, called the "Russo-Chinese Bank." The "Bank," which then proceeded to construct the "Chinese-Eastern Railway" across Manchuria, was for all practical purposes owned by the Ministry of Finance and operated by Sergei Witte.

Further events served to exacerbate Russo-Japanese relations. In 1897, responding to German annexation of a Chinese port, the Russians had seized Port Arthur, the city at the southern tip of the Liaotung Peninsula. This aggressive step was taken at the behest of the Minister of Foreign Affairs, and not supported by Witte. Nevertheless the Finance Minister quickly swallowed his distaste and convinced the Chinese to lease the entire peninsula, so recently denied Japan, to the Russians. Before long he was building the "South Manchuria Railway," a branch linking the Chinese-Eastern with Port Arthur. Then, in 1900, when the anti-foreigner Boxer Rebellion broke out in China, Russian troops were sent, ultimately at Witte's request, to occupy Manchuria and protect the railways. Manchuria had become, in effect, a Russian protectorate.

The Japanese, alarmed by the Russian advance and fearful for their own ambitions, began to take counter-measures. Almost immediately, they joined with Britain and the United States in trying to force a Russian pullback. Early in 1902 they concluded a defensive alliance with the British, a move obviously directed against the Russians. Their efforts finally bore fruit. On March 26, Russia signed a pact with the Chinese to evacuate its troops from Manchuria in three stages, over the next eighteen months. By September 26, 1903, all Russian soldiers were to have been withdrawn.

The appearance of resolution was deceiving. The evacuation agreement was a humiliation for Russia, and it marked the beginning of the end of Witte's control of Far Eastern policy. He continued to advocate peaceful penetration, insisting that Russia could still control Manchuria through economic exploitation and influence in Peking. The emperor, however, had begun to have doubts. Russia had sunk enormous sums into Manchuria; compliance with the evacuation agreement would jeopardize the entire investment. Nicholas was not yet ready to abandon his dreams of empire in the Far East.

In the wake of the evacuation agreement, therefore, there arose alternative proposals. One of these was a "compromise" plan advanced by the Minister of War. Kuropatkin insisted that Russia must keep its troops in Manchuria until it had guarantees, from the Chinese or Japanese, that the Russian sphere of influence could continue. He was opposed, at first, by Witte, and by Foreign Minister V. N. Lamsdorf, both of whom favored strict compliance with the withdrawal agreement. Eventually, however, at Kuropatkin's insistence, they agreed that Russia should continue to occupy at least the northern part of Manchuria.

A more aggressive policy was advocated by A. M. Bezobrazov, a chauvinist adventurer and "entrepreneur" who had impressed the tsar with his uncompromising views and vehement expression. Bezobrazov insisted that any "retreat" would be folly, and that instead Russia should strengthen its hold over Manchuria and seek to penetrate Korea. In the late 1890s, he had already managed to involve the emperor in an unsuccessful scheme to advance Russian interests in Korea through a private timber company. Now he revived this idea, centered around a

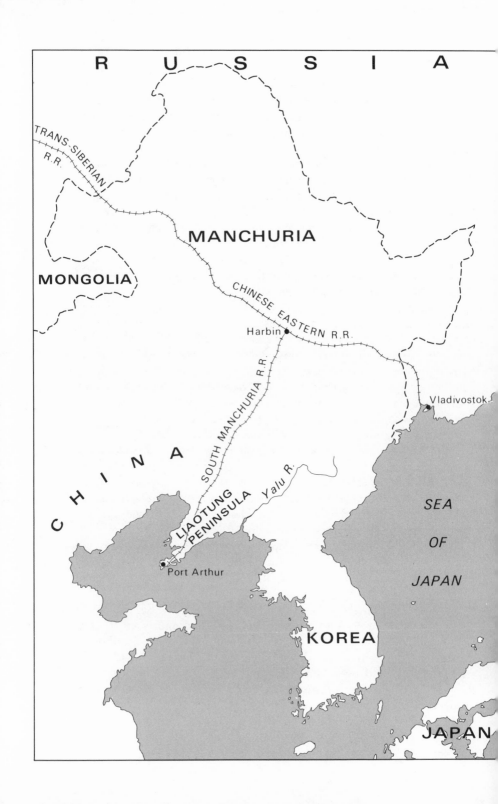

State Secretary A. M. Bezobrazov.

concession from the Korean crown to exploit timber resources along the Yalu River. Nicholas apparently was impressed. As he later confided to his Minister of War: "It was not easy for me to listen to Bezobrazov . . . when he told me we had chosen the wrong path in the Far East. But I recognized that he was right."[12]

As the stock of Bezobrazov rose, the influence of Witte diminished. The appointment of Plehve, coming only nine days after the withdrawal agreement, was a clear sign of this decline. Other portents soon followed. The Finance Minister's long report on Manchuria, presented after his journey there in fall of 1902, was ignored by Nicholas II. In January 1903, quite against his wishes, Witte was ordered to provide a huge credit to Bezobrazov from the Russo-Chinese Bank. Major decisions, including the creation of a Far Eastern Viceroyalty, were made without Witte's knowledge. Through it all, Bezobrazov constantly criticized the Minister of Finance, and inveighed against his policies. [13]

Throughout the latter part of 1902, then, and through all of 1903, Russian Far Eastern policy and diplomacy followed a tortuous course. Nicholas switched positions constantly, sometimes siding with Bezobrazov, other times supporting his ministers. He seemed, in fact, to be playing one side against the other, using Bezobrazov as a counterpoise to the ministerial "triumvirate" of Kuropatkin, Lamsdorf, and Witte. [14] Meanwhile, evacuation deadlines passed unheeded, Russian belligerence increased, and negotiations with Japan bogged down. The Japanese, profoundly distrustful of Russian intentions, would ultimately opt for war.

According to Witte, the real villain in this whole sad saga was none other than V. K. Plehve. As long as the ministers were united in opposition to adventurism, Witte argued, they had been able to counter the influence of Bezobrazov. Only after Plehve came on the scene and threw his support to Bezobrazov did the emperor change his mind and side with the adventurer. Witte even went so far as to suggest a reason for the Minister of Interior's stance: Plehve wanted a war in the Far East to ease internal pressures! "When Kuropatkin left the post of Minister of War . . . he admonished Plehve that he, Plehve, had been the only one of the ministers who had wanted this war, and the only one to side with the band of political adventurers. As he left, Plehve replied: 'Aleksei Nikolaevich, you do not know the internal situation in Russia. What we need to hold back revolution is a little, victorious war.' " [15]

Whether or not Plehve actually uttered these words, they are the most famous quote ever attributed to him. They have earned him a line in even the most cursory surveys of this period, [16] often followed by the observation that the war turned out to be neither "little" nor "victorious." More important than the words, however, is Witte's implication: the Russian government went to war hoping to solve its internal problems by engaging in foreign adventure. This, of course, explains why the Russians failed to respond to Japanese conciliatory gestures. It also squares well with the view of Plehve as a man who instigated pogroms in order to channel the discontent of the masses against the Jews rather than the government.

V. I. Gurko, Plehve's major apologist and a vituperative critic of Sergei Witte, presented a different picture. According to Gurko, Plehve's role in the whole matter was only peripheral, and the real villain was Witte. Witte, after all, was the one who created the Manchurian mess in the first place. He spent enormous sums of money, badly needed in European Russia, in that distant province; and he managed to get Russia into a situation from which it could not extricate itself without enormous loss of fortune and prestige. Plehve, to be sure, had caused some harm by supporting Bezobrazov, on one hand, as part of a maneuver to dispose of Witte, and on the other, in an attempt to dilute the adventurer's influence by getting him "attached to some official group." But Plehve, Gurko assured his readers, "was definitely opposed to war."[17]

PLEHVE, BEZOBRAZOV, AND THE FAR EASTERN VICEROYALTY

Actually V. K. Plehve did not begin to play a conspicuous role with regard to the Far East until early in 1903. After an entire career of dealing with internal matters, he had little experience or expertise in international affairs. In matters pertaining to the Far East, as he later admitted to War Minister Kuropatkin, he was "totally ignorant." Early in his ministry, therefore, he chose to remain largely in the background. He did, however, maintain contact with a certain V. M. Vonliarliarskii, a former subordinate of his in the Imperial Chancery and a cohort of Bezobrazov's in the original Yalu scheme. According to Gurko, "Vonliarliarskii kept in almost daily touch with Plehve and possibly found in him a certain support in their common opposition to Witte." No doubt he also kept Plehve apprised of Bezobrazov's activities and plans.[18]

Throughout 1902 and 1903, in fact, Russian Far Eastern policy seems to have operated on three different levels. On one level, that of formal diplomacy, the Russians sought to secure their interests in Manchuria through agreements with the Chinese and Japanese. Decisions on this level were made, at least until mid-1903, by Witte, Kuropatkin, and Lamsdorf, with the participation of other diplomatic and military officials. Plehve's involvement was minimal. On another level, that of adventurist expansionism, the Russians strove to extend their commercial and territorial empire through the guise of concessions granted to semi-private corporations. Policies on this level were suggested by Bezobrazov and his cohorts, with the general support of the emperor. Plehve, although not directly involved, did give his backing to Bezobrazov, finding him a convenient ally against Witte. On the third level, that of internal administration of the Far Eastern provinces, the government tried to eliminate inconsistencies and to consolidate state authority into a strong, unified, local source. This was the only level within Plehve's realm of competence, and the only one with which he was directly concerned. Unfortunately, however, things could not be kept separate, and actions taken on any one level profoundly affected the others.

Plehve's role in the conduct of formal diplomacy was almost non-existent. He did take part, along with Kuropatkin, Witte, and Lamsdorf, in a conference held at Yalta in October of 1902. The participants unanimously concluded that Manchuria must remain under Russian influence, despite the withdrawal agreement, but they came up with no definite policy. Plehve's views do not seem to have differed much from those of the other ministers.[19] He did not participate, however, in the important conference of January 25, 1903, which decided to postpone the second stage of the evacuation until the Chinese agreed to a list of conditions insuring Russian predominance.[20] This policy, arrived at by the Ministers of Foreign Affairs, Finance, and War, was a repudiation of the withdrawal agreement. When the Chinese, prompted by Japan, Britain, and the U.S.A., rejected these demands, the Russians were left with an awkward choice. They could either back down, and resume the evacuation, or they could leave their troops in Manchuria, and risk the possibility of war.

The Russian response was a fateful one. On April 13, 1903, six days after the Chinese rejection, Kuropatkin, Witte, and Lamsdorf met with several key diplomats to devise a new Manchurian policy. This time they accepted a proposal, made by Kuropatkin, to continue the occupation of northern Manchuria. Nine Russian battalions were to remain stationed in the vicinity of the Chinese-Eastern Railroad.[21] The significance of this was unmistakable. The "responsible" ministers, without the participation of Bezobrazov, Plehve, or even the emperor, had decided that Russia should unilaterally abrogate a major part of the evacuation agreement. The Chinese, in their weakened state, could do little but protest, but it was now essential for the Russians to reach an accord with Japan.

At this point, the other levels of Far Eastern policy began to come into play. Early in April, Bezobrazov arrived back in Saint Petersburg from a three-month trip to the Far East. While there he had behaved so extravagantly, throwing his money and weight around, that the emperor had finally recalled him. Before returning, however, the adventurer had sent a long memorandum, outlining his views and explaining his plans. It insisted that Russia must find some way to renege on the Manchurian withdrawal agreement, while occupying the territory bordering Korea so as to extend its influence into that country. The vehicle it offered, of course, was the Yalu timber concession. Bezobrazov envisioned a new organization, similar to a British "chartered company," which would unite all concessions in Manchuria and Korea under the direction of a special "state secretary." He also suggested, to eliminate interdepartmental inconsistencies, that all state authority in the Far East be consolidated in one source. [22]

On March 26, 1903, even before Bezobrazov's return—and before the Chinese had rejected Russia's "conditions"—the emperor held a meeting to discuss the memorandum. This time Plehve was present, along with Witte, Kuropatkin, Lamsdorf, and A. M. Abaza, the adventurer's cousin and cohort. The results were a defeat for Bezobrazov. It was decided that the Yalu timber concession should be conducted as a private enterprise, without a government charter, and should be restricted entirely to the river basin. Exploitation was to be delayed, pending diplomatic efforts to obtain a concession from China on the Manchurian bank of the river. Administrative authority was to be vested, not in a special "state secretary," but in the commander of Russian forces at Port Arthur. The notion of uniting all local authority apparently was shelved. Above all, it was agreed, "adventurism" could not be condoned, and conflict with Japan must be avoided. [23]

Plehve's views, expressed at this conference, are of particular interest. In one sense, with regard to the scheme, he supported the conclusions of Witte, Lamsdorf, and Kuropatkin. The Far Eastern question, he rightly pointed out, did not really concern his department, except to the extent that decisions made there would affect public opinion. In this area, at present, great caution was necessary, and adventurism should be avoided. On the other hand, some of Bezobrazov's findings made sense to him, and he suggested that it might be desirable to delay the evacuation temporarily while trying to ascertain the military capabilities of Japan. He also supported Bezobrazov's proposals that all Manchurian concessions be amalgamated, and that all local governmental authority be consolidated. With such great distances involved, he argued, it would certainly be beneficial to have a strong, unified, local administration.[24]

There are several reasons why Plehve may have supported a strong local authority. Such a proposal squared well with his overall goals of unifying local authority and removing administrative confusion. It also, if implemented, would have weakened the power of Witte, making it impossible for the Minister of Finance to continue to dominate Far Eastern affairs. Besides, Plehve knew that the tsar favored this proposal, since he had discussed it with him beforehand. Nicholas, as Plehve later admitted, had called him in and spoken to him about the need to organize a strong authority in the Far East, and had expressed displeasure at the constant opposition he was getting from the ministers.[25]

The meeting of March 26, in fact, was but a temporary setback for Bezobrazov. By the time of the next imperial conference, six weeks later, the entire situation had changed. The Chinese rejection of the Russian "demands," coming on April 7, had revealed the bankruptcy of the "ministerial" policy. Almost simultaneously, Bezobrazov had arrived back in Petersburg and begun to ply the emperor with his nationalist views and his forceful personality. Shortly thereafter, on April 15, Kuropatkin left on a mission of his own to the Far East, thereby removing one of Bezobrazov's most effective opponents from direct contact with the emperor. Before long Nicholas was once more under the influence of the expansionist schemer. This was made manifest to all when, in early May, it was announced that Bezobrazov had been given the title of "State Secretary of His Imperial Majesty."[26]

The conference which occurred at Tsarskoe Selo on May 7, 1903, was perhaps the most significant of all the Far Eastern conferences Plehve took part in. Unfortunately, no minutes were kept and the conference journal, composed by Bezobrazov, is probably inaccurate. Nevertheless, the broad outlines of what took place are clear. The conference apparently was called to give Bezobrazov a chance to report on his trip and explain his schemes to the ministers. A report was also heard from General K. I. Vogak, a Russian military agent in the Far East, who supported Bezobrazov's views. Participating in the conference, besides the emperor, were Plehve, Witte, Lamsdorf, Abaza, and Kuropatkin's stand-in as Minister of War.[27]

It seems that some of the results of the conference had been decided in advance. Several days beforehand, acting under the influence of Bezobrazov, Nicholas II had wired important new instructions to Admiral E. I. Alekseev, the Russian commander at Port Arthur. The admiral was directed to increase Russian "military preparedness" in Manchuria as quickly as possible, to take steps to prevent "the penetration of foreign influence" into Manchuria, and to begin supporting "the broad activity of Russian entrepreneurs in Manchuria." Alekseev was also told to prepare to concentrate in his own hands "supreme and responsible control in the Far East over all departments." It appears from the conference journal that these communications were read to the conferees. If so, they must have realized they were being presented with a *fait accompli,* and that control of Far Eastern policy, at least for the moment, was being removed from their hands.[28]

It was at this conference that Plehve revealed himself as a wholehearted backer of Bezobrazov. When Witte objected to the expenditure of treasury monies to support the new enterprises, Plehve replied that the treasury should participate to any extent "corresponding to the actual interests of the state." This was necessary, he felt, to "prevent the large-scale penetration of foreign capital into Manchuria before Russian interests there were secured." He called for the cautious introduction of Russian enterprises, and the nonadmission of foreigners, into Manchuria. He also supported the move to concentrate greater power in the hands of Admiral Alekseev. According to one report, he was downright bellicose: "It was not diplomacy that made Russia, but bayonets," he allegedly remarked, asserting that bayonets, too, would decide the issue in Manchuria.[29]

Plehve's reasons for supporting Bezobrazov appear to have been several. The most obvious was the desire to get the better of Witte. Observing that Bezobrazov had attained the status of imperial favorite, and that Witte had become vulnerable as a result of Far Eastern affairs, Plehve no doubt sensed an opportunity to dispose of his chief rival. It was only natural that he should join forces with Bezobrazov to attack their common enemy and, in Kuropatkin's words, to "settle accounts with Witte."[30]

It is also possible that Plehve was persuaded by Bezobrazov's arguments. He was, to be sure, no expert on foreign affairs, but years of experience in dealing with internal dissension had taught him one important lesson: it was better to stand firm than to retreat. Once you began to yield, he reasoned, you would inevitably continue to yield. After the conference of May 7 he explained himself to the director of his chancery: "Bezobrazov very logically demonstrated that the complications happening to us in the Far East are nothing else but a natural development of the adventures begun by Witte himself. . . . If we were to withdraw now, all the difficulties and millions expended on the railroad to Port Arthur and Dalny would be thrown out of the window. This opinion compels consideration. A policy of concession in foreign affairs, as in internal affairs, is always more dangerous than a firm, hard course."[31]

Another explanation of Plehve's conduct is the one he later gave as the "real" reason for his support of Bezobrazov. Imperial favorites, he insisted, were an inevitable feature of autocracy; it was a serious mistake for ministers openly to oppose such persons. Would it not be better to accept the inevitable, to appear to go along, all the while seeking a way to dilute the favorite's influence? In Bezobrazov's case, this could be accomplished easily enough by giving him a responsible position, and attaching him to some committee or other. "[O]nce he is appointed member of the Special Committee for Far Eastern Affairs," Plehve reportedly argued, "not only am I certain that his attitude to the Far Eastern problem will change, but I also think that his word will carry no greater weight with the Tsar than the word of any other committee member."[32]

Whatever his ultimate intention, however, it is unlikely that Plehve was guided by hopes of distracting attention from Russia's internal problems. He was undeniably concerned about domestic discontent—and about the new policy's effect on public opinion.[33] But his main concern here seems to have been avoiding public controversy. In conversation with Bezobrazov and Abaza a few weeks after the conference, he supported the conclusion that "the sooner we manage to attach a more complete form to the newly-projected arrangement, the more desirable it will be for local affairs and for public sentiment in the Center." According to the minister, public relations were best served by "a clear and habitual form for affairs, irrespective of the essential correctness of their orientation."[34]

It is doubtful, moreover, that he actually contemplated war at this time as an antidote to public unrest. In spring of 1903, war was still a rather remote possibility. Furthermore, the internal situation had not yet reached the critical stage. The Zubatov experiment still seemed to be working well, and there had been no serious turmoil in the countryside since the Khar'kov-Poltava riots of March 1902. It was not until summer of 1903 that the wave of strikes swept southern Russia. In the debates concerning the Factory Law of June 10, 1903, Plehve was sanguine enough to reassure the State Council that there was little immediate danger of serious internal disorder.[35]

At any rate, the views of Bezobrazov, supported by Abaza, Vogak, Plehve, and the emperor himself, prevailed at the May 7 conference. Despite the objections of Witte and Lamsdorf, several major changes were made in the areas of adventurism and administration. Bezobrazov's enterprise was given a freer hand: the limits on treasury support were removed, and the "possibility of involvement in other business" besides timber was foreseen. It was decided not to wait for formal concessions from the Chinese to begin exploitation on the Manchurian side of the Yalu. The participation of foreign capital, at Plehve's insistence, was now to be prohibited. And Admiral Alekseev, besides supervising the activity of the enterprise, was to be given "suitable authority and rights" to "cope with the present organization of affairs."[36] It was a victory for Bezobrazov, and a victory for Plehve.

The victory for adventurism appears to have been short-lived. Early in June, when Bezobrazov returned to the Far East to implement his plans, Nicholas began to have reservations. In fact, the adventurer's influence seems to have declined as soon as he left the capital. Even as he traveled eastward, he received a telegram from Abaza announcing that the emperor, in order to "avoid the risk of coming into conflict" with Japan, had "definitely decided to allow the Japanese complete possession of Korea." Arriving in Port Arthur, he ran into the combined opposition of Kuropatkin and Alekseev. A series of conferences was held during the month of June 1903, attended by Kuropatkin, Alekseev, Bezobrazov, the Russian ambassadors to China and Korea, and various other persons. Over Bezobrazov's objections, it was decided that the Yalu enterprise should be given "an exclusively commercial character." Officers in the Russian army were to be excluded from participation, and the business was to be managed by "persons not employed in the service of the Empire."[37]

Back in Saint Petersburg, however, the administrative part of the program—the part with which Plehve was directly concerned—met with considerable success. In accordance with the decisions of the May 7 conference, Abaza was commissioned to draw up a new statute for Far Eastern administration. Having no expertise in these matters, Abaza appealed to Plehve, who arranged to have Chancery Director Liubimov assist him with this project. Throughout the latter part of May and the first half of June, according to Liubimov's recollections, the two met almost daily. Using the Viceroyalty of the Caucasus and the Siberian Railway Committee as guides, they drafted two new statutes: one instituting a Viceroyalty of the Far East, and the other setting

up a Special Committee on Far Eastern Affairs. Their work, apparently, was kept confidential. By the end of June it was completed, and
the stage was set for imperial action. [38]

In July 1903, attention in Russia was focused not on the Far East
but on the cities of the south, where massive strikes were occurring,
and on the wilderness of Sarov, to which the emperor and his entou-
rage made a very remarkable pilgrimage. It seems that during the
previous summer the tsar's wife, the Empress Alexandra, had become
enamored of the legends surrounding the life of Serafim, a hermit of
Sarov. Through her husband, she had insisted that Serafim be declared
a saint, and that this should occur on the anniversary of his death, July
19. The Procurator of the Holy Synod had persuaded Nicholas to
postpone the ceremonies for a year. Finally, in mid-July 1903, the
imperial family traveled to Sarov. The Minister of Interior also attended the ceremonies. It is clear that the pilgrimage was a profound
experience for Nicholas II, and that it had repercussions which were
political as well as religious. The tsar returned to Saint Petersburg
determined, apparently, to move resolutely, and to take up the reins
of government himself. [39]

There followed a series of critical developments on every policy
level. The Japanese, pressured by their British allies, finally agreed to
negotiate with Russia on the issues of Manchuria and Korea. Talks
began in late July. Meanwhile, both Kuropatkin and Bezobrazov had
returned from the Far East. The former presented a detailed report on
the increasing strength of Japan, but asserted that the Japanese would
not go to war over Manchuria. Bezobrazov, in a separate memorandum, stressed the need for a "strategic screen on the Yalu." He also
sent letters to the tsar, ranting against the ministerial "triumvirate" and
their "defeatist" policies. These influences, and the tsar's "decisive"
mindset, appear to have been responsible for what happened next. [40]

On July 30, 1903, without prior warning, the imperial government announced the formation of a "Viceroyalty of the Far East," to
include the Port Arthur area and the territory north of Manchuria. The
action was taken suddenly, by a special decree, bypassing both the
State Council and the Committee of Ministers. It caught the ministers,
especially Witte and Kuropatkin, unawares. It could not have come as
a total surprise: the creation of a special authority in the Far East had
been discussed, in Witte's presence, at the conference of May 7, and
it had also come up during the Kuropatkin-Alekseev-Bezobrazov talks
in June at Port Arthur. The fact that the decision was made without
consulting the ministers rankled, however, and produced an unfavor-

able impression. Even Plehve claimed, in conversation with Kuropatkin, that he had not learned of the emperor's intentions until two days
before the announcement. Since it was his ministry that had drawn up
the statute, however, it is doubtful that he was surprised. On the
following day, July 31, Admiral Alekseev was appointed to fill the new
post.[41]

The announcement of the Viceroyalty had an immediate and far-
reaching impact. It served, on one hand, to undermine the Russo-
Japanese negotiations right from the beginning. The Japanese, whose
first formal proposal was made the day of Alekseev's appointment,
could not help but notice that the Viceroyalty included lands on either
side of Manchuria. Did this not signify that the Russians intended
eventual annexation? If so, what was the purpose of negotiation? It
also seemed to remove the Far Eastern provinces from the direct competence of the ministers, thus diluting the influence of Kuropatkin,
Lamsdorf, and Witte. However, as events soon made clear, it did not
dilute the influence of Plehve.

The influence of Plehve—as well as that of Bezobrazov—was
apparent in an event that rocked Saint Petersburg two weeks later:
Witte's dismissal as Minister of Finance. Both the minister and the
adventurer had lobbied for Witte's removal; both were informed of it
by Nicholas in advance. Bezobrazov was apprised by the emperor, at
the time of the Viceroyalty announcement, that Witte's situation was
"very transitory." Plehve learned of his rival's coming demise even
earlier, perhaps as early as the spring of that year. According to Gurko,
Nicholas told the Minister of Interior he had made up his mind,
suddenly and definitively, at a religious service inaugurating a new
battleship. "The Lord put into my heart," he allegedly remarked, "the
thought that I must not delay that which I was already persuaded to
do."[42]

THE COMING OF THE WAR

With the removal of Witte, the major purpose of Plehve's support of
Bezobrazov had been accomplished. Accordingly, this should have
marked the end of the Plehve–Bezobrazov alliance, in fact if not in
appearance. In fact, Bezobrazov had been more successful in the areas
of Plehve's concern—the Viceroyalty and the dismissal of Witte—
than he had in the realm of actual Russian policy vis-à-vis Manchuria

and Korea. Now, with Witte gone, Plehve's actions should have revealed themselves in skillful maneuvers to dilute the influence of Bezobrazov, and to avert the threat of war.

On September 30, the statute of the Special Committee on Far Eastern Affairs, intended to supervise the activities of the Viceroy, was finally confirmed. The committee was to be chaired by the emperor himself, and to include as members the Ministers of Interior, Finance, Foreign Affairs, and War, with the Viceroy himself as a member *ex officio*. On October 10, in addition to the statutory members, State Secretary Bezobrazov was appointed to the committee.[43]

This all would seem to square with Plehve's account of his own motivations. The committee did seem to give the responsible ministers a measure of control over Far Eastern affairs. It also might be expected to "lower" Bezobrazov to a position of equality with them. However, one has merely to look at the set-up of the committee to realize that this was not necessarily the intention. Plehve was chosen as vice-chairman, a clear indication of his influence in the creation of the committee. Abaza, Bezobrazov's relative and colleague, was appointed to the post of business manager: as head of the committee secretariat, he would be entrusted with the day-to-day business of the committee. His assistant was to be N. G. Matiunin, another supporter of Bezobrazov and one of the originators of the Yalu concession scheme.[44] It hardly seems likely that anyone interested in diluting Bezobrazov's influence would have arranged to have the key positions go to his closest cohorts.

It is apparent, in fact, that Bezobrazov and Plehve had worked together to bring these results. Early in June, on the eve of Bezobrazov's departure for the Far East, they had met to discuss "the circumstances of the future Special Conference on Far Eastern Affairs." On August 2 they again got together to discuss the implementation of the new Viceroyalty decree. On October 14, two weeks after the establishment of the Far Eastern Committee, Bezobrazov wrote to Nicholas II suggesting that "State Secretary Plehve . . . be appointed Your Majesty's deputy in the committee. . . ."[45]

It is also clear that Plehve's relationship with the "Bezobrazov clique" continued long after the formation of the Far Eastern Committee. A. M. Abaza, as business manager of this committee, was in a position to have regular contact with Plehve and the tsar. Viceroy Alekseev, when he began to fear in late October that his power was waning, was reassured by Bezobrazov's representative that "he could count on the sincerest cooperation" of Plehve, Bezobrazov, and Abaza.

In December, Foreign Minister Lamsdorf informed War Minister Kuropatkin that he had "reason to believe" Plehve was still supporting the "Bezobrazovists." As late as spring and summer of 1904, Abaza and Bezobrazov still looked on Plehve as an ally and protector, and were confident of his ability to salvage their Far Eastern plans. Plehve, for his part, was not so trusting: letters from Bezobrazov to his colleagues were intercepted and copied by the Ministry of Interior.[46]

And yet, whether Plehve intended it or not, the influence of Bezobrazov does seem to have declined after Witte's dismissal. In mid-August, Kuropatkin opined to Nicholas II that the adventurer's "usefulness" was over and that the time had come to "throw him out the window." The tsar apparently agreed. Although Bezobrazov continued to write the emperor, he took part in no more policy conferences, and he played no role in the negotiations with Japan. By October, even Witte was able to tell Kuropatkin that the tsar, exasperated by Bezobrazov's boasts, was "finished" with the Far Eastern schemer. That same month Bezobrazov himself left Russia, not to return for over a year. Meanwhile the Yalu timber enterprise, deep in debt and deprived of extensive state support, had for all intents and purposes ceased to function. By November, in fact, Abaza was heard to complain that even the Committee on the Far East was being bypassed in the negotiations with Japan.[47]

Unfortunately, the decline of Bezobrazov did not produce a major shift in Russian policy. The crucial negotiations with Japan were complicated by the new viceroy, Admiral Alekseev, who had to be consulted on every proposal and counter-proposal. Since he was in Port Arthur, and the tsar was traveling in Europe, this caused innumerable delays and resulted in some confusion as to what Russian policy really was. Alekseev, once considered an opponent of Bezobrazov, pressed for a hard line, while at the same time preparing for an eventual Japanese attack. It began to look as if the Russians were stalling, hoping merely to prolong negotiations until their military position could be improved.[48]

In September, the final evacuation deadline passed, but Russian troops remained in Manchuria. In October came a ray of hope: the Japanese put forth new proposals that seemed to point toward a compromise. They suggested, in effect, that Japan would agree to stay out of Manchuria in return for a Russian promise to stay out of Korea. A neutral zone was also proposed on either side of the Manchurian–Korean border. But Alekseev, distrustful of Japanese intentions, decided it would be contrary to Russian interests to sanction in any way

the Japanese occupation of Korea. The Russian counterproposals, submitted late in November, attempted to place restrictions on Japanese
rights in Korea while ignoring the subject of Manchuria. This response
destroyed the last real hope for peace. [49]

Meanwhile, even Plehve had begun to have second thoughts
about his support for Bezobrazov. In a conversation with Kuropatkin
on November 7 he admitted his ignorance of Far Eastern matters, and
seemed genuinely regretful of his association with the adventurers. He
claimed that he had gotten involved in spring of that year when, prior
to the conference of March 26, the emperor had expressed to him "the
necessity for establishing a strong authority in the Far East." He asserted that Bezobrazov's influence resulted from the ministers' opposition to the tsar, and he blamed the whole mess on Witte who, in his
opinion, had tried to set up under his own control a separate state in
Manchuria. Finally, voicing his uncertainty about the direction of Far
Eastern affairs, he agreed to support the War Minister's proposal that
Russia restrict itself to northern Manchuria. [50]

This ended the split among the ministers over the Far East.
Plehve had been the only responsible official—besides, of course, the
emperor—to side with the adventurers. His support for the War Minister, combined with Nicholas's renewed spirit of caution, made it
possible for Kuropatkin and the "responsible ministers" to regain full
influence over Far Eastern policy. Kuropatkin's proposal, put forth in
two special memoranda to Nicholas II, called for Russia to return
southern Manchuria to the Chinese, and to sell them the South Manchuria Railway, while retaining for itself the northern part of the
province. It had been endorsed by Witte in October; now it also had
Plehve's sanction. In the meantime, the emperor himself had sent
Alekseev a sharp telegram instructing him to avoid war at all costs,
and had agreed to restrict the Viceroy's war authority. But Alekseev—
although he gave some thought to resigning—still held for a forward
policy, and the unfortunate November counterproposal to Japan reflected his position, not the ministers'. A conference held on December 15, attended by Nicholas II, Kuropatkin, Lamsdorf, and Abaza,
repudiated Alekseev's position and agreed to Japanese demands to rein-
troduce Manchuria into the negotiations. The conference supported
the notion, expressed by the emperor himself, that "War is out of the
question, and time is our best ally." [51] At the end, it seems, the views
of Kuropatkin carried more weight than those of Bezobrazov or Alekseev.

This change in the Russian position came too late, and was of too little substance, to do any good. The conference of December 15 drafted a new proposal, by which the Russians agreed to recognize the rights of Japan in Manchuria. At Kuropatkin's insistence, however, the November proposal's limitations on Japanese use of Korea were retained. The new proposal was presented on December 24. But the Japanese had finally become frustrated with the negotiations, and were beginning to prepare for war. Their response of January 1, 1904, was uncompromising and belligerent, rejecting any limits on their use of Korea and insisting on Russian recognition of the "territorial integrity of China in Manchuria." Another Russian conference on January 15, attended by much the same group as before, drafted a new and more conciliatory proposal. Before it arrived in Tokyo, however, the Japanese had broken off diplomatic relations, and their fleet was already at sail. On January 26, 1904, without a declaration of war, Japanese torpedo boats launched a devastating attack on the Russian naval squadron at Port Arthur.[52] The Russo-Japanese War had begun.

V. K. Plehve does not appear to have been deeply involved in Far Eastern matters in the months just prior to the war. The minister's actions centered around his new administrative and peasant reforms, introduced in fall of 1903, as well as a trip to Poland and a tour of Western Siberia. It is possible, in fact, that his decision to back Kuropatkin was influenced by a desire to gain support for his provincial peasant conferences, being discussed by the Committee of Ministers. In any event, he did not participate in any of the December and January conferences which determined the Russian policy toward Japan.[53]

His exact attitude toward the Far Eastern question during this period is unclear. In November he had expressed great concern over the direction of events in Manchuria, and had decried the fact that, with the ascendancy of Bezobrazov, "influence had fallen into bad hands. . . ." In December he concurred with Kuropatkin's assessment that a war, especially if Russia suffered early setbacks, would result in greater internal disturbance than before.[54] On the other hand, many in Saint Petersburg, including Lamsdorf and Witte, were convinced that Plehve was counting on war to relieve internal pressures. The Russian ambassador to Japan, in fact, would later recall that this view was "generally accredited among people who were in a position to know. . . ."[55] Furthermore, the outbreak of war found the Minister of Interior in a jovial mood, buoyed by the patriotic demonstrations and convinced that, for the moment at least, all would go well on the domestic scene. It was not long afterward that he allegedly made his oft-quoted remark about the benefits of a "little victorious war."[56]

In the actual conduct of the war Plehve did not, of course, play a major role. He most likely was instrumental in the selection of Kuropatkin as Commander in the Far East—possibly because he doubted Alekseev's abilities as a military leader. He also had a continuing interest in countering revolutionary propaganda among the troops. Later, when it was decided to liquidate the Yalu timber company, Abaza tried—apparently without success—to frustrate this effort by having Plehve placed in charge of the operation. The fact that the mail of both Abaza and Bezobrazov was intercepted and monitored by the police suggests that the minister had something less than complete confidence in his erstwhile comrades.[57]

His confidence in an ultimate Russian victory, however, was never shaken, despite continuing news of Russian reverses in the Far East. In arguing for the new resettlement law of June 6, 1904, he confidently spoke of the vast new territories which it would soon be necessary to colonize. He steadfastly refused to consider the possibility that tiny Japan could defeat the mammoth Russian Empire. "Which is greater," he was known to ask, "fifty million people, or one hundred and fifty million?"[58]

Plehve was dead before the real answer to his question became evident, and before the real consequences of Russia's Far Eastern policy appeared. The Russians, suffering from poor preparation and five-thousand-mile supply lines, were defeated on land and at sea by the smaller nation. And the disastrous war eventually led to an increase in anti-government activity, and finally to revolution.

It is impossible to deny that Plehve's role in the coming of the war was an important one, and that the minister must therefore bear his part of the responsibility. In supporting Bezobrazov against the other ministers, he had only added to the confusion surrounding Russia's policy. In insisting that "foreigners" be denied access to Manchuria —as well as by persecuting the nationality groups and the Jews—he had helped deprive Russia of the sympathy and support of foreign governments.[59] In abetting the establishment of the Far Eastern Viceroyalty, he had helped erect what proved to be an indomitable obstacle to successful negotiations with Japan.

It is possible, however, to overestimate his role. The war of 1904–05 had many causes, dating back to the middle 1890s and before. These involve the conflicting aspirations of two imperialist powers in the Far East, and the desire of both to take advantage of a weakened China. They involve Witte's enormous expenditure of Russian time and money in Manchuria. They involve the resentment caused when Japan was forced to give up the Liaotung peninsula. They involve the Russian seizure of Port Arthur, the occupation of Manchuria, and the abrogation of the evacuation agreement. They involve Nicholas II's inability to chart a steady, resolute course, and his participation in a speculative and annexationist venture in Korea. They involve Bezobrazov's irresponsible demagoguery and chauvinist scheming, Alekseev's uncompromising and belligerent attitude, and even Kuropatkin's insistence that Russia must renege on part of its withdrawal pact with China. They involve, for that matter, the expansionist aspirations of the Japanese, and the backing given them by Great Britain. No doubt Plehve's support for an aggressive and adventurist policy contributed to the process which led to war. But it is untenable to suggest that his desire to distract attention from Russia's internal situation was the cause of the Russo-Japanese War.

Plehve's influence, of course, was important, but it was probably not the determining factor. He had not participated in the original formulation of Far Eastern policy, having become minister only after the signing of the evacuation agreement. Even as minister he was not involved in all the critical decisions, taking part neither in the conferences which approved the postponement of the troop withdrawal nor in the sessions which formulated the final proposals to Japan. There is no reason to think that it was Plehve's support for Bezobrazov that induced Nicholas II to side with the adventurer: Nicholas had been involved in the concession scheme since 1898. It is problematical, in fact, whether Plehve could have changed the emperor's mind if he had opted to oppose Bezobrazov. For that matter, there is no real assurance that the war would have been avoided even had Nicholas ignored Bezobrazov and followed the advice of Kuropatkin and the "responsible" ministers.

Nevertheless, if Plehve was not the ultimate villain described by Witte, neither was he the well-intentioned bystander that Gurko portrayed. His action in supporting Bezobrazov, no matter what his reasons, was irresponsible and inexcusable. Plehve was a very influential man in Russia during 1903: his opinions, apparently, carried great weight with the emperor. He was, by his own admission, "completely ignorant" of Far Eastern affairs. He was also a professed advocate of caution and gradualism. Perhaps, had he chosen to oppose Bezobrazov and to lobby with the tsar for a more cautious policy, he may have been able to reduce the schemer's impact. Perhaps, had he recognized the real threat a war would pose to Russia's internal stability, he might even have counseled a policy of withdrawal from the Far East. But Plehve had neither the vision nor the political courage to opt for such a course. Instead, anxious to get the upper hand with Witte, and unwilling to displease the tsar, he had thrown in his lot with a group of adventurers who were pushing Russia toward war.

8

The Plehve System

ADMINISTRATIVE REFORM AND PLEHVE'S "CONSTITUTION"

The interval after the fall of Witte marked something of a transition period for Plehve and his policies. The preliminary and preparatory stage was over; the time for implementation had arrived. Witte's departure had removed the main obstacle to the formation of a "Plehve system," and had signaled the emperor's willingness to give full support to his Minister of Interior. Plehve's plans to reform the imperial bureaucracy, and to revise peasant legislation, were both completed by fall of 1903, but both faced further discussion in councils, committees, or conferences. His labor policies, too, were in transition: the demise of the *Zubatovshchina*, and the summer strikes of 1903, meant a new approach to the worker question would have to be found.

Administrative reorganization was, in many respects, the key to Plehve's program. Russia could not begin to solve its problems, he contended, as long as the "creative forces" were working against each other, and as long as the Russian state was characterized by disorder and disunity. System and order were thus prerequisites for reform: in order for Russia to change and to modernize, there must be some organization with the power and authority to coordinate policy, preserve order, and implement the needed reforms. Whatever the faults of the imperial bureaucracy, it was the only organization capable of playing such a role. But it could not do this alone; it needed support and assistance from all loyal Russians, both to provide it with information and to carry out its programs.[1]

Unfortunately, he wrote in a letter shortly after Witte's fall, the imperial bureaucracy did not have public support. Since the reforms of the 1860s, the leaders of the state had had their hands full merely trying to adjust to "newly-arising relationships" brought on by "the growth of social consciousness" and the "breakdown of the social-economic structure." This had caused many in society to doubt the competence of the autocratic system, and to yearn for "a governmental order based on political freedom." "They began to see in this a panacea for all social ills," he complained, "and the best means for insuring cooperation between the authorities and the people." In reality, however, this movement had only compounded the disunity, opening the way for all sorts of "political careerists" and "centrifugal tendencies."[2]

The task of the government, then, was to regain public support and to "take away the meaning of existence from oppositional elements by creative work for the common good." If only the intellectuals, the zemstvos, and the various nationalities could be made to put aside their demands for freedom and autonomy, and rally around the banner of the autocracy, Russia could face its problems in an organized, controlled, and systematic way. Only then would it be possible to effect a "gradual" and "organic" reorganization of Russian life, and to "improve economic conditions without bringing disorder to society. . . . Only our historic autocracy can accomplish such a multi-faceted program as has fallen to the lot of our current generation. In these times it alone can achieve a just correspondence between all wants and needs. Only under its standard can harmonious work thrive."[3]

Despite his break with Shipov, then, and despite the increasing hostility of the zemstvos, the minister pressed ahead with his plans to achieve greater cooperation between state and society. He aroused much comment in the summer of 1903 by announcing his intention to lower zemstvo electoral qualifications; that is, in a sense, to make these bodies more "democratic." In July he offered to create a conference of zemstvo-men within his ministry to consider the problem of local roads, and in August he agreed to let the zemstvo assemblies discuss a new draft statute concerning these roads. That same month he approved a new statute for the municipal government of Saint Petersburg which, among other things, increased the number of qualified electors while granting the city governor greater control over the town council.[4] The message in all this was clear: Plehve wished to show favor to the zemstvos and town councils, to cooperate with them, and to expedite their work, but in return they must submit even more fully to the authority of state officials.

Finally, early in October, the Ministry of Interior made public the details of a major administrative reform. This reform, referred to in certain circles as the "Plehve constitution," was a fundamental pillar of the Plehve system. It had been preceded by a careful study of earlier proposals for popular representation. First put forth in the wake of the February 26 manifesto, this project had been worked out quietly while more sensational events were attracting public attention.[5]

The plan consisted primarily of an internal reordering of the Ministry of Interior. The ministry's Economy Department was to be consolidated with several other departments into a Main Office for Local Affairs. Along with this there was to be established a "Council on Local Affairs," to be chaired by the minister himself. It would include as members all department heads of the ministry, representatives from several other state departments, and twelve to fifteen "local persons" appointed to three-year terms. The council was to discuss: 1) projected new laws or changes in existing laws relating to "local economy," 2) measures proposed by zemstvos and town councils, 3) methods of uniting the policies of various departments, and 4) the general state of local affairs. Its recommendations were to be added to the list of proposals introduced by the ministry into the higher legislative process.[6]

The formation of this council had several major objectives. The first was to streamline the bureaucracy and unify policy by bringing together in one place matters dealing with local affairs. The second was to provide for the participation of local figures on a permanent and regular basis. It was also hoped, of course, that this policy would satisfy the strivings of the "more loyal" zemstvo elements, and thus help bridge the gap between government and society.[7]

The provision for participation of "local persons," it goes without saying, aroused the greatest interest in society. Unfortunately, although the concept itself was applauded, the actual procedure fell far short of what most zemstvo leaders would have liked. In the category of "local persons," Plehve's "constitution" included, besides zemstvo board chairmen and marshals of the nobility, persons "closely acquainted with the needs and interests of local economy." The selection of these persons was to be reserved to the discretion of the Minister of Interior, and in no way dependent on the zemstvos themselves; and the persons selected were not to convey any notion of formal representation. The council itself was to be purely advisory, and was not to restrict the activity of the minister in any way. These provisions, of course, did not meet the zemstvo demand for full-scale representation.

And, by making it possible for the minister to choose only the most "reliable" local representatives, they would give the government an opportunity to "falsify" public opinion.[8]

Plehve's project fell short, not only of zemstvo aspirations, but even of the earlier "constitutions" advanced by his predecessors. The plans of Valuev and Loris-Melikov had both been based, to a certain extent, on elected zemstvo representation, and had both involved public review of legislation prepared for the State Council. Plehve's plan differed in that the local persons were to be selected by the Minister of Interior and participate in the consideration of policy within his ministry. Whereas the earlier projects provided for representation of local interests and opinions—albeit on a very restricted basis—Plehve's proposal provided only for the incorporation of local expertise.

Plehve's "constitution" demonstrates the careful and bureaucratic nature of his administrative approach. His plan provided an expanded role for members of society, but only under the closest control of the Minister of Interior, who was to decide which public figures would participate and what they would discuss. The plan studiously avoided any hint at popular representation, or at zemstvo participation, in the discussion of state affairs. It was, of course, not a "constitution" at all; nor was it in any real sense a compromise with society. Needless to say, it won the government little support in local self-government circles.[9]

The minister nonetheless went ahead with his plans, and submitted the reform for legislative approval. In defending it before the State Council, he pictured it mainly as a move to increase administrative efficiency. The goal of improving government–zemstvo cooperation, originally one of his major concerns, was not really emphasized. He even helped defeat an amendment which would have provided for election of the council's "local" members by the zemstvo and nobility assemblies. Plehve's supporters insisted they should be chosen by the Minister of Interior, arguing that their purpose was not to provide "representation" but to allow for input from "persons acquainted with local life." By a vote of fifty to twelve, the Plehve position was upheld. The project was confirmed into law by Nicholas II on March 22, 1904.[10]

The immediate effect of this reform, like that of so many other Plehve projects, was negligible. The Main Office for Local Affairs was indeed established, and Khar'kov governor S. N. Gerbel', a former zemstvo-man, was chosen to be its head. However, the Council on

Local Affairs—the only part of the reform with any interest for local society—came into existence on paper only. It was not actually constituted until 1908, long after Plehve had departed from the scene.[11]

The other aspects of Plehve's administrative reforms—those involving local coordination and bureaucratic decentralization—did not fare any better. The proposals to unify provincial administration, worked out by the Plehve commission on provincial reform, were never even introduced for legislative consideration. These proposals, it will be recalled, were to give the governors greater control over local self-government and the local agencies of various ministries. Conscious of probable opposition, both from the zemstvos and from other ministries, the Minister of Interior kept the work solely within his department, hoping to avoid any premature discussion. As it turned out, however, its details were published in the émigré press early in 1904, and the project itself was suspended with the outbreak of the Japanese war.[12]

Meanwhile, the efforts at decentralization did achieve some modest results. True to the tsar's instructions, the various ministries did eventually draw up lists of matters for transfer to the decision of local authorities. These were in due course submitted to the Platonov commission and debated by the State Council. A number of these issues were in fact transferred by an imperial decree published in early 1904. In truth, however, little real authority changed hands: the governors gained sway over such things as the unloading of livestock and the confirmation of veterinarians. Not surprisingly, the ministries proved reluctant to divest themselves of any substantial decision-making power.[13]

The net results of all Plehve's administrative reform efforts, then, were minimal. A number of items of secondary importance were indeed devolved upon local authorities thus, if nothing else, reducing somewhat the flow of paperwork between the capital and the provinces.[14] An internal reorganization of the ministry and its Economy Department was enacted, and provision was made, at least on paper, for the possibility of regular local input. But, for the most part, coordination of provincial government, decentralization of the bureaucracy, and greater cooperation between state and society remained unrealized goals.

THE REVISION OF PEASANT LEGISLATION

Early in November 1903, about a month after the unveiling of Plehve's "constitution," came the announcement that the Ministry of Interior had completed its preliminary work on revision of peasant legislation. This, of course, was only a first step: according to the procedures set by the Manifesto of February 26, the project must still be submitted to provincial conferences of "deserving persons who enjoy public confidence." To facilitate discussion, therefore, the ministry published a series of materials, including V. I. Gurko's summary *Sketch* and, a bit later, several volumes of the *Works of the Editing Commission on the Revision of Peasant Legislation*. Volume I contained the texts of six pieces of legislation, including proposed statutes on peasant administration, courts, and land usage. The remaining volumes (of which there eventually were to be five) were for supplementary and explanatory materials. [15]

Although Plehve himself had not written this project, he did bear a share of the responsibility for its tone and content. From the beginning, he had played a supervisory role, selecting the individuals responsible for the various sections, holding frequent discussions with Gurko, the principal author, and continuously pressing for its speedy conclusion. He had read, and made corrections on, the preliminary drafts, moderating their criticisms of the existing order and giving the work a slightly more cautious tone. He had chaired the meetings at which these drafts were discussed, bringing in experts with more traditional views to counterbalance the "liberalism" of some of the authors. Realizing the project would undergo many changes, he had not concerned himself with every word and phrase, but he clearly approved of its overall thrust and supported it strongly in reports to the tsar. [16]

On the surface, the new peasant project represented a strong reaffirmation of the tutelage approach. "The revision of peasant legislation," insisted the Editing Commission, "must be based on the fundamental principles of the statutes of February 19, 1861." These principles, it went on to assert, were "1. the separate status of the peasant estate . . . , 2. the inalienability of peasant allotment lands, and 3. the inviolability of the basic forms of peasant land tenure. . . ." Indeed, the commission argued at some length that it was the legitimate successor to the legislators of 1861, and that its proposed "reform" was only a "perfection" and "completion" of the emancipation act of 1861. [17]

Of the project's three main principles, the first two were upheld
in their entirety. The separateness of the peasant class was seen as
resulting from "organic peculiarities" in its life-style and outlook, aris-
ing from centuries of attachment to the land. The project claimed that
in order to protect this class, especially its "weaker elements," the
government had set up an entire program of tutelage, including an
inalienable land fund and special credits. Consequently, it had a duty
to treat the peasants differently from the other classes: ". . . [T]o
those who provide tutelage belongs the right to supervision over
those who enjoy the benefits of this tutelage." Following the circle
a little further, the project argued that inalienability of peasant
lands was a natural outgrowth of the separateness of the peasant
class. If this protection were to be taken away, the experience of
other countries had shown, the land would soon either be bought
up by a few wealthy persons, or fragmented into miniscule plots.
Either way, it would "deprive the masses of their means of existence."[18]

Only with regard to the third principle—the inviolability of the
forms of land tenure—was there any significant change. Even here the
project refused to mount an open attack against the commune; in fact,
it endorsed it as the best type of land tenure under current conditions.
Rather than assailing the form of land *ownership*, with all its political
and legal ramifications, the project addressed itself to the question of
actual land *use*. And here, indeed, it found serious defects: the periodic
repartitions, the open-field farming of disconnected strips, and the
parcelization of peasant plots. But it did not see these as resulting from
the commune as such; indeed, the latter two defects were common to
both communal and hereditary ownership. And even if a system of
separate, consolidated, individual plots might be superior, the peasants
in most areas had not yet attained the cultural level necessary for such
a change. Therefore, the project reasoned, there was no need to alter
the basic system.[19]

And yet, alongside this ratification of the *status quo*, the project
adopted several changes and shifts of emphasis which could only lead
to a weakening of the commune, and a gradual changeover to a different type of land tenure. These nuances, buried in many cases amidst
the tutelage-oriented rhetoric, were nevertheless the most interesting
and important facets of the program. The most significant new emphases were three: the glorification of the *khutor*, or individual consolidated farmstead, as the most efficient and practical form of
landownership, the shift from open hostility to benevolent neutrality

toward the wealthy peasant, and the desire to inculcate in the peasants respect for the principle of property.

The favorable attitude toward the *khutor* flowed from the commission's perception of the causes of peasant inefficiency: open-field strip-farming and parcelized plots. In order to correct these defects, it would be necessary "to abolish the strip-farming system and the parcelization of individual peasant plots, to consolidate the property of each household into one separate plot, in a word, to transfer to a *khutor* economy, in which every individual proprietor can be truly free in economic relations to manage all the land in his use, and to employ upon it those agricultural methods which most correspond to his level of cultural development."[20]

Although reasoning that a massive, immediate changeover to individual farmsteads was impossible, the project did include steps to make it easier for individual peasant families to consolidate their plots or leave the commune. According to existing law, any householder had the right, at the time of repartition, to demand the detachment of his land from the commune. In the new draft statute, this provision was strengthened by two new stipulations: the land thus allotted was to be consolidated in one place, and it was to be transferred to hereditary tenure. By another new provision, any time at least one-fifth of the members of a land society decided to separate from the commune and consolidate their lands, they could do so, regardless of the wishes of the remainder. Such action had formerly required a two-thirds majority, making it very unlikely. The project also foresaw the possibility of special loans, tax incentives, and technical assistance for those who would consolidate and improve their lands.[21]

This was as far as the commission was willing to go. The project did not ease the existing requirements for whole villages to transfer from communal to hereditary tenure, retaining the provision that a two-thirds majority must approve this change. In fact, consistent with its championing of the *khutor*, it made such a change more difficult by requiring that all plots first be consolidated into separate, individual farms. In addition, by permitting separation only during repartitions —which could occur only once every twelve years—the project insured against too rapid a changeover from communal tenure, and too great a disruption of village life.[22]

Nevertheless, the steps toward easing departure, timid as they were, marked a real switch in government attitude. No longer was the commune seen as an indigenous form of land tenure, peculiar to the

Russian peasantry, which was immutable and constant. Despite the supposed "inviolability" of the commune, the project clearly recognized it as a transitory form of land tenure, linked with a certain level of peasant development, that would eventually be replaced by a more advanced form.[23] It was this change in attitude, more than any specific measure, which constituted the real innovation in the commission's work.

The switch in attitude could also be seen in relation to the wealthy peasants. Previously they had been looked upon as "just about the worst and most harmful element of the population," and the fear of them had been one of the main rationales for the tutelage approach. The project itself pointed out that the "popular masses" included "numerous weaker elements, who do not have sufficient strength or durability to withstand the impact upon them of persons endowed with great energy, and sometimes great unscrupulosity. . . ." But it also recognized the "indisputable" fact that the peasants were no longer a homogeneous mass, and that the "former, evenhanded distribution of wealth" had given way to "more and more inequality of property."[24]

Not only did the project recognize this fact, it viewed it as natural and beneficial. To obstruct this development, it concluded, would be to go against the "basic principles of economic life," which dictate that "the *accumulation of wealth* represents one of the most powerful tools for the economic and cultural progress of the people." "It must not be forgotten," argued the commission, "that the prosperous peasants, being directly interested in the *preservation of the property principle,* are everywhere the sturdiest bulwarks of the existing order, which their property interests compel them to protect and defend."[25] This key insight, within a few short years, would become the guiding principle of Russian peasant policy, embodied in Stolypin's "wager on the strong."

The Plehve reform project, haunted by fears of a "rural proletariat," did not go quite so far as the Stolypin program later would. While rejecting measures impeding the wealthy peasants, the commission still tried to protect the poorer ones. While making it easier for industrious peasants to consolidate their plots, it strove to place limits on the amount of peasant land any one family could acquire. Both lower and upper limits were set: the former to protect against excessive parcelization, the latter to prevent land speculation and monopolization. Limits for each locale were to be set by the zemstvo assembly and approved by the Committee of Ministers: any peasant who acquired more than the maximum was to be required to sell the excess. [26] This would help insure availability and protect poorer peasants from losing their land.

The third attitudinal change, the desire to implant respect for property, proceeded from the same considerations as the new posture toward the rich peasants. No doubt the desire to forestall wanton destruction such as had occurred in Khar'kov and Poltava also played an important part. ". . . [I]t is exceedingly important," concluded the project,

> that we strive to inculcate among the peasants the notion of the *right of property* which, as is well-known, lies at the basis of any cultural life. True conservatism consists in the proper guarding and development of this principle. It must not be forgotten that, along with religion and the family, property is one of the fundamental pillars of the existing order, and that it is precisely the absence of the proper respect for property among our peasants which serves as one of the major causes for the lawlessness . . . which has been noted in our rural life.

To this end, and in hope of fostering better relations between peasants and rural nobility, the project included a special statute on delimitation of peasant allotments from the lands of their non-peasant neighbors. Moreover, it reasoned, as their "level of cultural development and economic security" increased, so too would their "respect for the rights of others. . . ." [27] Nevertheless, because of the commission's dedication to "inalienability," the peasants' own property rights remained very restricted. Even those with hereditary tenure were permitted neither to rent nor to sell their plots to persons outside the peasant class without permission from the authorities. Furthermore, the form of property advocated was not "private" property at all, but "family" property. In this respect the Plehve program differed markedly from the subsequent Stolypin reforms, which championed private, individual ownership. Although it favored preservation of the strict patriarchal family, the Plehve project made clear that the owner of the property was not the "head of the household," but the family as a whole. [28]

Historical interpretations of the Plehve–Gurko project have generally divided over whether it should be viewed as a consolidation and clarification of the tutelage approach of the 1880s and 1890s, or as a forerunner of the Stolypin reforms of 1906–10. [29] Actually, in a very real sense, it was both. On one hand, it sought to codify and systematize the various regulations on peasant life and land tenure, to eliminate inconsistencies, and to bring them all together in one place. On the other hand, it both envisioned and endorsed a fundamental transformation of Russian rural life, from open-field, communal strip-farming villages to individual, consolidated, hereditary family farms. It strove simultaneously to encourage respect for property, to facilitate consolidation of plots, and to support the strong and innovative, while preserving the communal order, protecting the weaker elements, and preventing the widespread separation of peasants from the land. The more advanced peasants would be permitted and encouraged to unite, combine, and improve their lands, thus setting an example for their less industrious fellows. This would then insure the sort of gradual and organic improvement that Plehve so much preferred.

The proposed reform thus mirrored the personality and outlook of the Minister of Interior: it was perceptive enough to see that change was necessary and desirable, but it insisted that this change be gradual and directed from above. The government's role was not to cause, compel, or precipitate change, as the reformers of the 1860s—and Sergei Witte—had tried to do. Nor was it to prevent change and preserve the *status quo*, as the counter-reformers of the 1880s had done. The role of the government was to facilitate change, to supervise change, and above all to control change. This, at least, was the perception of V. K. Plehve.[30]

On the whole, it is true, the general tenor of the reform was supportive of the tutelage approach. Yet even here there was a subtle, yet very informative, shift. Traditionally tutelage had been provided by the local nobles, first as landlords and then, after the emancipation, as leaders of local affairs, members of local self-government, and eventually as land captains. But the new peasant project provided little role for the nobility: the government itself was to supervise, protect, and direct the peasant class.[31]

The Plehve–Gurko project was also, in many ways, a forerunner of the Stolypin reforms. For one thing, many of the same persons who worked on the 1903 peasant project would also be involved in preparing the later reforms. For another thing, the project's efforts to abolish strip-farming, to facilitate consolidation of plots, to prevent frequent repartitions, and to strike a more favorable posture toward the wealthy peasants, all pointed the way toward Stolypin's legislation. In the words of one close observer, "the project of the Stishinski Commission already included all the elements of the decree of November 9, 1906."

More important, perhaps, was the project's tacit admission that the commune eventually must go. Gurko, in fact, would later claim that the provisions on land tenure were intended as a "modest but decisive attack upon the commune," and that he and his colleagues had resorted to "camouflaging" the measure. It was their hope that when the project was examined in the provincial conferences, it would be replaced with "a more complete and speedy abolition of the commune."[32]

THE FURTHER COURSE OF PEASANT REFORM

Gurko's high hopes for the provincial conferences were not widely shared. Many persons, within the government and without, were dissatisfied with the reform project; some even feared it tended to "re-enserf" the peasants. Others objected to the conferences themselves, fearing that Plehve's governors would most certainly control things, and that input from other branches of government—including the Special Conference on Agricultural Industry—would largely be ignored. Therefore, when the plan to set up these conferences came before the Committee of Ministers, it encountered heavy opposition.[33]

The opposition was spearheaded by a familiar figure. The new Chairman of the Committee of Ministers, S. Iu. Witte, suddenly had an opportunity to test his diminished influence, and to try once again to obstruct his rival's plans. He immediately rose to the challenge. In response to the Minister of Interior's proposal, submitted on October 27, 1903, he had the committee's chancery draw up a "comparison" of the new peasant project with other legislation. The comparison, supposedly intended to facilitate discussion, was in fact an indirect attack on the Editing Commission's work, placing it all in an unfavorable light. In the actual debate, however, Witte ignored the provisions of the project, and instead sought to categorize it as "preliminary" material, requiring much further discussion and development. Any peasant legislation, he insisted, must take into account the work of the local committees on agricultural industry, which had only recently been compiled and published. Therefore, in his view, the new draft should be considered "either in a special high interdepartmental conference, or . . . at least in the departments most closely interested."[34]

Witte's efforts, however, were doomed to failure. Plehve himself admitted that the project was preliminary, and could indeed benefit from changes, but claimed that provincial conferences were the place to accomplish this. The materials of the local committees, he contended, were too general to be applied directly to the specific requirements of peasant legislation. Others made an even more telling argument: it would be "inexpedient," and even impertinent, to revise the policy so clearly set forth by the tsar himself in the Manifesto of February 26.[35] At any rate, with the emperor's support, Plehve could hardly lose.

On January 8, 1904, was published an imperial decree establishing "Conferences on the Revision of Peasant Legislation" in nearly every province. It was a decisive victory for the Minister of Interior. The principles of the Editing Commission, including the "preservation of the peasant class structure" and the "inalienability of allotment lands," were set down as guidelines. The conferences were to be chaired by the governor, and to include as members the provincial marshal of the nobility, the president of the circuit court, the heads of the various provincial administrations, the chairman of the provincial zemstvo board, representatives from the nobility and zemstvos, and at least four land captains. In addition, "persons who could contribute to the success of the conference by dint of their knowledge and experience" were to be invited by the governors. The order of work, regulation, and management was to be defined by special instructions from the Minister of Interior.[36]

The provisions of the decree showed Plehve's determination to prevent a recurrence of the problems with the agricultural committees. No county conferences, where outspoken criticism of the government might surface, were established. Control of the provincial conferences was placed firmly in the hands of the governors, who were given almost total discretion over which local persons would take part. The decree also marked the clear defeat of Witte's peasant policies. No longer could there be much doubt that the peasant reform was to be based on Plehve's modified tutelage approach, rather than on the self-reliance program favored by Witte, the Special Conference, and by local society in general. Apparently the work of the six hundred local committees, carried out, collected, and compiled at great effort and expense to the government, was to be ignored.

As if the decree of January 8, 1904, were not enough to insure "reliability," the Minister of Interior soon summoned to Saint Petersburg about half the governors who would serve as chairmen. The ostensible purpose was to "discuss" the upcoming conferences, but most of those summoned were ill-prepared to do so. Instead, the governors were treated to "explanatory" speeches from Plehve, Stishinskii, and Gurko, and instructed to use great care in selecting the members and ascertaining their attitudes. Items for discussion were carefully spelled out, with the *Works of the Editing Commission* serving as a guideline. The second half of the governors, scheduled to arrive in early February, never actually came: the war with Japan intervened and took precedence.[37]

The project, however, was by no means abandoned. On February 6, 1904, less than two weeks after the start of the war, the ministry issued a special instruction further defining the operations of the conferences. No "outsiders" would be allowed to participate in the conferences or their committees. No publication of any conference material in the press was to be permitted without prior consent of the governor. Although individual peasants might be invited to attend, the peasantry as such, despite the fact that it was the focus of the proposed legislation, was excluded from participation.[38]

Plehve's provincial conferences, as it turned out, did not actually begin to meet until spring and summer of 1904. The outbreak of war with Japan in January temporarily distracted public attention from the peasant question. With the country at war, it seems, the peasants and their problems had suddenly become a matter of secondary importance. It took prodding from Plehve just to get the sessions underway. Even when they did meet, the conferences did not generate the kind of excitement and controversy the local agriculture committees had: partly because of the war, of course, and partly because of their "bureaucratic" nature. Almost half of the members were government officials, another third came from assemblies of the nobility, and fewer than one-fifth of them were involved in zemstvos or town councils.[39]

Most of the conferences met in May, June, or July of 1904, discussed their general views, set up committees to deal with various topics, and resumed work in the fall. Surprisingly, perhaps, their views coincided largely with those of Witte's local committees on several important issues. Thirty-five of the forty-three conferences, for example, wished to encourage peasants to consolidate their plots into individual farmsteads, and only three opposed this. On the question of whether to make it easier to switch from communal to hereditary ownership, thirty-three expressed themselves in favor, and only nine were against. In other words, the "individualist" approach prevailed even in these "bureaucratic" conferences. By the time their work was finished, however, early in 1905, the political situation had changed a great deal, and Plehve was long in his grave. Not until 1906 were the results even compiled, and then not in their entirety.[40]

Meanwhile, however, Plehve's ministry did manage to carry through one major piece of peasant legislation: a new law concerning resettlement. Historically, large-scale relocation of peasants had been opposed by the Ministry of Interior, which feared that too much mobility might hamper law enforcement and give rise to social unrest. Plehve, however, during his 1902 trip to Khar'kov and Poltava, had begun to look on resettlement as a possible means of social control. One of the local governors, apparently, persuaded him that extensive migration was necessary to relieve the crowded conditions in the Center. Plehve may also have been influenced by A. V. Krivoshein, his talented and ambitious new Resettlement Director, and his collaborator in formulating a new resettlement policy.[41]

At any rate, in autumn of 1902, the Ministry of Interior had begun taking steps to revise its resettlement policy. In October, a circular was sent to the governors requesting their recommendations on this subject. By November, Plehve himself was openly touting resettlement as a solution to the "land-shortage" question. In December, during his centennial speech to the ministry, he went so far as to praise the Siberian Railway Committee for its work in directing peasant migration.[42] On the surface, at least, this brought him into accord with Witte, the author of the railway project, and a longtime advocate of extensive peasant resettlement.

Their agreement, however, was only superficial. Witte, interested in colonization and economic growth, had encouraged and assisted resettlement, but had not tried to control *who* should migrate, or *where* they should migrate from. Plehve, concerned with internal order, proposed to give the government a more active role. Henceforth, he insisted, the state should control the entire process: it should decide which peasants should migrate, where they should migrate from, and where they should settle. In so doing, the government could establish, within each province, the pattern and mix of population most suitable to its political interests, and to the interests of social stability. It could encourage the colonization of "insecure" districts, such as the Caucasus and the Far East, while relieving the "land-shortage" in the Center.[43]

During the course of 1903, then, resettlement policy—like so many other issues—became a hostage to the Witte–Plehve rivalry. On one score, Witte had emerged victorious: he had managed to frustrate Plehve's efforts to have relocation of poorer peasants assisted by the Peasant Bank. In the long run, however, Plehve was more successful. Early in the year, at the tsar's request, the Siberian Railway

Committee had begun to examine proposals for transferring peasants from the crowded Center to outlying regions. Seizing the opportunity, Plehve had his ministry compile several proposals, which he submitted in June of 1903. The result was a Special Conference on Resettlement, chaired by State Secretary A. N. Kulomzin, and including the Ministers of Finance, Agriculture, and Interior.[44]

The Kulomzin Conference did not actually meet until January 30, 1904—much to Plehve's advantage. By that time Witte had been dismissed and his successor, Pleske, was terminally ill: the Ministry of Finance was in no position to challenge anything. Meanwhile, Plehve and Krivoshein had had time to make a tour of resettlement areas in western Siberia, and their colleagues had had time to draft legislative proposals for submission to the conference. These proposals, in turn, served as a basis for the discussion, and to a large extent determined its outcome. Despite subsequent efforts to amend them by V. N. Kokovtsov, the new Minister of Finance, Plehve's project prevailed. It was passed by the State Council, with several revisions, in May, and confirmed into law by Nicholas II on June 6, 1904.[45]

The Resettlement Law of June 6, 1904, established the principle of government direction of the resettlement process. Henceforth, government assistance was to be provided only to settlers who were leaving an area felt by the government to be overcrowded, or who were moving to an area the government wished to colonize. Such areas were to be determined by agreement among the Ministers of Interior, Finance, and Agriculture. It was further laid down that these "privileged" settlers would be compensated for the land they left behind, either by the village community or by the individual acquiring the land. They were also to be given special privileges, including reduced railway rates, a five year exemption from various forms of taxation, and a three year exemption from military service for males over eighteen. No longer would resettlement be available only to the wealthier peasant: now, even the poor could move, as long as their colonization patterns fit the political needs of the state.[46]

The resettlement law, like the peasant reform project, revealed some changes in attitude. Most obviously, the age-old notion that order was best preserved by preventing peasant movement had been discarded. Less obviously, the old disdain for prosperous peasants had also been moderated, at least by implication. The law intended to restore prosperity in the Center by encouraging the *poor* to move *away*, thus relying for stability on the wealthier and sturdier elements. The law also signaled a shift in attitude toward the commune. In one sense, it provided a means to relieve "land-shortage" without sacrificing the communal structure. On the other hand, by providing assistance, loans, and privileges to emigrating peasants, it encouraged them, in effect, to leave their communes. Furthermore, it removed a major obstacle to their departure by providing that "privileged" resettlers must be compensated by the commune for the land they left behind. In their new locations, settlers would have the right to determine their form of land tenure—communal or hereditary—by a simple majority vote.[47]

Despite its nuances, however, the law's main objective was control. By facilitating the emigration of poorer peasants from areas of "land-shortage," it was designed to stabilize these areas. By helping Russian peasants resettle in areas dominated by other nationalities, it intended to increase the "reliability" of these regions. Above all, by selective granting of privileges and assistance, it meant to place the resettlement process under the full supervision of the government.

The resettlement law was the only part of Plehve's peasant program actually enacted into law. The work of the Editing Commission, although it may have provided something of a basis for later legislation, suffered much the same fate as the work of Witte's local committees. The new political orientation following Plehve's death in 1904, the steady stream of Russian reverses in the Far East, and finally the revolutionary tide of 1905, all combined to push Plehve's peasant project far into the background. When it re-emerged, the political situation had changed, and so had the nature of peasant reform. Even the resettlement law, when finally implemented, would have a much different impact than originally intended.[48]

THE SEARCH FOR A LABOR POLICY

Along with administrative reorganization, and attempts at peasant reform, the last part of Plehve's ministry also witnessed a search for an effective labor policy. On one hand, it was a time of opportunity: with Witte out of the way, the Minister of Interior was in a better position to press for full control over worker affairs. Without this, he reasoned, labor reform would be impossible.[49] On the other hand, it was a period of adjustment: with Zubatov gone and his experiment discredited, the future course of worker–state relations was very much in doubt.

After Witte's dismissal, Plehve wasted little time in seeking to extend his powers. One day, toward fall of 1903, he appeared at the apartment of his old collaborator, labor expert Ivan Ianzhul, and proceeded to put forth a plan that he had developed. "I am considering a broad reorganization of my department . . . ," he explained. "Among other things . . . all information and legislation concerning the workers is to be concentrated in one department of the Ministry of Interior. From the Ministry of Finance, and from other departments, everything relating to the workers must be transferred to a special section, or Department of Labor."

Realizing that such a reform would meet with sharp opposition, Plehve had decided to introduce it somewhat surreptitiously. "Of course it is necessary to do everything gradually, so that no one becomes frightened," he told Ianzhul, "therefore I propose to begin the reorganization with the Central Statistics Committee, which must gradually be converted into a *central department* of labor. In the meantime, however, it will not be called this, but it must go by its old name. Little by little, I think, *it is possible to broaden the rights of the workers and to satisfy many of their demands.*" The role of the director of this department would be crucial, he felt, and he wanted the best possible man. Would not Ianzhul accept the directorship of the labor department, for the time being to remain known as the Central Statistics Committee?[50]

Unfortunately, perhaps, the minister's plans were never to be fulfilled. Ianzhul ultimately accepted the proposal, but only after revealing that he was suspected of "conspiratorial activity" by Grand Duke Sergei. As it turned out, Plehve never responded to his friend's acceptance. To a subsequent inquiring letter from Ianzhul, the minister replied that, against his wishes, the matter had taken a different turn, and the offer would have to be rescinded.[51]

Why did Plehve abandon his scheme? Ianzhul's liberal friends speculated that, having learned that the professor was under suspicion, the minister quickly abandoned the plan rather than risk his own position. Ianzhul himself noted that Plehve appeared agitated when told of the unfavorable report. But the minister had been considering this appointment for quite some time—it is unlikely that he had been completely unaware of his old friend's "indiscretions."[52]

There was another obstacle which may have had a greater impact: the continued opposition of the Ministry of Finance. Plehve knew that Witte's successor, E. D. Pleske, was unlikely to cooperate with him, but Pleske was a dying man. The Minister of Interior need only bide his time, and work to insure that the next Finance Minister would be more to his liking. By February 1904 his patience had borne fruit: V. N. Kokovtsov, Plehve's friend and successor as Imperial Secretary, was named Minister of Finance. There was little doubt that Plehve had a hand in this appointment: he had visited the emperor the day before, and he had even phoned Kokovtsov to inform him in advance. However, when he broached to Kokovtsov the idea of transferring the factory inspectorate, the new Finance Minister objected in the strongest terms. Such a move, he felt, would turn the inspectorate into a tool of the police, and "would have a disastrous effect on our entire industry." Even when informed that Nicholas II had provisionally approved the plan, Kokovtsov vowed to oppose it. "I had no idea," responded Plehve, "that after helping you to rise to the head of the finance administration I should be given proof of your intractability . . . and should not find in you the support I was entitled to count on."[53]

The conversation destroyed both the Kokovtsov–Plehve friendship and the prospects of Plehve's labor program. The Minister of Finance, true to his word, relayed his objections to the tsar and Plehve, deprived of the support of his colleague, decided not to pursue the plan any further. The war, by this time, had distracted attention away from domestic reforms. For some time the angry Plehve pointedly ignored Kokovtsov, and the two remained at odds until July of 1904. Only then did the Minister of Interior apologize, and ask that their former friendly relations be restored.[54] In spite of his success at removing Witte, therefore, Plehve never did manage to gain full control over worker affairs. The only concrete result of his efforts was the statistical work of A. V. Pogozhev, and even that was not completed by the time of Plehve's death.

The other side of Plehve's labor policy, the Zubatovshchina, had disintegrated with the general strikes of the summer of 1903. The demise of the Independents marked the end of the experiment in Odessa, Vilnius, and Minsk, and the fall of Zubatov led Trepov to return to proven methods of police repression in dealing with Moscow strikers. Nevertheless, the remnant of the Moscow worker organization continued to function, albeit in a restricted fashion, for several more years.[55] Despite his attainment of preeminence among the ministers, Plehve was still unwilling to risk a clash with Moscow governor-general Grand Duke Sergei.

Only in Saint Petersburg did the movement begun by Zubatov actually grow and expand. At first, things had looked bleak: Zubatov's

departure in August of 1903 left the movement leaderless and disorga-
nized. The "Saint Petersburg Society of Workers in Mechanical Production," crippled by rumors of police collaboration and widespread
worker distrust, had never really gotten off the ground. Plehve had
postponed his approval of the society's by-laws, and as a result attempts to set up a mutual aid fund and a lecture series had come to
naught. Meanwhile, however, one of Zubatov's associates had decided
to take the lead in establishing a new worker group. Father G. A.
Gapon, an Orthodox priest who had come to view the factory workers
as his own special ministry, was fairly well known among the workers
of the capital. Despite his distrust of Zubatov, he had associated himself with the latter's movement earlier in 1903 in hopes of furthering
the development of worker organizations. He had met often with the
Head of the Special Section, and he had even received some financial
support from him. In August of 1903, shortly before Zubatov's dismissal, Gapon had rented a hall and begun to hold meetings of factory
laborers. [56]

By November Gapon and his workers were able to present the
city-governor with the draft by-laws of a proposed "Assembly of Russian Factory-Plant Workers of the City of Saint Petersburg." Its stated
aims were to provide the workers with "rational and sober" ways to
spend their off-hours, to increase their "enlightenment," and to improve their living and working conditions. To accomplish these goals,
the Assembly proposed to hold weekly meetings, and to establish
lectures and discussions, concerts and reading rooms, mutual aid
funds, consumer shops, and even burial societies. In February 1904 the
new city-governor, impressed by the proposal, presented to the Minister of Interior arguments in favor of confirming the assembly. [57]

In spite of his disenchantment with the *Zubatovshchina*, Plehve
responded favorably. Perhaps he drew a distinction between the essentially conservative and Orthodox Moscow and Saint Petersburg movements, which might still be of value, and the discredited Jewish
Independent movement of Minsk, Vilnius, and Odessa. Perhaps the
increased activity of the Social Democrats in the capitals convinced
him of the continuing need to attract the workers away from the
Marxists, or at least to divide the labor movement. Perhaps, with
Zubatov and Witte both out of the picture, he no longer feared that
the societies might get out of control, or that his sponsorship of them
might be used against him. At any rate, in January of 1904 he finally
gave his long-delayed confirmation to the various mutual assistance
associations of Moscow workers. On February 15, in a move which

was to have major consequences, he approved the statutes of Gapon's "Assembly of Factory-Plant Workers of the City of Saint Petersburg."[58]

The success of Gapon's "Assembly" was immediate and significant. The opening meeting was held in April, and the first local branch of the assembly began to operate in May. Over the course of 1904 eleven branches were set up throughout Saint Petersburg, making Gapon and his workers an important political and social force in the capital. City-governor Fullon continued to praise the society to Plehve as a "firm bulwark" against the spread of socialism. A report of the Saint Petersburg Okhrana also described the advantages of such a society, calling it an "excellent influence" upon the workers. In May of 1904, on the occasion of the official opening of the assembly's first branch, Plehve even presented the emperor with an expression of "most humble feelings of love and devotion" from the Gapon-led workers.[59]

By July, however, Plehve had reason to doubt the wisdom of supporting Gapon. Anxious to expand his organization to other cities, the intrepid priest had traveled to Moscow to explore the possibilities of uniting with that city's worker council. Arriving on June 19, 1904, he had begun to attend worker meetings without first receiving permission from the authorities. He criticized the Moscow societies for their dependence on the authorities, and for their failure to attract widespread support. To improve their operations, he suggested that they reorganize along the more independent and more effective lines of his "Saint Petersburg Assembly." He also proposed that they send a liaison man to Saint Petersburg, in order to increase communication and cooperation between the worker groups in the two cities.[60]

Gapon's activities, meanwhile, had been closely observed by the Moscow police and the office of the governor-general. The latter, on July 6, 1904, sent a terse letter to the Minister of Interior describing and criticizing the priest's activities. Plehve in turn ordered city-governor Fullon to recall Gapon to Saint Petersburg and to warn the priest that, "in case of further agitation by him among the workers," he would be subjected to administrative exile. This turn of events had the combined effect of terminating Gapon's visit to Moscow, and of convincing the minister once again of the dangers inherent in government-sponsored worker societies. A few days later, however, Plehve himself was gone, and the Gapon worker organization continued to function and spread throughout Saint Petersburg.[61]

Plehve's inability to implement his own worker program, and his continued support of the discredited *Zubatovshchina*, are symptomatic of the real weakness of his position during the last part of his administration. His defeat of Witte and attainment of imperial favor had made him, in the eyes of many contemporaries, an "all-powerful dictator."[62] In reality, though, he was nothing of the sort. Even within the government he was less than almighty, as Kokovtsov's successful opposition had demonstrated. And the government itself was losing control over the course of events. Plehve had initiated a number of reforms, but he had either been unable to carry them through, or they had failed to accomplish their objectives. In this last period, then, he seems to have been grasping at straws, hoping to find some combination that would reverse the anti-government trend. He did not necessarily confirm the Gapon assembly because he favored its approach: his dismissal of Zubatov suggests that this was probably not the case. He approved it, evidently, because he had been unable to carry out any worker program of his own.

UNITY, ORDER, AND REFORM

For all Plehve's efforts, then, and for all his determination, he accomplished relatively little in terms of administrative, peasant, or worker reform. Viewed in this context, no "Plehve system" ever really came into effect. Enough was accomplished, however, to provide a glimpse of what the Russia of Plehve might ultimately have looked like.

It would perhaps be going too far to impute to Plehve a grand design, or a coherent vision of Russia's future. He was, after all, a practical politician rather than a revolutionary, a repairman rather than an architect. His job was to preserve and perfect the system, not to tear it down; to improve the existing order, not to erect a new one. Still, as he was wont to admit, the system was functioning poorly: change and adaptation were needed if the autocratic order was to survive.[63]

Plehve's passions, as an administrator, were for unity and order. In his view, the government could hardly function well when each ministry went in its own direction, when each local official answered to a different department, when the zemstvos acted independently of the government. Unity, he felt, must somehow be imposed. Emperor and subject, nobleman and peasant, industrialist and worker, policeman and factory inspector, Ministry of Finance and Ministry of Interior, governor and zemstvo—all must work together, must function as a team. Although they might differ in their short-term needs, they must subordinate these to the overriding, long-term goals of the Russian government.

The government envisioned by Plehve would be a strong, unified, and authoritarian one, based on an effective, streamlined bureaucracy which controlled nearly every aspect of people's lives. Gone would be the divisions and conflicts between the agencies of one ministry and those of another, between the central government and its local organs, between the autocracy and the zemstvos. The key official in the Plehve system, next to the emperor himself, would be the Minister of Interior, a sort of superminister who would possess real power to get things done and to unify policy. He would have general supervisory authority over almost all local officials, from policemen to zemstvo board chairmen to factory inspectors. Even the other ministers, although autonomous within their departments, would be expected to follow his lead.[64]

On the provincial level, the governors would act as the unifying force, coordinating all state authority within their provinces. Educators and officials, tax inspectors and factory inspectors, gendarmes and policemen all would come under their sway. The zemstvos and town councils would play an expanded role, not as autonomous, self-governing institutions, but as local branches of the state administration. Within their provinces, they would be supervised and coordinated by the governors, like all other local institutions. On the interprovincial level, supervision and coordination would be provided by the Ministry of Interior, which would receive information on local conditions through the governors, the police and local officials, and the Council on Local Affairs.

Like a good parent, however, the government would also be flexible, responsive to growth and change, and sensitive to the needs of its "children." Nationality groups, once they subordinated themselves to the need for imperial unity, could retain some of their customs and conventions. Factory workers, if they refrained from strikes and violence, would be protected and aided by a benevolent state. Peasants, as they sought to escape from poverty, would be given loans, assistance, and protection. Nobles, provided they were loyal and served the government, would retain their privileged status. Zemstvos, once they abandoned their dreams of independence, would be given greater responsibility. Modernization and improvement would be facilitated and encouraged, but gradual transformation would preclude disruptive change.

On the whole, Plehve's state-oriented system reflected the tradition of the Ministry of Interior, over which he presided, and of which he was a product. His vision of a strong and orderly Russia, its people united in common purpose by a benevolent and authoritative bureaucracy, was consistent with the legacies of Valuev, Loris-Melikov, and especially Tolstoi. It differed mainly in that Plehve went even further than any of his predecessors in seeking to extend bureaucratic control. His administrative, labor, police, peasant, and nationalities policies all sought in some way to expand the powers of the Ministry of Interior or extend bureaucratic operations on the provincial and local levels. Those who hoped for greater autonomy—for the workers, the peasants, the zemstvos, the nationalities, or even the landed nobility—would find little to applaud in the system of Plehve.

9

Repression Versus Reform

PLEHVE'S REPRESSIVE POLICIES

The last part of Plehve's administration, from the end of 1903 to July of 1904, was one of irony and contradiction. On one hand, the former Warsaw schoolboy and obscure assistant procurator had reached the pinnacle of success: he was unquestionably the most powerful minister in Russia. He had prevailed in a bitter struggle against Russia's ablest statesman, and he was now engaged in carrying out his own program to save the Russian autocracy. On the other hand, in a very real sense, his policies had already failed. For, while ingratiating himself with the emperor, he had aroused the bitter wrath of every sector of Russian society, not to mention the undying hatred of the Finns, the Armenians, and the Jews. His worker policy had erupted in disaster during the summer months of 1903, and revolutionary propaganda was making serious inroads among the factory population. The situation was yet worsened by the war which, after the first flush of patriotic fervor, brought a succession of defeats and a growing hostility toward the government. The solidifying of his position should have allowed Plehve to begin the orderly implementation of his reforms. Instead it was followed by an increase in confrontation between the monarchy and its subjects, and by an ever-widening application of the tactics of repression.

Repression, in fact, was the most visible feature of Plehve's administration. From the very beginning, having been called to his post to restore order and combat sedition, he had used force, and the threat of force, to silence criticism and suppress discontent. This approach, apparent from his handling of the Khar'kov-Poltava disorders, had been revealed further in his treatment of the statisticians, the participants of the May 1902 zemstvo conference, and the local agricultural committees. It had also manifested itself in the frequent use of troops and firepower to put down worker disorders, in his support for the russification excesses of Bobrikov in Finland and Golitsyn in the Caucasus, and, in a different sense, in his tolerant attitude toward the perpetrators of anti-Semitic outrages.

More than this, repression had underlain many of the day-to-day operations of his ministry. Under Plehve, for example, the laws on censorship were applied systematically and severely. Any publication —liberal or conservative—which dared to criticize any state official or policy, or which presumed to discuss sensitive topics, could expect warning, censure, or suspension. In July of 1902 a confidential circular was sent to "the editors of uncensored periodical publications" listing nineteen subject areas they were prohibited from discussing. These included government documents, military affairs, political crimes and criminals, student or worker disorders, and a number of other categories. Rarely a week passed in which there did not appear an "Order of the Minister of Interior" temporarily prohibiting non-subscription sale of one periodical, or warning and fining the editors of another. Even such loyal monarchists as A. A. Stolypin and A. S. Suvorin, publishers of the two major Saint Petersburg dailies, were not immune from intimidation.[1]

In addition, Plehve made personal threats to such opposition publicists as liberal scholar P. N. Miliukov, populist-socialist writer N. K. Mikhailovskii, and progressive legal publisher I. V. Gessen. Miliukov was called in from jail for an amicable chat with the minister, during which Plehve astonished his guest by offering him the post of Minister of Education. The scholar refused, and was sent back to prison, but a week later he was released by the minister with the following words: "I have drawn the conclusion from our conversation that you shall not make peace with us. But at least do not come out into open battle against us. If you do, we will smash you." Similar sentiments were expressed by the minister to Gessen, whose journal, *Law (Pravo)*, was seen by Plehve as "properly speaking, a branch of [the illegal émigré journal] *Liberation*." To Gessen's objections that there was no foundation for such a charge, the minister replied: "If I had a foundation, we would not be talking in this room, but you would be sitting in the defendant's bench."[2]

In his conversation with Mikhailovskii, in December of 1902, the minister was even more explicit. "I know as well as you do," he told the famous populist, "that a writer is capable, by means of allusions, circumlocutions and omissions, of dealing with this subject, and this subject is revolution. . . . In general the students, the young people, the workers and the peasants—they are all cannon fodder. The press is the moving force. It must pay for all the disorders, and it will pay; I just want to warn you about it in advance." Thus did Plehve justify his persecution of the press: it was futile for him to try to combat anti-government activity by naive youths and ignorant peasants and workers, while the real villains, the publicists, were free to continue their work. Something had to be done to shut off the flow of ideas and theories. "As long as you are only a writer I will not touch you," he warned Mikhailovskii, "but if you should start some sort of disorder I will not stop short of banishments, and I will not be detained by their number."[3]

More repressive even than the censorship, perhaps, was the surveillance of persons "with views not corresponding to those of the government." This group, which included some of the empire's most eminent public men, was kept under constant watch. Information on their activities and ideas was collected systematically by the police, compiled and coordinated by the Minister's Chancery, and presented in the form of special reports to the tsar. Most of this information came from simple observation, but some of it was obtained through the opening, reading, and recopying of private mail. This practice, known as "perlustration," was of course concealed by the government, but the fact that it was done was fairly common knowledge. Plehve privately justified it as necessary for the good of the state, objecting only that it had been conducted so haphazardly that it revealed almost nothing. He claimed, in fact, that it was actually quite legal: it was permitted by a secret imperial decree which had been given to D. A. Tolstoi and each succeeding Minister of Interior. As minister, Plehve expanded and perfected the perlustration apparatus, placed it under the supervision of his own personal bodyguard, and used it to gather information on anyone who might be in a position to frustrate his plans.[4]

Plehve's relations with society, meanwhile, continued to deteriorate. The minister was not oblivious to the need for public support: ". . . every government," he had written, "and even more so the individuals who make it up, require for their success public approval and cooperation. . . ." But the government could only win this support by pursuing sound policies based on Russia's real needs. Ironically, however, the bureaucracy did not have the knowledge and resources to initiate and implement such policies on its own.[5] Without public assistance, in other words, it could not win public support. But many members of society, despite Plehve's efforts to accommodate, had continued to criticize, oppose, and even plot against the government. The more outspoken their criticism, the more repressive the minister became, and the more he repressed them, the more he was opposed by society as a whole.

Realizing the irony of his position, the minister did strive to retain the backing of some more conservative groups. In the capital, for example, he cultivated the support of several "salons": groups of intellectuals and public figures who met regularly to discuss current policies. One of these, the circle of K. F. Golovin, took his side in the struggle against Witte; others, such as that of Prince Meshcherskii, did not. Plehve also kept on friendly terms with certain influential Slavophiles. He established good relations with F. D. Samarin, a Moscow zemstvo-man and Slavophile who had broken with Shipov over the growing influence of the liberals and third element. Having "examined" Samarin in a Moscow hotel in spring of 1903, he then brought this Slavophile to Petersburg to help with the peasant project. He also maintained close contact with another Slavophile, A. A. Kireev, a retired general who cherished Plehve as Russia's "last trump card." All this, however, was to little avail: the bulk of Russian society, convinced the minister was "deceiving" men like Kireev, increasingly aligned itself in open opposition to Plehve and his policies.[6]

This was especially true of the zemstvo-men. In April of 1903, during their fire insurance conference in Petersburg, representatives of twenty-three provincial zemstvo boards had gotten together to work out a common program. Disturbed by Plehve's notion of government–zemstvo cooperation, they decided to call upon all zemstvo assemblies to petition the tsar that any legislation pertaining to local life must first be approved by the zemstvos. Furthermore, they went on, any time zemstvo-men were called in by the ministry, there should be invited representatives "elected for this purpose" from *all* provincial zemstvos. The following month, Orel Marshal of the Nobility M. A. Stakhovich sent the tsar a "most devoted address," couched in the most humble and loyal terms, calling for similar concessions. Plehve's response was hostile and abrupt: pointing out that the "address" concerned areas beyond the scope of the zemstvos, he directed the Orel governor to prevent any future such episodes.[7]

The summer of 1903 had brought even further occasions for

discord. In July Plehve made a proposal, consistent with his view on gubernatorial authority, that all zemstvo doctors and pharmacists be confirmed by the local governor. That same month he forbade the Kaluga zemstvo to publish a brochure on the emancipation of the serfs, claiming that this would exceed the zemstvo's "limits of jurisdiction." In the provinces of Tambovsk, Vologda, Saratov, Kursk, and Kaluga, the governors stepped in to prevent various other activities by the zemstvos. In August there occurred in Iaroslavl a regional agricultural convention, which the zemstvo leaders took advantage of to hold another "congress." The mood of the congress, especially in secret sessions, was one of opposition to the government, and the Iaroslavl governor reported as much to the Minister of Interior. Plehve responded with reprisals: throughout the summer, large numbers of searches and arrests were made by the gendarmes.[8] As the zemstvos became more dissatisfied, the minister seemed to become more determined than ever to keep them under restraint.

But it was not just the zemstvos that turned against the minister; Plehve managed to alienate the nobility as a whole. His harsh treatment of marshals like Evreinov and Stakhovich, and his arrests of aristocrats like Dolgorukov, were widely viewed as violations of nobility privilege. Even more disconcerting to the first estate was the advance of bureaucratic absolutism. The provincial reform, in increasing the powers of the governors, would have lessened the influence of the marshals, especially in the area of education. Similarly, a change in procedures for procuring land captains, sponsored by Plehve, gave the governors and ministry even greater influence over these officials, and even broader scope in appointing persons who were not from the local nobility. Disturbed by Witte's stress on industry, dismayed by agrarian decline, and disquieted by peasant unrest, the nobles now found themselves deprived of their rightful preeminence by the Minister of Interior. As time went on, even men like Kireev and Golovin came to question Plehve's policies.[9]

Despite all this, it was not until after Witte's dismissal that repression became the overriding, dominant theme of Plehve's government. Prior to this there at least had been the promise of reform, the hope of accommodation between state and society, and the prospect of a positive relationship between the government and the workers. But the promise of reform had diminished as the content of Plehve's reforms became known, and the worker situation had deteriorated with the strikes of 1903. The hope for reconciliation between state and society, never too bright, had been extinguished by the disintegration of

Plehve's arrangement with Shipov. The removal of Witte may itself have damaged Plehve's standing: hitherto the Minister of Finance, long perceived as the major enemy of zemstvos and nobility, had received much of the blame for government policy. Now, with Witte gone and the government clearly in Plehve's hands, all hatred and resentment could be channeled toward the Minister of Interior. [10]

Plehve was not unaware of the seriousness of the situation. As early as January of 1903 he had admitted to a colleague that "in Russia, with the exception of a rather small number of people who receive a good salary and have occasion to be honored by imperial favor, the entire population is generally dissatisfied with the government." [11] His intelligence told him that reforms were needed to change this situation. But his police instincts also told him that to permit criticism was to invite trouble, and that to make concessions could only lead to further yielding. He persisted, therefore, in repression: the more active and outspoken the opposition became, the more vigorous and vindictive were his reactions.

The period following the dismissal of Witte witnessed, on one hand, an increased assertiveness on the part of society and, on the other, a vigorous attack on the most troublesome zemstvos by the Ministry of Interior. The former expressed itself in the actions of the zemstvo-men who participated in the "Commission on the Center" of October 1903, and in the resolutions of the provincial zemstvo assemblies which met at the end of that year. The latter commenced with the "inspection" of several provincial zemstvos by ministry officials.

The Commission to Investigate the Question of the Decline of the Welfare of the Central Agricultural Provinces, popularly known as the "Commission on the Center," had been founded in 1901, but did not actually convene until October of 1903. Its chairman was V. N. Kokovtsov, the current Imperial Secretary and the future Minister of Finance. It included, besides the representatives of the various ministries, a fairly large delegation from society: the chairmen of the zemstvo boards of all eighteen provinces in the Center were invited to attend. Plehve, whose ministry had by this time completed its peasant project, had no great interest in this conference; his main concern was to prevent it from becoming a platform for the zemstvo-men to discuss political questions. [12]

In this he was not entirely successful. The zemstvo board chairmen, seizing on Kokovtsov's proposal to hear their considerations first, drafted a long memo outlining the zemstvo position. Disregarding the framework of the commission, they directed their attention to the legal, social, cultural, and educational status of the peasant class. Insisting that the peasants be granted full equality with the other classes, they went on to give a long list of restrictions which, they felt, must be abolished. They also called for expanded peasant education, state funding of the zemstvos, the granting of credits to small land holders, and a lowering of the redemption dues. Their demands were published by the press, occasioning a rather broad public discussion of the peasant question. [13]

Commission Chairman Kokovtsov was a friend of Plehve's and, having previously benefited from his support, did not care to antagonize the minister. He demonstrated, however, a good deal of tact, avoiding the confrontation which characterized Plehve's relations with society. Accepting the zemstvo memorandum as a whole, he proceeded to direct discussion only towards its economic and non-political aspects. The commission's work was then submitted to the Conference on Agricultural Industry, which largely ignored the zemstvo note, since it dealt with issues "beyond the scope of the conference." The only measure it approved was the lowering of redemption dues, and even this was postponed by the outbreak of war with Japan. [14]

The regular annual sessions of the provincial zemstvo assemblies, meeting at the end of 1903, provided another opportunity for the zemstvo-men to express their views. In assembly after assembly, responding to the call of the provincial board chairmen, members raised the issue of petitioning the government for a greater zemstvo role in the legislative process. In several instances, discussion of these questions was blocked by the assembly chairman (the provincial marshal of the nobility); in other cases the resolutions were actually passed, only to be dismissed out of hand by the governors. Nevertheless, the point they made was clear enough: Plehve's "constitution" was unacceptable to the zemstvos. The government, they insisted, must consult *elected* representatives of *all* provincial zemstvos, not just a handful of selected local persons. [15]

The minister, meanwhile, using his inspection authority, was accelerating his efforts to force the zemstvos into submission. Not surprisingly, the Moscow zemstvo was the first to feel the effects. In October of 1903 Assistant Minister N. A. Zinov'ev and ten ministry officials were dispatched to Moscow to conduct an inspection. Zinov'ev and his staff paid particular attention to the activities of the professional zemstvo employees, and the relationship between the provincial and county zemstvo institutions. The assistant minister behaved in an assertive and overbearing fashion. He viewed the indepen-

Assistant Minister of Interior Senator N. A. Zinov'ev.

dence given the third element as evidence of irresponsibility, and he was critical of the centralization of authority in the hands of the provincial board. Nevertheless, on November 11, in his concluding speech to the members of the board, he reported that his overall impressions had not been unfavorable. He also promised to inform them of his conclusions as soon as possible, so they could correct any mistaken impressions before the report was published. As it turned out, however, no such information ever was forthcoming and the report—finally published in May of 1904—was extremely critical of the zemstvo.[16]

It was in Tver province, where the nobles had a reputation for radicalism, that the next inspection took place. It was conducted by Department of General Affairs Director Sturmer, himself a former chairman of the Tver provincial zemstvo board. Although Sturmer's inspection apparently was accomplished without rancor, it provided an excuse for Plehve to launch an all-out attack on the Tver zemstvo. On January 8, 1904, the minister presented the emperor with a report incorporating Sturmer's findings. The Tver provincial zemstvo, he alleged, had set up illegal executive bodies composed mainly of third element people, had hired politically unreliable teachers who were turning local children against the church and state, and had cut off support for the Tver county zemstvo when the latter placed its schools under church control.

To rectify the situation, Plehve suggested severe countermeasures. The minister himself, he felt, should be permitted to appoint the members of the Tver provincial zemstvo board, and to banish "persons who have a harmful influence on the course of zemstvo administration." The Tver governor, meanwhile, should be given the authority to dismiss from public service any zemstvo-man he considered injurious to "state order and public tranquility." The emperor agreed, and on January 16 a special decree was issued ordering the implementation of these recommendations.[17]

The dissolution of the elected zemstvo board, and its replacement by a board of Plehve's appointees, aroused widespread indignation. According to the law, it was claimed, a new election should have been held; Plehve had therefore exceeded his authority. By moving against the *elected* representatives, he had also demonstrated that it was not just the third element that he intended to pursue. This became even more apparent when a number of liberal zemstvo-men from Tver were either banished from the province or removed from public activity.[18]

Other actions of the minister were directed against the third element and the liberal intelligentsia. In September of 1903 it became known that Plehve had been given the authority to suspend statistical operations in any province at his own discretion. In January of 1904 the Third Congress of Activists in the Field of Technical Education, attended by a large number of radically-inclined educators, was closed down by the police. A similar assembly of doctors, the Ninth Congress of the Pirogov Society of Russian Physicians, was permitted to continue, but at the end of the congress the government stepped in to prevent its resolutions from being read. These actions, which further widened the gulf between government and society, were futile: while attention was focused on the congresses, both held in Saint Petersburg, representatives of various opposition groups were holding a secret congress of the "Union of Liberation" elsewhere in the city.[19]

THE WAR AGAINST THE ZEMSTVOS

By early 1904 it was apparent that Plehve had abandoned any hopes for reconciliation with society, and that he was placing his hopes in government by force. His bent for repression had developed almost into an obsession. Frustrated, perhaps, by the failure of his attempts to gain support from society, and driven by his desire to prevent united zemstvo activity, he reacted with hostility even to the "loyal" elements. His personal power, in some respects, had never been greater: in appointing a new Education Minister, the emperor pointedly instructed the man to "come to an understanding with Plehve."[20] Ironically, however, Plehve's failure to solve Russia's problems, and his inability to control events, had never been more apparent.

For a short time after the outbreak of war with Japan, events seemed to be playing into Plehve's hands. The surprise Japanese attack, a clear violation of international convention, temporarily united all but the most radical behind the government. Large patriotic demonstrations took place in several cities; some of these were police-inspired, but others were quite spontaneous. The funeral of populist writer Mikhailovskii, a few days after the declaration of war, aroused scarcely a murmur—much to the delight of Plehve. In normal times, he recognized, this would have served as an occasion for all sorts of anti-government demonstrations.[21]

Throughout Russian society there was an upsurge of patriotism and a lull in criticism of the government. For weeks following the beginning of hostilities, the newspapers were filled with declarations of loyal support from various zemstvos and nobility assemblies. Conservatives, moderates, and liberals agreed that any "initiative for . . . new reforms" should be postponed until "after the defeat of the foreign enemy." Even *Liberation*, the radical émigré journal which had spearheaded the opposition, took an ambivalent position favoring defense of the fatherland but continued opposition to its government. Only the most radical dared call for defeat of the Russian war effort—and their voices were drowned temporarily by the sudden wave of patriotism.[22]

This situation should have worked to Plehve's advantage. Here was his chance to split the opposition, to separate the wheat from the chaff and the "turbid" from the "pure." Here was his chance to draw the loyal elements into "useful state work," while "relentlessly pursuing" the rest. Indeed, the government took a faltering step in this direction by promising to excuse anyone "under police supervision" who agreed to join the Far Eastern army. But soon, by continuing his regimen of repression, Plehve had managed to drive the loyal forces once more into opposition.[23]

Unfortunately, Plehve's distrust of the zemstvos had by this time become an obsession. On February 28, 1904, in the Special Conference on the Needs of Agricultural Industry, he launched into a bitter attack on the zemstvos in general, and the third element in particular. At issue was a proposal, which Plehve had previously favored, to submit a new law on local roads to the zemstvo assemblies for discussion. Under the current system, he alleged, the zemstvos were a long way from being truly representative of the people. Although the assemblies themselves were elected, their actual work was done by hired bureaucrats who were, "upon analysis, worse than the people in Saint Petersburg." If the proposal on local roads would be considered by the zemstvos, the views expressed would not be those of "local people" at all: they would be the "abstract" and "doctrinaire" views of another "bureaucracy" made up of hired "outsiders." "It is possible to tell in advance what kind of replies we will get . . . ," he asserted. "It will be pointed out that under the contemporary tenor of state life no reform of roads is possible, and that once the governmental structure is changed the roads will improve all by themselves. At present all issues are approached from this point of view; even the reform of peasant legislation is tied to the general legal order."

He did not mean to imply, of course, that these "alien elements" had taken control of every zemstvo, but he did feel that in many cases the responses would be written "by all sorts of statisticians, medical aides and, at best, public instructors, who are under police surveillance." The local representatives, after all, were "not especially skillful in written explanations," and so they ordinarily entrusted this kind of work to those who, "in the course of long terms in jail, with plenty of leisure time, have become practiced in the composition of all sorts of essays." [24]

A minor incident which took place five weeks after the outbreak of war served as a portent of things to come. In March 1904 the Ministry of Interior convened another zemstvo fire insurance conference for the purpose of concluding an inter-zemstvo agreement. A special preparatory commission, made up of third element personnel, was formed, but immediately trouble arose concerning the fire inspector from Tver. The insurance workers from the other provinces refused to have anything to do with him, since he represented the new, Plehve-appointed Tver zemstvo board. Several of these workers soon found themselves in jail: their rude treatment of the Tver zemstvo employee was seen by the ministry as a "protest against an imperial order." On this occasion, the zemstvos gave in—the rest of the third element members went home, while the elected zemstvo representatives stayed on and continued the conference. [25]

The next clash between the ministry and society was not to be settled so simply. The trouble began, as so often before, within the Moscow zemstvo. A number of patriotic zemstvo-men, searching for an appropriate role in the war effort, had decided that the zemstvos should provide aid to wounded soldiers, and assistance to the families of the dead. Meanwhile, the Russian Red Cross had encountered some difficulties, and appealed to the zemstvos for help. In response, several zemstvo officials—led by the ubiquitous D. N. Shipov—decided to establish an "All-Zemstvo Organization" to provide war relief to soldiers and their families. By April, a "Society of Zemstvo-Organizations to Aid Wounded Soldiers," and special "zemstvo detachments" to work in the Far East, had been formed. [26] Shipov, as might have been expected, was chosen to preside, but due to complications he was unable to accept.

In February, Shipov had been elected to a fifth three-year term as Chairman of the Moscow Provincial Zemstvo Board, but he had not yet been confirmed by the Minister of Interior. On April 12, during a visit to Saint Petersburg, he called on Plehve to inquire about the delay. The minister, explaining that such a decision required "a good deal of consideration," announced that he had finally decided not to confirm Shipov at all. One reason, of course, was that the Moscow Board Chairman had "created for himself the position of the self-ordained chairman of the All-Russian Zemstvo," and was thus "violating the will of the Sovereign." "The second reason I consider your activity harmful," Plehve told Shipov, "is contained in the situation where you bring persons into zemstvo affairs who are newcomers, and who have no connection whatsoever with local interests. Under the zemstvo boards there have been formed cadres of *sansculottes* who have acquired a dominating influence in zemstvo affairs, shoving aside those elements which have been summoned by law to local self-government." The zemstvo-man protested, but to no avail: on April 20, the non-confirmation of Shipov was formally announced.[27]

Meanwhile, leadership of the "All-Zemstvo Organization" had fallen to Shipov's elected assistant, Prince G. E. L'vov. On April 27, the emperor granted an audience to L'vov, who was asked to transmit the tsar's gratitude and support to his colleagues in the war relief effort. Indeed, it would seem impossible to have found fault with such humanitarianism and patriotism.

Plehve, however, managed to do just that. On April 17, shortly before L'vov's audience with the tsar, he instructed the governors to supervise the organization closely, to make sure that "unreliable persons" were not included in the detachments, and to prevent any new zemstvos from joining. Whatever their patriotic impulses, he commented, the zemstvos were restricted by law to the boundaries of their individual provinces. It was "necessary to take measures" so that "joint zemstvo activity" did not spread to other areas, or take place "outside the surveillance of the governor." Plehve was not just concerned about united zemstvo activity; he had reason to fear that radicals in the zemstvo detachments were intent on turning the soldiers against the government.[28]

The indignation aroused by Plehve's circular, and by his refusal to confirm Shipov, was great. The first conference of the "All-Zemstvo Organization," held on May 2, decided to ignore the minister's instructions. Acting on the basis of the emperor's remarks to Prince L'vov, they continued to enlist new members and expand their organization. The Moscow provincial board at first refused to elect a new chairman: the majority continued to vote for Shipov during the first several ballots. One prominent board member, M. V. Chel'nikov, resigned in disgust, while protest petitions were filed by a number of other zemstvos and town councils. The Moscow board finally selected F. A.

Golovin, a constitutionalist who was considerably more radical than Shipov, and who made it clear that he had no intention of abandoning Shipov's policies. Despite this, to the surprise of nearly everyone, Golovin was immediately confirmed by the Minister of Interior.[29]

This move was puzzling even to the constitutionalists: what could the minister hope to gain by replacing Shipov with the more radical Golovin? The answer, most probably, is that Shipov, despite his monarchist and Slavophile views, occupied a central position in the zemstvo movement that no one else could fill. Golovin may have been more determined to oppose the government, but he did not command the universal respect of his predecessor, nor could he hope to assume Shipov's position as the spokesman for the "All-Russian Zemstvo."

Plehve's repressive actions, therefore, had intimidated neither the "All-Zemstvo Organization" nor the Moscow provincial board. The supposedly all-powerful minister was able to issue commands and threats, and to submit individuals to dismissal, banishment, or jail. But he had little ability to alter the general course of events. Indeed, his actions accomplished the opposite of what they had been intended to do. By turning the Slavophiles against the government they helped resolve the split in society, strengthening the opposition movement and hastening the process which was leading toward revolution.[30]

The opposition movement was also strengthened by the news from the Far East. Russian forces suffered defeat after disastrous defeat. General Kuropatkin arrived in Manchuria in the middle of March, surrounded by hopes that he could somehow reverse the military situation. But after his arrival things only got worse. On March 31 the battleship *Petropavlovsk* was sunk by a Japanese mine, taking with it the life of Admiral Makarov, Russia's most capable naval commander. On April 18 the Russian armies were routed at the Battle of the Yalu River. Similar defeats followed at Nanshan and Tellisu, as the Japanese drove the Russians back into the interior. Port Arthur itself came under siege. Meanwhile, the army's inability to deal effectively with the lightly regarded enemy was serving only to highlight the incompetence and weakness of the regime.

Faced with growing discontent and increasingly vocal criticism, Plehve's only real response was more repression. Besides Shipov, he also refused to confirm the Chairman of the Vologda Provincial Zemstvo Board. Zemstvo inspections, similar to those which had taken place in Moscow and Tver, were conducted in the provinces of Viatka and Kursk, and in the county of Sudzha. The first two, like the one in

Moscow, were carried out by Assistant Minister Zinov'ev, who apparently treated the zemstvo-men with discourtesy and disrespect. The last was conducted by Kursk vice-governor Kurlov. Both came out strongly against the work, attitude, and influence of the third element, and were especially critical of the type of education provided by zemstvo schools. Rural children, it seems, were being taught not about the emperor and God, but about "abstract notions" and vague philosophies. "You burden the peasant with tools he cannot repair, and education he does not need," was Zinov'ev's remark to the Viatka board. Finally, as if to emphasize the tsar's approval of these inspections, Zinov'ev and Sturmer were presented with a special resolution of "imperial gratitude" for their work. [31]

In May, after an extended delay, was published Zinov'ev's report on his October inspection of the Moscow provincial zemstvo. Although it did note some positive aspects, especially in the areas of road-building and medical care, its overall tone was sharply critical. Two major deficiencies were noted. The first was extreme centralization, by which the provincial board strove to control all the activities of the entire province, to appoint all county officials, and to supervise closely the operations of the county zemstvos. This had led, in Zinov'ev's opinion, to excessive spending, to inefficiency and waste, to friction between the county and provincial zemstvos, and to the stifling of local initiative. The second major fault was the tendency to entrust important affairs to the hired zemstvo employees, who were in many cases actually in control of zemstvo affairs. This third element, it was pointed out, had no legal status to deal with such issues. [32]

THE HARVEST OF NATIONAL DISCONTENT

The war with Japan, besides increasing government–zemstvo tensions, provided the first real test of Plehve's nationality policies. By any possible measure, they were a serious failure. The Armenians and Finns in general refused to support the war effort. Among nationality groups, government attempts to manufacture "patriotic demonstrations" met with indifference and hostility, while opposition parties boldly called for Japanese victory. [33]

The war was also widely opposed within the Jewish community, but this did not prevent the government from inducting Jews into the army. This led, in some cases, to the grossest injustice: Jewish women and children were deported to the Pale because their husbands and fathers, the ones who had obtained the privilege to live outside, had left their families to join the war effort. Even Plehve could not justify this, and on March 6, 1904, a circular signed by himself and Lopukhin temporarily rescinded the orders to deport Jews illegally residing in central Russia. The war may also have led the minister to take strict measures to prevent new pogroms: at any rate, despite widespread rumors and anti-Semitic proclamations, Easter of 1904 passed without incident.[34]

Ironically, the outbreak of war may have hampered Plehve's efforts to "improve the lot of Jews." Toward the end of 1903, he had argued in the Committee of Ministers for a further extension of Jewish residence rights within the Pale. In January of 1904, he had summoned to the capital sixty representatives of the Jewish community, and asked them to indicate the most necessary reforms. That same month, he had constituted a special commission to revise Jewish legislation, with a view toward removing "needless restrictions."[35]

The summoning of the Jewish leaders was a good example of Plehve's notion of the public's role in government. First, the dignitaries assembled and drafted a resolution calling for a freer Jewish access to higher education, and more liberal rights of residence. The minister then received a delegation from this "Jewish parliament." In the one-hour interview, according to a later report, Plehve did most of the talking. He told them that he considered the Jews a "higher race" than the Russians, not a lower one, and that the limitations on Jews were therefore necessary to prevent them from accumulating too much power. He also blamed the Jews for recent murders and terrorist acts. But he did go on to promise that the government "was prepared to improve the situation of the Jews," although only "slowly and gradually." "You must not think about equal rights," he allegedly told them; "what good would it do to give you equal rights today and then tomorrow have a repetition of Kishinev or Gomel?"[36]

The commission on Jewish legislation was a bit more substantive. Prince I. M. Obolenskii, the former Khar'kov governor who had crushed the peasant riots, was chosen to preside. Other members included Police Director Lopukhin, Moscow Police Chief Trepov, and the governors of various provinces in the Pale, such as Pahlen of Vilnius and Urusov of Bessarabia. The discussions that ensued were wide-ranging and argumentative. Several members, including Lopukhin, Pahlen, and Urusov, wished to go beyond Plehve's propositions and remove all restrictions against the Jews. Obolenskii, despite his "repressive" reputation, proved tolerant and fair-minded. It was proposed to start afresh by ignoring the multitude of existing laws and retaining only those restrictions the commission felt necessary. But before anything could be accomplished, the war with Japan broke out, and the governors returned to their provinces with no conclusions having been reached.[37]

In the long run, the work of the commission, and that of the "Jewish parliament," were not entirely in vain. Although Plehve himself did not live long enough to complete his revision of Jewish laws, several important steps were taken in summer of 1904. In July, restrictions on Jewish residence close to the western border were removed. And, that same month, the Committee of Ministers approved Plehve's request that certain categories of Jews be exempted from various "unnecessary" and "impractical" provisions of the anti-Jewish legislation. These exemptions were approved by Emperor Nicholas II on August 20, 1904—five weeks after Plehve's death.[38] In an ironic twist of fate, a measure of relief for certain Jews had been part of Plehve's legacy.

In Finland, the coming of the war followed close on the heels of new russification efforts. In October 1903 the governor-general had begun presiding over the Finnish Senate, and deliberations of this body were thenceforth conducted in Russian. That same month, an imperial resolution had made it possible for any Russian subjects except Jews to own land in Finland. In November, Bobrikov had been granted additional authority to exile administrative and educational officials of the middle civil service ranks. In January 1904 had begun the changeover to Russian language in Finnish schools, and the connection of the Finnish railroads to the imperial railway system.[39]

The war itself provided new opportunities for repression. Many Finns, seeing the war as a "liberation" force, openly hoped for Japanese victory, while continuing to resist induction. Plehve responded with new repressive measures against draft-evading Finnish students, while Bobrikov imposed even stricter censorship on the Finnish press.[40]

Toward the summer of 1904, however, Plehve seems to have had some second thoughts about the wisdom of Russian policy. With a view to stabilizing the situation, he resurrected an idea which had been considered briefly by him and Bobrikov four years earlier. In an instruction to the local governors, he asked their views about a plan to separate from Finland the province of Vyborg, and to incorporate it fully into the Russian empire. Vyborg, which guarded the access to Saint Petersburg, was the only part of Finland needed by Russia for defensive and strategic purposes. Once this was done, he reasoned, it might be possible to restore a large measure of autonomy to the rest of the Grand Duchy.[41]

Although nothing ever came of this proposal, the summer of 1904 did bring a measure of relief to the Finns. On June 3, at 11:05 A.M., on the premises of the Finnish Senate, N. I. Bobrikov was assassinated by the son of a former senator. The hated "dictator" and governor-general was finally removed. Plehve responded by securing the appointment of Prince I. M. Obolenskii. But Obolenskii, already the victim of one assassination attempt, had no desire to follow in Bobrikov's footsteps. He accepted the post, but refused to continue the repression. And so, as a result of one of Plehve's last major decisions, the Finns were provided with a mild respite from extreme russification policies.[42]

Meanwhile in the Caucasus the turmoil continued. Ferment among Armenians, which had reached a high point in fall of 1903 following the confiscation of Armenian Church property, persisted throughout the winter and spring of 1904. It even disrupted the war effort: numerous troops were "squandered" keeping order in the Caucasus, while Armenians in the lower ranks either deserted with their rifles or rebelled against their superiors. Efforts by local authorities to quell the disorders were only partially successful: the situation stabilized somewhat by summer of 1904, but this did not prevent the assassination of the Vice-Governor of Elizavetpol in July.[43]

It is clear that, by the middle of 1904 if not long before this, Plehve had lost control of the situation. He seems to have been merely reacting to events, striking out blindly against forces beyond his control. He blamed Russia's demise on Witte and hoped, once all traces of Witte's influence were removed, that the danger to Russia would be over.[44] But it was not Witte alone who had alienated the nobility and society. Plehve, by seeking to extend the bureaucracy and by using repressive tactics, had contributed greatly to their disenchantment with the government.

Plehve, in fact, had managed to turn every sector of the Russian public—the nobility, the peasants, the workers, the Jews, the nationalities, and the intellectuals—against the government. As opposition had increased, so had repression; as repression became more widespread, the opposition movement became stronger. Even members of the imperial bureaucracy were coming to realize that something would have to give, that "things could not go on like this much longer."

Plehve himself was vaguely aware of the problem. In talking with Shipov in April he admitted that some sort of change would be necessary in the not-too-distant future. In July, seeking to restore good relations with Kokovtsov, he expressed a strange uncertainty. "Now is not the time for us to break with one another," he told the Finance Minister. ". . . The Lord knows how long we shall work together. You do not know much, nor do I, perhaps, of what is going on around us."[45]

10

The Minister and the Terrorists

THE BATTLE ORGANIZATION OF THE SOCIALIST REVOLUTIONARIES

Shortly after his appointment as Minister of Interior, V. K. Plehve granted an interview to a well-known French reporter. During the course of the interview, the journalist remarked that it certainly must have taken great courage for Plehve to assume his new post, in light of what had happened to Sipiagin. "Yes, I am aware that our security is constantly threatened," the minister allowed, "but no one is so well guarded as the Minister of Interior." Besides, the danger of further terrorist acts would soon be decreased. "As far as these attacks go, perhaps they will occur for yet another month or so, but after that they will become much rarer. . . . You see, sir, the revolutionary parties are strong only because of the weakness of the police. . . . The former head of the police did not know his business. He was too weak, so I replaced him. I have absolute confidence that the new director of the police will do an outstanding job." Plehve's confidence arose primarily out of his own experience as Director of Police in "similar circumstances" during the early eighties. At that time, he boasted to the Paris correspondent, "it took me only a few days to discover the key to the entire revolution."[1]

Plehve's notion that the revolutionary situation of 1902 was very much like that of 1881 turned out to be incorrect. The movement of 1881 had indeed consisted mainly of "small bands"; and it had effectively been destroyed by Plehve and his police. But the revolutionary movement that had arisen out of its ruins during the 1890s was far

218

broader and deeper. Not only were the revolutionary groups themselves larger and more numerous, but their message was finally beginning to win adherents among peasants and factory workers.

Still, Plehve's conception of "small bands of revolutionary ringleaders" is not entirely incomprehensible. In 1902, the Russian revolutionaries were only beginning to form themselves into the broad-based political parties that would emerge in the revolution of 1905. It is true that they were making rapid progress, and that "central committees" and "party newspapers" had already come into existence. But these committees and newspapers as often as not were the work of émigré revolutionaries residing in Western Europe. There were formulated grandiose plans for well-organized and tightly-structured parties, revolutionary hierarchies, and "iron discipline," but as of yet these existed more in the minds of the émigrés than they did in the reality of Russia. Inside Russia, individual revolutionaries and radical groups, although beginning to align themselves into larger organizations, still functioned with a great deal of autonomy.

There had emerged, however, two broad tendencies which already bore the name, and most of the trappings, of revolutionary political parties. The Marxists, or "Social Democrats," were active among the industrial workers in the major cities, trying to instill in them a "political" consciousness, and to turn them not just against their employers, but also against the government. Although relatively few in number, they had achieved some success in organizing strikes and worker disorders in various industrial centers. The Socialist Revolutionaries, or "SRs," on the other hand, were intent on bringing peasants as well as workers into the revolutionary picture. Their ideology attempted to merge revolutionary Marxism with the traditions of Russian populism and the peculiar realities of Russian life. In 1901 the major SR groups had managed to amalgamate into a rudimentary party, with a program calling for the overthrow of the autocracy and the "socialization" of the land.[2]

The latter group, the Socialist Revolutionaries, posed a very grave problem for Plehve. This had nothing to do with their ideology which, from the government's point of view, differed little from that of the Marxists. Nor did it involve their numerical strength which, like that of the Social Democrats, was hardly overwhelming. The main threat posed by the SRs was that they, unlike the Marxists, believed in the usefulness of terror as a tactic in the revolutionary struggle.

In autumn of 1901 there had been formed, under the SR central committee, a semi-autonomous "Battle Organization" whose sole purpose was the practice of terror. It was made up of dedicated men and women, most of them quite young, who were willing to sacrifice even their lives in the struggle against autocracy. It was so secretive that its members often did not know each other's real names. A plan for a central organ uniting various local agencies was conceived, but never carried out. Throughout its existence, the Battle Organization functioned on an opportunistic and improvisational basis, adapting its rules and its tactics to the situation at hand.[3]

At the heart of the Battle Organization was Grigorii A. Gershuni, the most effective and most charismatic revolutionary of his time. Of the three main leaders of the SR movement, Gershuni was the activist, the organizer, the agitator, and the practical worker. The other two —Viktor Chernov and Mikhail Gots—were theoreticians and polemicists. While they spent their time in Western Europe, discussing SR policy and editing the party newspaper, Gershuni boldly traveled about Russia organizing local revolutionary cells and urging the people on against autocracy. He was vibrant, flamboyant, energetic, and sincere, the kind of dynamic revolutionist who easily attracted devoted followers from among the impatient, idealistic, and romantic Russian youths. He was also a genius in the "art" of political terror.[4]

The murder of Minister of Interior Sipiagin was the first public act of the Battle Organization. Toward the end of 1901 Gershuni, with the aid of SR activist Mikhail Mel'nikov, had conceived a plan for the "execution" of both Sipiagin and Procurator of the Holy Synod Pobedonostsev. Military uniforms were to be secured and two young volunteers, dressed as aides-de-camp, were to approach their intended victims during official functions and shoot them dead. One of the volunteers, Stepan Balmashev, was a former Kiev student who had come under Gershuni's influence and joined the terrorist group a few months earlier. On April 2, 1902, he successfully carried out the murder of Sipiagin. Due to a misunderstood communication, however, the projected attack on Pobedonostsev never was made. Gershuni hastily contrived a new plot to murder both the procurator and Saint Petersburg Governor Kleigels, but this too went awry. The cautious Pobedonostsev failed to show up at Sipiagin's funeral and the would-be assassins, Grigor'ev and Iurkovskaia, lost their nerve.[5]

On the day following Sipiagin's murder, the Battle Organization issued a proclamation taking full credit for the deed. The use of terror was defended as "the only possible response to our ministers." "We consider it not just our right, but even our sacred duty," the terrorists proclaimed ". . . to avenge the blood of the people with the blood of

Terrorist leader G. A. Gershuni.

the oppressors." Shortly thereafter, having safely escaped abroad, Gershuni was lauded by the SR central committee and placed in charge of all terrorist activities. They officially declared him "dictator" of the Battle Organization. Then, in issue number seven of the SR organ *Revolutionary Russia*, the party leaders publicly espoused the use of terror, and endorsed the program of the Battle Organization.[6]

Having taken over for the slain Sipiagin, V. K. Plehve wasted little time in formulating his response. One of his first acts as minister was to have his predecessor's assassin bound over to the military for trial. The court-martial itself was brief: Balmashev admitted his "responsibility," but denied any "guilt." The sentence, too, was swift and summary: on April 26, 1902, Stepan Balmashev was condemned to death. A week later, on May 3, he was hanged in the Schlusselburg fortress.[7] The deadly battle between Plehve and the terrorists had begun.

In this struggle, as in his earlier confrontation with the revolutionaries, the minister achieved convincing results. The pattern, in fact, was very similar. The perpetrator of the recent atrocity—like the murderers of Alexander II—was hanged, a new Director of Police was appointed, and the police espionage apparatus was hastily and energetically reorganized. A new Sudeikin was found, in the person of Sergei Zubatov, to direct the undercover operations. Agents and collaborators were used, arrests were made, and intensive interrogations followed. Finally, there was a break: a prisoner succumbed to police "persuasion" and agreed to talk. This was followed, as before, by the arrest of the terrorist leader and the decimation of the terrorist ranks. Thirteen months after Sipiagin's assassination the police finally caught up with Grigorii Gershuni who, like Vera Figner before him, was the heart and soul of the terrorist movement. Plehve's remarks to the French correspondent were certainly no idle boast.

The new minister's first move, after initiating the Balmashev trial, was to appoint a new Director for the Police Department. This was Lopukhin, the energetic procurator whose abilities Plehve would later praise to the Parisian journalist. But Lopukhin, although an intelligent and capable prosecutor, had only limited experience with counterrevolutionary police work. This he had acquired during the investigation and prosecution of political cases in Moscow, where he had been favorably impressed by the work of the famed Okhrana Chief, Zubatov. Soon, with Plehve's approval, Zubatov was transferred to Saint Petersburg and placed in charge of the Police Department's "Special Section," which was then rapidly transformed into an all-Russian Okhrana. Zubatov's system of spies and collaborators was expanded and applied on an empire-wide basis.[8]

Plehve's next move was to infiltrate the terrorist ranks with police agents. As in 1881, the groundwork for his success had been laid even before he took office. Already one of Zubatov's agents, a Jewish engineer named Evno Azef, had managed to gain the confidence of the leaders of the SR party. Azef had secretly been in the employ of the police since 1893, and had already provided the Okhrana with much valuable information. He had been responsible, among other things, for the police seizure of the main SR printing press in Tomsk in 1901. Behaving with great circumspection, Azef had even managed to befriend Gershuni, and he was thus in a position to perform even greater services for the police. In July of 1902, around the time of Zubatov's transfer to Saint Petersburg, Azef was ordered by the police to join the Battle Organization. Plehve himself apparently approved this commission, even though it went against a departmental rule that agents should not become actively involved in the leadership and direction of revolutionary activities.[9]

Gershuni and his terrorists, meanwhile, had not been idle. From the day of his appointment, Plehve had become their primary target, and they had turned their attention toward planning his removal. Prince Obolenskii's merciless flogging of peasants during the spring 1902 riots had made the Khar'kov governor, too, a candidate for revolutionary vengeance. Gershuni decided, most probably because it would be less difficult, that Obolenskii should be disposed of first. A young worker and recent terrorist recruit named Foma Kachura was selected for the job. He and Gershuni then traveled to Khar'kov where, on July 29, Kachura made his attempt. It was a failure: his shots missed Obolenskii, and instead wounded the local police chief. Nevertheless, it made the desired impression. Kachura, although refusing to give the police his name, identified himself immediately as a member of the Battle Organization. On his person was found a declaration stating that Obolenskii had been sentenced to death by the SR terrorists for his treatment of the Khar'kov peasants. Gershuni, who had managed to avoid apprehension, then turned his attention to the Minister of Interior.[10]

Plehve's decision to have Azef join the terrorists, therefore, came at an opportune moment. It was not long before it paid handsome dividends. In October 1902 Azef traveled to Kiev and joined his new comrades in devising a plan for Plehve's assassination. His presence, apparently, was welcomed by Gershuni. The plot they hatched was a simple one: two young cavalry officers—one of them the same Grigor'ev who had earlier failed to kill Pobedonostsev—were to attack Plehve's carriage from horseback. The attack, thanks to Azef's timely warning to the police, was never carried out. In January 1903 the terrorists Mel'nikov and Kraft, who had participated in the conspiratorial meeting at Kiev, were arrested. The following month Grigor'ev and Nadarov, the two officers who were to execute the plan, were also picked up by the police. Azef's warnings, it was evident, had saved Plehve's life.[11]

The questioning of the suspects produced a further reward. Grigor'ev, it turned out, was not of the mettle of which terrorists are made. Confronted by the fact that his interrogators were obviously well informed about the Battle Organization, he broke down and confessed his crimes. He then went on to name many of his comrades, and to confirm something that the police already suspected: that Grigorii Gershuni was the leader of the Battle Organization. The persons implicated by Grigor'ev were arrested, and the manhunt for Gershuni was intensified.[12]

The search for the terrorist leader took on an almost personal dimension for Plehve. Gershuni's arrest, it might well be expected, would lead to the end of the Battle Organization and its danger to the minister. On Plehve's desk, according to one associate, there stood a framed photograph of Gershuni. During the reports of Lopukhin and Zubatov, Plehve liked to point to this picture and declare that it would stay there until the terrorist was arrested. He even got to the point where he would ask them about Gershuni's health, referring to the revolutionary—as if he were an acquaintance—by his first name and patronymic.[13]

Gershuni's photograph, as a result of Plehve's insistence, was also distributed to police detectives throughout the Russian empire. It was rumored that a handsome reward for his arrest had been offered by the emperor. Pressure was brought to bear on Azef to discover and reveal the whereabouts of the fugitive.[14] Still, the artful conspirator managed to evade the police traps, and he even succeeded in carrying out a new political murder.

This attack, the third one made by the Battle Organization, was directed against Ufa governor N. M. Bogdanovich. The latter, during the infamous Zlatoust strike of March 1903, had ordered his troops to fire into a crowd of demonstrating workers. Gershuni could not let this atrocity go unavenged. He hastened to Ufa, where he found that a local revolutionary group had already conceived a plan and selected two "executioners." Gershuni gave it his approval and, on May 6, 1903, the two assassins gunned down the governor while he was walking in a public garden.[15]

Bogdanovich's murderers escaped unharmed, but Gershuni, this time, was not so lucky. From Ufa he went to Kiev where, almost by chance, he fell into the hands of the police. He refused, of course, to reveal his name, but A. I. Spiridovich, the Chief of the Kiev Okhrana, recognized him by sight. The erstwhile head of the Battle Organization was then taken to Saint Petersburg to join his previously arrested comrades.[16]

As if the arrest of Gershuni were not good news enough for the minister, it was followed by a most extraordinary development. It seems that the terrorist leader, before leaving for Ufa, had made arrangements for a successor to replace him in case he should be captured or killed. These had been communicated abroad to Mikhail Gots, who saw to it that Gershuni's wishes were carried out. In June 1903, at Geneva, the SR leaders acknowledged as the new head of the Battle Organization Gershuni's self-appointed successor: Evno Azef. Incredibly, an agent of the imperial police had become the head of the revolutionary terrorists.[17] Plehve's victory over the revolutionaries seemed to be assured: with Azef in control, the threat from the Battle Organization should soon disappear. In little more than a year, Plehve had managed to arrest all the main leaders of the terrorist movement, and to replace his most fearsome antagonist with an agent of the police. As he had done two decades earlier, it appeared, Plehve had broken the back of the revolutionary terrorists.

THE ROLE OF EVNO AZEF

The destruction of the People's Will, it will be remembered, had had an unexpected sequel: the "traitor" Degaev, to atone for his betrayal, had planned and helped execute the murder of Sudeikin. The sequel to the arrest of Gershuni was no less strange. Only this time it was not the head of the Okhrana, but the Minister of Interior himself who paid the terrible price.

Certainly, with Azef now directing the Battle Organization, the minister should have had little to worry about. This agent now should have no trouble warning of new assassination plots. He also would be in position to report on the activities of the SR leaders abroad, to find out the location and resources of SR groups in Russia, and—in a relatively short period of time—to allow the police to put an end to the entire SR movement. Okhrana leaders now brimmed with confidence: such devoted Plehve servants as Skandrakov, the head of the minister's personal guard, and Spiridovich, chief of the Kiev Okhrana, were strangely complacent when the Battle Organization issued a new death sentence naming Plehve as its target. Even the minister was not particularly disturbed: "We shall know about these attacks in due time," he is said to have remarked when questioned about his own safety. [18]

There were, however, several flaws in the minister's reasoning. One of these was his misjudgment of the strength of the revolutionary movement and the depth of popular dissatisfaction. The hatred of the government in general, and of Plehve in particular, was so bitter, and so widespread, that the revolutionaries had little trouble finding new recruits to fill the terrorist ranks. The situation should have been obvious to Plehve in summer of 1902 when Prince Sviatopolk-Mirskii, then still Assistant Minister, was sent to Siberia to interview youths who had been exiled thither for anti-government activity. The Prince was empowered to pardon any of those who were willing to repent their "sedition." He met with the coldest of receptions. Almost to a man, the prisoners refused to come to terms with the government, even though such an accommodation could have won for them their freedom. [19]

The arrest of Gershuni, then, although it was followed by a lapse of more than a year in Battle Organization attacks, did not spell the end of the terror. In fact, within a few months after this arrest, several events had occurred which were to have a direct bearing on Plehve's future. In spring of 1903 a young Social Democrat named Boris Savinkov, having been exiled to Vologda for seditious activity, switched allegiances and joined the SRs. Under the influence of Ekaterina Breshkovskaia, a close associate of Gershuni's, he determined to devote his life to terror. In June he escaped abroad, made his way to Geneva, and offered his services to Mikhail Gots. In August, finally, he was introduced to Evno Azef, and became a member of the Battle Organization. That same month another young revolutionary, exiled to Siberia for participating in student disorders, made good his escape from Irkutsk province. Egor Sazonov then made his way to Western Europe, where he, too, decided to join the Battle Organization. The former eventually would direct, and the latter would execute, the murder of Plehve. [20]

Police agent and terrorist leader Evno Azef.

Another miscalculation made by the minister and his police officials was their trust in Evno Azef. The latter was a mercenary—a
revolutionary who betrayed his comrades for profit. He had no particular devotion either to the government or to Plehve; if he had alle-

giance to any official at all it was to Zubatov. But this had not stopped him from deceiving the police in the past: although well aware of Gershuni's role as leader of the Battle Organization, he had consistently concealed this fact from the authorities. Perhaps he, too, had come under the spell of the charismatic revolutionary and was loath to betray him; perhaps he was merely protecting himself or holding out for a higher price. At any rate, it was not until Grigor'ev's confession that the police became fully aware of Gershuni's real role. Azef was confronted by both Zubatov and Lopukhin about this, but he responded only with counter-accusations that his reported information was not being used correctly. Either this was enough to satisfy the police leaders or they thought Azef valuable nevertheless, for, as it turned out, no action was taken against him.[21]

In reality, Azef's only real allegiance was to himself. He sat in a very dangerous position, especially after Gershuni's arrest, and he had to think first of his own safety. A continual series of arrests, and a long train of assassination attempts gone awry, could only help convince his SR colleagues that they had a traitor in their midst. If he were found out, his game would be over; and so, most probably, would be his life. On the other hand, if he could successfully plan and accomplish the murder of Plehve, his position among the SRs would be secured. Azef had little love for Plehve: as a Jew, he could not help but resent the Kishinev pogrom and the minister's reputed role. With Zubatov's dismissal in August of 1903, the only police official to whom Azef had any loyalty was gone. A short time later, the Battle Organization resumed its plans to assassinate the Minister of Interior, this time under the guidance and direction of Evno Azef.[22]

Another mistake made by Plehve was his appointment of L. A. Rataev to head the Foreign Okhrana. As head of the Special Section of the Department of Police, Rataev had been ineffective; he had also acquired a reputation as a shirker and *bon vivant*. Plehve himself had been critical of Rataev and had taken the opportunity, in summer of 1902, to have him removed in favor of Zubatov. Instead of being discharged, however, Rataev was transferred to the Paris Okhrana post recently vacated by Rachkovskii. Even so, he apparently resented this irreverent treatment. Lacking Rachkovskii's ability and devotion to duty, he carried out his tasks perfunctorily; he was not the man to suspect the motives, or control the actions, of an informer like Azef. As a police employee who spent most of his time abroad, Azef made very frequent reports to Rataev, either in person or by letter. By playing upon Rataev's resentments, by feeding him only the information he wanted Rataev to know, and by skillfully plying the police official for information on Okhrana activities, Azef was able to "use" the head of the Foreign Okhrana for his own purposes. Rataev, unwittingly, became an accomplice in the collaborator's intrigues.[23]

In fall of 1903, Azef devised an elaborate scheme for doing away with Plehve. Gone were the days of the isolated assassin with a pistol: the Battle Organization now turned to conspiracies involving numerous participants and the use of explosive devices. Young volunteers came to Saint Petersburg and took jobs as street-peddlers, cab drivers, and merchants. The purpose of this elaborate ruse was to observe the comings and goings of Plehve, and to determine when and where it would be best to strike against him. "If there is no traitor among us," Azef reportedly remarked, "von Plehve will be killed."[24]

The police, meanwhile, seemed to be making real progress in their struggle against the revolutionaries. Plehve's reorganization of the department, the establishment of "Okhranas" in all the major cities, the systematic collection of data and the surveillance of revolutionary suspects all appeared to be bearing fruit. During the course of 1903, besides the arrests of Gershuni and the members of the Battle Organization, entire revolutionary groups were seized in places such as Kiev, Odessa, Saint Petersburg, Kursk, Saratov, Ekaterinoslav, and Moscow. Secret printing presses were also discovered and destroyed. Many of the best revolutionary workers were removed from action. Even SR leader Mikhail Gots was arrested for a while in Italy, although the tsarist government failed in its efforts to have him extradited to Russia.[25]

Plehve and his minions also had success in breaking the will of the arrested terrorists. Besides Grigor'ev, they also managed to obtain a confession from Foma Kachura, the young worker who had attempted to murder Prince Obolenskii. Kachura, sentenced to death but spared through the intercession of his intended victim, finally admitted that it was Gershuni who directed the attack against the Khar'kov governor. Gershuni himself, however, did not break, even under the most intensive interrogation. At one point, according to the terrorist's own account, Plehve himself visited Gershuni's cell in the Schlusselberg fortress. "What do you have to say to me?" the minister asked as he confronted the man who had been plotting to kill him. The surprised terrorist could only respond with a contemptuous question. "To you?" he asked; after which the minister silently turned and left. Further questioning by police officials revealed nothing: Gershuni refused to name his accomplices, even though he was told that this was the only way to save his life. [26]

The trial of Gershuni and his associates, the "Case of the So-Called Battle Organization of the Socialist Revolutionary Party," took place finally in February 1904. It was decided not to hold a large trial of SR members, who might attract public sympathy, but to try only a few persons who were implicated in outright crimes such as murder and attempted assassination. The government's case was not strong: it was based on the testimony of Grigor'ev, himself one of the accused, and on the confession of Kachura, who appeared at the trial to be confused and unstable. Nevertheless, Gershuni, Mel'nikov, and even Grigor'ev—the latter despite his cooperation with the police—were sentenced to death. The sentence was soon commuted to life imprisonment, as the government apparently decided not to make martyrs of the convicted assassins. [27]

Other events seemed also to show that the police had the upper hand, and that the life of the Minister of Interior was secure. In January of 1904 another plot to assassinate Plehve was exposed by Evno Azef. Serafima Klichoglu, a former associate of the Battle Organization, had formed her own small terrorist band late in 1902. Learning through party channels that she was preparing an attack on the minister, Azef immediately informed Rataev of the conspiracy. The two then traveled to Saint Petersburg, where the collaborator even went so far as to meet with Klichoglu, learn the details of her plans, and report on them to the police. Azef, apparently, did not want any competition for his Battle Organization, especially since a successful attack by Klichoglu might destroy his rapport with the police without winning him the admiration of the revolutionaries. The exposure of the plot, on the other hand, would solidify his standing with the police. Klichoglu and her accomplices were arrested; charts of the minister's itinerary and floorplans of the Winter Palace were found in their possession. [28] The value of Azef's work was proven anew: once more the master spy had "saved" Plehve's life.

Another attack on the Minister of Interior was attempted in March, this time by Azef's own minions. The group of young conspirators in Saint Petersburg, among them Boris Savinkov and Egor Sazonov, had grown impatient with their time-consuming surveillance. Their observations had led them to conclude that the easiest time to assassinate the minister would be on Thursday, when he traveled by carriage to make regular reports to the tsar. Over Azef's objections, they concocted a plan to murder the minister when he returned to the Police Department building from his visit to the emperor on Thursday, March 18, 1904. Unable to dissuade the young enthusiasts, Azef finally went along. A number of bombs were prepared and, on the appointed day, three bomb-throwers stationed themselves near the entrance to the Police Department building. Accomplices were posted at prominent places to signal them when Plehve's carriage was approaching.[29]

Azef's activity during all this was strange, but shrewd. He personally reported the basic outlines of the plan to the Director of the Police Department, but he made out that Lopukhin, and not Plehve, was the intended victim. He neglected, however, to give the exact details, including the time and the date. Apparently he was playing both sides of the fence, trying to protect himself in any eventuality. As it turned out, the assassination attempt was a failure. One of the terrorists, fearful that he was being watched, had left his post; the other two bomb-throwers missed their chance when Plehve's coach went speeding by. The minister, unknowingly, had survived another attempt. But this time the conspirators were not arrested; they escaped undetected, and were now free to redesign and perfect their plot.[30]

Disconcerted by their failure, and by rumors of Azef's arrest, the terrorists lost their composure, and the group split in two.[31] One faction, under Savinkov, decided to give up on Plehve and assassinate Kiev governor-general Kleigels. Another band, of which Sazonov was a member, was to remain in the capital and make a new attack on Plehve. The latter group planned two attempts, one for Thursday, March 24, and another for April 1. The first misfired when they failed to encounter the minister's carriage. The second was abandoned when one of the conspirators accidently blew himself up while preparing his bomb.

Meanwhile, under increasing suspicion from the SR leaders, Azef had definitely decided that Plehve must be sacrificed. He caught up with Savinkov and his comrades in Kiev, persuaded them to abandon the useless Kleigels venture, and reassembled the entire group in Khar'kov. Here he proposed to them a new, elaborate, and hopefully foolproof plan. They were to return to the capital, rent an apartment, take up various posts, and meticulously chart the exact route of the minister on his visits to the emperor. Savinkov, disguised as a wealthy English businessman, was placed in charge of the operation. All was accomplished according to the plan.

In June 1904, finally, the conspirators met with Azef in Moscow to work out the final details. There were to be four bomb-throwers who would meet Plehve's carriage along its route to the Warsaw station, whence the minister normally embarked on the short train ride to Peterhof. The first was to let the carriage go by; the second was to throw his bomb. If, for some reason, he failed or missed and the carriage went on, the third and fourth terrorists were to complete the task. If the carriage turned around and headed back, the first bomb-thrower would be in a position to strike. Savinkov was to supervise the operation; Sazonov, as the second bomb-thrower, was to play the principal role. The attempt was set for July 8, but once again it miscarried, this time because Sazonov failed to show up at the appointed time.

A new attempt was fixed for the following week. On Thursday, July 15, between 8:00 and 9:00 in the morning, the four bomb-throwers met with Savinkov at the Warsaw station. To avoid suspicion, they were dressed in the uniforms of railway employees, enabling them to blend with the crowd. The bombs were passed out, and the four then left and took up their appointed stations along the Izmailovskii Prospekt. They walked approximately forty paces apart, waiting for the minister's carriage to arrive. This time there would be no failure.

THE END OF THE MINISTER

Ever since his appointment as minister V. K. Plehve had, of necessity, been preoccupied with his own safety. This was only to be expected, for it was common knowledge that the terrorists were plotting his murder. Any public appearance, any trip by train or carriage, might well be his last. Even the arrest of Gershuni and his replacement by Azef did not totally allay the danger: aside from the Battle Organization attacks on Sipiagin, Obolenskii, and Bogdanovich, there occurred a number of isolated attempts on the lives of various other persons. These included unsuccessful attacks on Vilnius governor von Wahl, Kiev gendarme chief Novitskii, and anti-Semitic publisher Krushevan, the severe wounding of Caucasus Governor-General Golitsyn, and the successful mid-1904 murders of Finland Governor-General Bobrikov and Elizavetpol Vice-Governor Andreev. Plehve himself was so thoroughly despised, by such a large number of people, that the possibility of a vengeful attack by some lone, disgruntled person could never be ruled out.

Shortly after taking over the ministry, Plehve had chosen Alek-
sandr Spiridonovich Skandrakov—an old colleague from his days at
the Police Department—as his personal bodyguard. Skandrakov, an
experienced police official who had served as a gendarme officer in
Kiev and as chief of the Moscow Okhrana, may well have been the
only man that Plehve completely trusted. Besides acting as a bodyguard, he was also reportedly in charge of perlustration, observing the
activities and reading the mail of everyone from anti-government activists to imperial ministers. He even spied on Plehve's own Director
of Police.[32]

Unreservedly devoted to his chief, Skandrakov set up an extensive system of personal security for the minister. For most of the year,
Plehve lived in the Police Department building itself, in the impressive
home that Sipiagin had constructed within the edifice on the Fontanka
River. Here he was constantly surrounded by police, as well as by
special guards: P. N. Miliukov later recalled being led through dark
corridors, and through doorways guarded by muscular lackeys, on his
way to the minister's office.[33] In summer Plehve lived at his *dacha* on
Aptekarsk Island, but here, too, he was continually protected by
guards.

The minister never went about in public unless the utmost precautions had been taken. A special carriage, with iron-lined window
shades, was used to transport Plehve on his infrequent ventures. His
destinations, his routes, and the times of his coming and going were
not revealed beforehand. His carriage was always accompanied by a
number of detectives, who rode alongside on bicycles and watched for
suspicious activity. On railroad trips, he traveled in a separate railway
car, surrounded by police, which rolled through towns with its shades
drawn and doors locked. "Suspicious persons" in the towns through
which he passed were rounded up by police beforehand.[34]

The constant existence as a hunted man, the ever-present fear
that each day might be his last, could not help but have its effect on
Plehve's personality. It was only natural that he should develop something of a "siege mentality." On one of his visits to Aptekarsk Island,
for instance, labor expert Pogozhev noticed that the minister was
wearing some sort of protective body armor underneath his shirt. "Do
you suppose," Plehve had asked his guest, "that I would simply decide
to let you come to see me, and that I would remain alone with you for
a long period of time, without taking all the necessary precautions?
What if you should suddenly thrust a dagger at me?" Conversely, the
minister was known to take isolated walks on occasions when he was

outside the capital—evidently in an effort to escape the continual confinement of his position. At times he even gave vent to a kind of gallows humor: he refused to have the black bunting, which had been used for the funeral of Sipiagin, removed from the staircase of his Fontanka home. When it was suggested that the cloth be taken down, the minister replied: "No, you'd better save it; you can still use it for me."[35]

By the middle of 1904, Plehve had already survived at least six assassination plots. Two of these he was aware of: the Grigor'ev–cavalry officer conspiracy and the aborted Klichoglu plan. Four others, all arranged by the Azef-Savinkov band, had not been brought to his knowledge. These included the proposed attempts of March 18, March 25, April 1, and July 8—all of which had failed due to simple chance or terrorist bungling. He was unaware, then, that he had already four times been spared. He was also unaware of the new attack which the Battle Organization was planning to execute on Thursday, July 15, 1904.

The morning of July 15 was clear and sunny. Plehve, as usual, set out punctually for his weekly report to the emperor. As usual, he rode in his special carriage; as usual, his bicycle detectives rode close at hand, with Skandrakov following in a small coach. The last part of the minister's route would take him down the Izmailovskii Prospekt to the Warsaw station, where he was to catch the 10:00 train for Peterhof.[36]

There is no evidence that he was particularly worried about his safety that morning. The recent murders of Bobrikov and Andreev, coming more than a year since the last previous successful assassination, had again raised the specter of terror. But with a police collaborator at the head of the Battle Organization, Plehve had reason to expect that he would be warned in advance of any serious threat to his life. As it was, Azef had reported to Rataev as recently as June 19 that the assassination plans had been called off due to a "lack of bombs." It would, he had added, take considerable time for the new bombs to be prepared.[37]

Events were soon to demonstrate the falsity of this report. Somewhere along the Prospekt, as it neared the railway station, Plehve's carriage passed by Borishanskii, the first of Savinkov's bomb-throwers. The minister, unknowingly, had entered the terrorist trap. A short time later, at about twenty minutes before ten, he saw a young man dressed as a railway worker running toward his coach. The man was carrying a heavy object, wrapped in newspaper. Plehve quickly

Remains on street following Plehve's assassination.

changed positions, trying to avoid his fate. Briefly, his eyes met those of his assassin. The young man collided momentarily with one of the bicycle detectives, and lost his balance; but he still managed to throw his package toward the window of the carriage. Moments later there was a terrific explosion.[38]

Several eyewitnesses have described the ensuing scene. "Suddenly, the monotonous sound of the street was broken by a strange, heavy ponderous thud," wrote Boris Savinkov. "It sounded like a cast-iron hammer striking against a cold iron plate. At the same second, the broken panes in the windows began to clank in complaint. I watched as there ascended from the earth a thin funnel column of

Remains of carriage following Plehve's assassination.

grayish-yellow smoke, almost black at the edges. The column spread
out and covered the whole street, up to a height of five stories. It
dissipated as quickly as it had come. It seemed to me that I saw in the
smoke some sort of blackened ruins." A British reporter, who also
claimed to have been present, spoke of a "tremendous sound, as of
thunder," followed by the noise of breaking glass. "A dead horse, a
pool of blood, fragments of a carriage and a hole in the ground," he
went on, "were parts of my rapid impressions."[39]

The minister's carriage, it developed, had been shattered by the
force of the explosion. His coachman had been thrown over the horses
and killed on the spot. Debris was scattered over a wide area. A nearby
guard officer, and the bomb-thrower himself, were seriously wounded.

A number of passers-by, too, sustained injuries, as did the detective on the bicycle.[40]

On the street, near the place of the explosion, lay the body of its principal victim. The minister's face was mutilated, his arm was half torn off, and a gaping wound opened in his side. His body was covered with lacerations, and a splinter from the carriage was imbedded in his skull. Death, apparently, had been instantaneous. Egor Sazonov's bomb had done its work. Viacheslav Konstantinovich Plehve was no more.

11

The Legacy of Plehve

EPILOGUE

The assassination of Plehve produced a profound impression, both in Russia and abroad. Almost everywhere, it seems, the reaction was one of joy and relief. The sensitive Dmitri Shipov, one of the few who did not share this emotion, was appalled by the open rejoicing in Russian society over a political murder. Among the émigré revolutionary groups, the response was one of outright jubilation. The Socialist Revolutionaries issued their usual proclamation, listing the "crimes" for which Plehve had been "executed." Azef, Savinkov, Sazonov, and their associates became the heroes of the day. SR matriarch Ekaterina Breshkovskaia, who disliked Azef intensely, greeted him with a profound bow. All the criticism and suspicion directed toward the Battle Organization was forgotten in this moment of victory.[1]

Even among government officials, there appears to have been no great sorrow over Plehve's demise. Witte, who could hardly suppress his satisfaction, remarked that it was the slain coachman, and not the minister, who deserved public sympathy. Lopukhin, who owed his position to Plehve, grumbled that the minister had been "stifling everybody." Only the most loyal functionaries, men like Liubimov and Skandrakov, seem to have been genuinely aggrieved. Others, like Gurko, were more afraid that their work would suffer now that its sponsor was gone.[2]

The emperor himself, despite rumors that he was happy to be freed from Plehve's "tyranny," was quite saddened by the event. "In the person of good Plehve," he wrote in his diary for July 15, 1904, "I have lost a friend and an irreplaceable Minister of Interior. How severely the Lord visits us with His Wrath! In such a short time, to have lost two such devoted and useful servants. But it is His Holy Will!" If Nicholas had any inkling of the importance of this event, his diary gives no indication. It continues, as usual, with trivia: "Aunt Marusia came to lunch. . . . We went for a walk with Mama, and for a ride with Misha to the sea. We dined on the balcony—it was a lovely evening."[3]

Following the assassination, Plehve's corpse was returned to the Police Department by Skandrakov, who had been following the minister in his own carriage. The body was dressed, and the series of requiems began. Plehve's wife and son, who had been on their way to Kostroma province, hastily returned to the capital. The funeral itself took place on Sunday, July 18. In attendance were the emperor and grand dukes, the officials of the ministry, the diplomatic corps, and nearly all the high state officials—with the exception of Witte, who happened to be in Berlin on imperial business.[4]

Egor Sazonov, the minister's assassin, was taken half-dead to a hospital. He soon recovered, however, and was questioned by the police. The fourth bomb-thrower, S. V. Sikorskii, had also been arrested when he was observed trying to dispose of his bomb in the Neva River. The other two escaped, as did Boris Savinkov. Sazonov and Sikorskii, it was widely expected, would soon be sentenced to death.

But already things were beginning to change. On July 30, the Empress Alexandra gave birth to a son: the long-awaited male heir had finally arrived. Nicholas was in no mood for vindictiveness. The christening of the baby was accompanied by a manifesto proclaiming an outright ban on corporal punishment, and a cancelling of outstanding arrears in redemption dues.[5] A few weeks later, the emperor appointed the conciliatory Prince Sviatopolk-Mirskii to replace Plehve as Minister of Interior. Mirskii was given a mandate to make concessions, and to heal the rift between the government and society. He also strove to restore some semblance of legality to police operations. He decided that the suspected assassins should not be bound over for military court-martial, but should instead be tried in the criminal courts. The trial, which took place in November 1904, featured a dramatic speech by defense attorney Karabchevskii, who announced that Sazonov's bomb was "filled not with dynamite, but with the tears and sufferings of the entire Russian people. . . ." Sazonov was sentenced to life imprisonment, while Sikorskii was given twenty years at hard labor.[6]

Evno Azef, incredibly, escaped the suspicion of the police. Apparently, there was no serious attempt made to investigate his role, even though it was well known that his Battle Organization had accomplished the murder. Lopukhin and others accepted the spy's lame excuses and countercharges, and Azef was allowed to continue in his position. His reputation among the revolutionaries now secure, he continued to play his double role for four more years.

The death of Plehve brought about the end of some of his policies. His oppressive censorship was eased, his "zemstvo inspections" ceased, the Tver zemstvo's autonomy was restored, and most of the zemstvo workers exiled by Plehve were pardoned. Many of his top assistants, including Stishinskii, von Wahl, Zinov'ev, and Sturmer, were removed from their posts. His project for increasing the authority of the governors was stillborn, and an attempt to revive the issue in 1905 came to naught. His Council on Local Affairs, the heart of his "constitution," did not actually meet until 1908.[7]

This is not to deny that Plehve's regime had an important impact on late imperial Russia. Many of his programs, if not successful themselves, became the precursors of even wider reforms. Plehve's peasant project, although never directly implemented, did serve as groundwork for future legislation. In fact, some of its main contributors—men like Gurko, Lykoshin, and Krivoshein—were to play a leading role in drafting the 1906 laws which became the foundation of "Stolypin's land reforms." Similarly, Plehve's Resettlement Law became the foundation of a much broader policy: a special supplement of March 10, 1906, extended its "privileges" to all peasant resettlers, regardless of where they came from or where they settled. What had begun as an attempt to regulate and control migration became, in effect, a guarantee of the peasants' right to resettle at state expense.[8]

Although Plehve's "labor department" plan had largely been abandoned, some of its goals eventually were realized. In 1905 was established a Ministry of Trade and Industry, separate from both Interior and Finance, to which were transferred all departments dealing with workers and industry, including the factory inspectorate. In 1906, the workers were even given the right to form unions, but these were closely restricted and expressly forbidden to strike. Plehve's reorganization of the imperial police, his establishment of an empire-wide Okhrana, and his use of collaborators and secret agents were continued by his successors. The russification of Finland, although decelerated

Plehve's assassin, Egor Sazonov.

significantly under Governor-General Obolenskii, was never completely abandoned. The policy of restricting Jews, although eased very slightly by Plehve's own late efforts, was continued and expanded.

More significantly, the hostility toward the government engendered by Plehve's policies could not be erased by his successors. The repression of the zemstvos and the conflict with society were rejected by Sviatopolk-Mirskii, but it proved to be too late to undo the harm. By expanding the bureaucracy, restricting the zemstvos, and repressing even the nobility, Plehve had convinced many of the need for political change. By trying to force cooperation he had engendered confrontation; by striving to impose control he had fostered disarray. Indeed, by arousing or increasing the enmity of almost every segment of the population, he had set in motion the forces which led to the Russian revolution of 1905.

Several other aspects of his policies, in fact, qualify him as a principal author of this revolution. The war with Japan, for which Plehve must bear a share of the blame, continued to go poorly after his assassination. The Russian surrender of Port Arthur in December of 1904 was a major blow to the prestige of the regime, demonstrating to one and all the government's weakness and inability to deal with its enemies. The following month, the spark to set off the revolution was produced by another remnant from the Plehve era. At the beginning of January 1905, Father Gapon's Assembly of Factory-Plant Workers of the City of Saint Petersburg organized a massive strike in the capital. On Sunday, January 9, a huge crowd of workers under Gapon's direction converged on the Winter Palace to present a petition to the monarch. The imperial troops, however, fired into the crowd, killing and wounding several hundred workers—and destroying once and for all the myth of the emperor's innocent benevolence. Less than six months after the minister's demise the revolution had begun, set in motion by an organization confirmed by Plehve and financed by his police.

CONCLUSIONS

V. K. Plehve came to the Ministry of Interior in April 1902 full of self-confidence and vigor. He had, after all, achieved notable success in every post he had held during his long career. What reason was there to expect that this one, a position toward which he had been striving for more than twenty years, would prove to be an exception?

Since he was so suddenly thrust into this post, Plehve had no carefully conceived plans nor detailed prescriptions for curing Russia's ills. Based on his long experience in government, however, he did have some definite ideas on how things should proceed. He was concerned, above all, with order and control. Russia was in the midst of a difficult transition, and faced with enormous problems; this was no time for dissension and discord. The problems could only be resolved, and the necessary reforms enacted, if the various elements could be made to put aside their differences, stifle their complaints, and work together for the good of all. His job, as Minister of Interior, would be to supervise, direct, and coordinate these efforts.

Plehve's vision of Russia's future, as it emerged from his developing programs, was that of a strong autocracy gradually adapting itself to changing conditions. It was basically an authoritarian vision: although it recognized the need for reform and modernization, it insisted that any changes be made "gradually," and "from above." It allowed for no differences of opinion, little variety of national custom, and no criticism of the government. It envisioned cooperation between the state and society, and between the Russians and the nationalities, but not on equal terms: society and the nationalities were expected to forego their autonomy and submit to the will of the government. It foresaw an expanded role for the zemstvos and town councils, but only under the strict supervision of the administrative authorities.

To attain this vision, certain things had to be accomplished. The revolutionaries had to be stopped, that much was clear. State policy had to be unified, and government control consolidated. The monarchy had to win back to its side the nobility, which was rapidly becoming estranged, and to engage the forces of society in "useful work for the common good." A new peasant program had to be devised, and agrarian poverty relieved. Industrial workers, so susceptible to revolutionary propaganda, had to be protected, assisted, and convinced that the government was on their side. The empire had to be made more unified and homogeneous, and the nationalities had to be made more patriotic and loyal.

During his rather brief tenure in office, then, Plehve set out to meet these various objectives. In order to combat sedition, the political police were revitalized and expanded, and the use of spies and agents was increased. In order to unify local policy, the ministry worked out a plan to concentrate more power in the hands of the governors. In order to facilitate cooperation between state and society, a series of conferences within the Ministry of Interior were held, and a Council on Local Affairs was set up to regularize this process. Peasant reforms, which foresaw the gradual transition from communes to farm-steads and resettlement aid for poor villagers, were initiated in the ministry. Several laws to assist factory workers were passed, and work-ers in various cities were encouraged to form mutual-aid societies. Efforts were made to abet Jewish emigration and ease Jewish restraints, while Finnish and Armenian autonomy was further restricted.

While this may not have been a particularly bold program, it nevertheless represented a serious and responsible attempt to address Russia's problems. It sought not so much to impose change as to direct it; it strove to combine modernization with the maintenance of order. It was consistent with the ministry's traditional approach in its drive for bureaucratic control, yet it went beyond this in its plans to assist rural change, transfer authority to the provinces, and simultaneously expand and subordinate the activities of local self-government. In these respects it pointed the way to the reforms of P. A. Stolypin, pursued with some success from 1906 to 1911.

Plehve, however, laboring under several constraints, achieved very little success. Before he could concentrate on his policies, he first had to secure his position and prevail in his struggle against Witte. And by the time he finally succeeded, the actions taken to defeat his rival had damaged his own position. His harassment of the local com-mittees, for instance, enabled him to undermine Witte, but at the same time upset his agreement with Shipov and antagonized the no-bility. His abandonment of Zubatov allowed him to parry Witte's intrigues, but it also cut some ground from under his own worker program. His support for Far Eastern adventurism helped dislodge Witte from the Ministry of Finance, but it also helped push Russia into the disastrous war with Japan.

In another sense, Plehve's failure was inherent in his own person-ality. The very traits that had secured him in his post—the desire and ability to please his superiors, and the unwillingness to jeopardize his career—also served to weaken his programs. Wary of offending those "above" him, he hesitated to put forth any far-reaching changes.[9] Faced with a growing crisis, he insisted on caution and gradualism. "I am extremely cautious by nature . . . ," he once remarked; "As in the Russian proverb, I try on a suit ten times before I have it tailored."[10]

As a result, the reforms that Plehve finally did propose were so cautious and gradual they were bound to be ineffective. Important changes, such as the alteration in attitude toward the commune, were carefully buried amidst traditionalist rhetoric. Attempts to involve society in decision-making, such as the zemstvo-ministerial conferences, the provincial conferences on peasant legislation, and the Council on Local Affairs, were so strictly controlled as to frustrate their purpose. An imaginative policy, such as sponsorship of the *Zubatovshchina*, was quickly disavowed as soon as it ran into problems. Even his provincial reform, so important for administrative unity, never made it out of his ministry.

In the meantime, Plehve's attempts at reform and reconciliation were being undercut by the negative, repressive side of his program. If his reform program was distinguished by caution, his repression was marked by severity. Determined to suppress any and all opposition, intent on preserving the powers of the bureaucracy, and convinced that concession was a sign of weakness, he proceeded to alienate even those upon whose support he depended. Here the ambivalence and inner contradictions of his approach were most apparent. The same man who wished to improve the lot of the peasants gave public approval to the governor who had them flogged. The defender of the workingman, and the author of Russia's "progressive" factory laws, did not hesitate to have striking workers dispersed by whips and rifle fire. The "champion" of the nobility was quick to dismiss, exile, or arrest any nobleman who dared to express views "contrary to those of the government." The man who admitted that Finnish culture was "too deeply rooted" to be eradicated, [11] and that the impoverishment of Jews was creating more revolutionaries, continued to russify, repress—and thus to further alienate—these nationalities.

Even had he had the requisite power and character, it is doubtful if Plehve could have succeeded. Many of the forces at work in Russia —the growth of population, the emergence of nationalism, the spread of Western ideals—were largely beyond the government's control. Repressive policies could deal only with the external manifestations of such forces. The most they might accomplish would be to drive the problems beneath the surface, while the government implemented reforms to deal with the discontent. But the repressive tactics also served to turn more and more of the population against the government, making reform increasingly difficult. Even Stolypin would achieve no lasting success: in the long run his personal fate, and the fate of his programs, would be little better than Plehve's.

Especially in the last months of Plehve's ministry did his weakness and helplessness become apparent. No longer did he have any control over events: he was reduced to striking out fiercely against the government's critics, while hoping out loud that the war—or some other external force—would restore popular allegiance to the regime. He had the power to place persons under surveillance, to make arrests and exiles, to conduct inspections, to censor books and periodicals, to refuse to confirm public officials, and more. But he was powerless to stop the spread of ideas, to force the nationalities to be loyal, to compel the zemstvo-men to narrow their horizons, or to make the revolutionaries cease their "seditious" activity. By trying to prevent discussion of sensitive subjects, he only attracted more attention to them. By trying to russify the nationalities, he only made them more anti-Russian. By fostering official anti-Semitism, he made the Jews into a dangerous, hostile force. By using repressive tactics against the liberal and radical elements, he drove more and more moderates to join the opposition. By having troops shoot at striking workers, he only helped swell the revolutionary ranks. Most ironically of all, by infiltrating the terrorists with an agent of his police, he helped set the stage for his own assassination.

Notes

ABBREVIATIONS USED IN NOTES

GBL	Gosudarstvennaia Biblioteka SSSR imeni V. I. Lenina, Otdel Rukopisei
GPB	Gosudarstvennaia Publichnaia Biblioteka imeni M. E. Saltykova-Shchedrina, Otdel Rukopisei
Otchet Gos. Sov.	Russia, Gosudarstvennyi Sovet, *Otchet po deloproizvodstvu Gosudarstvennago Soveta*
Prolog Voiny	*Prolog Russko-Iaponskoi Voiny: Materialy iz arkhiva grafa S. Iu. Vitte*
PSZRI	Russia, Laws, Statutes, etc., *Polnoe sobranie zakonov rossiiskoi imperii* (3rd edition)
Trudy Red. kom.	Russia, Redaktsionnaia kommissiia po peresmotru zakonopolozhenii o krest'ianakh, *Trudy Redaktsionnoi kommissii po peresmotru zakonopolozhenii o krest'ianakh*
TsGAOR	Tsentral'nyi Gosudarstvennyi Arkhiv Oktiabrskoi Revoliutsii SSSR
TsGIA	Tsentral'nyi Gosudarstvennyi Istoricheskii Arkhiv SSSR

1—THE MINISTER OF INTERIOR

1. D. N. Liubimov, "Russkaia smuta nachala deviatisotykh godov, 1902–1906gg.," pp. 2–3, 6–7.

2. A. S. Suvorin, *Dnevnik*, p. 290; V. I. Gurko, *Features and Figures of the Past*, p. 107.

3. For discussions of the imperial government prior to 1905, see N. P. Erosh-kin, *Ocherki istorii gosudarstvennykh uchrezhdenii dorevoliutsionnoi Rossii*, pp. 248–325; G. L. Yaney, *The Systematization of Russian Government*, pp. 250–65, 305–14, 331–70; N. M. Korkunov, *Russkoe gosudarstvennoe pravo*, 2: 61–157, 235–56, 346–487; N. B. Weiss-man, *Reform in Tsarist Russia*, pp. 7–20; P. A. Zaionchkovskii, *Rossiiskoe samoderzhavie v kontse xix stoletiia*, pp. 98–117, 158–68, 336–428; and G. B. Sliozberg, *Dorevoliutsionnyi stroi Rossii*, pp. 109–12, 138–41, 143–48, 150–90. See also Gurko, pp. 30–32.

4. See S. Iu. Witte, *Vospominaniia: Tsarstvovanie Nikolaia II*, 1: 3–4, 9–12; 2: 228, 289–90, 291–93; Gurko, pp. 221–22; and A. A. Mosolov, *At the Court of the Last Tsar*, pp. 6–11, 28–31, 125, 234.

5. See S. Iu. Witte, "A Secret Memorandum on the Industrialization of Imperial Russia," pp. 64–74; T. H. Von Laue, *Sergei Witte and the Industrialization of Russia*, pp. 71–119; Stuart R. Tompkins, "Witte as Minister of Finance, 1892–1903," pp. 590–606.

6. The figures used are those cited by Von Laue, pp. 262–72.

7. Gurko, pp. 52–68; Von Laue, pp. 167–73, 276–90.

8. Von Laue, pp. 211–22, 249–50.

9. Various aspects of this rivalry are discussed in Jeremiah Schneiderman, *Sergei Zubatov and Revolutionary Marxism*, pp. 32–47; Yaney, pp. 287–90, 312–14; and Von Laue, pp. 157–62, 222–23, 252.

10. See E. M. Feoktistov, *Vospominaniia E. M. Feoktistova*, pp. 205, 226; Witte, *Tsarstvovaniia Nikolaia II*, 1: 27–28; and Zaionchkovskii, *Rossiiskoe samoderzhavie*, pp. 136–37, 151–52, 183–84, 294–96, 306–7, 411–16, 421–24.

11. See Schneiderman, pp. 32–39; I. Kh. Ozerov, *Politika po rabochemu voprosu v Rossii za poslednie gody*, pp. 29–33, 157–65, 171–72; and *PSZRI* 19, no. 16439 (February 1, 1899).

12. Von Laue, pp. 157–62; Gurko, p. 78.

13. Gurko, pp. 86–87; B. B. Veselovskii, *Istoriia zemstva*, 3: 533–34; Ozerov, pp. 64–72, 262–63.

2—VIACHESLAV KONSTANTINOVICH PLEHVE

1. Theodor Herzl, *The Complete Diaries of Theodor Herzl*, 4: 1522; A. V. Pogozhev, "Iz vospominanii o V. K. fon-Pleve," p. 260.

2. Details of Plehve's early life are taken primarily from his service record, found in TsGIA, f. 1162, op. 6, d. 419, ll. 163–79 and TsGAOR, f. 586, op. 1, d. 2, ll. 1–30; and from *Pamiati Viacheslava Konstantovicha Pleve*, a eulogistic biography anonymously written by D. N. Liubimov. See Liubimov, pp. 165–67.

3. Herzl, *Complete Diaries*, 4: 1536.

4. Rumors later arose that Plehve was of Catholic or Jewish background, that he was orphaned in early childhood, that he had cynically changed religions and betrayed his childhood guardians. See *Osvobozhdenie*, July 2, 1902, p. 28; Aug. 19, 1902, p. 66; Carl Joubert, *The Truth about the Tsar and the Present State of Russia*, pp. 244–45; and Witte, *Tsarstvovanie Nikolaia II*, 1: 30, 194. They are denied by sources close to Plehve: A. A. Lopukhin, *Otryvki iz vospominanii*, p. 11; Liubimov, pp. 164–67;

Pamiati Pleve, pp. 43–44. They also seem to be contradicted by his later correspondence with his parents, who died in 1893 and 1901, and by the fact that he was eventually buried next to them in Moscow. TsGAOR, f. 586, op. 1, d. 450, ll. 1–9; *Peterburgskii Nekropol'*, 3: 427.

5. *Pamiati Pleve*, pp. 7–8; GBL, f. 169, d. P73, no. 2.

6. For discussions of the judicial system see Samuel Kucherov, *Courts, Lawyers and Trials under the Last Three Tsars*, pp. 21–106; I. V. Gessen, *Sudebnaia Reforma*, pp. 50–141; and M. Vydria and V. Ginev, "Sudebnaia sistema dorevoliutsionnoi rossii," pp. 509–11.

7. Gessen, *Sudebnaia Reforma*, pp. 143–44; Zaionchkovskii, *Rossiiskoe samoderzhavie*, p. 152.

8. TsGAOR, f. 586, op. 1, d. 2, ll. 1, 4, 8.

9. TsGAOR, f. 586, op. 1, d. 15, ll. 1, 5–7.

10. V. G. Korolenko, *Sobranie sochinenii*, 6: 275; 7: 147–48; TsGAOR, f. 586, op. 1, d. 2, ll. 17–18.

11. *Pamiati Pleve*, p. 9; *Novoe Vremia*, April 6, 1902, p. 2; July 16, 1904, p. 2.

12. D. T. Orlovsky, *The Limits of Reform*, pp. 173–74, 179–81, 186, 191–94.

13. TsGAOR, f. 586, op. 1, d. 2, l. 18; d. 16, ll. 1–2; E. J. Dillon, *The Eclipse of Russia*, pp. 78, 118; "K delu 1 marta 1881 goda," pp. 23–47; *Pamiati Pleve*, p. 10.

14. "K delu 1 marta 1881 goda," p. 24; TsGIA, f. 1284, op. 241, d. 82, ll. 225–26.

15. TsGAOR, f. 586, op. 1, d. 2, ll. 18–19; V. P. Meshcherskii, *Moi Vospominaniia*, 3: 16.

16. TsGIA, f. 1284, op. 241, d. 82, l. 225; P. A. Zaionchkovskii, *Krizis samoderzhavie na rubezhe 1870–1880 godov*, pp. 341–42.

17. *Pamiati Pleve*, pp. 10–11, 13.

18. Meshcherskii, 3: 25–26.

19. TsGAOR, f. 586, op. 1, d. 27; f. 730, op. 1, d. 3675, l. 1.

20. *PSZRI*, 1, no. 350 (August 14, 1881); Zaionchkovskii, *Krizis*, pp. 400–7.

21. TsGAOR, f. 730, op. 1, d. 3675, l. 2; M. Klevenskii, "Okhrannoe otdelenie," pp. 705–6.

22. TsGAOR, f. 586, op. 1, d. 22, l. 1; A. I. Georgievskii, *Materialy po istorii studencheskago dvizheniia v Rossii*, 1: 2.

23. V. K. Plehve, "Zapiska po universitetskomu voprosu," pp. 224–25; TsGAOR, f. 730, op. 1, d. 3675, ll. 2–3.

24. Georgievskii, 1: 57–59.

25. N. K. Mikhailovskii, *Vospominaniia*, p. 24.

26. TsGAOR, f. 543, op. 1, d. 227, ll. 1, 20.

27. E. M. Feoktistov, *Vospominaniia*, pp. 241–42; Zaionchkovskii, *Rossiiskoe samoderzhavie*, pp. 289–90.

28. "K delu 1 marta 1881," pp. 23–69; Stepan S. Volk, *Narodnaia Volia 1879–1882*, pp. 115–16, 142–43, 334; Zaionchkovskii, *Rossiiskoe samoderzhavie*, pp. 166–68; Ia. V. Stefanovich, "Pis'mo Ia. V. Stefanovicha k V. K. Pleve," pp. 410–11; V. N. Figner, *Zapechatlennyi trudy*, 1: 362.

29. On the Degaev-Sudeikin affair see N. P. Makletsova (Degaeva), "Sudeikin i Degaev," pp. 264–72; Figner, 1: 338–42, 356–59, 368–70; Anna Pribyleva-Korba, "Sergei Petrovich Degaev," pp. 1–17; N. A. Troitskii, "Degaevshchina," pp. 125–33; Volk, pp. 147–49; GBL, f. 215, no. 2, d. 2, ll. 106–7.

30. Pribyleva-Korba, p. 17; TsGAOR, f. 586, op. 1, d. 24, l. 6; *The Times* (London), April 19, 1884, p. 9.

31. TsGIA, f. 1162, op. 6, d. 419, l. 168.

32. A. A. Polovtsov, *Dnevnik gosudarstvennogo sekretaria A. A. Polovtsova*, 1: 440; Gurko, p. 108; Feoktistov, pp. 205, 226, 229, 273; A. V. Bogdanovich, *Tri poslednik samoderzhtsa*, pp. 94–95; Meshcherskii, 3: 47.

33. Meshcherskii, 3: 101–2; TsGAOR, f. 586, op. 1, d. 1156, ll. 19, 38, 45–130 *passim*; Polovtsov, *Dvevnik*, 1: 376; 2: 87, 120, 122, 266; Bogdanovich, p. 74.

34. Feoktistov, pp. 229, 273.

35. Iu. B. Solov'ev, *Samoderzhavie i dvorianstvo v kontse XIX veka*, p. 65; GBL, f. 126, d. 11, ll. 116–17; Polovtsov, *Dvevnik*, 2: 194.

36. TsGAOR, f. 586, op. 1, d. 688, ll. 12–61, 68–139 *passim*; Gurko, p. 208; Polovtsov, *Dvevnik*, 2: 204; Witte, *Detstvo; Tsarstvovanie Aleksandra II i Aleksandra III*, p. 273.

37. Feoktistov, pp. 229–30; GBL, f. 126, d. 13, l. 253.

38. TsGIA, f. 1162, op. 6, d. 419, ll. 168–73.

39. *PSZRI* 6, no. 3769 (June 3, 1886); 9, no. 6198 (July 13, 1889); TsGAOR, f. 586, op. 1, d. 44, ll. 2–5; d. 404, ll. 5–7; Polovtsov, *Dvevnik*, 2: 387, 387n.; *Novoe Vremia*, January 12, 1894, p. 1; Zaionchkovskii, *Rossiiskoe samoderzhavie*, pp. 189–93, 203–4; Richard G. Robbins, Jr., "Russia's Famine Relief Law of June 12, 1900: A Reform Aborted," pp. 26–30; E. C. Thaden, ed., *Russification in the Baltic Provinces and Finland*, pp. 66, 159; *Pamiati Pleve*, p. 15; TsGIA, f. 1149, op. XI-1893, d. 77, ll. 256–59.

40. *PSZRI* 9, no. 6196 (July 12, 1889). For various views on this law and its purposes, see Zaionchkovskii, *Rossiiskoe samoderzhavie*, pp. 369–401; A. P. Korelin, *Dvorianstvo v poreformennoi Rossii*, pp. 196–99; Weissman, pp. 19–20; Yaney, pp. 365–76.

41. *PSZRI* 10, no. 6927 (June 12, 1890); 12, no. 8708 (June 11, 1892).

42. Feoktistov, pp. 272–74; Zaionchkovskii, *Rossiiskoe samoderzhavie*, pp. 367, 385, 392; TsGIA, f. 1162, op. 6, d. 419, ll. 170, 171; Polovtsov, *Dvevnik*, 2: 120–23, 266, 414; E. M. Brusnikin, "Podgotovka zakona 14 dekabria 1893 o neotchuzhdaemosti krest'ianskikh nadel'nykh zemel'," pp. 355–56.

43. Zaionchkovskii, *Rossiiskoe samoderzhavie*, pp. 16, 27, 135; TsGIA, f. 1162, op. 6, d. 419, l. 171; S. M. Dubnov, *A History of the Jews in Russia and Poland*, 2: 380–82, 399–402; H. Rogger, "Russian Ministers and the Jewish Question," pp. 30–35; Polovtsov, *Dvevnik*, 2: 314.

44. TsGAOR, f. 586, op. 1, d. 73, l. 5; dd. 70, 80, 1155; Richard G. Robbins, Jr., *The Famine in Russia, 1891–1892*, pp. 100–9; Polovtsov, *Dvevnik*, 2: 408, 413, 422.

45. TsGAOR, f. 1463, op. 1, d. 1115, l. 155; f. 586, op. 1, d. 1, l. 1; d. 2, ll. 22–30; TsGIA, f. 1151, op. XII-1896, d. 1a, ll. 247, 254–55, 272–73, 276, 285–88, 294–95, 298–99, 319–21.

46. *Gosudarstvennyi Sekretar'*. TsGIA, f. 1162, op. 6, d. 419, l. 174.

47. Russia, Gosudarstvennaia Kantseliariia, *Gosudarstvennaia Kantseliariia 1810–1910*, pp. 1–6, 364–66, 461–66; Gurko, pp. 35–47; GBL, f. 126, d. 12, l. 19.

48. Gurko, pp. 35–36, 47–48; GBL, f. 126, d. 11, l. 303.

49. *Novoe Vremia*, January 11, 1894, p. 2; *Pamiati Pleve*, pp. 19–22.

50. Gurko, p. 47; Witte, *Tsarstvovanie Nikolaia II*, 2: 234.

51. *Pamiati Pleve*, pp. 24–25; Russia, Gosudarstvennyi sovet, *Gosudarstvennyi sovet*

1801–1901, pp. 205, 208; *Gosudarstvennaia kantseliariia, 1810–1910*, pp. 396–98, 405–6, 420–25; TsGIA, f. 1283, op. 1, dd. 4, 229; op. 6, d. 419, l. 175.

52. Witte, *Tsarstvovanie Nikolaia II*, 1: 28.

53. *Ibid.*, 1: 29–31.

54. *Ibid.*, 1: 150, 185.

55. TsGIA, f. 1283, op. 1, d. 229, ll. 1–4, 10–15, 56–62; Gurko, pp. 48, 61–62; Solov'ev, pp. 295–304.

56. Witte, *Tsarstvovanie Nikolaia II*, 1: 28; TsGIA, f. 1622, op. 1, d. 446, ll. 2–3.

57. Witte, *Tsarstvovanie Nikolaia II*, 2: 221–22, 229; J. R. Fisher, *Finland and the Tsars, 1809–1899*, pp. 116, 150–51; Thaden, pp. 80–82; V. Semennikov, "Nikolai Romanov i Finliandiia," p. 226; Gurko, p. 48.

58. *Gosudarstvennaia kantseliaria 1810–1910*, p. 407; GPB, f. 586, d. 1, l. 1; TsGAOR, f. 586, op. 1, d. 445, I, 1–2; Witte, *Tsarstvovanie Nikolaia II*, 2: 231; Gurko, p. 48; Fisher, pp. 152–57.

59. *Gosudarstvennaia kantseliariia, 1810–1910*, pp. 407–9; M. M. Borodkin, *Iz noveishei istorii Finliandii*, p. 224.

60. GPB, f. 586, d. 11, ll. 6–9; TsGIA, f. 1162, op. 6, d. 419, l. 176; Witte, *Tsarstvovanie Nikolaia II*, 2: 230.

61. Fisher, pp. 158–59; Borodkin, p. 215.

62. *Pamiati Pleve*, p. 27; GPB, f. 586, d. 11, l. 26; Gurko, pp. 50, 133n.

63. GPB, f. 586, d. 11, ll. 17–18, 49–50; TsGAOR, f. 586, op. 1, d. 445, II, 19–20, 36–37; Borodkin, pp. 129–31, 140–49, 150–53.

64. Thaden, pp. 436–37.

65. Borodkin, pp. 84–92; Witte, *Tsarstvovanie Nikolaia II*, 2: 232–35; Polovtsov, "Dnevnik A. A. Polovtseva," pp. 76–77; PSZRI 21, no. 20456 (June 29, 1901).

66. M. Russobtovskii, *Istoricheskoe osveshchenie finliandskago voprosa*, pp. 86, 91; *Novoe Vremia*, April 9, 1902, p. 4; April 19, 1902, p. 4; April 30, 1902, p. 4; Borodkin, p. 337; Thaden, pp. 438–39.

67. Polovtsov, "Dnevnik," p. 138.

68. Witte, *Detstvo*, p. 273; Gurko, p. 108; *Pamiati Pleve*, p. 50; TsGAOR, f. 634, op. 1, d. 10, ll. 97–98; Feoktistov, p. 229.

69. D. M. Wallace, *Russia*, 2: 447; Witte, *Tsarstvovanie Nikolaia II*, 1: 28; Pogozhev, p. 263; *Pamiati Pleve*, p. 50.

70. TsGAOR, f. 826, op. 1, d. 45, l. 239; Gurko, p. 111; S. D. Urusov, *Memoirs of a Russian Governor*, p. 9.

71. *Novoe Vremia*, April 6, 1902, p. 2.

72. Gurko, p. 110; Pogozhev, pp. 263, 265; Herzl, *Complete Diaries*, 4: 1522–26, 1528–32, 1534–40; Wallace, 2: 234, 373.

73. Gurko, pp. 108–9, 121–22; GBL, f. 126, d. 13, l. 244.

74. *Pamiati Pleve*, p. 51; Gurko, p. 108; Witte, *Tsarstvovanie Nikolaia II*, 2: 14. See also discussion in R. T. Manning, "The Russian Provincial Gentry in Revolution and Counterrevolution, 1905–1907," p. 51.

75. Gurko, pp. 47, 108–10; Solov'ev, p. 65.

76. Witte, *Tsarstvovanie Nikolaia II*, 1: 29; Feoktistov, pp. 229–30; GBL, f. 126, d. 13, l. 253.

77. Bogdanovich, p. 144; Gurko, p. 111; Feoktistov, p. 230.

78. Polovtsov, *Dnevnik*, 2: 41; Bogdanovich, p. 185.

79. Feoktistov, p. 230.

80. TsGAOR, f. 543, op. 1, d. 227, l. 1; *Pamiati Pleve*, pp. 11, 20, 46; V. K. Plehve, "Pis'mo k A. A. Kireevu," pp. 201–2.

81. *Novoe Vremia*, January 11, 1894, p. 2.

82. TsGAOR, f. 1283, op. 1, d. 229, l. 3; Plehve, "Pis'mo k Kireevu," pp. 202–3.

83. Liubimov, p. 72; Gurko, p. 109; Plehve, "Pis'mo k Kireevu," pp. 202–3.

84. GPB, f. 586, d. 11, l. 26; *Pamiati Pleve*, pp. 11–12.

85. Gurko, pp. 110, 234, 309.

86. L. Tikhomirov, "25 let nazad," p. 59.

3—THE PEASANT QUESTION AND THE ZEMSTVOS

1. Liubimov, pp. 1–5.

2. A. A. Polovtsov, "Dnevnik," p. 138.

3. TsGAOR, f. 1463, op. 1, d. 1115, l. 345; TsGIA, f. 721, op. 3, d. 13, l. 10; Liubimov, p. 8; *Novoe Vremia*, April 6, 1902, p. 1.

4. *Novoe Vremia*, April 8, 1902, p. 1.

5. Liubimov, p. 9; GBL, f. 126, d. 13, l. 133; *Grazhdanin*, April 11, 1902, p. 27; Bogdanovich, p. 278; TsGAOR, f. 586, op. 1, d. 7, l. 20.

6. TsGAOR, f. 634, op. 1, d. 10, ll. 97–98; GBL, f. 126, d. 13, l. 133.

7. *Novoe Vremia*, April 13, 1902, p. 1; April 11, 1902, p. 1; Nicholas II, Emperor, "Pis'mo P. S. Vannovskomu," pp. 60–61; GBL, f. 126, d. 13, ll. 133–34; Maurice Bompard, *Mon Ambassade en Russe*, p. 66.

8. *Novoe Vremia*, April 11, 1902, p. 4; April 18, 1902, pp. 3, 4; GBL, f. 126, d. 13, l. 134.

9. TsGAOR, f. 634, op. 1, d. 10, ll. 97–98; f. 586, op. 1, d. 953, ll. 3–4; *Novoe Vremia*, April 17, 1902, p. 2.

10. *Osvobozhdenie*, July 2, 1902, p. 28; Liubimov, pp. 9–10, 152–53.

11. *Krest'ianskoe dvizhenie v Poltavskoi i Khar'kovskoi guberniiakh v 1902g.*, pp. xx, 67–69, 79–84, 163–65; GBL, f. 215, no. 2, d. 2, l. 101; *Novoe Vremia*, April 18, 1902, p. 4; April 21, 1902, p. 5.

12. Yaney, pp. 41–43; *Krest'ianskoe dvizhenie*, pp. 79–80.

13. *Krest'ianskoe dvizhenie*, pp. xvi–xviii, 55–56, 82–93.

14. *Krest'ianskoe dvizhenie*, pp. xviii–xix, 67–78; L. I. Emeliakh, "Krest'ianskoe dvizhenie v Poltavskoi i khar'kovskoe guberniakh v 1902g.," p. 171; *Novoe Vremia*, April 29, 1902, p. 2.

15. Liubimov, p. 11.

16. *Novoe Vremia*, May 1, 1902, p. 2; TsGIA, f. 1263, op. 2, d. 5560, ll. 52–55.

17. For discussions of the peasant question, see James Y. Simms, Jr., "The Crisis of Russian Agriculture at the End of the Nineteenth Century," pp. 377–98; G. T. Robinson, *Rural Russia Under the Old Regime*, pp. 94–242; Yaney, pp. 38–45; Von Laue, pp. 169–78, 272–74; Gurko, pp. 138–41, 158–60.

18. See *Trudy Red. kom.*, 1: 10–28.

19. See Gurko, pp. 171–72; Von Laue, pp. 173–76; M. S. Simonova, "Bor'

ba techenii v pravitel'stvennom lagere po voprosam agrarnoi politiki v kontse XIXv.,"
pp. 77–79.

20. Shmuel Galai, *The Liberation Movement in Russia*, pp. 37–42; TsGIA, f. 1233,
op. 1, d. 78, ll. 163–65; Shipov, pp. 167–68; Manning, pp. 29–45.

21. Simonova, "Bor'ba," pp. 74–81; Von Laue, pp. 167–77, 227–29.

22. TsGIA, f. 1283, op. 1, d. 24, l. 3; Polovtsov, "Dnevnik," p. 144.

23. TsGIA, f. 1291, op. 122, d. 70. I, ll. 24–44, 51–56, 70–71, 81–87, 88–
89; *Trudy Red. kom.*, 1: 7–8.

24. Polovtsov, "Dnevnik," p. 114; G. G. Savich, ed., *Novyi gosudarstvennyi stroi
Rossii*, p. 1.

25. Polovtsov, "Dnevnik," p. 116.

26. *Ibid.*, p. 121; TsGIA, f. 1233, op. 1, d. 20, ll. 65–66, 70–71, 153–55.

27. TsGIA, f. 1233, op. 1, d. 20, ll. 76–77, 84–85.

28. Witte, *Tsarstvovanie Nikolaia II*, 2: 64–66; Gurko, pp. 130, 141, 153–55,
178, 180–81, 184–85.

29. *Novoe Vremia*, September 18, 1902, pp. 1, 4; Gurko, pp. 190–92, 295.

30. GBL, f. 126, d. 13, ll. 170, 171, 209; TsGAOR, f. 1463, op. 1, d. 1115,
l. 344.

31. *Novoe Vremia*, May 11, 1902, pp. 1, 4; May 22, 1902, p. 1; September 27,
1902, p. 1; October 5, 1902, p. 1; Gurko, pp. 130, 178, 188–90, 192–97; GBL,
f. 126, d. 13, ll. 209–10.

32. TsGIA, f. 1291, op. 122, d. 70. I, l. 108; *Trudy Red. kom.*, 1: 8–10; Gurko,
pp. 146–47, 156, 620.

33. TsGIA, f. 1284, op. 241, d. 222, ll. 17–18; f. 1291, op. 122, d. 70. I,
l. 108; f. 1233, op. 1, d. 23, l. 47.

34. TsGIA, f. 1284, op. 241, d. 222, ll. 16–17; Gurko, pp. 134–41; *Novoe
Vremia*, September 27, 1902, p. 1.

35. The book was serialized in *Novoe Vremia*, November 21 through December
1, 1901, and later published under the title *Ustoi narodnogo khoziaistva Rossii* (St. Petersburg: A. S. Suvorin, 1902). See especially pp. 51–56, 176–81.

36. Solov'ev, pp. 203–6; Gurko, pp. 133, 159–61, 165, 171–73.

37. TsGIA, f. 1291, op. 122, d. 70. I, l. 110.

38. Plehve, "Pis'mo k Kireevu," pp. 202–3; D. N. Shipov, *Vospominaniia i dumy
o perezhitom*, pp. 174–75.

39. For discussions of the zemstvos and their views see Yaney, pp. 70–71,
230–32, 355; N. M. Pirumova, *Zemskoe liberal'noe dvizhenie*, pp. 74–124; Manning, pp.
75–86; Weissman, pp. 15–18; Gurko, pp. 123–26, 242–44.

40. TsGIA, f. 1151, op. XII-1896, d. 1a, ll. 255, 272, 276, 294–95; I. P.
Belokonskii, *Zemskoe dvizhenie*, p. 140; Gurko, pp. 227–33.

41. Shipov, pp. 174–75, 178–79, 183–84, 209–10, 218–21; TsGIA, f. 1233,
op. 1, d. 16, ll. 71–72, 311–12; Belokonskii, pp. 104–5, 153–54, 161–63; Plehve,
"Pis'mo k Kireevu," pp. 201–3.

42. *Krest'ianskoe dvizhenie*, pp. 53–55; Belokonskii, pp. 132–33; *Novoe Vremia*,
April 29, 1902, p. 2; June 5, 1902, p. 4.

43. F. Danilov, "Obshchaia politika pravitel'stva i gosudarstvennyi stroi k nachalu xx veka," pp. 469–71; Liubimov, p. 160; Galai, *Liberation*, pp. 31–32, 155.

44. TsGAOR, f. 586, op. 1, d. 1085, ll. 1–4; Shipov, pp. 157–68.

45. E. D. Cherminskii, "Zemsko-Liberal'noe dvizhenie nakanune revoliutsii
1905–1907gg.," p. 47.

46. Shipov, pp. 169–70; Belokonskii, p. 102.

47. Gurko, pp. 121–23, 236; *Novoe Vremia*, December 30, 1902, p. 3; Shipov, pp. 174–175; Belokonskii, pp. 132–33, 163.

48. Belokonskii, p. 102.

49. Galai, *Liberation*, pp. 39–42; V. A. Maklakov, *Vlast' i obshchestvennost' na zakate Staroi Rossii*, p. 317; Shipov, pp. 136–52, 176–78.

50. The following account of Plehve's conversation with Shipov is taken from Shipov, pp. 171–84.

51. Nicholas II, "Pis'mo Vannovskomu," p. 61.

52. Shipov, pp. 185–92, 193; Belokonskii, pp. 104–5.

53. TsGIA, f. 1263, op. 2, d. 5560, ll. 235–37; *Novoe Vremia*, July 19, 1902, p. 1, August 14, 1902, pp. 1, 3; Gurko, pp. 186–87.

54. *Novoe Vremia*, August 31, 1902, pp. 1, 2; Gurko, pp. 227–28.

55. *Novoe Vremia*, September 1, 1902, p. 2; *Grazhdanin*, September 12, 1902, pp. 15–16; Belokonskii, pp. 139–40.

56. *Novoe Vremia*, August 31, 1902, p. 1.

57. *Novoe Vremia*, September 5, 1902, p. 4; Belokonskii, p. 140.

4—PLEHVE, WITTE, AND SOCIETY

1. Gurko, p. 228; TsGAOR, f. 601, op. 1, d. 244, l. 88.

2. Von Laue, pp. 39, 43.

3. Von Laue, pp. 42–49, 69–70. Plehve found Witte's marriage "very original." GPB, f. 586, d. 18, l. 1.

4. See discussions in Yaney, pp. 288–90 and Von Laue, pp. 1–5, 63.

5. *Novoe Vremia*, January 11, 1894, p. 2.

6. Liubimov, p. 72.

7. Simonova, "Bor'ba," p. 76; TsGIA, f. 1283, op. 1, d. 229, ll. 57–59.

8. Witte, *Tsarstvovaniia Nikolaia II*, 1: 195, 258; TsGIA, f. 1233, op. 1, d. 21, ll. 180–81, 185–89, 277–78, 370; M. S. Simonova, "Otmena krugovoi poruki," pp. 185–86; TsGAOR, f. 634, op. 1, d. 11, l. 66.

9. Savich, pp. 1, 2; Belokonskii, pp. 94–96.

10. TsGIA, f. 1233, op. 1, d. 20, l. 84.

11. *Ibid.*, p. 85; *Novoe Vremia*, August 12, 1902, p. 1.

12. S. S. Ol'denberg, *Tsarstvovanie Imperatora Nikolaia II*, 1: 184–87.

13. Belokonskii, pp. 106–12, 115, 118–22.

14. Shipov, pp. 195–96; TsGIA, f. 1282, op. 2, d. 1007, ll. 19–20; d. 1008, ll. 8–9, 16–18, 20–28, 42–46, 102–7, 112–16; Liubimov, pp. 28–29, 59, 63–64; Belokonskii, pp. 115–18, 141–45.

15. TsGIA, f. 1282, op. 2, d. 1005, ll. 1–10, 21, 22–26, 44–45, 50–53, 61–62, 130–35; Liubimov, pp. 59–62; Belokonskii, pp. 112–13.

16. The following account is taken from Liubimov, pp. 66–76.

17. *Novoe Vremia*, December 30, 1902, p. 3; October 3, 1903, p. 3; Belokonskii, pp. 154, 161–63, 166–67.

18. Liubimov, pp. 72–73.

19. Belokonskii, p. 104.

20. TsGIA, f. 1282, op. 2, d. 1008, l. 115; Shipov, pp. 193–94; Belokonskii, p. 146, 146n.

21. *Grazhdanin*, October 3, 1902, pp. 20–21; October 17, 1902, p. 16; Simonova, "Politika tsarizma v krest'ianskom voprose nakanune revoliutsii 1905–1907gg.," p. 214.

22. Russia, Osoboe soveshchanie o nuzhdakh sel'sko-khoziaistvennoi promyshlennosti, *Trudy mestnykh komitetov o nuzhdakh selsko-khoziaistvennoi promyshlennosti* (58 vols. (Saint Petersburg, 1903).

23. For discussions of tsarist local government see Weissman, pp. 7–39; Korelin, pp. 179–233; Yaney, pp. 319–80; S. A. Korf, *Administrativnaia iustitsiia v rossii,* 1: 424–30.

24. Plehve, "Pis'mo k Kireevu," pp. 202–3.

25. Korf, 1: 424–26.

26. Orlovsky, pp. 135–37, 165–66.

27. *Ibid.*, pp. 178–80, 185–89, 191–96.

28. Pirumova, pp. 38–47.

29. *Ibid.*, pp. 93–111; Manning, pp. 79–86.

30. Gurko, p. 122; Korf, pp. 423, 430; Weissman, p. 47.

31. Korf, pp. 423–30; Weissman, pp. 47–50.

32. *Novoe Vremia*, November 13, 1902, p. 13; November 10, 1902, p. 3.

33. *Novoe Vremia*, December 30, 1902, p. 3.

34. *Ibid.*

35. *Novoe Vremia*, December 30, 1902, pp. 2, 3; January 2, 1903, pp. 1, 2, 4; Polovtsov, "Dnevnik," pp. 162–64; Kuropatkin, "Dnevnik," pp. 17, 19; GBL, f. 126, d. 13, ll. 198–99.

36. *Novoe Vremia*, November 12, 1902, pp. 1, 4; Von Laue, pp. 220–22.

37. Gurko, pp. 217, 219–20; Liubimov, pp. 51–54.

38. See text of manifesto in *Novoe Vremia*, February 27, 1903, p. 1.

39. *Ibid.*, pp. 2–3; Kuropatkin, "Dnevnik," p. 43; TsGIA, f. 1099, op. 1, d. 7, l. 59.

40. Simonova, "Otmena," pp. 184–88, 189–90; Polovtsov, "Dnevnik," pp. 141–42, 144; *PSZRI* 23, no. 22629 (March 12, 1903).

41. Liubimov, p. 52; Gurko, pp. 157–59, 219.

42. Gurko, pp. 161–62; GBL, f. 265, d. 124.7, ll. 35–38; TsGIA, f. 1284, op. 242, d. 222, l. 75.

43. TsGIA, f. 1273, op. 1, d. 433, l. 2; *Osvobozhdenie*, April 18, 1903, pp. 349–50.

44. TsGIA, f. 592, op. 44, d. 422, ll. 89, 91; *Osvobozhdenie*, April 18, 1903, pp. 349–50.

45. *Osvobozhdenie*, April 18, 1903, pp. 350–52; Danilov, p. 476.

46. Gurko, pp. 213–14; TsGIA, f. 592, op. 44, d. 422, ll. 93, 96, 100, 101, 103, 106.

47. *Novoe Vremia*, March 2, 1903, p. 2; V. K. Plehve, *Usilenie gubernatorskoi vlasti,* p. 1.

48. Liubimov, pp. 42–45; Plehve, *Usilenie*, pp. 6–7; Weissman, p. 52.

49. Liubimov, p. 45; Korf, 1: 441–48nn.

50. TsGAOR, f. 586, op. 1, d. 360, ll. 1–2; Plehve, *Usilenie*, pp. 21–30.

51. *PSZRI* 23, no. 23041 (May 30, 1903); no. 22757 (April 2, 1903); Gurko, pp. 216–17, 601; Danilov, p. 474.

52. *PSZRI* 23, no. 22906 (May 5, 1903); *Novoe Vremia*, July 2, 1903, p. 2.

53. *Otchet Gos. Sov. 1902/3*, 1: 209–10, 214–15, 222–23, 225; Weissman, pp. 64–65; *Novoe Vremia*, July 2, 1903, p. 2.

54. TsGIA, f. 1234, op. 1, delo po Osobomu Soveshchaniiu pod predsedatel'stvom S. F. Platonova, ll. 2–4.

55. *Ibid.*, ll. 4–5, 270–77. See also *Osvobozhdenie*, June 18, 1903, pp. 11–12; Weissman, pp. 55–56; and Gurko, 129.

56. Plehve, "Pis'mo k Kireevu," pp. 202–3.

57. Shipov, pp. 199–202.

58. *Ibid.*, p. 216; Belokonskii, pp. 153–54.

59. Shipov, p. 213.

60. *Ibid.*, pp. 220–21; Belokonskii, pp. 161–63.

61. *Novoe Vremia*, May 5, 1902, p. 5; August 9, 1902, p. 3; TsGAOR, f. 810, op. 1, d. 492, ll. 33–34; Shipov, pp. 199, 202.

62. TsGAOR, f. 102, d. 9.27.A., ll. 171–72; *Osvobozhdenie*, June 18, 1902, pp. 7–12, 13–14; July 2, 1902, pp. 30–31.

63. Shipov, pp. 193–94, 197, 207n.; Weissman, pp. 86–88.

64. *Ibid.*, p. 207n.; *Osvobozhdenie*, September 18, 1902, pp. 100–2; November 2, 1902, pp. 148–50; February 16, 1903, pp. 289–91; Pirumova, pp. 202–4.

65. See Galai, *Liberation*, p. 144.

66. Shipov, p. 201.

67. Pirumova, pp. 158–74, 199–211; Manning, pp. 82–86.

68. Shipov, p. 199.

69. *Ibid.*, pp. 196–97; *Russkiia Vedomosti*, February 23, 1903, p. 3.

70. The account of this discussion is taken from Shipov, pp. 206–10.

71. *Ibid.*, pp. 210–13.

72. GBL, f. 265, d. 124.7, ll. 29–34; f. 126, d. 13, l. 209.

5—THE JEWISH, FINNISH, AND ARMENIAN QUESTIONS

1. *Novoe Vremia*, April 9, 1903, p. 3.

2. Louis Greenberg, *The Jews in Russia*, 2: 50–51.

3. *Ibid.*, p. 51; *The Times* (London), May 6, 1903, p. 7; May 18, 1903, p. 5; May 19, 1903, p. 3; May 20, 1903, p. 7; May 27, 1903, p. 6.

4. Zaionchkovskii, *Rossiiskoe samoderzhavie*, p. 27; Dubnov, 2: 247–58, 380–82, 385–86, 399–402; *PSZRI* 12, no. 8708 (June 11, 1892); Rogger, "Russian Ministers," pp. 30, 35; Witte, *Tsarstvovanie Nikolaia II*, 1: 192.

5. *Materialy dlia istorii antievreiskikh pogromov v Rossii*, 1: 11–12, 14, 40–42, 44; Urusov, pp. 45–56, 76–82; *Osvobozhdenie*, December 2, 1903, p. 225; December 25, 1903, p. 262.

6. Urusov, pp. 80–81; A. N. Kuropatkin, "Dnevnik A. N. Kuropatkina," p. 43.

7. *The Times* (London), May 18, 1903, p. 20.

8. *The Times* (London), May 22, 1903, p. 3; May 27, 1903, p. 7; *New York Times*, May 21, 1903, p. 8; May 27, 1903, p. 3; Urusov, pp. 12–26.

9. *Novoe Vremia*, April 29, 1903, p. 1; *Materialy*, 1: 169–70, 176–77, 178–82,

258, 261–62; 323–24, 333–34; Urusov, pp. 74–75; Osvobozhdenie, June 18, 1903, p. 15.

10. Lopukhin, Otryvki, pp. 76, 86–89; Witte, Tsarstvovanie Nikolaia II, 1: 192, 193, 316; 2: 13–74.

11. Greenberg, 2: 50–52; Dubnov, 3: 68–71.

12. Hans Rogger, "The Jewish Policy of Late Tsarism: A Reappraisal," pp. 44–45; Materialy, 2: 8–173 passim.

13. Witte, Tsarstvovanie Nikolaia II, 1: 192–93. See also below, pp. 105–10.

14. Novoe Vremia, May 13, 1903, p. 4; June 20, 1903, p. 1; Urusov, pp. 77–78; Schneiderman, pp. 220–21, 228–29.

15. Lopukhin, Otryvki, p. 88; Witte, Tsarstvovanie Nikolaia II, 1: 193.

16. Lopukhin, Otryvki, p. 15.

17. Liubimov, p. 85; Gurko, pp. 247, 248; Lopukhin, Otryvki, pp. 15–16; Urusov, p. 78.

18. Materialy, 1: 281–82; 334; Urusov, pp. 15, 17, 57–58; Liubimov, pp. 80–81, 82–83; Gurko, p. 248.

19. Lopukhin, Otryvki, p. 16; Liubimov, p. 85; Gurko, p. 248.

20. Urusov, pp. 15, 78; Materialy, 1: 335–46.

21. Urusov, pp. 4, 10, 12, 15–18, 23, 33–34, 45–47, 75–76, 77–78.

22. Ibid., pp. 15, 77.

23. Cited in A. S. Tager, The Decay of Czarism, pp. 9–10.

24. Urusov, pp. 80–81, 82.

25. Ibid., p. 55.

26. Gurko, pp. 246, 248; L. A. Rataev, "Evno Azef: Istoriia ego predatel'stva," p. 198.

27. Thaden, pp. 16–18.

28. V. K. Plehve, "A Defense of Russia's Policy in Finland," p. 577.

29. Herzl, The Diaries of Theodor Herzl, p. 389.

30. For Plehve's stated views on the nationalities question see Plehve, "Defense," pp. 577–80; Pamiati Pleve, pp. 27–28; and Herzl, Diaries, pp. 389–90, 399–400.

31. Thaden, pp. 66, 159; Gurko, p. 50; Borodkin, pp. 231–33.

32. See H. J. Tobias, The Jewish Bund in Russia from its Origins to 1905, pp. 2–8; Rogger, "Jewish Policy," pp. 46–50; A. F. Koni, "Sergei Iul'evich Vitte," pp. 272–73; Herzl, Diaries, pp. 389–90; G. B. Sliozberg, Dela minuvshik dnei, 3: 53–54.

33. Greenberg, 1: 187–200; 2: 19, 33–35, 38, 39–44, 48; Polovtsov, Dnevnik, 2: 314.

34. I. I. Ianzhul, "Vospominaniia I. I. Ianzhul o perezhitom i vidennom," pp. 488–90.

35. Koni, pp. 272–74.

36. Grazhdanin, November 7, 1902, pp. 15–16; Osvobozhdenie, March 19, 1903, p. 340; Novoe Vremia, May 24, 1903, p. 2; Rogger, "Russian Ministers," p. 41.

37. N. A. Bukhbinder, "O Zubatovshchine," pp. 289–301; Dubnov, 3: 45.

38. Dubnov, 3: 45; Herzl, Diaries, p. 390n.

39. Osvobozhdenie, September 18, 1903, p. 125; Greenberg, 2: 180.

40. Herzl, Diaries, p. 387; Greenberg, 2: 178–79.

41. Herzl, Complete Diaries, 4: 1522–23, 1525, 1527; Liubimov, p. 88; Herzl, Diaries, pp. 392, 394–97.

42. Herzl, Complete Diaries, 4: 1520, 1532, 1533.

43. Herzl, *Diaries*, p. 391; *Complete Diaries*, 4: 1538–39, 1550–51.

44. Herzl, *Complete Diaries*, 4: 1551; *Diaries*, pp. 407–8.

45. Dubnov, 3: 84, 88–90; *New York Times*, October 2, 1903, p. 5; *Osvobozhdenie*, October 2, 1903, pp. 133–36.

46. *Osvobozhdenie*, October 2, 1903, pp. 149–50; Urusov, pp. 142, 165–66; Rogger, "Russian Ministers," p. 43; Herzl, *Complete Diaries*, 4: 1583–84.

47. Herzl, *Complete Diaries*, 4: 1587–88.

48. Dubnov, 3: 84; Greenberg, 2: 180; *Osvobozhdenie*, August 19, 1903, pp. 87–88; H. Heilbronner, "Count Aehrenthal and Russian Jewry," p. 398.

49. E. K. I. Jutikkala, *A History of Finland*, pp. 200–9, 214–17, 218–19, 222–23; Thaden, pp. 31–32, 76–82; Fisher, *Finland*, pp. 98–104.

50. Borodkin, pp. 84–85, 92, 94, 125, 145, 149, 151–53, 188–89, 215, 225; *Novoe Vremia*, April 13, 1902, p. 13.

51. Russobtovskii, pp. 86, 91; Borodkin, p. 377; *Novoe Vremia*, April 9, 1902, p. 4; April 29, 1902, p. 4.

52. TsGAOR, f. 586, op. 1, d. 445, II, 7–8, 10–11, 18; Gurko, p. 50; Borodkin, pp. 68–69, 130–31, 176–77, 222, 230–31, 233–35.

53. Borodkin, pp. 231–33; TsGAOR, f. 586, op. 1, d. 445, II, 36–37; Thaden, p. 53.

54. Borodkin, pp. 233–35.

55. *Novoe Vremia*, July 9, 1902, p. 5; Russobtovskii, pp. 96–97.

56. Nicholas II, Emperor, *The Secret Letters of the Last Tsar*, pp. 158–59.

57. Borodkin, p. 230.

58. *Ibid.*, p. 225; GPB, f. 586, d. 12, l. 28; d. 13, l. 48.

59. Evgenii Fedorov, *Podgotovka finliandskoi revoliutsii 1899–1905gg.*, pp. 27–35; *Novoe Vremia*, July 30, 1902, p. 4; September 29, 1902, p. 3.

60. Borodkin, pp. 381–83; GPB, f. 586, d. 13, l. 50; *Novoe Vremia*, April 6, 1903, p. 5.

61. *Novoe Vremia*, February 15, 1903, p. 13; March 13, 1903, p. 4; April 19, 1903, p. 13; May 27, 1903, p. 4; June 7, 1903, p. 4; June 26, 1903, p. 4; Jutikkala, pp. 238–39.

62. Jutikkala, pp. 238–39; Borodkin, pp. 102–3; *New York Times*, April 19, 1903, p. 5; June 19, 1903, p. 7; Plehve, "Defense," pp. 577–78.

63. Plehve, "Defense," pp. 577–79.

64. *Ibid.*, pp. 579–80.

65. *Osvobozhdenie*, November 2, 1903, pp. 178–79; December 25, 1903, pp. 241–42.

66. Borodkin, pp. 199–200.

67. Interview in *Die Post*, cited in Borodkin, pp. 218–19.

68. For background on the Armenian question see G. Harutunian, *Revoliutsionnoe dvizhenie v Armenii 1905–1907gg.*, pp. 54–55, 68–75; Simon Vratzian, *Armenia and the Armenian Question*, pp. 18–20; R. Hovannisian, *Armenia on the Road to Independence*, pp. 7–18; *Osvobozhdenie*, September 18, 1903, pp. 116–17.

69. Gurko, p. 246; *Osvobozhdenie*, September 18, 1903, pp. 116–17.

70. Witte, *Tsarstvovanie Nikolaia II*, 1: 187–88; *Novoe Vremia*, July 12, 1903, pp. 2, 4.

71. Hovannisian, p. 18; Harutunian, pp. 57–59; *Osvobozhdenie*, October 2, 1903, pp. 139–40; September 18, 1903, p. 117.

72. *Osvobozhdenie*, September 18, 1903, pp. 117–18.

73. L. Villari, *Fire and Sword in the Caucasus*, pp. 156–57; Urusov, pp. 87–88.

74. *Osvobozhdenie*, October 2, 1903, pp. 139–41; November 12, 1903, p. 198; November 24, 1903, p. 207; Harutunian, pp. 59–60; Kuropatkin, "Dnevnik," pp. 91–92; Hovannisian, pp. 18–19.

75. Urusov, p. 88; Villari, pp. 157–58; Gurko, p. 236.

76. Kuropatkin, "Dnevnik," p. 92; Gurko, p. 50n.

6—THE WORKER QUESTION AND THE POLICE

1. Witte, *Tsarstvovanie Nikolaia II*, 1: 195; *Otchet Gos. Sov. 1902/3*, 2: 196–97; Bogdanovich, p. 290.

2. *Otchet Gos. Sov. 1902/3*, 2: 195–96; A. G. Rashin, *Naselenie Rossii za 100 let*, pp. 321–25; R. S. Livshits, *Razmeshchenie promyshlennosti v dorevoliutsionnoi Rossii*, pp. 198–206.

3. Schneiderman, pp. 39–43.

4. *PSZRI 5*, no. 3013 (June 3, 1885); 6, no. 3769 (June 3, 1886); F. C. Giffen, "The Role of the Pleve Commission in the Russian Factory Laws of 1885 and 1886," pp. 143–50; Ianzhul, *Iz vospominanii i perepiski fabrichago inspektora*, pp. 68–69.

5. Ozerov, pp. 140–41; TsGAOR, f. 586, op. 1, d. 42, ll. 1–11.

6. Ozerov, pp. 24–25, 29–33, 131–42, 146–52, 157–65, 171–72; *Otchet Gos. Sov. 1896/7*, pp. 189–95; Schneiderman, pp. 33–34, 35–44.

7. Ozerov, pp. 177–78, 262–63; *Otchet Gos. Sov. 1902/3*, 2: 187–92.

8. Ianzhul, "Vospominaniia," pp. 269–72.

9. Ozerov, pp. 262–64; *Otchet Gos. Sov. 1902/3*, 2: 187–89.

10. *Otchet Gos. Sov. 1902/3*, 2: 195–97.

11. *PSZRI 23*, no. 23122 (June 10, 1903); Ozerov, pp. 64–72.

12. *PSZRI 23*, no. 23060 (June 2, 1903); M. Grigor'evskii, *Sbornik statei*, pp. 222–27.

13. TsGAOR, f. 826, op. 1, d. 45, l. 395.

14. *Novoe Vremia*, November 20, 1902, p. 2; March 16, 1903, p. 2; Gurko, p. 246.

15. Kuropatkin, "Dnevnik," p. 40.

16. Ianzhul, "Vospominaniia," p. 491.

17. Gurko, pp. 215–16; Pogozhev, pp. 259–60.

18. TsGAOR, f. 586, op. 1, d. 570, l. 20; *PSZRI 23*, no. 23041 (May 30, 1903); Ozerov, pp. 166–69; Gurko, pp. 216–17; Pogozhev, p. 275.

19. Gurko, p. 226; Ianzhul, "Vospominaniia," p. 492; Pogozhev, pp. 259–60, 263.

20. Pogozhev, pp. 261–62, 265, 268–69, 270.

21. *Ibid.*, pp. 268, 269–70.

22. *Ibid.*, pp. 268, 270; Ianzhul, "Vospominaniia," p. 497.

23. Zaionchkovskii, *Rossiiskoe samoderzhavie*, pp. 164–65; Eroshkin, chart 6.

24. For Zubatov's early career see M. R. Gots, "S. V. Zubatov (stranichka iz perezhitago)," pp. 63–68, 393–94; A. I. Spiridovich, "Pri tsarskom rezhime," p. 123; Schneiderman, pp. 49–55.

25. S. V. Zubatov, "Pis'mo," pp. 434–35; Zubatov, "Zubatovshchina," pp.

160–61; *Osvobozhdenie,* February 16, 1903, pp. 294–95; Witte, *Tsarstvovanie Nikolaia II,* 1: 195; Gurko, p. 119.

26. M. Rakovskii, ed., "Zubatov i Moskovskie gravery (1898–1899gg.)," pp. 204–5, 207–8, 209–14, 230–32; Schneiderman, pp. 93–95; Ozerov, pp. 195–99.

27. Ozerov, pp. 200–1, 205–7, 213–15, 217–24; *Osvobozhdenie,* March 2, 1903, pp. 317–19; March 19, 1903, pp. 331–32; Schneiderman, pp. 112–24.

28. "Stachka rabochikh zavoda br. Bromlei v 1903g.," p. 141n.; Bukhbinder, "K istorii zubatovshchiny," pp. 171–72; Bukhbinder, "Zubatovshchina v Moskve," pp. 96–99.

29. Bukhbinder, "Nezavisimaia evreiskaia rabochaia partiia," pp. 208–21; D. Zaslavskii, "Zubatov i Mania Vil'bushevich," pp. 100–23.

30. Bukhbinder, "Zubatovshchina v Moskve," pp. 103–6, 119–33; Liubimov, pp. 34–35; Schneiderman, p. 135; TsGIA, f. 1282, op. 1, d. 704, ll. 2–25.

31. Witte, *Tsarstvovanie Nikolaia II,* 1: 195.

32. Zubatov, "Pis'mo," pp. 435–36; Gurko, pp. 113, 119.

33. Gurko, pp. 112–13; *Novoe Vremia,* May 11, 1902, pp. 1, 4; *Delo A. A. Lopukhina v osobom prisutstvii pravitel'stvuiushchago senata,* p. 113.

34. Bukhbinder, "O zubatovshchine," pp. 289–301, 303–6; S. Piontkovskii, ed., "Novoe o zubatovshchine," pp. 299–306; A. I. Chemeriski, M. Rafes and M. Frumkina, "Vospominaniia o 'evreiskoi nezavisimoi rabochei partii'," pp. 318–19, 323–24; Bukhbinder, "Nezavisimaia," pp. 229–31.

35. Ozerov, p. 222; Bukhbinder, "Zubatovshchina v Moskve," pp. 106, 115; *Osvobozhdenie,* October 2, 1902, pp. 122–23; Schneiderman, pp. 169–72; Zubatov, "Zubatovshchina," pp. 162–63.

36. B. I. Nikolaevskii, *Istoriia odnogo predatelia,* pp. 18, 118–20; "Kar'era P. I. Rachkovskago: Dokumenty," pp. 78–82, 85–86; TsGAOR, f. 1463, op. 1, d. 115, ll. 347–48; Polovtsov, "Dnevnik," pp. 156–57, 158–60.

37. See TsGAOR, f. 634, op. 1, d. 10, l. 156; Schneiderman, pp. 172–73; V. I. Shtein, "Neudachnyi opyt (Zubatovshchina)," pp. 240–42; Ianzhul, "Vospominaniia," pp. 491–92; Gurko, p. 119.

38. Zubatov, "Pis'mo," p. 436; Gurko, p. 191.

39. A. P., "Departament politsii v 1892–1908gg.: Iz vospominanii chinovnika," pp. 19–21. See also V. D. Novitskii, "Zapiska gen. Novitskago," pp. 73–74.

40. Lopukhin, *Nastoiashchee i budushchee russkoi politsii,* p. 34; Novitskii, pp. 73–74.

41. Novitskii, pp. 74–75; Gurko, pp. 113, 119–20; A. P., pp. 20–21.

42. "Istoriia 'legalizatsii' rabochago dvizheniia," p. 86.

43. Ozerov, pp. 224–28; *Osvobozhdenie,* April 18, 1903, pp. 361–63; "Stachka . . . Bromlei," pp. 140–42; Schneiderman, pp. 268–73; Bukhbinder, "O zubatovshchine," pp. 300–2, 320, 326–28.

44. "Istoriia 'legalizatsii'," pp. 89–91; Bukhbinder, "Nezavisimaia," pp. 230–32, 281–83; Bukhbinder, "O zubatovshchine," pp. 311–12; Schneiderman, pp. 299–307.

45. "Istoriia 'legalizatsii'," pp. 87–88; Schneiderman, pp. 174–81; *Revoliutsionnaia Rossiia,* no. 16 (January 15, 1903), pp. 14–15.

46. Bukhbinder, "O zubatovshchine," pp. 294, 306; Novitskii, pp. 80–84; Gurko, p. 212; Witte, *Tsarstvovanie Nikolaia II,* 1: 257.

47. Bukhbinder, "O zubatovshchine," pp. 230, 289, 294; Koni, pp. 273–75;

"Istoriia 'legalizatsii'," pp. 87, 89–90; Bukhbinder, "Nezavisimaia," pp. 230–31; Novitskii, pp. 81–83.

48. *Novoe Vremia*, April 9, 1903, p. 3; Novitskii, pp. 107–8.

49. Bukhbinder, "Zubatovshchina v Moskve," pp. 102, 108; Bukhbinder, "K istorii 'Sobraniia russkikh fabrichno-zavodskikh rabochikh g. S. Peterburga'," p. 299.

50. Lopukhin, "Zapiska po delu o stachkakh i besporiadkakh proizkhodivshikh v iiule 1903 godu v gorodakh Odesse, Kieve i Nikolaeve," p. 289; Chemeriskii et al., pp. 320–22; Bukhbinder, "Nezavisimaia," pp. 265–66; Schneiderman, pp. 281–84.

51. Chemeriskii et al., p. 321; D. Shlossberg, "Vseobshchaia stachka 1903g. na Ukraine," pp. 67–68.

52. For accounts of the Odessa strike, see S. A. Ratova, "Vseobshchaia stachka v 1903 godu na Kavkaze i Chernomorskom poberezh'e," pp. 106–10; Lopukhin, "Zapiska," pp. 385–91; Bukhbinder, "Nezavisimaia," pp. 231–35; Shlossberg, "Vseobshchaia stachka," pp. 62–66; Schneiderman, pp. 312–32; *Revoliutsionnaia Rossiia*, no. 29 (August 5, 1903), pp. 6–7; no. 30 (August 20, 1903), pp. 8–9; *Osvobozhdenie*, August 2, 1903, appendix, pp. 2–3.

53. Lopukhin, "Zapiska," pp. 387–88, 389; *Osvobozhdenie*, August 2, 1903, appendix, p. 3; *Iskra*, no. 45 (August 2, 1903), p. 6; no. 46 (August 15, 1903), pp. 5–6; Shlossberg, pp. 63–64; Schneiderman, pp. 317, 326; Ratova, p. 112.

54. Lopukhin, "Zapiska," pp. 391–92; Ratova, pp. 110, 112–14; Bukhbinder, "Nezavisimaia," p. 234.

55. "Istoriia 'legalizatsii'," pp. 92, 93; Ratova, p. 115; Bukhbinder, "Nezavisimaia," p. 241.

56. Shlossberg, pp. 66–67; Bukhbinder, "Nezavisimaia," p. 234.

57. Bukhbinder, "Nezavisimaia," pp. 233, 234, 235.

58. *Ibid.*, p. 234; Russia (USSR), Tsentral'nyi Arkhiv Revoliutsii, *Vseobshchaia stachka na iuge Rossii v 1903 godu*, pp. 90–92; *Revoliutsionnaia Rossiia*, no. 28 (July 15, 1903), pp. 2–3; no. 31 (September 1, 1903), pp. 7–9.

59. Shlossberg, pp. 62–79; Lopukhin, "Zapiska," pp. 385–95; Ratova, pp. 98–117; *Iskra*, no. 45 (August 1, 1903), pp. 6–8.

60. *Vseobshchaia stachka*, pp. 33, 43–45; "K istorii vseobshchei stachki na iuge Rossii v 1903g.," pp. 80–87; Ratova, pp. 98–105, 116–17; Lopukhin, "Zapiska," pp. 392–95; *Osvobozhdenie*, August 2, 1903, appendix, pp. 3–4.

61. *Novoe Vremia*, August 2, 1903, p. 4; *Vseobshchaia stachka*, pp. 42–48; Lopukhin, "Zapiska," pp. 385, 391–92.

62. Lopukhin, "Zapiska," pp. 386–89.

63. Zubatov, "Pis'mo," p. 436; Witte, *Tsarstvovanie Nikolaia II*, 1: 196.

64. Witte, *Tsarstvovanie Nikolaia II*, 1: 196; Lopukhin, *Otryvki*, pp. 73–75. See also P. E. Shchegolev, *Okhranniki i avantiuristy*, p. 119; "Prikliucheniia I. F. Manuilova," p. 21.

65. Zubatov, "Doklad Direktoru Departamenta Politsii," pp. 93–94.

66. *Ibid.*, pp. 94–96.

67. "Istoriia 'legalizatsii'," p. 92; Pogozhev, pp. 267–68.

68. Witte, *Tsarstvovanie Nikolaia II*, 1: 197.

7—THE FALL OF WITTE AND THE FAR EASTERN QUESTION

1. Witte, *Tsarstvovanie Nikolaia II*, 1: 218–19; Kuropatkin, "Dnevnik," p. 55.

2. Witte, *Tsarstvovanie Nikolaia II*, 1: 219; *Novoe Vremia*, August 18, 1903, p. 2; V. N. Kokovtsov, *Out of My Past*, p. 7.

3. Witte, *Tsarstvovanie Nikolaia II*, 1: 3, 9–12, 127, 218–19; 2: 228.

4. *Ibid.*, 1: 28–29, 192–93, 214, 444, 461; Gurko, p. 234; Polovtsov, "Dnevnik," pp. 168–69.

5. Kokovtsov, pp. 30–31; Witte, *Tsarstvovanie Nikolaia II*, 1: 194, 199, 422.

6. Kuropatkin, "Dnevnik," p. 45; Gurko, p. 278; V. L. Glazov, "Dva razgovora," pp. 216–17.

7. Witte, *Tsarstvovanie Nikolaia II*, 1: 197, 258; TsGAOR, f. 1463, op. 1, d. 1115, ll. 361–62; GBL, f. 126, d. 13, l. 148; *Novoe Vremia*, May 29, 1902, p. 1.

8. Kuropatkin, "Dnevnik," pp. 59–60; Witte, *Tsarstvovanie Nikolaia II*, 1: 204–11, 220, 222–23, 258, 282.

9. Kuropatkin, "Dnevnik," pp. 59–60.

10. Witte, *Tsarstvovanie Nikolaia II*, 1: 218; Kuropatkin, "Dnevnik," p. 60.

11. This review of Russian involvement in the Far East is based on: B. A. Romanov, *Rossiia v Man'chzhurii*, chs. 1–6; R. R. Rosen, *Forty Years of Diplomacy*, 1: 189–239; Kuropatkin, *Zapiska o russko-iaponskoi voine*, pp. 144–87; Witte, *Vynuzhdenyia Raz'iasneniia po povodu otcheta Gen.-Ad. Kuropatkina o voine s Iaponei*, pp. 50–100; Andrew Malozemoff, *Russian Far Eastern Policy 1881–1904*, chs. 4–9; John A. White, *The Diplomacy of the Russo-Japanese War*, pp. 1–131.

12. *Prolog Voiny*, pp. 248–60; Kuropatkin, "Dnevnik," pp. 45, 58, 81.

13. Malozemoff, pp. 196, 200, 208–9; Witte, *Tsarstvovanie Nikolaia II*, 1: 214–15.

14. Kuropatkin, "Dnevnik," pp. 45, 58, 81; Gurko, pp. 272–75.

15. Witte, *Tsarstvovanie Nikolaia II*, 1: 262.

16. See, for example, Lionel Kochan, *Russia in Revolution 1890–1918*, pp. 67, 166; Ol'denburg, 1: 234; *Istoriia SSSR*, 2: 264; Melvin C. Wren, *The Course of Russian History*, p. 477; Hovannisian, p. 83; S. A. Piontkovskii, *Ocherkii istorii SSSR*, p. 261; and especially David Walder, *The Short Victorious War*.

17. Gurko, pp. 253, 278, 286–91.

18. Kuropatkin, "Dnevnik," p. 83; Gurko, p. 272; Romanov, "Kontsessiia na Ialu," p. 103.

19. Witte, *Vynuzhdenyia*, pp. 73–74; *Prolog Voiny*, p. 242.

20. "Zhurnal Osobogo soveshchaniia 25 ianvaria 1903g.," pp. 120–23.

21. Kuropatkin, "Dnevnik," p. 43.

22. Kuropatkin, "Dnevnik," pp. 11–12, 33–34, 37–38, 81; *Prolog Voiny*, pp. 254–68, 277–79; Romanov, *Rossiia*, pp. 404–7; Liubimov, pp. 95–98.

23. *Prolog Voiny*, pp. 246–47, 277–82; Liubimov, pp. 95–105.

24. Liubimov, pp. 101–3; *Prolog Voiny*, pp. 281–82.

25. Kuropatkin, "Dnevnik," p. 83.

26. Romanov, *Rossiia*, pp. 409–10; *Russko-iaponskaia voina: Iz dnevnikov A. N. Kuropatkina i N. P. Linevicha*, p. 8; *Prolog Voiny*, pp. 282, 309.

27. Witte, *Vynuzhdennyia*, pp. 85–86; *Prolog Voiny*, pp. 282–85; *Russko-iaponskaia voina*, p. 9.

28. *Russko-iaponskaia voina,* pp. 9, 24–25; Romanov, *Rossiia,* pp. 409, 410n.; *Prolog Voiny,* p. 286.

29. *Russko-iaponskaia voina,* pp. 24–25; *Prolog Voiny,* pp. 286–87; Malozemoff, p. 307.

30. *Russko-iaponskaia voina,* p. 25.

31. Liubimov, pp. 106–7, 108.

32. Gurko, pp. 277–78. See also Kuropatkin, "Dnevnik," p. 45.

33. Kuropatkin, "Dnevnik," pp. 27, 40, 42.

34. *Russko-iaponskaia voina,* pp. 143–44.

35. *Otchet Gos. Sov. 1902/3,* 2: 196.

36. *Russko-iaponskaia voina,* pp. 21–25; *Prolog Voiny,* pp. 282–86.

37. Malozemoff, p. 220; Witte, *Vynuzhdennyia,* pp. 79, 81, 93–94; *Prolog Voiny,* pp. 292–93, 295, 305; *Russko-iaponskaia voina,* pp. 29–32.

38. Romanov, *Rossiia,* pp. 432–33, 433n.; Liubimov, pp. 108–9.

39. Polovtsov, "Dnevnik," p. 157; *Novoe Vremia,* July 20, 1903, pp. 1–2; Nicholas II, *Dnevnik,* p. 21.

40. Kuropatkin, "Dnevnik," pp. 44–45; Kuropatkin, *Zapiski,* p. 174; *Prolog Voiny,* pp. 311–14, 346; *Russko-iaponskaia voina,* pp. 41, 148–59.

41. Witte, *Tsarstvovanie Nikolaia II,* 1: 214; *Prolog Voiny,* pp. 287, 294; *Russko-iaponskaia voina,* pp. 31–32, 34; Kuropatkin, "Dnevnik," p. 45; *Novoe Vremia,* August 1, 1903, pp. 1, 3.

42. *Russko-iaponskaia voina,* p. 157; Romanov, *Rossiia,* p. 443; Gurko, p. 225.

43. *Novoe Vremia,* October 6, 1903, pp. 1, 2; October 17, 1903, p. 1.

44. Romanov, *Rossiia,* p. 461n.

45. *Russko-iaponskaia voina,* pp. 143–44, 156–57, 162.

46. Romanov, *Rossiia,* p. 457; Witte, *Detstvo,* p. 264; Romanov, ed., "Bezobrazovskii kruzhok letom 1904," pp. 70, 74–80; Kuropatkin, "Dnevnik," p. 94.

47. Kuropatkin, "Dnevnik," pp. 58, 81, 86–87, 93; Romanov, *Rossiia,* pp. 454–60.

48. Kuropatkin, "Dnevnik," pp. 84–87; Malozemoff, p. 225; Gurko, pp. 282–83.

49. Malozemoff, pp. 241–42, 243–44.

50. Kuropatkin, "Dnevnik," p. 83.

51. *Russko-iaponskaia voina,* pp. 35–36; Kuropatkin, *Zapiski,* pp. 177–82; Kuropatkin, "Dnevnik," pp. 79, 84, 86, 87–89, 91, 95–97.

52. Kuropatkin, "Dnevnik," pp. 95–97, 103–5; *Russko-iaponskaia voina,* pp. 52–53; Malozemoff, pp. 246–49.

53. *Novoe Vremia,* October 21, 1903, p. 2; *Osvobozhdenie,* March 7, 1904, pp. 339–40; Kuropatkin, "Dnevnik," pp. 84, 86, 95–97, 103–4, 107–8; Gurko, pp. 193, 291.

54. Kuropatkin, "Dnevnik," pp. 83, 94.

55. *Russko-iaponskaia voina,* p. 41; Rosen, 1: 220.

56. Liubimov, pp. 141–42; Witte, *Tsarstvovanie Nikolaia II,* 1: 262.

57. Kuropatkin, "Dnevnik," pp. 94–95; "Iz istorii revoliutsionnogo dvizheniia v armii nakanune 1905g.," pp. 172–73; Romanov, "Bezobrazovskii kruzhok," pp. 70–71, 74–79.

58. *Otchet Gos. Sov. 1903/4,* 1: 323–24; Urusov, p. 178.

59. *Russko-iaponskaia voina,* p. 25.

264 NOTES

8—THE PLEHVE SYSTEM

1. V. K. Plehve, "Pis'mo k Kireevu," pp. 202–3.
2. Ibid.
3. Ibid.
4. A. A. Kizevetter, Na rubezhe dvukh stoletii, pp. 345, 348; Shipov, pp. 221–22; Novoe Vremia, July 10, 1903, p. 2; August 9, 1903, p. 4; August 21, 1903, p. 2; Weissman, pp. 82–83.
5. Gurko, p. 122; Novoe Vremia, March 19, 1903, p. 4.
6. Novoe Vremia, October 3, 1903, pp. 2–3.
7. Ibid., p. 3; Gurko, pp. 125, 130; Weissman, p. 81.
8. Belokonskii, p. 166; Gurko, pp. 125–26.
9. Gurko, pp. 125–26; GBL, f. 126, d. 13, l. 268.
10. Otchet Gos. Sov. 1903/4, pp. 71, 74–80, 92–97; PSZRI 24, no. 24253 (March 22, 1904).
11. Novoe Vremia, April 9, 1904, pp. 1, 4; Veselovskii, 3: 582–83.
12. Liubimov, pp. 46–47; Weissman, p. 54; Osvobozhdenie, January 19, 1904, pp. 275–79; Veselovskii, 3: 583.
13. TsGIA, f. 1234, op. 1, delo po Osobomu Soveshchaniiu pod predsedatel'stvom S. F. Platonova, ll. 2–5, 270–77; Weissman, p. 56; Gurko, p. 59; Novoe Vremia, February 23, 1904, p. 2.
14. Gurko, p. 129.
15. TsGIA, f. 1284, op. 241, d. 222, ll. 94, 98; f. 1291, op. 122, d. 70.l, ll. 190–212; Trudy Red. kom., Gurko, pp. 162–64.
16. Gurko, pp. 162–63, 171–72; GBL, f. 265, d. 124.7, ll. 34–39; TsGIA, f. 1284, op. 241, d. 222, ll. 74–75, 94–98.
17. Trudy Red. kom., 1: 1–9, 10–11.
18. Ibid., 1: 12, 15–16, 17–19.
19. Ibid., 1: 19, 22–23, 26, 27.
20. Ibid., 1: 23–24.
21. Ibid., 1: 374, 377; 5: 337–44, 368–75, 379–80; D. A. J. Macey, "The Russian Bureaucracy and the 'Peasant Problem'," pp. 277–78; P. I. Liashchenko, "Krest'ianskoe delo i poreformennaia zemleustroitel'naia politika," pp. 136–37.
22. Trudy Red. kom., 1: 367, 378–79; 5: 225, 368–69, 391–93; Simonova, "Politika," pp. 220–21.
23. Trudy Red. kom., 1: 22–27, 89–91; Simonova, "Politika," p. 219; Macey, pp. 257–60.
24. Trudy Red. kom., 1: 14–15; 5: 450–51.
25. Ibid., 5: 450.
26. Ibid., 1: 383–84; 5: 451, 453, 455; Macey, pp. 274–77.
27. Trudy Red. kom., 5: 416–17; 1: 23–24, 94; 6: 7–9; Macey, pp. 270, 272–73.
28. Trudy Red. kom., 1: 353–55; 5: 33–34, 37–43, 50–54, 412, 428–32.
29. Gurko, pp. 159–63, 171–73, 176–77; Liashchenko, pp. 141–42; I. V. Chernyshev, Agrarno-krest'ianskaia politika Rossii za 150 let, p. 273; S. M. Dubrovskii, Stolypinskaia zemel'naia reforma, pp. 70–71; Simonova, "Politika," pp. 212–14, 220–21; Macey, pp. 262–68.
30. See discussion in Macey, pp. 260–62.

31. *Trudy Red. kom.*, 1: 12–19; Weissman, pp. 74–75.

32. Simonova, "Politika," pp. 216–17; Dubrovskii, pp. 121–22; GBL, f. 265, d. 124.7, l. 38; Gurko, pp. 158–60, 165, 176–77, 461–62, 474–77, 499–502.

33. Kuropatkin, "Dnevnik," p. 84; Gurko, pp. 163–66; TsGAOR, f. 586, op. 1, d. 431, ll. 1–9; Simonova, "Politika," p. 221.

34. TsGIA, f. 1263, op. 2, d. 5630, ll. 19–130; TsGAOR, f. 586, op. 1, d. 432, l. 2.

35. TsGAOR, f. 586, op. 1, d. 432, ll. 3, 4.

36. *Novoe Vremia*, January 10, 1904, p. 1.

37. TsGIA, f. 1291, op. 122, d. 70.I, ll. 221, 222–23, 236–38; Gurko, pp. 168–69; Urusov, pp. 173–75.

38. Russia, MVD, *Poriadok obsuzhdeniia proektov vyrabotannykh Redaktsionnoi kommissiei*, pp. 5–6.

39. Simonova, "Politika," p. 222; *Novoe Vremia*, February 27, 1904, p. 2; TsGIA, f. 1291, op. 122, d. 70.I, ll. 239–40; Macey, pp. 281–82.

40. Macey, pp. 282–84.

41. Witte, *Detstvo*, pp. 399–400; TsGIA, f. 1273, op. 1, d. 443, l. 2; Gurko, pp. 192–97.

42. *Novoe Vremia*, October 27, 1902, p. 3; December 30, 1902, p. 3; TsGIA, f. 1233, op. 1, d. 23, ll. 44–45.

43. TsGAOR, f. 586, op. 1, d. 404, l. 28; TsGIA, f. 1273, op. 1, d. 443, l. 2.

44. TsGIA, f. 1273, op. 1, d. 443, ll. 496–97; V. A. Stepynin, "Iz istorii pereselencheskoi politiki samoderzhavie," p. 162.

45. Gurko, p. 193; TsGAOR, f. 586, op. 1, d. 404, ll. 1–46; TsGIA, f. 1273, op. 1, d. 443, ll. 5, 109–20, 598–609, 626–29, 652–53; *Otchet Gos. Sov. 1903/4*, pp. 323–25.

46. *PSZRI* 24, no. 24701 (June 6, 1904); Stepynin, pp. 163–64.

47. TsGAOR, f. 586, op. 1, d. 404, l. 79; Simonova, "Politika," p. 222; *PSZRI* 24, no. 24701 (June 6, 1904), arts. 9, 10, 16.

48. Stepynin, p. 164; below, p. 240.

49. Ianzhul, "Vospominaniia," p. 491.

50. *Ibid.*, pp. 497–98.

51. *Ibid.*, pp. 498, 499.

52. Ianzhul, "Vospominaniia," p. 498; Pogozhev, p. 275; GBL, f. 586, d. 8, no. 2.

53. Kokovtsov, pp. 9–10, 12–13, 26–27.

54. *Ibid.*, pp. 28–30.

55. Ozerov, pp. 221–28.

56. N. A. Bukhbinder, ed., "K istorii Sobraniia'," pp. 292, 296–97, 299; G. A. Gapon, *Zapiski Georgiia Gapona*, pp. 33–36, 39–40, 43–44; Walter Sablinsky, *The Road to Bloody Sunday*, pp. 77–82.

57. A. A. Lopukhin, "Doklad Direktora Departamenta Politsii Lopukhina Ministru Vnutrennikh Del o sobytiakh 9-go ianvaria," pp. 330–31; Gapon, pp. 47–48.

58. Bukhbinder, "K istorii 'Sobraniia'," pp. 297, 299; Sablinsky, p. 97.

59. Lopukhin, "Doklad," p. 331; Gapon, pp. 46–48; Bukhbinder, "K istorii 'Sobraniia'," p. 299.

60. Bukhbinder, "K istorii 'Sobraniia'," p. 300; Gapon, pp. 50–51.

61. Bukhbinder, "K istorii 'Sobraniia'," pp. 300–1, 300n.; Pogozhev, pp. 267–68; Sablinsky, pp. 114–17.
62. Osvobozhdenie, March 7, 1904, attachment.
63. Plehve, "Pis'mo k Kireevu," pp. 202–3.
64. See Glazov, p. 214.

9—REPRESSION VERSUS REFORM

1. Osvobozhdenie, September 2, 1902, p. 96; September 18, 1902, p. 103; December 2, 1902, p. 200; Bogdanovich, pp. 279, 284–85.
2. P. N. Miliukov, Vospominaniia 1859–1917, 1: 202–4; I. V. Gessen, V dvukh vekakh, pp. 174–75.
3. Mikhailovskii, p. 25.
4. Liubimov, pp. 22–24, 25–31; Shipov, pp. 207, 207n.; Spiridovich, "Pri tsarskom rezhime," p. 153; "Nikolai II i samoderzhavie v 1903g.," pp. 190–222.
5. Plehve, "Pis'mo k Kireevu," p. 203; Novoe Vremia, December 30, 1902, p. 3.
6. Gurko, pp. 229–33; GBL, f. 265, d. 124.7, ll. 29–40; f. 126, d. 13, ll. 168, 210, 273, passim.
7. Belokonskii, pp. 159–60, 165.
8. Novoe Vremia, July 3, 1903, p. 4; Belokonskii, pp. 167–70, 172–73.
9. Gurko, pp. 123–24, 233–34; Weissman, pp. 49, 74–76, 87–89; GBL, f. 126, d. 13, ll. 273, 316, 323, 325. See also G. M. Hamburg, "The Russian Nobility on the Eve of the 1905 Revolution," pp. 325–36.
10. Gurko, pp. 227, 233; Galai, Liberation, pp. 149–51.
11. Polovtsov, "Dnevnik," p. 168.
12. TsGIA, f. 1233, op. 1, d. 78, l. 105; Gurko, p. 242.
13. Novoe Vremia, October 22, 1903, p. 3; October 23, 1903, p. 3; Gurko, pp. 242–43.
14. Simonova, "Politika," p. 215; Gurko, pp. 242–43.
15. Shipov, p. 226; Belokonskii, pp. 177–83.
16. Shipov, pp. 227–28; below, p. 213.
17. Belokonskii, pp. 193–95; Novoe Vremia, January 17, 1904, p. 1.
18. Gurko, p. 240.
19. Novoe Vremia, September 3, 1903, p. 4; Belokonskii, pp. 184–92; Galai, Liberation, pp. 188–89.
20. Glazov, p. 214.
21. Liubimov, pp. 141–42, 143, 146–47; Novoe Vremia, January 30, 1904, p. 2; February 1, 1904, p. 5.
22. Novoe Vremia, January 29–February 4, 1904 passim; Galai, Liberation, pp. 199–206.
23. Plehve, "Pis'mo k Kireevu," p. 202; Belokonskii, p. 197.
24. Shipov, pp. 221–24. Plehve's remarks may have been removed from the conference transcript: TsGIA, f. 1233, op. 1, d. 16, ll. 65–66.
25. Novoe Vremia, March 3, 1904, p. 4; Osvobozhdenie, April 2, 1904, p. 382.
26. Belokonskii, p. 198.
27. Shipov, pp. 233–34; Novoe Vremia, April 20, 1904, p. 2.

28. *Osvobozhdenie*, May 21, 1904, p. 425; July 19, 1904, pp. 35–36; Belokonskii, pp. 198–99.

29. Belokonskii, pp. 199, 200–2; *Novoe Vremia*, May 27, 1904, p. 1.

30. Galai, *Liberation*, p. 206; Gurko, pp. 244–46.

31. Belokonskii, p. 203; *Novoe Vremia*, June 30, 1904, p. 1.

32. *Novoe Vremia*, June 30, 1904, pp. 2, 4.

33. S. Galai, "The Impact of the Russo-Japanese War on the Russian Liberals, 1904–1905," pp. 88–89; *Osvobozhdenie*, February 19, 1904, pp. 323–26; March 7, 1904, pp. 338–39.

34. *Osvobozhdenie*, April 18, 1904, p. 406; May 2, 1904, pp. 422–23; June 2, 1904, p. 455; Urusov, pp. 47–52, 54–55.

35. TsGIA, f. 1263, op. 2, d. 5626, l. 203; *Osvobozhdenie*, March 7, 1904, p. 337; Urusov, *Memoirs*, pp. 171, 175.

36. *Osvobozhdenie*, March 7, 1904, p. 337.

37. *Novoe Vremia*, January 18, 1904, p. 4; Urusov, pp. 171, 175–77.

38. *Novoe Vremia*, July 7, 1904, p. 4; TsGIA, f. 1263, op. 2, d. 5732, ll. 228–31.

39. *Novoe Vremia*, October 19, 1903, p. 5; October 22, 1903, p. 1; November 11, 1903, p. 5; November 28, 1903, p. 5; December 4, 1903, p. 5; December 11, 1903, p. 1.

40. *Osvobozhdenie*, March 7, 1904, pp. 338–39; June 2, 1904, p. 456; July 2, 1904, pp. 29–30.

41. Borodkin, pp. 199–200; Gurko, pp. 50–51.

42. *Osvobozhdenie*, July 19, 1904, pp. 45–46; Witte, *Tsarstvovanie Nikolaia II*, 2: 237–38.

43. Kuropatkin, "Dnevnik," pp. 91–92; *Osvobozhdenie*, April 2, 1904, pp. 374–77; *Novoe Vremia*, January 27, 1904, p. 6; February 11, 1904, p. 13; July 6, 1904, p. 2.

44. Belokonskii, p. 204.

45. Gurko, p. 176; Shipov, p. 234; Kokovtsov, p. 29.

10—THE MINISTER AND THE TERRORISTS

1. *Osvobozhdenie*, July 19, 1904, p. 46. The interviewer was Gaston Leroux of *Le Matin*.

2. See J. L. H. Keep, *The Rise of Social Democracy in Russia*, pp. 67–76, 96–103; Oliver H. Radkey, *The Agrarian Foes of Bolshevism*, pp. 50–64.

3. V. M. Chernov, *Pered burei: Vospominaniia*, pp. 162–64; Allison Blakely, "The Socialist Revolutionary Party, 1901–1907," pp. 81–86.

4. Chernov, pp. 132–41; Blakely, pp. 82–83.

5. Chernov, pp. 169–70; G. A. Gershuni, *Iz nedavniago proshlago*, pp. 63–67.

6. A. I. Spiridovich, *Histoire du Terrorisme Russe*, p. 153; *Revoliutsionnaia Rossiia*, no. 7 (June 1902), pp. 2–5.

7. *Osvobozhdenie*, July 19, 1902, p. 47.

8. *Delo Lopukhina*, p. 114; above, pp. 134–39.

9. *Delo Lopukhina*, pp. 9–10, 40, 55, 114–15; Nikolaevskii, pp. 62, 62–63nn.; Rataev, p. 196.

10. Spiridovich, *Histoire*, pp. 158–60; "K delu Fomy Kochury," pp. 103–6; Gershuni, pp. 71–74.
11. Nikolaevskii, p. 64; Spiridovich, *Histoire*, p. 161.
12. Rataev, pp. 196–97; Gershuni, pp. 57–58, 60–62.
13. Liubimov, pp. 151–52.
14. A. I. Spiridovich, *Zapiski zhandarma*, pp. 122–23; Nikolaevskii, p. 69.
15. Spiridovich, *Histoire*, p. 161; Nikolaevskii, p. 71.
16. Spiridovich, *Zapiska*, pp. 125–28; Gershuni, pp. 8–18.
17. Spiridovich, *Histoire*, pp. 171–73.
18. Liubimov, p. 152; Nikolaevskii, p. 102.
19. *Osvobozhdenie*, December 19, 1902, pp. 211–12.
20. B. V. Savinkov, *Vospominaniia terrorista*, pp. 11–13; E. S. Sazonov, *Materialy dlia biografii*, p. 8.
21. Nikolaevskii, pp. 31–38, 68–70; Rataev, pp. 196–99.
22. Rataev, p. 198; Savinkov, p. 13.
23. Nikolaevskii, pp. 79–82; E. F. Azef, "Doneseniia Evno Azefa: Perepiska Azefa s Rataevym v 1903–1905 gg.," pp. 198–99, 200–8; *Delo Lopukhina*, pp. 55–56.
24. Savinkov, pp. 13–14ff.
25. Spiridovich, "Pri tsarskom rezhime," pp. 154–57; Chernov, pp. 150–52.
26. Gershuni, pp. 35–43, 45.
27. *Ibid.*, pp. 34, 74–81; *Osvobozhdenie*, April 2, 1904, p. 383.
28. TsGAOR, f. 102.III, d. 3421/1904, ll. 17–20; Rataev, pp. 199–200, 204.
29. Savinkov, pp. 24–26.
30. Nikolaevskii, pp. 85–87; Savinkov, pp. 27–29.
31. This description of the group's activities from March through July 1904 is based on Savinkov, pp. 33–57.
32. Spiridovich, *Zapiski*, p. 104; P. P. Zavarzin, *Zhandarmy i revoliutsionery*, p. 66.
33. Miliukov, 1: 202.
34. Savinkov, pp. 28, 32, 43–44, 57; *Osvobozhdenie*, March 7, 1904, pp. 339–40.
35. Pogozhev, pp. 262–63; *Pamiati Pleve*, pp. 43–44; Liubimov, p. 161.
36. Savinkov, pp. 56–57.
37. Azef, p. 206; Spiridovich, *Histoire*, pp. 180–81.
38. Sazonov, pp. 9–10; *Pamiati Pleve*, pp. 51–52.
39. Savinkov, p. 57; Dillon, p. 133.
40. *Pamiati Pleve*, pp. 52–53.

11—THE LEGACY OF PLEHVE

1. Shipov, pp. 238–39; *Osvobozhdenie*, August 2, 1904, pp. 63–64; Nikolaevskii, pp. 97–99.
2. Suvorin, p. 312; Liubimov, pp. 157–58, 163–64; Gurko, pp. 175–76.
3. Nicholas II, *Dnevnik*, p. 161.
4. *Pamiati Pleve*, pp. 53–57; Witte, *Tsarstvovanie Nikolaia II*, 1: 198.
5. *Novoe Vremia*, August 28, 1904, pp. 1, 2; M. N. Kovalenskii, *Russkaia revoliutsiia v sudebnykh protsessakh i memuarakh*, pp. 46, 49, 51.

6. Nikolaevskii, pp. 102–5.
7. Gurko, pp. 295, 298; Veselovskii, 3: 583; Liubimov, pp. 46–47.
8. Gurko, pp. 499–501; Dubrovskii, pp. 121–22; Stepynin, p. 164.
9. GBL, f. 126, d. 13, l. 314; Gurko, p. 278; Shipov, pp. 174–75.
10. Polovtsov, "Dnevnik," p. 169.
11. Herzl, Diaries, p. 389.

Bibliographical Note

Since V. K. Plehve did not live to write his memoirs, and since there exists no single central source for his activities and attitudes, it has been necessary to pull together information from a wide variety of sources. Historical materials relating to Plehve are numerous, yet diverse. They include archival holdings, published documents, memoirs and diaries of Plehve's associates, and secondary literature concerning persons and developments with which he was involved.

The most extensive collection of relevant materials is the *fond V. K. Pleve* (fond 586) of the Central State Archive of the October Revolution (Ts-GAOR) in Moscow. This is a varied assortment of documents, memoranda, reports, minutes, and letters, most relating to Plehve's political career. It includes letters to Plehve from persons such as D. A. Tolstoi, I. N. Durnovo, N. V. Murav'ev, and S. Iu. Witte, as well as several letters from Plehve to these and other persons. It also contains a number of documents on various state activities in which Plehve was involved, such as the enactment of exceptional security measures in 1881, the organization of famine relief efforts in 1891–1892, the elaboration of a new resettlement law in 1904, and various plans to reorganize provincial government and revise peasant legislation. Although this collection sheds more light on Plehve's activities than it does on his motives and ideals, items such as his 1881 memo on police measures and his 1899 letter on the Finnish question do provide important insights into his thought.

Much useful information may also be found elsewhere in the Soviet archives. The Archive of the October Revolution contains, besides the Plehve papers, the correspondence of N. P. Ignat'ev and D. N. Shipov, the diary of revolutionary-turned-Slavophile Lev Tikhomirov, the papers from the Tsarskoe Selo palaces, and several memoirs touching on Plehve's career and character. The Manuscript Section of the Saltykov-Shchedrin State Public Library (GPB) in Leningrad houses a number of Plehve's private letters to family

271

members and associates, the most interesting of which are his numerous and revealing letters to Finnish Governor-General N. I. Bobrikov. The Central State Historical Archive (TsGIA) in Leningrad contains a wide range of government documents, including the records of the Obolenskii Commission on the Peasant Land Bank, the Platonov Conference on Decentralization, the Kulomzin Commission on Resettlement, and the Committee of Ministers. It also houses the stenographic transcripts of the Special Conferences on the Affairs of the Nobility and the Needs of Agricultural Industry, in both of which Plehve played a prominent role. The Manuscript Section of the State Lenin Library (GBL) in Moscow includes, among other things, the diaries of A. A. Kireev, a retired Slavophile general who corresponded and conversed with Plehve, and the memoirs of F. D. Samarin, a conservative Moscow zemstvo-man whom Plehve recruited to help on his peasant project.

A number of documents containing relevant information have been published in various journals and collections. The Soviet periodical *Krasnyi Arkhiv* printed assorted letters, memoranda, reports, and minutes relating to events, policies, and conferences in which Plehve was involved. Other useful collections include *Materialy dlia istorii antievreiskikh pogromov v Rossii* (two volumes of letters and documents concerning government involvement in anti-Semitic activities), *Krest'ianskoe dvizhenie v Poltavskoi i Khar'kovskoi guberniakh v 1902g.* (state documents and reports relating to the Khar'kov and Poltava peasant riots of 1902) and *Vseobshchaia stachka na iuge Rossii v 1903 godu: Sbornik dokumentov* (a similar collection dealing with general strikes in southern Russia during summer of 1903). Prerevolutionary publications of interest in this regard are *Delo A. A. Lopukhina v osobom prisutstvii pravitel'stvuiushchago senata*, which contains testimony from the trial of Plehve's police chief, and *Prolog Russko-Iaponskoi Voiny: Materialy iz arkhiva S. Iu. Vitte*, a collection of Witte's papers dealing with the background of the Russo-Japanese War. Among the official publications of the imperial Russian government, the most helpful are the *Trudy* (Works) of the Editing Commission for Revision of Peasant Legislation, and the *Otchet po deloproizvodstva Gosudarstvennago Soveta*, which gives synopses of State Council deliberations on the proposals brought before it. Many relevant documents and reports, of course, were published in the Russian newspapers (e.g., *Novoe Vremia*) and the émigré press (e.g., *Osvobozhdenie*).

Memoir literature also provides a rich source for the student of Plehve. The most supportive memoirs are those of D. N. Liubimov ("Russkaia smuta nachala deviatisotykh godov, 1902–1906"), the Minister of Interior's Chancellor, who sheds important light on Plehve's relations with Witte and society, and on the workings of Plehve's ministry. Liubimov also wrote a brief, eulogistic biography (*Pamiati Viacheslava Konstantinovicha Plehve*), which was published by the Ministry of Interior shortly after Plehve's death. The most thorough and illuminating memoirs are those of V. I. Gurko (*Features and Figures of the Past*), the head of the ministry's Land Section, who provides numerous insights into Plehve's character, ideas, and policies, especially those concerning the peasants. The most critical are those of S. Iu. Witte (*Vospo-minaniia: Tsarstvovanie Nikolaia II*), the brilliant Finance Minister, who makes no effort to hide either his bitter resentment of Plehve or his conviction that Plehve was largely responsible for most of Russia's ills. All three, of course, were written much later than the events they describe by men with faulty memories and strong points of view; all three, however, are invaluable sources on Plehve and his times.

Other memoirs provide significant glimpses into various aspects of Plehve's activities. The minister's handling of the imperial police, for instance, is discussed in the reminiscences of police officials Spiridovich and Novitskii, and in the short, polemical fragment by Police Director Lopukhin. His approach to the worker question is illuminated by the memoirs of labor experts Ianzhul, Pogozhev, and Ozerov, as well as in the fragmentary recollections of Zubatov and Gapon. His relations with "society" are described by zemstvo activist Shipov, who recounts in detail his encounters with Plehve, and to a lesser extent by Kizevetter, Maklakov, Miliukov, and Samarin. His attitudes and actions toward the Jews are dealt with by Prince S. D. Urusov, appointed by Plehve as Governor of Bessarabia in the wake of the Kishinev pogrom, and by liberal lawyer A. F. Koni, who gives an account of Plehve's dispute with Witte on this issue. His character and relations with other state officials are discussed in the memoirs of E. M. Feoktistov, who was censorship director during Plehve's early years in the Ministry of Interior, and in those of V. N. Kokovtsov, Witte's successor as Minister of Finance. His relations with revolutionaries, and the events leading to his assassination are recorded in the reminiscences of revolutionaries V. N. Chernov, G. A. Gershuni, and Boris Savinkov, the last of whom describes in detail the elaborate and successful assassination plot which he personally supervised.

Several of Plehve's associates kept diaries, which provide more immediate accounts of impressions and conversations. Foremost among these is the journal of War Minister A. N. Kuropatkin (published in *Krasnyi Arkhiv*), which provides an important first-hand account of Russia's drift into war with Japan, and Plehve's role therein. Likewise the diaries of the Russian official A. A. Polovtsov and the Zionist leader Theodor Herzl record the contents of their discussions, and the nature of their relations, with Plehve. Of less help, but still useful, are the published diaries of A. V. Bogdanovich, A. S. Suvorin, and Emperor Nicholas II.

With regard to secondary literature, although there has hitherto been no comprehensive treatment of Plehve, there have been a number of books and articles which touch upon his activities. His administrative reforms, for example, were described in part by S. A. Korf, and have more recently been thoroughly and thoughtfully treated in the work of N. B. Weissman. His relations with the zemstvos are considered from various perspectives by I. P. Belokonskii, Shmuel Galai, E. D. Chermenskii, and N. M. Pirumova, while Iu. B. Solov'ev has shed some light on his attitude toward the nobility. Varying interpretations of his peasant program have been put forth by M. S.

Simonova, I. V. Chernyshev, and D. A. J. Macey, while V. A. Stepynin has described his resettlement policy. His activities toward the Jews, depicted by historians like Dubnov, Sliozberg, and Greenberg, have been carefully reconsidered in several articles by H. Rogger. M. M. Borodkin, a contemporary of Plehve's, has extensively and sympathetically recounted his dealings with the Finns, while some aspects of his earlier career have been dealt with in works and articles by P. A. Zaionchkovskii, R. G. Robbins, and F. C. Giffen. Biographies of Plehve's associates, including T. H. von Laue's classic study of Witte and J. Schneiderman's solid work on Zubatov, also shed light on his programs and policies. Finally, books such as those by D. T. Orlovsky, G. L. Yaney, W. Pintner, and D. K. Rowney, although they do not deal directly with Plehve, provide valuable insights into the workings of the Russian Government.

Bibliography

ARCHIVAL COLLECTIONS

Gosudarstvennaia Biblioteka SSSR imeni V. I. Lenina, Otdel Rukopisei (GBL). (USSR State Lenin Library, Manuscript Section)

    fond 126 (A. A. Kireev—diaries)
    fond 169 (D. A. Miliutin—correspondence)
    fond 215 (M. M. Osorgin—memoirs)
    fond 265 (F. D. Samarin—memoirs)

Gosudarstvennaia Publichnaia Biblioteka imeni M. E. Saltykova-Shchedrina, Otdel Rukopisei (GPB). (Saltykov-Shchedrin State Public Library, Manuscript Section)

    fond 586 (V. K. Plehve—correspondence)

Tsentral'nyi Gosudarstvennyi Arkhiv Oktiabrskoi Revoliutsii SSSR (Ts-GAOR). (USSR Central State Archive of the October Revolution)

    fond 102 (Department of Police—files)
    fond 543 (Tsarskoe Selo Palace—papers, memoranda)
    fond 586 (V. K. Plehve—papers, correspondence)
    fond 601 (Emperor Nicholas II—diaries)
    fond 634 (L. A. Tikhomirov—diaries)
    fond 730 (N. P. Ignat'ev—correspondence)
    fond 810 (D. N. Shipov—correspondence)
    fond 826 (B. F. Dzhunkovskii—memoirs)
    fond 1463 (A. N. Mosolov—memoirs)

Tsentral'nyi Gosudarstvennyi Istoricheskii Arkhiv SSSR (TsGIA). (USSR Central State Historical Archive)

    fond 592 (Obolenskii Commission on Peasant Land Bank)
    fond 1099 (A. A. Klopov—correspondence)

fond 1151 (Abaza Commission on nobility landownership)
fond 1162 (service records)
fond 1233 (Special Conference on the Needs of Agricultural Industry)
fond 1234 (Platonov Conference on decentralization)
fond 1263 (Committee of Ministers)
fond 1273 (Resettlement Law of 1904—materials)
fond 1282 (Ministry of Interior—reports, local agriculture committees)
fond 1283 (Ministry of Interior—reports, conference on nobility)
fond 1284 (Ministry of Interior—reports, peasant affairs)
fond 1291 (Ministry of Interior—reports, peasant affairs)
fond 1622 (S. Iu. Witte—papers and correspondence)

DOCUMENTS

Delo A. A. Lopukhina v osobom prisutstvii pravitel'stvuiushchago senata: Stenograficheskii otchet. Saint Petersburg: Tip. R. I. Artsivi, 1910.

Krest'ianskoe dvizhenie v Poltavskoi i Khar'kovskoi guberniakh v 1902g. Sbornik dokumentov. Khar'kov: Khar'kovskoe knizhnoe izdatel'stvo, 1961.

Materialy dlia istorii antievreiskikh pogromov v Rossii. Edited by S. M. Dubnow and G. Ia. Krasnyi-Admoni. 2 vols. Petrograd and Moscow: Tipografiia "Kadima" and Gosudarstvennoe izdatel'stvo, 1919, 1923.

Prolog Russko-Iaponskoi Voiny: Materialy iz arkhiva grafa S. Iu. Vitte. Edited by B. B. Glinskii. Petrograd: Tipografiia Aktsionernago Obshchestva "Brokgauz-Efron," 1916.

Russia. Gosudarstvennyi Sovet. *Otchet po deloproizvodstvu Gosudarstvennago Soveta 1869–1905/6.* 41 vols. Saint Petersburg: Gosudarstvennaia tipografiia, 1870–1906.

Russia. Laws, statutes, etc. *Polnoe sobranie zakonov rossiiskoi imperii.* 33 vols. 3rd ed. Saint Petersburg: Gosudarstvennaia tipografiia, 1885–1916.

Russia. Ministerstvo vnutrennykh del. *Ocherk rabot Redaktsionnoi kommissii po peresmotru zakonopolozhenii o krest'ianakh.* Saint Petersburg: Tipografiia Ministerstva vnutrennikh del, 1904.

Russia. Ministerstvo vnutrennykh del. *Poriadok obsuzhdenie proektov vyrabotannykh Redaktsionnoi kommissiei po peresmotru zakonopolozhenii o krest'ianakh.* Saint Petersburg: Tipografiia Ministerstva vnutrennikh del, 1904.

Russia. Redaktsionnaia komissiia po peresmotru zakonopolozhenie o krest'ianakh. *Trudy redaktsionnoi kommissii po peresmotru zakonopolozhenii o krest'ianakh.* 6 vols. Saint Petersburg: Tipografiia Ministerstva vnutrennikh del, 1903–1904.

Russia (USSR). Tsentral'nyi Arkhiv Revoliutsii. *Vseobshchaia stachka na iuge Rossii v 1903 godu: Sbornik dokumentov.* Moscow: Gosudarstvennoe izdatel'stvo politicheskoi literatury, 1938.

Savich, G. G., ed. *Novyi gosudarstvennyi stroi Rossii: Spravochnaia kniga.* Saint Petersburg: Tipografiia akts. obshch. Brokgauz-Efron, 1907.

BOOKS AND ARTICLES

A. P., "Departament politsii v 1892–1908gg.: Iz vospominanii chinovnika." *Byloe,* No. 5–6 (27–28) (1917): 17–24.

Ascher, A. "The Coming Storm: The Austro-Hungarian Embassy on Russia's Internal Crisis." *Survey,* No. 53 (October 1964), pp. 148–64.

Azef, E. F. "Doneseniia Evno Azefa: Perepiska Azefa s Rataevym v 1903–1905gg." *Byloe,* No. 1 (23) (1917): 196–228.

Belokonskii, I. P. *Zemskoe dvizhenie.* 2nd ed. Moscow: Zadruga, 1914.

Blakely, Allison. "The Socialist Revolutionary Party, 1901–1907: The Populist Response to the Industrialization of Russia." Ph.D. dissertation, University of California, 1971.

Bogdanovich, A. V. *Tri poslednik samoderzhtsa.* Moscow and Petrograd: Izdatel'stvo L. D. Frenkel', 1924.

Bompard, Maurice. *Mon Ambassade en Russie (1903–1908).* Paris: Libraire Plon, 1937.

Borodkin, M. M. *Iz noveishei istorii Finliandii: Vremia upravleniia N. I. Bobrikova.* Saint Petersburg: T-vo P. Golike i A. Vil'borg, 1905.

Brusnikin, E. M. "Podgotovka zakona 14 dekabria 1893g. o neotchuzhdaemosti krest'ianskikh nadel'nykh zemel." *Uchenye zapiski Gor'kovskogo Gosudarstvenogo Universiteta* 72 (1972).

Bukhbinder, N. A., ed. "K istorii 'Sobraniia russkikh fabrichno-zavodskikh rabochikh g. S. Peterburga.'" *Krasnaia Letopis',* No. 1 (1922): 288–329.

———. ed. "K istorii zubatovshchiny v Moskve." *Istoriia Proletariata SSSR,* Sbornik 2 (1930): 169–98.

———. "Nezavisimaia evreiskaia rabochaia partiia (po neizdannym arkhivnym materialam)." *Krasnaia Letopis',* No. 3–4 (1922): 208–84.

———. "O Zubatovshchine." *Krasnaia Letopis',* No. 4 (1922): 289–335.

———. ed. "Zubatovshchina v Moskve." *Katorga i Ssylka* 14 (1925): 96–133.

Chemeriskii, A. I., Rafes, M. and Frumkina, M. "Vospominaniia o 'evreiskoi nezavisimoi rabochei partii.'" *Krasnyi Arkhiv* 1 (1922): 315–18.

Chermenskii, E. D. "Zemsko-liberal'noe dvizhenie nakanune revoliutsii 1905–1907gg." *Istoriia SSSR,* No. 5 (1965): 41–60.

Chernov, V. M. *Pered burei: Vospominaniia.* New York: Izdatel'stvo imeni Chekhova, 1953.

Chernyshev, I. V. *Agrarno-krest'ianskaia politika Rossii za 150 let.* Petrograd: Tipografiia Ministerstva Putei Soobshcheniia, 1918.

Danilov, F. "Obshchaia politika pravitel'stva i gosudarstvennyi stroi k nachalu XX veka." *Obshchestvennoe dvizhenie v Rossii v nachale XX-go veka.* Edited by L. Martov, P. Maslov, and A. Potresov. Vol. 1. Saint Petersburg: Tipografiia t-va "Obshchestvennaia Pol'za," 1909.

Dillon, E. J. *The Eclipse of Russia.* London and Toronto: J. M. Dent and Sons, 1918.

Dubnov, S. M. *A History of the Jews in Russia and Poland from the Earliest Times until the Present Day.* 3 vols. Translated by I. Friedlaender. Philadelphia: Jewish Publication Society of America, 1916–1920.

Dubrovskii, S. M. *Stolypinskaia zemel'naia reforma: Iz istorii sel'sko khoziaistva i krest'ianstva Rossii v nachale XX veka.* Moscow: Izdatel'stvo Akademii nauk SSSR, 1963 [First published, 1925].

Emeliakh, L. I. "Krest'iansko dvizhenie v Poltavskoi i Khar'kovskoi Guberniakh v 1902g." *Istoricheskie Zapiski* 38 (1951): 154–75.

Eroshkin, N. P. *Ocherki istorii gosudarstvennykh uchrezhdenii dorevoliutsionnoi Rossii.* Moscow: Gosudarstvennoe uchebno-pedagogicheskoe izdatel'stvo ministerstva prosveshcheniia RSFSR, 1960.

Fedorov, Evgenii. *Podgotovka finliandskoi revoliutsii 1899–1905gg.* Saint Petersburg, [n. p.], 1907.

Feoktistov, E. M. *Vospominaniia E. M. Feoktistova: Za kulisami politike i literatury, 1848–1896.* Edited by Iu. G. Oksman. Leningrad: "Priboi," 1929.

Figner, V. N. *Zapechatlennyi trud: Vospominaniia.* 2 vols. Moscow: Izdatel'stvo Sotsial'no-ekonomicheskoe literatury "Mysl," 1964.

Fisher, J. R. *Finland and the Tsars, 1809–1899.* London: Edward Arnold, 1899.

Galai, Shmuel. "The Impact of the Russo-Japanese War on the Russian Liberals, 1904–1905." *Government and Opposition* 1 (1965): 85–109.

——— . *The Liberation Movement in Russia, 1900–1905.* Cambridge: At the University Press, 1973.

Gapon, G. A. *Zapiski Georgiia Gapona: Ocherk rabochago dvizheniia v Rossii 1900-kh godov.* Moscow: Tipografiia Vil'de, 1918.

Georgievskii, A. I. *Materialy po istorii studencheskago dvizheniia v Rossii.* 2 vols. London and Saint Petersburg: Izdatel'stvo "Svobodnaia mysl," 1906.

Gershuni, G. A. *Iz nedavniago proshlago.* Paris: Tribune Russe, 1908.

Gessen, I. V. *Sudebnaia Reforma.* Saint Petersburg: Tipo-Litografiia F. Vaisberga i P. Gershunina, 1905.

——— . *V dvukh vekakh: Zhiznenyi otchet.* Berlin: Speer und Schmitt Buchdruckerei, 1937.

Giffen, Frederick C. "The Role of the Pleve Commission in the Russian Factory Laws of 1885 and 1886." *European Studies Review* 2 (1972): 143–50.

Glazov, V. L. "Dva razgovora: Iz dnevnikov V. L. Glazova." Edited by S. F. Platonov. *Dela i Dni* 1 (1921): 209–18.

Gots, M. R. "S. V. Zubatov (stranichka iz perezhitago)." *Byloe*, No. 9 (1906): 63–68.

Greenberg, Louis. *The Jews in Russia: The Struggle for Emancipation.* 2 vols. New Haven and London: Yale University Press, 1944, 1951.

Grigor'evskii, M. ("Lunts, M. G."). *Sbornik statei.* Moscow: F. Ia. Burche, 1909.

Gurko, V. I. *Features and Figures of the Past: Government and Opinion in the Reign of Nicholas II.* Translated by Laura Matveev. Edited by J. E. Wallace Sterling, Xenia Joukoff Eudin, and H. H. Fisher. Stanford: Stanford University Press, 1939.

Hamburg, G. M. "The Russian Nobility on the Eve of the 1905 Revolution," *Russian Review* 38 (July 1979): 323–38.

Harutunian, G. *Revoliutsionnoe dvizhenie v Armenii, 1905–1907gg.* Erevan: Izdatel'stvo "Asiastan," 1970.

Heilbronner, Hans. "Count Aehrenthal and Russian Jewry." *Journal of Modern History* 38 (1966): 394–406.

Herzl, Theodor. *The Complete Diaries of Theodor Herzl.* Translated by Harry Zohn. 5 vols. New York and London: Herzl Press and Thomas Yoseloff, 1960.

———. *The Diaries of Theodor Herzl.* Edited and translated by Marvin Lowenthal. New York: Dial Press, 1956.

Hovannisian, Richard G. *Armenia on the Road to Independence, 1918.* Berkeley: University of California Press, 1967.

Ianzhul, I. I. *Iz vosponinanii i perepiski fabrichnago inspektora.* Saint Petersburg: Tip. Akts. Obshch. Brokgauz-Efron, 1907.

———. "Vospominaniia I. I. Ianzhul o perezhitom i vidennom." *Russkaia Starina* 144 (1910): 258–72, 485–500.

"Istoriia 'legalizatsii' rabochago dvizheniia: Spravka Osobago Otdela Departamenta Politsii." *Byloe*, No. 1 (23) (1917): 86–87.

Istoriia SSSR: Uchebnik dlia pedagogicheskikh institutov. 2 vols. Moscow: Izdatel'stvo "Prosveshchenie," 1964.

"Iz istorii revoliutsionnogo dvizheniia v armii nakanune 1905g." *Krasnyi Arkhiv* 63 (1930): 168–73.

Joubert, Carl. *The Truth about the Tsar and the Present State of Russia.* London: Eveleigh Nash, 1905.

Jutikkala, E. K. I. *A History of Finland.* Translated by Paul Sjöblom. New York: Frederick A. Praeger, 1962.

"Kar'era P. I. Rachkovskago: Dokumenty." *Byloe*, No. 8 (30) (1918): 78–87.

"K delu Fomy Kochury." *Byloe*, No. 6 (1906): 102–7.

"K delu 1 marta 1881 goda: Neizdannye doklady grafa Loris-Melikova, V. K. Pleve, A. V. Komarova." *Byloe*, No. 10–11 (32–33) (1918): 12–69.

Keep, J. L. H. *The Rise of Social Democracy in Russia.* Oxford: Clarendon Press, 1963.

"K istorii vseobshchei stachki na iuge Rossii v 1903g." *Krasnyi Arkhiv* 88 (1938): 75–122.

Kizevetter, A. A. *Na rubezhe dvukh stoletii: Vospominaniia 1881–1914.* Prague: Izdatel'stvo "Orbis," 1929.

Klevenskii, M. "Okhrannoe otdelenie." *Bol'shaia Sovetskaia Entsiklopediia.* 1939. Vol. 43.

Kochan, Lionel. *Russia in Revolution 1890–1918.* London: Weidenfeld and Nicolson, 1966.

Kokovtsov, V. N. *Out of My Past: The Memoirs of Count Kokovtsov.* Translated by Laura Matveev. Edited by H. H. Fisher. Stanford: Stanford University Press, 1935.

Koni, A. F. "Sergei Iul'evich Vitte." *Sobranie sochinenii.* Vol. 5. Moscow: Izdatel'stvo "Iuridicheskaia literatura," 1968.

Korelin, A. P. *Dvorianstvo v poreformennoi Rossii.* Moscow: Izdatel'stvo "Nauk," 1979.

Korkunov, N. M. *Russkoe gosudarstvennoe pravo.* 2 vols. Saint Petersburg: Tipografiia M. M. Stasiulevicha, 1913–1914.

Korolenko, V. G. *Sobranie sochinenii.* 10 vols. Moscow: Gosudarstvennoe izdatel'stvo khudozhestvennoi literatury, 1953–1955.

Kovalenskii, M. N. *Russkaia revoliutsiia v sudebnykh protsessakh i memuarakh.* Moscow: Kooperativnoe izdatel'stvo "Mir," 1925.

Kucherov, Samuel. *Courts, Lawyers and Trials under the Last Three Tsars.* New York: Frederick A. Praeger, 1953.

Kuropatkin, A. N. "Dnevnik A. N. Kuropatkina." *Krasnyi Arkhiv* 2 (1922): 5–117.

———. *Zapiska generala Kuropatkina o russko-iaponskoi voine: Itogi voiny.* Berlin: J. Ladyschnikow, 1911.

Liashchenko, P. I. "Krest'ianskoe delo i poreformennaia zemleustroitel'naia politika." *Tomskii gosudarstvennyi universitet izvestiia,* Book 66. Tomsk: Tipolitografiia Sibirskago T-va Pechatnago Dela, 1917.

Liubimov, D. N. "Russkaia smuta nachala deviatisotykh godov, 1902–1906." Manuscript in archives of the Hoover Library on War, Revolution and Peace, Stanford, California.

Livshits, R. S. *Razmeshchenie promyshlennosti v dorevoliutsionnoi Rossii.* Moscow: Izdatel'stvo Akademiia Nauk SSSR, 1955.

Lopukhin, A. A. "Doklad Direktora Departamenta Politsii Lopukhina Ministru Vnutrennikh Del o sobytiakh 9-go ianvaria," *Krasnaia Letopis',* No. 1 (1922): 330–38.

———. *Nastoiashchee i budushchee russkoi politsii.* Moscow: Izdanie V. M. Sablina, 1907.

———. *Otryvki iz vospominanii: Po povodu "Vospominanii" gr. S. Iu. Vitte.* Moscow: Gosudarstvennoe izdatel'stvo, 1923.

————. "Zapiska Direktora Departamenta Politsii, deistvitel'nogo sovetnika Lopukhina, po delu o stachkakh i bezporiadkakh, proizkhodivshikh v iiule 1903 goda v gorodakh Odesse, Kieve, i Nikolaeve." *Krasnaia Letopis'*, No. 4 (1922): 385–95.

Macey, David Anthony James. "The Russian Bureaucracy and the 'Peasant Problem:' The Pre-history of the Stolypin Reforms, 1861–1917." Ph.D. dissertation, Columbia University, 1976.

Maklakov, V. A. *Vlast' i obshchestvennost' na zakate Staroi Rossii: Vospominaniia sovremennika*. Paris: Izdanie zhurnala Illiustrirovannaia Rossiia, 1936.

Makletsova (Degaeva), N. P. "Sudeikin i Degaev." *Byloe*, No. 8 (1906): 265–72.

Malozemoff, Andrew. *Russian Far Eastern Policy, 1881–1904, with Special Emphasis on the Causes of the Russo-Japanese War*. Berkeley and Los Angeles: University of California Press, 1958.

Manning, Roberta Thompson. "The Russian Provincial Gentry in Revolution and Counterrevolution, 1905–1907." Ph.D. dissertation, Columbia University, 1975.

Meshcherskii, V. P. *Moi Vospominaniia. III 1881–1894*. Saint Petersburg: Fotoninko-kromo-lito-tipografiia F. Krozh, 1912.

Mikhailovskii, N. K. *Vospominaniia: I. Vera Figner; 2. V. K. Pleve*. Berlin: Izdanie Gugo Shteinitsa, 1906.

Miliukov, P. N. *Vospominaniia 1859–1917*. 2 vols. New York: Collier Books, 1955.

Mosolov, A. A. *At the Court of the Last Tsar*. Translated by F. W. Dickes. Edited by A. A. Pilenco. London: Methuen and Co., Ltd., [1935].

Nicholas II, Emperor of Russia. *Dnevnik Imperatora Nikolaia II, 1890–1906gg*. Berlin: Knigoizdatel'stvo "Slovo," 1923.

————. "Pis'mo Nikolaia II P. S. Vannovskomu, 1902 god." *Byloe*, No. 7 (29) (1918): 60–61.

————. *The Secret Letters of the Last Tsar*. Edited by E. J. Bing. New York and Toronto: Longmans, Green and Co., 1938.

Nikolaevskii, B. I. *Istoriia odnogo predatelia: Terroristy i politicheskaia politsiia*. Berlin: Petropolis, 1932.

"Nikolai II i samoderzhavie v 1903g.: Iz itogov perliustratsii." *Byloe*, No. 8 (30) (1918): 190–222.

Novitskii, V. D. "Zapiska gen. Novitskago." *Sotsialist-Revoliustionner*, No. 2 (1910): 53–113.

Ol'denberg, S. S. *Tsarstvovanie Imperatora Nikolaia II*. 2 vols. Belgrade: Izdanie obshchestvo rasprostraneniia russkoi natsional'noi i patrioticheskoi literatury, 1939.

Orlovsky, Daniel T. *The Limits of Reform: The Ministry of Internal Affairs in Imperial Russia, 1802–1881*. Cambridge, Mass: Harvard University Press, 1981.

Ozerov, I. Kh. *Politika po rabochemu voprosu v Rossii za poslednie gody.* Moscow: Tipografiia T-va I. D. Sytina, 1906.

Pamiati Viacheslava Konstantinovicha Pleve. Saint Petersburg: Tip. Ministerstva vnutrennikh del, 1904.

Peterburgskii Nekropol'. 3 vols. Saint Petersburg: Tipografiia M. M. Stasiulevicha, 1912.

Pintner, Walter, and Don Karl Rowney, eds. *Russian Officialdom.* Chapel Hill: University of North Carolina Press, 1980.

Piontkovskii, S., ed. "Novoe o zubatovshchine," *Krasnyi Arkhiv* 1 (1922): 289–314.

Piontkovskii, S. A. *Ocherki istorii SSSR XIX i XX vv.* Moscow: Gosudarstvennoe sotsial'no-ekonomicheskoe izdatel'stvo, 1935.

Pirumova, N. M. *Zemskoe liberal'noe dvizhenie: sotsial'nye korni i evoliutsiia do nachala XX veka.* Moscow: Izdatel'stvo Nauka, 1977.

Plehve, V. K. "A Defense of Russia's Policy in Finland." *American Monthly Review of Reviews* 28 (1903): 577–80.

———. "Pis'mo min. vnutr. del. V. K. Pleve na imia voennogo min. A. N. Kuropatkina ot 5/XI 1903g." *Krasnyi Arkhiv* 63 (1930): 171–73.

———. "Pis'mo V. K. Pleve k A. A. Kireevu." *Krasnyi Arkhiv* 18 (1926): 201–3.

———. *Usilenie gubernatorskoi vlasti: Proekt fon Pleve.* Paris: Osvobozhdenie, 1904.

———. "Zapiska V. K. Pleve po universitetskomu voprosu." *Byloe,* No. 21 (1907): 215–25.

Pogozhev, A. V. "Iz vospominanii o V. K. fon-Pleve." *Vestnik Evropy* 46 (1911): 259–80.

Polovtsov, A. A. "Dnevnik A. A. Polovtseva." *Krasnyi Arkhiv* 3 (1923): 75–172.

———. *Dnevnik gosudarstvennogo sekretaria A. A. Polovtsova.* Edited by P. A. Zaionchkovskii. 2 vols. Moscow: Izdatel'stvo "Nauka," 1966.

Pribyleva-Korba, Anna. "Sergei Petrovich Degaev." *Byloe,* No. 4 (1906): 1–17.

"Prikliucheniia I. F. Manuilova: Po arkhivnym materialam." *Byloe,* No. 5–6 (27–28) (1917): 236–86.

Radkey, O. H. *The Agrarian Foes of Bolshevism: Promise and Default of the Russian Socialist Revolutionaries, February to October, 1917.* New York: Columbia University Press, 1958.

Rakovskii, M., ed. "Zubatov i Moskovskie gravery (1898–1899gg.)." *Istoriia Proletariata SSSR, Sbornik* 2 (1930): 199–232.

Rashin, A. G. *Naselenie Rossii za 100 let, 1811–1913gg.: Statisticheskii ocherki.* Moscow: Gosudarstvennoe statisticheskoe izdatel'stvo, 1956.

Rataev, L. A. "Evno Azef: Istoriia ego predatel'stva." *Byloe*, No. 2 (24) (1917): 187–210:

Ratova, S. A. "Vseobshchaia stachka v 1903 godu na Kavkaze i Chernomorskom poberezh'e." *Byloe*, No. 18 (1907): 97–117.

Robbins, R. G., Jr. *The Famine in Russia 1891–1892: The Imperial Government Responds to a Crisis*. New York and London: Columbia University Press, 1975.

————. "Russia's Famine Relief Law of June 12, 1900: A Reform Aborted." *Canadian-American Slavic Studies* 10 (1976): 25–37.

Robinson, G. T. *Rural Russia under the Old Regime*. Berkeley and Los Angeles: University of California Press, 1967.

Rogger Hans. "The Jewish Policy of Late Tsarism: A Reappraisal." *Weiner Library Bulletin* 25 (1971): 42–51.

————. "Russian Ministers and the Jewish Question, 1881–1917," *California Slavic Studies* 8 (1975): 15–76.

Romanov, B. A., ed. "Bezobrazovskii kruzhok letom 1904." *Krasnyi Arkhiv* 17 (1926): 70–80.

————. "Kontsessiia na Ialu." *Russkoe Proshloe*, No. 1 (1923): 87–108.

————. *Rossiia v Man'chzhurii, 1892–1906: Ocherki po istorii vneshnei politiki samoderzhaviia v epokhu imperializma*. Leningrad: Leningradskii vostochnii institut imeni A. S. Enukidze, 1928.

Rosen, Baron R. R. *Forty Years of Diplomacy*. 2 vols. New York: Alfred A. Knopf, 1922.

Russia. Gosudarstvennaia kantseliariia. *Gosudarstvennaia kantseliariia, 1810–1910*. Saint Petersburg: Gosudarstvennaia tipografiia, 1910.

Russia. Gosudarstvennyi Sovet. *Gosudarstvennyi Sovet 1801–1901*. Saint Petersburg: Gosudarstvennaia tipografiia, 1901.

Russko-iaponskaia voina: Iz dnevnikov A. N. Kuropatkina i N. P. Linevicha. Edited by M. N. Pokrovskii. Leningrad: Gosudarstvennoe izdatel'stvo, 1925.

Russobtovskii, M. *Istoricheskoe osveshchenie finliandskago voprosa*. Saint Petersburg: Tip. "Rodnik," 1910.

Sablinsky, Walter. *The Road to Bloody Sunday*. Princeton, N. J.: Princeton University Press, 1976.

Savinkov, B. V. *Vospominaniia terrorista*. Khar'kov: Izdatel'stvo "Proletarii," [1926].

Sazonov, E. S. *Materialy dlia biografii*. Edited by S. P. Mel'gunov. Moscow: Izd. zhurnala "Golos Minuvshago," 1919.

Schneiderman, Jeremiah. *Sergei Zubatov and Revolutionary Marxism*. Ithaca and London: Cornell University Press, 1976.

Semennikov, V. "Nikolai Romanov i Finliandiia." *Krasnyi Arkhiv* 27 (1928): 225–33.

Shchegolev, P. E. *Okhranniki i avantiuristy*. Moscow: Izdatel'stvo politkator-zhan, 1930.

Shipov, D. N. *Vospominaniia i dumy o perezhitom*. Moscow: Tovarishchestvo "Pechatnaia S. P. Iakovleva," 1918.

Shlossberg, D. "Vseobshchaia stachka 1903g. na Ukraine." *Istoriia Proletariata SSSR*, No. 7 (1931): 52–85.

Shtein, V. I. "Neudachnyi opyt (Zubatovshchina)." *Istoricheskii Vestnik* 29 (1912): 221–55.

Simms, J. Y., Jr. "The Crisis of Russian Agriculture at the End of the Nineteenth Century." *Slavic Review* 36 (1977): 377–98.

Simonova, M. S. "Bor'ba techenii v pravitel'stvennom lagere po voprosam agrarnoi politiki v kontse XIX v." *Istoriia SSSR*, No. 1 (1963): 65–82.

———. "Otmena krugovoi poruki." *Istoricheskie Zapiski* 83 (1969): 159–95.

———. "Politika tsarizma v krest'ianskom voprose nakanune revoliutsii 1905–1907gg." *Istoricheskie Zapiski* 75 (1965): 212–42.

Sliozberg, G. B. *Dela minuvshikh dnei: Zapiski russkago Evreia*. 3 vols. Paris: Imprimerie Pascal, 1933–1934.

———. *Dorevoliutsionnyi stroi Rossii*. Paris: Maison du Livre Étranger, 1933.

Solov'ev, Iu. B. *Samoderzhavie i dvorianstvo v kontse XIX veka*. Leningrad: Izdatel'stvo "Nauka," 1973.

Spiridovich, A. I. *Histoire du Terrorisme Russe, 1886–1917*. Translated by V. Lazarevskii. Paris: Payot, 1930.

———. "Pri tsarskom rezhime." *Arkhiv Russkoi Revoliutsii* 15 (1924): 85–206.

———. *Zapiski zhandarma*. [Khar'kov]: Izdatel'stvo "Proletarii," [1928].

"Stachka rabochikh zavoda br. Bromlei v 1903g.," *Krasnyi Arkhiv* 56 (1933): 138–44.

Stefanovich, Ia. V. "Pis'mo Ia. V. Stefanovicha k V. K. Pleve." *Krasnyi Arkhiv* 4 (1923): 410–11.

Stepynin, V. A. "Iz istorii pereselencheskoi politiki samoderzhavie v nachale xx veka," *Istoricheskie Zapiski* 75 (1965): 161–64.

Suvorin, A. S. *Dnevnik A. S. Suvorina*. Edited by M. Krichevskii. Moscow and Petrograd: Izdatel'stvo L. D. Frenkel', 1923.

Tager, A. S. *The Decay of Tsarism: The Beiliss Trial*. Philadelphia: Jewish Publication Society of America, 1935.

Thaden, Edward C., ed. *Russification in the Baltic Provinces and Finland, 1855–1914*. Princeton, N. J.: Princeton University Press, 1981.

Tikhomirov, Lev. "25 let nazad: Iz dnevnikov L. Tikhomirova." *Krasnyi Arkhiv* 38 (1930): 20–69.

Tobias, H. J. *The Jewish Bund in Russia from its Origins to 1905*. Stanford: Stanford University Press, 1972.

Tompkins, S. R. "Witte as Minister of Finance, 1892–1903." *Slavonic and East European Review* 11 (1933): 590–606.

Urusov, Prince S. D. *Memoirs of a Russian Governor.* Translated and edited by Herman Rosenthal. London and New York: Harper and Brothers, 1908.

Veselovskii, B. B. *Istoriia Zemstva.* 4 vols. Saint Petersburg: Izdatel'stvo O. N. Popovoi, 1909–1911.

Villari, Liugi. *Fire and Sword in the Caucasus.* London: T. Fisher Unwin, 1906.

Volk, S. S. *Narodnaia Volia 1879–1882.* Moscow and Leningrad: Izdatel'stvo Nauka, 1966.

Von Laue, T. H. *Sergei Witte and the Industrialization of Russia.* New York and London: Columbia University Press, 1963.

Vratzian, Simon. *Armenia and the Armenian Question.* Translated by J. G. Mandalian. Boston: Hairenik Publishing Company, 1943.

Vydria, M., and Ginev, V. "Sudebnaia sistema dorevoliutsionnoi rossii." A. F. Koni, *Sobranie sochinenii,* Vol. I Moscow: Izdatel'stvo "Iuridicheskaia literatura," 1966.

Walder, David. *The Short Victorious War: The Russo-Japanese Conflict of 1904–1905.* London: Hutchinson, 1973.

Walkin, Jacob. *The Rise of Democracy in Pre-Revolutionary Russia: Political and Social Institutions under the Last Three Czars.* New York: Frederick A. Praeger, 1962.

Wallace, Sir D. M. *Russia.* 2 vols. London: Cassell and Company, Ltd., 1905.

Weissman, Neil B. *Reform in Tsarist Russia: The State Bureaucracy and Local Government, 1900–1914.* New Brunswick, N.J.: Rutgers University Press, 1981.

White, J. A. *The Diplomacy of the Russo-Japanese War.* Princeton, N.J.: Princeton University Press, 1964.

Witte, Sergei Iu. "A Secret Memorandum of Sergei Witte on the Industrialization of Imperial Russia." Edited by T. H. Von Laue. *Journal of Modern History* 26 (1954): 60–74.

———. *Vospominaniia: Detstvo; Tsarstvovanie Aleksandra II i Aleksandra III, 1849–1894.* Berlin: Knigoizdatel'stvo "Slovo," 1923.

———. *Vospominaniia: Tsarstvovanie Nikolaia II.* 2 vols. Berlin: Knigoizdatel'stvo "Slovo," 1922.

———. *Vynuzhdenyia Raz"iasneniia po povodu otcheta Gen.-Ad. Kuropatkina o voine s Iaponiei.* Moscow: Tipografiia T-va J. D. Sytina, 1911.

Wren, M. C. *The Course of Russian History.* New York: Macmillan, 1958.

Yaney, G. L. *The Systematization of Russian Government.* Urbana, Chicago, and London: University of Illinois Press, 1973.

Zaionchkovskii, P. A. *Krizis samoderzhavie na rubezhe 1870–1880 godov.* Moscow: Izdatel'stvo Moskovskogo universiteta, 1964.

———. *Rossiiskoe samoderzhavie v kontse XIX stoletiia: Politicheskaia reaktsiia* 80-*kh-nachala* 90-*kh godov*. Moscow: Izdatel'stvo "Mysl," 1970.

Zakharova, L. G. "Krizis samoderzhaviia nakanune revoliutsii 1905 goda." *Voprosy Istorii*, No. 8 (1972): 119–40.

———. *Zemskaia kontrreforma*. Moscow: Izdatel'stvo Moskovskogo Universiteta, 1968.

Zaslavskii, D. "Zubatov i Mania Vil'bushevich." *Byloe*, No. 9 (31) (1918): 99–128.

Zavarzin, P. P. *Zhandarmy i revoliutsionery: Vospominaniia*. Paris: Payot, 1930.

"Zhurnal Osobogo soveshchaniia (7 fevraliia) 25 ianvariia 1903g." *Krasnyi Arkhiv* 52 (1932): 110–24.

Zubatov, S. V. "Doklad Chinovnika Osobykh poruchenii V klassa pri Departamentie Politsii S. V. Zubatova Direktoru Departamenta Politsii." *Byloe*, No. 1 (23) (1917): 93–99.

———. "Dva dokumenta iz istorii Zubatovshchiny." *Krasnyi Arkhiv* 19 (1926): 210–11.

———. "Pis'mo." *Vestnik Evropy* 41 (1906): 432–36.

———. "Zubatovshchina." *Byloe*, No. 4 (26) (1917): 157–78.

NEWSPAPERS

Grazhdanin. Saint Petersburg.

Iskra. Leipzig, Munich, London, Geneva.

New York Times. New York.

Novoe Vremia. Saint Petersburg.

Osvobozhdenie. Stuttgart, Paris.

Revoliutsionnaia Rossiia. Tomsk, Geneva.

Russkiia Vedomosti. Moscow.

The Times. London.

Index

Abaza, A. M., 162, 164, 165–66, 168–69, 170, 172
Administrative reform. *See* Russian Government
Agrarian reform. *See* Peasants
Aleksandropol, 119
Alekseev, E. I., 163, 165, 166–67, 168, 169–70, 172
Alexander II, Emperor: impressed by Plehve, 15; assassinated, 16, 33, 222; and reform, 68–69, 73; and Finland, 111; memorialized, 133
Alexander III, Emperor: and Witte, 7; and Plehve, 17, 20, 22, 23, 35, 103–4; and Loris-Melikov, 17–18; death of, 27; and Finland, 111; and Meschcherskii, 152; and "perlustration," 201
Alexander Mikhailovich, Grand Duke, 77, 153
Alexandra Fedorovna, Empress, 136, 166, 239
"All-Zemstvo Organization," 210–12
Andreev (Elizavetpol Vice-Governor): murdered, 216, 232, 234
Anti-Semitism. *See* Jews
Aptekarsk Island, 56, 233
Armenian-Gregorian Church, 117, 118–20, 216
Armenian Revolutionary Union (*Dashnak*), 118

Armenians: under Russian rule, 102, 117–118; struggle for autonomy, 118–21, 213, 216, 244; mentioned, 153, 199
Assembly of Factory-Plant Workers of the City of Saint Petersburg, 194–95, 196, 242
Autocracy. *See* Russian Government
Azef, Evno: Okhrana spy, 223; plans attacks on Plehve, 223–24, 230–32, 234, 238; deceives police, 224, 227–29, 231, 234, 241; heads SR Battle Organization, 225, 226; photo, 227

Baku, 120, 146, 147
Balmashev, Stepan, 1, 39, 220, 222
Baltic Germans, 102, 103
Baltic provinces, 23, 84, 104
Baratynskii, acting Moscow Governor, 67
Basel, 105, 107, 108–9
Battle Organization: and the use of terror, 219–22, 232; and the police, 222–25, 228–31; and Evno Azef, 223, 225, 234; and Plehve's murder, 226, 228, 229–31, 234–37, 238, 241
Batum, 146

Bessarabia, 93, 96, 120, 214
Bezobrazov, A. M.: supported by
  Plehve, 152, 153, 159, 160, 161–
  62, 163–64, 167–68, 172;
  undermines Witte, 153, 155–57,
  158, 162, 163; and Yalu timber
  scheme, 155–57, 160, 161–
  62, 166, 173; and Committee on
  the Far East, 168–70; photo, 157
Black-earth provinces. See Center
Bobrikov, N. I.: and russification of
  Finland, 30, 31, 111, 114–15, 215;
  collaborates with Plehve, 30–31,
  113–15, 200; assassinated, 216,
  232, 234; mentioned, 32, 118, 272
Bogdanovich, N. M., 224, 232
Borishanskii, A., 234
Boxer rebellion, 155
Breshkovskaia, Ekaterina, 226, 238
Bunakov, N. F., 67–68
Bund, Jewish, 132–33
Bureaucracy. See Russian Government

Catherine the Great, Empress, 32, 82
Caucasus, 63, 118, 120, 146–47, 189,
  216, 232
Censorship. See Main Office on Affairs
  of the Press
Center (region): disorders in, 40–41;
  land-shortage in, 43; Plehve seeks
  to assist, 80–81, 189–91;
  commission discusses, 204–5;
  mentioned, 60, 164
Central Statistics Committee, 129,
  130, 192
Chambers of Justice, 13
Chancery of the Minister of Interior,
  49, 83, 165, 201
Chel'nikov, M. V., 86, 211
Chernov, V. M., 220, 273
China, 154, 155, 159, 160, 161, 162,
  171, 173
Chinese-Eastern Railway, 154–55, 160
Chita, 154
Circuit courts, 13
Citizen, 39, 71, 152. See also
  Meshcherskii, V. P.

Collective liability. See Krugovaia poruka
Colleges, provincial, 73
Commission for the Support of Noble
  Landownership, 25
Commission on Factory Legislation,
  23, 123–24
Commission on food provisions, 23
Commission on Jewish Legislation
  (1883–90), 23–24
Commission on Jewish Legislation
  (1904), 214–15
Commission on provincial
  administration, 82–84
Commission on the Center, 204–5
Committee of Ministers: centennial of,
  77; and Armenian Church, 119;
  and Far Eastern Viceroyalty, 166;
  Witte appointed Chairman, 150;
  and Jewish restrictions, 214, 215;
  mentioned, 1, 3, 4, 38, 183
Committee on Famine Relief, 23, 25
Commune. See Peasant commune
Complete Collection of Laws, 27
Compliants (in Finland), 31, 111, 112,
  113, 114, 115. See also Fennomen
Congress of Activists in the Field of
  Technical Education (1904), 208
Constitutionalists. See Zemstvo
  Constitutionalists
Cossacks, 120, 144, 146
Council of Workers in Mechanical
  Production (Moscow), 132, 139
Council on Local Affairs: Plehve's
  "constitution," 86, 177, 197, 244;
  criticized by society, 177, 245; not
  formed until 1908, 178–79, 241
Crimea, 68

Dalny, 164
Dashnak. See Armenian Revolutionary
  Union
Darmstadt, 116
Degaev, Sergei, 21, 225
Delianov, I. D., 19
Delo, 20
Department of General Affairs, 60,
  207

"Department of Labor," 130, 192, 241
Department of Police. *See* Police
Desiatskie ("teners"), 84
Dolgorukov, P. D., 67, 203
Durnovo, I. N.: opposes Witte, 9;
  presses counterreforms, 9, 73–74;
  champions nobility, 9, 27; Plehve
  plays key role under, 22, 25, 36,
  75, 94; dismissed, 28; mentioned,
  10, 21, 271
Durnovo, P. N., 48

Echmiadzin, 117, 119
Economy Department, 86, 177, 179
Editing Commission on the Revision of
  Peasant Legislation: formed, 45,
  49, 80; publishes *Works*, 180;
  champions *khutor* over commune,
  181, 182–83; stresses property
  rights, 184; foreshadows Stolypin
  laws, 185–86; work sent to
  provincial conferences, 186–88;
  mentioned, 191, 272. *See also*
  Peasants; Provincial Conferences on
  Revision of Peasant Legislation
Ekaterinoslav, 229
Elizavetpol, 120, 216, 232
Emancipation Act of 1861, ix, 42, 72,
  180
Emperor, 5–6. See also Alexander II,
  Emperor; Alexander III, Emperor;
  Nicholas II, Emperor
Erevan, 120
Ermolov, A. S., 85, 190
Estonians, 103
Evreinov, A. V., 67, 203

Factory elders. *See* Factory laws
Factory inspectors: Goremykin seeks
  control over, 9; under governors'
  supervision, 83, 84; established,
  123–24; Plehve seeks control over,
  125, 128–30, 192–93, 196–97;
  report to Witte, 146; transferred to
  Ministry of Trade and Industry, 241

Factory laws, x; June 3, 1885, 23, 123;
  June 3, 1886, 23, 123–24, 126;
  June 10, 1903 (Factory elders),
  124–25, 126, 164; others, 127
Factory owners. *See* Industrialists
Far East: Russian setbacks in, 1, 191,
  212, 244; Witte and Plehve differ,
  63; Witte ignored, 77; Russian
  expansionism in, 154–58, 163,
  174; Plehve supports expansion in,
  153, 159–60, 161–62, 163–64,
  168–69, 172, 173, 174, 189; map,
  156; volunteers offered pardon,
  209; zemstvo detachment to, 210
Far Eastern Viceroyalty, 158, 165,
  166, 167, 172
Farmstead. See *Khutor*
Fennomen, 103, 110–11, 113
Feoktistov, E. M., 273
Figner, Vera, 21, 222
Finland. *See* Finns
Finns: discontent toward Russia, 1, 32,
  39, 114, 116, 199, 213, 215;
  autonomy of, 29, 102, 113; Plehve
  seeks to subdue, 30–31, 103, 112,
  215–16; russification of, 31–32,
  111–12, 215, 241–42, 244, 245;
  divisions among, 103, 110–11;
  Plehve hated by, 199; mentioned,
  104, 153, 274
Finnish Conscription Act of 1901,
  111–12; 114, 115
Finnish Diet, 29–30
Finnish party. *See* Fennomen
Finnish Senate, 31
Fire insurance conference, 86, 87
Fiscal chamber, provincial, 83
"Flying squadron," 131, 137. *See also*
  Okhrana
Fontanka River, 233, 234
Food provisions commission, 23
France, 4, 154
Frish, E. V., 27
Fullon, I. A., 194–95

Gagarin, K. D., 22
Gapon, G. A., 140, 194–95, 196, 242

Gendarmes, 3, 71, 83, 130, 134, 137–39, 197, 203, 233. *See also* Okhrana; Police
Geneva, 225
Gentry. *See* Nobility
Georgians, 102
Gerbel', S. N., 178
Germans: in Russian Empire, 102
Germany, 4, 154
Gershuni, G. A.: heads Battle Organization, 220, 222, 223; police search for, 222, 224, 225; and Evno Azef, 223, 225, 228; arrest and trial of, 225, 226, 229–30, 232; photo, 221; mentioned, 273
Gesse, P. P., 152
Gessen, I. V., 200
Golitsyn, G. S., 118–20, 200, 232
Golovin, F. A., 211–12
Golovin, K. F., 202, 203
Gomel pogrom, 109, 214
Goremykin, I. L., 9–10, 28, 58, 125
Gots, Mikhail, 220, 225, 226, 229
Goujon, I., 133
Governors, provincial; supervised by Minister of Interior, 2, 4; and zemstvos, 24, 83, 203, 205, 211; and local committees on agriculture, 65, 67, 71; efforts to increase powers of, 73, 75, 77, 82–85, 87, 179, 196–97, 203, 241, 244, 245; consulted by Plehve, 82–83, 187–88, 189; and Jewish restrictions, 96, 107, 214–15; expropriate Armenians, 120; and provincial conferences on peasant legislation, 186, 187–88
Great Britain, 155, 160, 166, 173
Grigor'ev (terrorist), 220, 223–24, 228, 229, 230, 234
Gurko, V. I.: appointed to head Land Section, 49; and peasant reform, 50–51, 78, 79, 80, 180, 185–86, 187–88, 238, 241, 253n35; explains and defends Plehve, 98–99, 119, 159, 173, 272; mentioned, 137, 167

Helsingfors, 112
Helsingfors University, 11, 31
Herzl, Theodor, 107–10, 273
His Majesty's Personal Chancery, 3
Holy Synod, 3, 28, 102
Holy Trinity Monastery, 40
"Hundreders" (*sotskie*), 84

Ianzhul, I. I., 123–24, 125, 127, 128, 129, 136, 192, 273
Iaroslavl, 203
Ignat'ev, N. P., 18, 34, 94, 371
Imperial Chancery, 26–27
Imperial commission. *See* Commission
Imperial government. *See* Russian Government
Imperial Manifesto. *See* Manifesto
Imperial Secretary: functions of, 26
Independents (Jewish Independent Labor Party): in Minsk and Vilnius, 133, 139–40, 141, 142–43, 193, 194; in Odessa, 144–46, 147, 148, 193, 194; and Zubatov's dismissal, 147–49
Industrialists, 136, 139, 146, 196–97
Industrialization, ix, x, 7–8, 62, 122. *See also* Witte, S. Iu.
Iurkovskaia (terrorist), 220
Izmailovskii Prospekt, 232, 234–35

Japan: opposes Russian expansionism, 154, 155, 158, 160, 167, 169, 171, 173; Russians seek agreement with, 159, 161, 165, 166, 169–70; inflicts defeats on Russia, 171, 172, 212, 242, 244; mentioned, 188
Jewish Colonial Trust, 109
Jewish Independent Labor Party. *See* Independents
Jews: repression and alienation of, x, 23, 24–25, 142–43, 144, 172, 199, 213–14, 228, 242, 246; Plehve raised among, 13, 284n4; and Witte, 65, 108, 153; in

revolutionary movement, 69, 105–
6, 121, 132–33, 140, 245, 246;
and Kishinev pogrom, 93–96, 100;
Plehve's attitude toward, 69, 95–
99, 104–106; and Independents,
140, 142–43, 144, 148; Plehve
seeks to ease restraints on, 214–15,
244; mentioned, 122, 274. *See also*
Zionists
Judicial Reform of 1864, ix, 13
Justices of the peace, 13

Kachura, Foma, 223, 229, 230
Kaluga province, 13, 203
Karabchevskii, N. P., 239
Keller, F. E., 82–83
Khar'kov, 40, 223, 231
Khar'kov-Poltava riots: described, 39–
41; help focus concern on peasants,
42–43, 47, 184, 189; show Plehve's
repressive tendencies, 41–42, 100,
200; Plehve blames statisticians for,
53–54, 55, 61; show weakness of
local police, 84; mentioned, 1,
164, 223, 272
Khutor (farmstead), 181–82, 188, 244
Kiev, 75, 137, 146–47, 223–24, 225,
229, 231, 232
Kireev, A. A., 202, 203, 272
Kishinev, 93–94, 101, 137
Kishinev pogrom: described, 93–94;
photo, 95; Plehve's role in, 94–
101; undermines and discredits
Plehve, 94, 101, 106, 107, 120,
143, 228; mentioned, 122, 214
Kleigels, N. V., 220, 231
Klichoglu, Serafima, 230, 234
Kokovtsov, V. N., 190, 193, 196,
204–5, 217, 273
Korea, 153, 156, 165, 170, 171,
173
Kostroma province, 239
Kraft (terrorist), 224
Kristi, Moscow governor, 67, 91
Krivoshein, A. V., 49, 80–81, 189,
190, 241

Krugovaia poruka (Collective liability),
42, 65, 79
Krushevan, P. A., 94–95, 97, 98, 232
Kulomzin, A. N., 190, 272
Kurlov, P. G., 213
Kuropatkin, A. N.: and Finnish army
incorporation, 31–32;
conversations with Plehve, 78–79,
95–96, 98, 127, 158, 159, 170,
171, 273; and Far Eastern policy,
155, 157, 158, 159–62, 163, 165,
166, 167, 169, 170, 171; explains
Witte's dismissal, 153; as
commander of armies, 172, 212
Kursk, 60, 61, 62, 67, 71, 78, 92,
203, 212–13, 229

Lamsdorf, V. N.: and Far Eastern
policy, 155, 159–62, 167, 170;
opposes Bezobrazov, 158, 161,
165; feels Plehve backs
adventurism, 169, 171
Land captains, 2, 4, 43, 67, 72, 73–
74, 187, 203
Land captain law of 1889, 23–24, 43
Land Section, 45, 49, 50, 272
"Land-shortage," 43, 80–81, 189, 191
Latvians, 103
Law on Exceptional Measures, 18–19,
20, 42
Leroux, Gaston, 218, 267n1
Levendal, Kishinev Okhrana chief, 95,
97
Liaotung Peninsula, 154, 156, 173
Liberation (Osvobozhdenie) 88, 200, 209,
272
Liubimov, D. N., 49, 68–70, 78, 98–
99, 165–66, 238, 248n2, 272
Local committees on agriculture. *See*
Special Conference on the Needs of
Agricultural Industry
Local self-government. *See* Zemstvos;
Town councils
Lopukhin, A. A.: as Khar'kov
procurator, 40; appointed to head
police, 39, 134, 222; helps prepare

Lopukhin, A. A.: as Khar'kov (cont.) manifesto, 78; and Jews, 98–99, 100–101, 214; photo, 135; and gendarmes, 137; and worker disorders, 143, 145, 147; and terrorists, 218, 224, 228, 231, 238, 241; spied on by Plehve, 233; mentioned, 272
Loris-Melikov, M. T.: appointed "dictator", 15; reform plans of, 16, 17–18, 73, 74, 178, 198; recommends Plehve, 17, 34; resigns, 17–18; and pogroms, 97
L'vov, G. E., 211
Lykoshin, A. I., 50, 241

Main Office for Local Affairs, 177, 178
Main Office of Commercial Navigation, 77
Main Office on Affairs of the Press (censorship department), 20, 49, 64, 96, 200, 241
Makarov, S. O., 212
Manchuria, 1, 153, 154, 156, 158, 159–62, 163, 166, 167, 169–71, 172–73, 212
Manifesto of February 3, 1899, 30, 115
Manifesto of February 26, 1903, 78–79, 80, 81, 82, 180, 187
Marie Fedorovna, Empress, 114, 153
Mariinskii Palace, 1, 38
Marshals of the Nobility, 5, 47, 65, 75, 86, 88, 177, 187, 203, 205
Martynov, S. V., 67–68
Marxists, 15, 118, 136, 140. See also Social Democrats
Matiunin, N. G., 168
Mel'nikov, Mikhail, 220, 224, 230
Meshcherskii, V. P., 34, 39, 49, 71, 152–53, 202
Mikhail Nikovaevich, Grand Duke, 27
Mikhailovo railway station, 146
Mikhailovskii, N. K., 20, 200–201, 208
Military reforms of 1874, ix

Miliukov, P. N., 200, 233, 273
Ministry of Agriculture, x, 3, 23, 85, 119, 190
Ministry of Education, x, 2, 39, 58, 118–19, 200, 208
Ministry of Finance, 2, 3, 77, 150, 154, 190; clashes with Interior, 7–11, 63–64, 80–81, 85, 124, 190, 192, 196–97, 244. See also Witte, S. Iu.; Kokovtsov, V. N.
Ministry of Interior: powers of, 2–6, 24, 72; and zemstvos, 2, 24, 53, 55, 59, 75, 82, 85–87, 177–79, 202, 203, 204, 205–7, 210, 212–13, 244; clashes with Finance, 7–11, 63–64, 66, 80–81, 85, 124, 126, 127, 128–30, 190, 192, 196–97, 241, 244; and administrative reform, 16, 73, 75–77, 82–85, 177–79, 196–98, 243–44; and peasant reform, 43–44, 45–46, 47, 49–51, 61, 78, 79–80, 81, 180–86, 187, 188, 189–91; and local committees on agriculture, 66–68; and Kishinev pogrom, 94–97; and Armenians, 119–20; and factory workers, 124, 126, 127, 128–30, 143–44, 145–46, 191–96, 241; and perlustration, 169, 201, 233; and terrorists, 222–25, 229–30; mentioned, 242–43, 272
Ministry of Justice, 3, 13–14, 85
Ministry of Trade and Industry, 241
Ministry of War, 3, 29. See also Kuropatkin, A. N.
Minsk, 106, 133, 134, 139, 140, 141, 142–43, 144, 193, 194
Mkrtich, Catholicos, 117, 119–20
Modernization, ix, x, 197, 243
Moscow, 14, 19, 54–55, 63, 67, 93, 131–32, 134–36, 139, 193, 194, 205–7, 214, 229, 231–32
Moscow Okhrana. See Okhrana
Moscow provincial zemstvo, 87, 88, 205–7, 210–11, 213. See also Shipov, D. N.; Zemstvos
Moscow University, 13, 134
Municipal dumas. See Town councils
Murav'ev, N. V., 26, 85, 271

Nadarov (terrorist), 224
Nakashidze, Prince, 120
Nanshan, 212
Nationalities, ix, x, 39, 63, 101–103, 176, 197, 198, 216, 243, 246. See also Armenians; Finns; Jews; Ukrainians
Neva River, 239
New Times (Novoe Vremia), 33, 39, 200
Nicholas II, Emperor, 1, 25, 28, 42, 119, 141, 166, 193, 208, 273; indecisiveness of, 6, 46, 65, 173; and Witte, 7–8, 28, 46, 65, 71, 77–78, 146, 149, 150–51, 152, 158, 167, 169; appoints Plehve, 10–11, 30, 32, 38; and zemstvos, 10, 55–56, 60–61, 89, 211, 213; and Finns, 29, 30, 31–32, 114, 115, 116; and peasant question, 45, 46–47, 51, 71, 79, 187, 189–90; and administrative reform, 62, 75, 78–79, 84, 85, 128; and Far East, 77, 154, 155, 157, 158, 162–63, 165, 169–70, 173; and Jews, 100, 101, 110, 215; and Plehve's assassination, 234, 238–39
Nikolaev, 146, 147
Nikon, archimandrite, 40
Nobility: role and status of, 5, 9, 23, 25, 44, 50, 52, 60–61, 65, 187; Plehve's attitude toward, 25, 34, 45, 63–64, 67, 69, 80, 86, 185, 196–98, 243; disenchanted with government, 64, 203–4, 216, 242, 244, 245; patriotism of, 209; mentioned, 273
Notes of the Fatherland, 20
Novgorod, 67
Novitskii, V. D., 141, 232, 273

Obolenskii, A. D, 80–81, 272
Obolenskii, I. M., 40, 41, 214, 216, 223, 229, 232
Odessa: general strike in, 122, 142, 143–46, 147, 149; Independents active in, 134, 139, 140, 141, 142,

143–46, 193, 194; mentioned, 63, 137, 229
Okhrana, 3, 19, 130, 134, 137–39, 147–48, 222, 223, 225, 226, 229, 241; in Moscow, 19, 130, 131–33, 137, 233; in Saint Petersburg, 19, 20–21, 130, 137, 195; in Warsaw, 19, 130, 137; in Kishinev, 95, 137; in Paris, 136, 228–29; in Kiev, 137, 225; in Odessa, 137; in Vilnius, 137. See also Gendarmes, Police
Orel, 202
Orthodox Church, 78–79
Orzhevskii, P. V., 21–22
Osvobozhdenie. See Liberation
Ozerov, I. Kh., 132

Pahlen, K. I., 14, 24–25
Pahlen, Vilnius governor, 214
Pale of Settlement, 104–5, 106, 213–14
Palestine, 106, 107
Peasant commune, 42–43, 44–45, 64, 66, 79, 180–83, 185, 186, 191, 244, 245
Peasant Land Bank, 80, 81, 86, 189, 272
Peasant resettlement, x, 23, 81, 189–91, 241, 244, 272
Peasants: unrest among, x, 1, 39–41, 201, 203, 216, 219, 223; reform of legislation concerning, x, 46, 50, 60, 61, 66, 67, 71, 76–77, 78, 79, 142, 175, 180–86, 187, 188, 189–91, 204–5, 209, 239, 241, 244, 245; condition and status of, 2, 5, 8, 23, 42–44, 46, 47, 63–64, 72–73, 80–81, 84, 122–23, 196–98, 239; and Jews, 101, 105; mentioned, 142
People's Will, 16, 17, 20–21, 225, 230
Pereleshin, D. A., 68
Perlustration, 201, 233
Peterhof, 234
Petropavlovsk, battleship, 212

Philippe, 136, 152
Pikunov, V. I., 140
Pirogov Society of Russian Physicians, 208
Platonov, S. F., 85, 179, 272
Plehve, E. M. (mother of V. K.), 12
Plehve, E. V. (daughter of V. K.), 14, 34
Plehve, K. G. (father of V. K.), 12
Plehve, N. V. (son of V. K.), 14, 34, 239
Plehve, V. K.: appearance, 12; family, 12–13, 14, 34, 284n4; as student, 13; as procurator, 14–17; as assistant minister, 21–26; as Imperial Secretary, 26–27; passed over for minister, 28–29; appointed minister, 10–11, 32, 38; assassinated, 234–37, 238; mentioned, 271–74
—Administrative reform: expansion of bureaucratic power, x, 53, 74–75, 102–3, 175–76, 177–79, 244; coordination of local authority, x, 72, 74–75, 78, 82–85, 102–3, 176, 179, 243–44; decentralization, 82, 85, 179; failure to implement, 196, 245. See also Russian Government
—Character: energy and talent, ix, x, 16, 17–18, 32–33, 35, 37, 242–43; careerism and opportunism, 10–11, 14, 22, 34–35, 37, 40, 166, 173–74, 244; harshness, 33–34; caution and gradualism, 35, 38–39, 244; passion for unity and order, 36–37, 64, 100–101, 185, 196–97, 243; cordiality, 58–59, 107–8; uncertainty, 58–59, 216–17, 233–34
—Labor policies: revision of factory legislation, x, 23, 123–24, 126–27, 128–30; Zubatovshchina, x, 93, 130, 133–34, 136–37, 140–42, 147–48, 149, 194–95, 242; transfer of factory inspectorate, 125, 128–

30, 191–93; suppression of worker disorders, 127, 142–43, 143–46, 147. See also Workers, industrial; Zubatov
—Nationalities policies: repressive tendencies, x, 102–4, 120–21; repression of Jews, x, 23, 24–25, 94, 104–5; attitude toward Jews, 13, 25, 97–98, 104–6, 108, 110; russification of Finns, 29–31, 31–32, 102–4, 111–12, 116; and Kishinev pogrom, 93, 94–97, 98–101; and relief for Jews, 105–6, 108, 109–10, 214–15; and Zionism, 106–7, 108, 109–10; and relief for Finns, 112–13, 114, 116–17, 215–16; russification of Armenians, 117, 119–20, 216. See also Finns; Jews
—Peasant policies: revision of peasant legislation, x, 45, 47–48, 49–51, 76–77, 78–79, 180–84, 187–88, 191; resettlement, x, 189–91; land captains, 23–24; repression of riots, 41–42; abolition of collective liability, 65, 79; reform of Peasant Bank, 80–81; Commission on Center, 204–5; compared to Stolypin reforms, 183, 184–86, 244. See also Peasants
—Relations with society: seeks cooperation, x, 51–52, 55–61, 70, 71, 75–77, 85–87, 176, 201–2, 209; represses and alienates, 23–24, 42, 47, 55–56, 66–68, 69–70, 88–92, 204, 205–7, 208, 210–11, 212–13, 216, 245; supports nobility, 28–29; few ties with nobility, 36, 53; distrusts society, 69–70. See also Society, Zemstvos
—Rivalry with Witte: struggle for influence, 10–11, 28, 29, 59, 62–65, 66, 71, 147–48, 151–53, 157, 163, 167, 195–96, 244; differences in style, 33, 34–35, 60, 62–64, 108, 151–52, 185,

254n3; over Finland, 31–32; over agriculture, 47–48, 59, 64–65, 66–67, 68–70, 80–81, 89, 186–87, 189; over labor policy, 84, 125–28, 130, 141, 147–49; over Far East, 158–59, 160–62, 163–64, 165, 166–67, 168, 170–72, 173–74. *See also* Far East; Witte, S. Iu.
—Social control: struggle against revolutionaries, 16, 18–19, 20–21, 39, 40, 215, 218–19, 222–23, 224, 225–26, 227–31, 232, 233, 234–37; reorganization of police, 17–19, 134, 136, 137–39; preservation of order, 19, 20, 36–37, 39, 41–42, 100–101, 142–44, 145–46, 199–202, 212–13, 245–46; censorship, 20, 49, 96, 200–201, 241; perlustration, 201, 233. *See also* Okhrana; Police
Plehve, Z. N. (wife of V. K.), 14, 239
Pleske, E. D., 150–51, 190, 192
Pobedonostsev, K. P., 28, 102, 166, 220, 224
Pogozhev, A. V., 128–30, 149, 193, 233
Poland, 12, 63, 102, 171
Police, 2, 48, 49, 196–98, 208–10; limitations and weakness of, 4, 72, 84, 93–94, 218; reform of, 16, 19, 70, 84–85, 137–39, 222, 241, 243; and Jews, 95–96, 98, 101, 107; and workers, 124–25, 129, 132–33, 134, 136, 139, 140–41, 142, 145, 146, 193–95, 242; and terrorists, 222–25, 226, 229–30, 231, 223–35, 246. *See also* Gendarmes, Okhrana
Poltava. *See* Khar'kov-Poltava riots
Port Arthur, 154, 155, 164, 166, 169, 171, 173, 212, 242
Poznan, 12
Pravo, 200
Procurators, 13–15, 40
Proletariat. *See* Workers, industrial
Pronin (Kishinev agitator), 94–95, 97, 98

Provincial Conferences on Revision of Peasant Legislation, 51, 60, 78, 180, 186–87, 187–88, 245
Provisioning conference, 86

Raaben. *See* von Raaben
Rachkovskii, P. I., 136, 228
Rataev, L. A., 136, 228–29, 234
Red Cross, Russian, 210
Redemption dues, 43, 205, 239
Resettlement. *See* Peasant resettlement
Resettlement Administration, 49
Resettlement Law of 1904, 190–91, 241
Restel' foundry, 140, 143
Revolution of 1905, 242
Revolutionaries, 2, 8, 64, 69, 131, 219, 243, 245, 246; and Jews, 105, 110, 121; and workers, 199, 218–19; and terrorism, 220, 222–25, 226, 238. *See also* Battle Organization; Marxists; Social Democrats; Socialist Revolutionaries
Revolutionary Russia, 222
Rostov-on-Don, 127
Ruling Senate, 3, 99
Russian Gazette, 91
Russian Government, ix–x, 1, 3, 4, 6, 72, 196–98, 216, 274; and need for control, ix–x, 36–37, 53, 123–24, 196–98, 201, 208, 243, 244; and administrative reform, x, 3, 62, 72, 74, 78, 82–84, 85, 175, 177, 179, 185, 197–98, 245; and society, 25, 52–53, 55, 62, 64, 66–70, 72, 74, 75–76, 77, 87, 90, 91, 123–24, 196, 201–2, 203, 204, 211, 216, 242, 244; and peasant reform, 46, 50, 60, 61, 66, 67, 71, 76–77, 78, 79, 142, 175, 180–86, 188, 189–91, 204–5, 239, 241, 244, 245; and non-Russian nationalities, 96, 100–101, 102–3, 104–5, 111–15, 118–20, 215, 216; and factory workers,

Russian Government (cont.)
122–24, 125, 131, 147, 193–95,
242; and the Far East, 155, 160,
161, 166, 167, 169, 170, 171, 172,
209, 211, 212, 242; and terrorism,
220, 222–25, 226, 227, 229–30,
238
Russification, 102–4, 105, 111–15,
200, 241–42, 246
Russo-Chinese Bank, 154, 158
Russo-Japanese War, 110, 171, 179,
188, 199, 205, 208–9, 212, 213,
215, 242, 244, 246, 272

Saint Petersburg, 13, 15, 19, 31, 34,
37, 130, 137, 139, 141, 148, 176,
193–95, 215, 229, 230–31
Saint Petersburg Society of Workers in
Mechanical Production, 194
Samarin, F. D., 202, 272
Saratov, 203, 229
Sarov, 166
Savich, G. G., 50
Savinkov, Boris, 226, 230–32, 234,
234–36, 238, 273
Sazonov, Egor, 226, 230–31, 232,
234–37, 238, 239–41
Schlusselburg fortress, 222, 229
Security sections. See Okhrana
Semenov, D. P., 49–50
Serafim of Sarov, 166
Sergei Aleksandrovich, Grand Duke,
131, 133–34, 136, 139, 192, 193,
195
Shaevich, G. I., 140, 141, 143, 144–
46, 148, 149
Shamaev, Mikhail, 12
Shcherbin, F. A., 67–68
Shingarev, A. I., 67
Shipov, D. N., 54–55, 176, 202,
203–4, 211–12, 238, 244, 271,
273; discussions with Plehve, 56–
60, 88–92, 210–11, 216–17
Siberia, 7, 9, 154, 171, 190, 226
Siberian Railway Committee, 3, 151,
165–66, 189–90
Sikorskii, S. V., 239–41

Sino-Japanese War, 154
Sipiagin, D. S., 2, 28–29, 45–46, 48–
49, 84, 118–19, 125, 126, 133,
152, 218, 222, 234; murder of, 1,
32, 38, 220, 232; and Witte, 10,
47
Skandrakov, A. S., 201, 226, 233,
234, 238, 239
Slavophiles, 18, 53, 56, 61, 74, 89,
92, 102, 202, 212
Slieptsov, Voronezh governor, 67–68
Social Democrats, 144–45, 146, 147,
194, 219, 226. See also Marxists
Socialist Revolutionaries (SRs), 219,
222, 225–26, 228, 230, 238
Society, 2, 51–52, 239, 242; Plehve
seeks cooperation with, x, 62, 75–
76, 77, 85–87, 92, 201–2, 203–4,
208–9, 243–44; clashes with
bureaucracy, 66, 69–70, 90, 92,
176, 177–78, 187, 190, 201–2,
208, 212, 216, 238
Society of Zemstvo Organizations to
Aid Wounded Soldiers, 210–12
Sotskie ("hundreders"), 84
South Manchuria Railway, 154–55,
156, 170
Special Committee on Far Eastern
Affairs, 164, 165–66, 168
Special Conference on Resettlement,
190
Special Conference on the Needs of
Agricultural Industry, 45–46, 49,
71, 76, 81, 151, 186, 187, 205,
209–10, 272; local committees
of, 47, 51, 54, 65–70, 71, 72, 88–
89, 90–91, 186, 187, 188, 191,
244
Special Conference on the Needs of
the Nobility, 27, 272
Special Section, 130, 136, 194, 222–
23, 228. See also Okhrana; Police;
Zubatov, S. V.
Spiridovich, A. I., 225, 226, 273
Stakhovich, M. A., 56, 202, 203
State Controller, 77–78
State Council, 3, 4, 26, 27, 31–32,
46, 73, 77, 84, 126, 164, 166,
178, 179, 190, 272

State-Secretariat for Finland, 30–31, 111–12
Stead, W. T., 115–16
Steppes, 23
Stishinskii, A. S., 48, 49, 50–51, 79–80, 137, 185–86, 187–88, 241
Stolypin, A. A., 200
Stolypin, P. A., 183, 244, 245
Stolypin reforms, 183, 184, 185–86, 241
Strazhniki (police guards), 84
Student unrest, 8, 19–20, 39, 153, 201
Sturmer, B. V., 60, 92, 207, 213, 241
Stuttgart, 88
Sudeikin, G. D., 20–21, 131, 222, 225
Sudzha county, 67, 91, 212–13
Suvorin, A. S., 200, 273
Svecomen, 103, 110–11, 113
Sviatopolk-Mirskii, P. D., 48, 226, 239, 242

Tambovsk, 203
Tellisu, 212
"Teners" (desiatskie), 84
Terrorism, 2, 16–17, 64, 122, 219–22, 232. See also Battle Organization
Third element, 54, 59, 61, 74, 86, 90, 200, 202, 203, 205–7, 207–8, 209–10, 211, 213, 241
Tiflis, 120, 146
Tikhoretsk, 127
Times (London), 96
Tolstoi, D. N.: as Minister of Interior, 18, 20–22, 23, 73–74, 97, 102, 201; Plehve builds on legacy of, 34–35, 36, 75, 198; mentioned, 28, 271
Tomsk, 223
Town councils, ix, x, 2, 5, 16, 52; efforts to restrict autonomy of, 9, 23–24, 82, 83, 176, 177, 188, 197, 243, 244
Trans-Siberian Railway, 7, 154
Trepov, D. F., 131, 133–34, 139, 193, 214

Tsarist regime. See Russian Government
Tsarskoe Selo, 1, 162–63, 165
Tula, 14
Turkey, 108, 109, 110, 118
"Tutelage," 43–44, 66, 181, 184–85, 187
Tver zemstvo, 60, 207, 210, 241

Ufa province, 127, 224–25
Uganda, 108–9
Ukraine, 1, 40–41, 146
Ukrainians, 102, 140
Union of Armenian Social Democrats, 118
Union of Liberation, 208
United States, 155, 160
Universities, 19, 64
Urusov, S. D., 99–100, 101, 120, 214, 273

Valuev, P. A., 73, 74, 75, 178, 198
Vannovsky, P. S., 39, 58
Vasil'chikov, B. A., 82
Veterinary Law of 1902, 86, 88, 90
Viatka, 212–13
Viceroyalty of the Caucasus, 165–66
Viceroyalty of the Far East, 158, 165, 166, 167, 172
Vil'bushevich, Mania, 133, 134, 140, 141, 148
Vilnius, 105–6, 134, 137, 139–40, 193–94, 214, 232
Vishnegradskii, Ivan, 124
Vladimir, 14
Vladivostok, 154
Vogak, K. I., 162, 165
Volkonskii, M. S., 20
Vologda, 14, 203, 212, 226
Vonliarliarskii, V. M., 159
Von Raaben, Governor of Bessarabia, 94, 95, 96, 97, 98–99
Von Wahl, V. K., 48, 67, 97, 137, 138, 147, 148, 232, 241

Voronezh, 67–68, 71
Vuich, N. I., 34
Vyborg province, 116–117, 215–16

Wahl. See Von Wahl, V. K.
Warsaw, 12–13, 14–15, 19, 130, 137,
   199
Warsaw Station, 232, 234
Winter Palace, 15, 230, 242
Witte, S. Iu., 7–10, 77–78, 122, 150–
   51, 185, 188, 193, 271–74;
   encourages industry, 7–8, 44–45,
   63, 203; rivalry with Plehve, 10–
   11, 22, 28–29, 32, 34–35, 52, 59,
   62–65, 65–66, 68–70, 71, 80–81,
   89, 94, 97, 98, 108, 151–53, 158,
   163, 167, 171, 173, 195–96, 244;
   and society, 29, 52–53, 54, 56, 59,
   65–66, 68–70, 89, 203, 204, 216;
   and Finland, 31, 32; and peasant
   question, 45–46, 47, 49, 64, 65,
   79, 80–81, 186, 187, 189; and
   bureaucracy, 84, 85, 90; and Jews,
   94, 97, 98, 108; and Armenians,
   118–19; and factory affairs, 124–
   25, 126–27, 128, 130, 191–92,
   194; and Zubatovshchina, 131, 133,
   136, 141, 143, 146, 147–48,
   149; dismissed from Finance,
   150–51, 167, 175, 191–92; and
   Far East, 154–55, 157–58,
   159–62, 163, 165, 166, 169, 170,
   171; and Plehve's murder, 238,
   239
Workers, industrial, 2, 122–23, 241,
   242; legislation concerning, x, 9–
   10, 23, 123–24, 126–27, 241;
   Plehve's approach to, x, 63, 93,
   106, 126–27, 142, 175, 191–92,
   196–97, 198, 200, 243, 244, 245;
   unrest among, 2, 8, 39, 122–25,
   143–45, 146–47, 199, 201, 203,
   216, 219, 246; conditions among,
   123, 128–30; and Zubatov
   societies, 131–33, 140, 142, 148,
   193–95

Works of the Editing Commission on
   the Revision of Peasant Legislation,
   180–86, 188
World Zionist Congresses, 105, 107,
   108–9

Yalta, 68–70, 160
Yalu River, battle of, 212
Yalu River concession, 157, 159, 161,
   162, 165, 168, 169, 172

Zamiatnin, D. N., 14
Zemskii sobor, 18, 67
Zemstvos, ix, 2, 5, 23, 51–53, 72, 73,
   78, 209, 273; seek to expand role,
   2, 16, 54–55, 67, 74, 203, 205,
   211, 243; discontent among, 8, 54,
   74, 79, 84, 88–92, 177–78, 202–
   3, 211–12, 245, 246; government
   seeks to restrict, 9, 10, 23–24, 43,
   56, 61, 64, 71, 73–74, 82, 83, 84,
   88, 89, 92, 176, 188, 196–98,
   200, 203, 204, 205–7, 211, 213,
   241, 242; and peasant reform, 44,
   47, 65, 183, 187, 188; Plehve seeks
   accommodation with, 56–61, 77,
   85–87, 92, 93, 142, 176, 177,
   196–98, 243; Plehve distrusts, 69,
   179, 209–10, 211
Zemstvo constitutionalists, 53, 74,
   88–90, 92, 212
Zemstvo detachments, 210, 211
Zemstvo statisticians, 53–54, 61, 200,
   208
Zenger, G. E., 39
Zinov'ev, I. A., 109, 110
Zinov'ev, N. A., 48, 68, 80, 86, 205–
   7, 212–13, 241
Zionist Congresses, 105, 107, 108–9
Zionists, 105, 106–7, 133, 142–43,
   144
Zlatoust, 127, 224–25

Zubatov, S. V., 98, 164, 274; as Chief
of Moscow Okhrana, 131–34;
and worker societies, 133, 134,
140, 141, 142, 148, 193–95; as
Head of Special Section, 136,
137–39, 222–23, 224, 228; and
Plehve, 136, 139, 141–42,
147–48, 149, 153, 175, 191,
244, 245
Zubatovshchina, 132, 133, 134, 140,
142, 145, 149, 175, 193–95, 245.
See also Zubatov, S. V.
Zverev, N. A., 49
Zvolianskii, S. E., 132, 134, 139, 218

PLEHVE

was composed in 11-point Mergenthaler Weiss and leaded one point,
with display type also in Weiss,
by Dix Type Inc.;
printed by sheet-fed offset on 50-lb., acid-free Glatfelter Antique Cream,
Smythe-sewn and bound over boards in Joanna Arrestox B,
by Maple-Vail Book Manufacturing Group, Inc.;
and published by

SYRACUSE UNIVERSITY PRESS
SYRACUSE, NEW YORK 13210